P9-BVC-502

Adapt, Fragment, Transform

ADAPT,
FRAGMENT,
TRANSFORM

Corporate Restructuring

and System Reform

in Korea

Edited by
Byung-Kook Kim, Eun Mee Kim,
and Jean C. Oi

THE WALTER H. SHORENSTEIN
ASIA-PACIFIC RESEARCH CENTER

THE WALTER H. SHORENSTEIN ASIA-PACIFIC RESEARCH CENTER
(Shorenstein APARC) is a unique Stanford University institution focused on the
interdisciplinary study of contemporary Asia. Shorenstein APARC's mission is to
produce and publish outstanding interdisciplinary, Asia-Pacific–focused research;
to educate students, scholars, and corporate and governmental affiliates; to
promote constructive interaction to influence U.S. policy toward the Asia-Pacific;
and to guide Asian nations on key issues of societal transition, development,
U.S.-Asia relations, and regional cooperation.

The Walter H. Shorenstein Asia-Pacific Research Center
Freeman Spogli Institute for International Studies
Stanford University
Encina Hall
Stanford, CA 94305-6055
tel. 650-723-9741
fax 650-723-6530
http://APARC.stanford.edu

*Adapt, Fragment, Transform: Corporate Restructuring and System Reform
in Korea* may be ordered from:
The Brookings Institution
c/o DFS, P.O. Box 50370, Baltimore, MD, USA
tel. 1-800-537-5487 or 410-516-6956
fax 410-516-6998
http://www.brookings.edu/press

Walter H. Shorenstein Asia-Pacific Research Center Books, 2012.

Copyright © 2012 by the Board of Trustees of the
Leland Stanford Junior University.

All rights reserved. No part of this publication may be reproduced, stored in
a retrieval system, or transmitted in any form or by any means, electronic,
mechanical, photocopying, recording, or otherwise, without written permission
of the publisher.

Library of Congress Cataloging-in-Publication Data
Adapt, fragment, transform : corporate restructuring and system reform in Korea / edited by
Byung-Kook Kim, Eun Mee Kim, and Jean C. Oi.
      p. cm.
Includes bibliographical references and index.
ISBN 978-1-931368-21-6
1. Corporate reorganizations—Korea (South) 2. Corporate governance—Korea (South)
3. Industrial policy—Korea (South) I. Kim, Pyong-guk, 1959 Mar. 18– II. Kim, Eun Mee, 1958–
III. Oi, Jean Chun.
HD2908.A63 3012
338.6095195—dc23

2012010255

First printing, 2012.

Typeset by Classic Typography in 10.5/13 Sabon MT Pro

To the Memory of Walter H. Shorenstein

Contents

Tables and Figures

Tables

Figures

Abbreviations

AEFSO	Act on the Establishment of Financial Supervisory Organization
AFC	Asian financial crisis
BAI	Board of Audit and Inspection
BOK	Bank of Korea
CCE	Citizens' Coalition for Economic Justice
CGCG	Center for Good Corporate Governance
CME	coordinated market economy
CRA	Corporate Restructuring Accords
CSIP	Capital Structure Improvement Plan
DLP	Democratic Liberal Party
DP	Democratic Party
DPJ	Democratic Justice Party
DRP	Democratic Republican Party
EPB	Economic Planning Board
FDI	foreign direct investment
FEB	Finance and Economy Board
FISIA	Financial Industry Structure Improvement Act
FKI	Federation of Korean Industries
FKTU	Federation of Korean Trade Unions
FLC	forward-looking approach to asset classification
FSC	Financial Supervisory Commission
FSS	Financial Supervisory Service

FTC	Fair Trade Commission
GATT	General Agreement on Tariffs and Trade
GDP	gross domestic product
GNP	Grand National Party
HCI	heavy and chemical industrialization
IMF	International Monetary Fund
ISB	Insurance Supervisory Board
KAMCO	Korea Asset Management Corporation
KCCI	Korean Chamber of Commerce and Industry
KCIA	Korean Intelligence Agency
KCTU	Korean Confederation of Trade Unions
KDI	Korea Development Institute
KEA	Korean Employers Association
KEF	Korea Employers Federation
KEPCO	Korea Electric Power Corporation
KERI	Korea Economic Research Institute
KFB	Korea First Bank
KFIU	Korean Financial Industry Union
KMWF	Korean Metal Workers' Federation
KOTRA	Korea Trade Investment Promotion Agency
KT	Korea Telecom
KT&G	Korea Tobacco and Ginseng Corporation
KWAU	Korean Women's Association United
KWDI	Korean Women's Development Institute
LME	liberal market economy
M&A	merger and acquisition
MCB	main creditor bank
MCI	Ministry of Commerce and Industry
MHA	Ministry of Home Affairs
MHSA	Ministry of Health and Social Affairs
MME	mixed market economy
MOCI	Ministry of Commerce and Industry
MOCIE	Ministry of Commerce, Industry, and Energy
MoF	Ministry of Finance
MOFE	Ministry of Finance and Economy

MOGE	Ministry of Gender Equality
MOGEF	Ministry of Gender Equality and Family
MOHW	Ministry of Health and Welfare
MoL	Ministry of Labor
MOSF	Ministry of Strategy and Finance
MPB	Ministry of Planning and Budget
MPC	Monetary Policy Committee
MRFTA	Monopoly Regulation and Fair Trade Act
MTI	Ministry of Trade and Industry
MTIR	Ministry of Trade, Industry, and Resources
NBFI	nonbank financial institution
NBIC	Non-bank Insurance Corporation
NBLS	National Basic Livelihood Security
NBO	National Budget Office
NCB	nationwide commercial bank
NCNP	National Congress for New Politics
NDRP	New Democratic Republic Party
NGO	nongovernment organization
NKP	New Korea Party
NPA	National Police Agency
NPL	nonperforming loan
NPP	New Party by the People
OBSE	Office of Banking Supervision and Examination
OECD	Organisation for Economic Co-operation and Development
OPM	Office of the Prime Minister
PBC	Planning and Budget Commission
PCFR	Presidential Commission for Financial Reform
PCIRR	Presidential Commission on Industrial Relations Reform
POSCO	Pohang Iron and Steel Co.
PPD	Party for Peace and Democracy
PSPD	People's Solidarity for Participatory Democracy
PTB	principal transactions bank
RCRILL	Research Committee on the Revision of the Labor Law
ROA	return on assets
ROE	return on equity

ROI	return-on-investment
SFC	Securities and Futures Commission
SMDP	single-member district plurality
SME	small- and medium-sized enterprise
SSB	Securities Supervisory Board
TBTF	"too big to fail"
UDP	Unification Democratic Party
ULD	United Liberal Democrats
UR	Uruguay Round
VoC	varieties of capitalism
WTO	World Trade Organization

Glossary

amakudari "descent from heaven" in Japan

chaebŏl family-owned business group

chaeya dissident

Chŏlla region of Korea

ch'ongsu imperial

ch'ongsu ch'eje corporate governance structure

Hannaradang Grand National Party

hoesa nojo company union

isa director

kamsa auditor

Keidanren Japan Federation of Economic Organizations

kŭmyungdan financial association

kŭmyungdan h'yŏpjŏng financial association agreement

kungmin kiŏp company owned by the people

kwanch'i kŭmyung financial structure

kyeyŏ lhwa interfirm relations

myŏngbun moral justification

nakhasan insa "parachute" appointment

Nikkeiren Japan Federation of Employers' Associations

ŏyŏng   patronized

ŏyong nojo   union leadership (or pro-state)

pŏpjŏng kwalli   court receivership

pudo yuye hyŏbyak   bankruptcy protection

sach'ae   private curb market loans

samgŭm   three prohibitions (on workers' basic rights)

samje   three systems

segyehwa   globalization

shuntō   spring offensive

Sinmindang   New Democratic Party

Sŏngŏp Kongsa   Korea Asset Management Corporation

taejung kyŏngjeron   mass economics

taema pulsa   the big never die (too big to fail)

yŏsin kwalli chedo   credit control system

Contributors

Editors

BYUNG-KOOK KIM teaches comparative political theory at Korea University and currently serves as chancellor of the Korea National Diplomatic Academy. Dr. Kim served on the Presidential Commission on Policy Planning (1994–1998), taught at the John F. Kennedy School of Government, Harvard University, as the Ralph I. Straus Visiting Professor (2003), and was an executive council member of the International Political Science Association (2006–2009). His recent edited English-language publications include *Power and Security in Northeast Asia: Shifting Strategies* (2007) and *The Park Chung Hee Era: The Transformation of South Korea* (2011). Dr. Kim founded and directed the East Asia Institute before serving as senior secretary for foreign affairs and national security in the Lee Myung-bak presidency and president of the Korea Foundation.

EUN MEE KIM is dean and professor at the Graduate School of International Studies and the director of the Institute for Development and Human Security (IDHS) at Ewha Womans University. She is currently principal investigator on a research grant comparing emerging and traditional donors, and the relationship between human security and development. This research is supported by the WCU (World Class University) program through the National Research Foundation of Korea, funded by the Ministry of Education, Science, and Technology of the Republic of Korea. Prior to Ewha, she was professor in sociology at the University of Southern California, and a visiting scholar at Harvard University and Brown University. Her research interests include East Asian development; globalization; development cooperation; multiculturalism, and *chaebŏl*. Books include *Multicultural Society* *of Korea* (Nanam Publishing, 2009, co-authored in Korean); *Corporate Restructuring and Networks in Korea After the Financial Crisis* (Seoul National University Press, 2005, co-authored in Korean); *Big Business, Strong State: Collusion and Conflict in South Korean Development, 1960–1990* (State University of New York Press, 1997); and an edited book, *The Four Asian Tigers: Economic Development and the Global Political Economy Development* (Academic Press, 1998).

JEAN C. OI is the William Haas Professor in Chinese Politics in the Department of Political Science and a senior fellow at the Freeman Spogli Institute for International Studies at Stanford University. She directs the Stanford China Program at the Walter H. Shorenstein Asia-Pacific Research Center and is the director of the newly-established Stanford Center at Peking University. Her work focuses on comparative politics, with special expertise on Chinese political economy. Her books include *Going Private in China: The Politics of Corporate Restructuring and System Reform* (2011), an edited volume and the first in a series on corporate restructuring in China, Japan, and Korea; *Growing Pains: Tensions and Opportunity in China's Transformation* (2010), co-edited with Scott Rozelle and Xueguang Zhou; *Rural China Takes Off: Institutional Foundations of Economic Reform* (1999); *Property Rights and Economic Reform in China* (1999), co-edited with Andrew Walder; and *State and Peasant in Contemporary China: The Political Economy of Village Government* (1989). Currently, Professor Oi continues her research on rural finance and local governance in China and has started a new project on the logic of administrative redistricting in the Chinese countryside.

Contributors

DUKJIN CHANG is associate professor in the Department of Sociology and the director of the Institute for Social Development and Policy Research at Seoul National University (SNU). He received his PhD in sociology from the University of Chicago in 1999. Before joining the faculty at SNU in 2002, he was assistant professor at Ewha Womans University and visiting associate professor at Harvard University. His research interests have centered on social network theory and analysis, with applications to business groups, political networks, social movements, and social-networking sites. His ongoing research projects are twofold. One is an assessment of social quality across OECD countries, a nine-year project funded by the National Research Foundation of Korea. The other is a social network analysis of all Korean Twitter users (currently over 4 million) with an evaluation of their political impact on major elections. His books include *The Experiment of the Rho*

Moo Hyun Government: Unfinished Reform (Hanul Publishing, 2011, co-authored in Korean), *Risk Society, Risk Politics* (Seoul National University Press, 2010, co-authored in Korean), *Korea's Power Elite* (Hwanggum Nachimban, 2006, co-authored in Korean), and *Corporate Restructuring and Networks in Korea After the Financial Crisis* (Seoul National University Press, 2005, co-authored in Korean).

HEON JOO JUNG is an assistant professor in the Department of East Asian Languages and Cultures and an adjunct assistant professor in the Department of Political Science at Indiana University, Bloomington. He received his PhD in political science from the University of Pennsylvania in 2008. His research interests include the political economy of Korea and Japan, politics of economic crisis and reform, and East Asian regionalism. His recent publications include "The Rise and Fall of Anti-American Sentiment in South Korea: Deconstructing Hegemonic Ideas and Threat Perception" (2010), "Financial Regulatory Reform in South Korea Then and Now" (2009), and "Financial Regionalism in East Asia: Regional Surveillance Cooperation and Enforcement Problem" (2009). He is currently working on a book manuscript that examines the politics of financial regulatory reform in South Korea and Japan from a comparative perspective.

JOO-YOUN JUNG is an assistant professor in the Department of Political Science and International Relations at Korea University. After receiving her PhD in political science from Stanford University, Dr. Jung worked as postdoctoral fellow at the Weatherhead East Asian Institute (WEAI) at Columbia University and assistant professor in the Department of Political Science at the University of Alberta. Dr. Jung's major field is comparative political economy, with expertise in China and South Korea. Her research interests include the economic role of the state, the state bureaucracy, and the politics of institutional and economic reform. Her recent publications have appeared in journals such as *China Review, Pacific Focus,* and *Korean Journal of Defense Analysis,* and edited volumes such as *Going Private in China: The Politics of Corporate Restructuring and System Reform* (2011) and *Methods and Methodology in China Studies* (2010, in Korean).

NAHEE KANG is a lecturer at the Institute of Development Policy and Management (IDPM), University of Manchester. Prior to joining IDPM, she was an Economic and Social Research Council (ESRC) postdoctoral fellow at the International Centre for Corporate Social Responsibility, Nottingham University Business School, and a temporary lecturer in the Faculty of Social and Political Sciences, University of Cambridge. She obtained her PhD in social and political sciences from the University of Cambridge, funded by the Cambridge Political Economy Society Trust. Her research interests include comparative capitalism, corporate governance, and the private sector and development with a focus on East Asia. She has published in *New Political Economy*, *Socio-Economic Review*, and *Economy & Society*.

JI HYUN KIM is a PhD candidate in the Graduate School of International Studies at Ewha Womans University. She was a visiting fellow at the East-West Center at the University of Hawai'i at Manoa and is currently participating in research projects of the Institute for Development and Human Security (IDHS). Her research interests include development cooperation and foreign aid and the political economy of official development assistance (ODA).

JUNG KIM is a senior research fellow at the East Asia Institute (EAI) in Seoul, South Korea. Prior to joining the EAI, he worked at the Institute for Far Eastern Studies of Kyungnam University as a government-nominated researcher (1996–2002) and held a visiting research position in Advanced Social and International Studies at University of Tokyo as a Fox International Fellow (2004–2005). He earned his undergraduate degree in political science from Korea University and is expected to graduate from Yale University with his doctoral degree in political science. He has published numerous articles in academic journals and edited volumes, including *Asian Perspective*, *Asian Survey*, and *Korea and World Politics*.

CHUNWOONG PARK is currently a PhD candidate at the University of Illinois, at Urbana-Champaign. His area of interest includes historical sociology, cultural sociology, professions, and economic sociology. His dissertation investigates how doctors and lawyers in Korea's early modern period (1894–1945) were formed and what cultural reconfiguration took place in the process. He also studies Korean *chaebŏl*, in particular how the founding families of Korean *chaebŏl* assign their equity shares and control their firm networks.

ITO PENG is a professor of Sociology and Public Policy, and also an associate dean of Interdisciplinary & International Affairs in the Faculty of Arts and Science, University of Toronto. She teaches political sociology, comparative welfare states, and public policy, focusing especially on East Asia, Europe, and North American comparisons. Her published articles have appeared in *Politics and Society*, *Social Politics*, *International Labor Review*, *Social Policy and Administration Journal*, *Development and Change*, *Journal of East Asian Studies*, and others. Her current research includes a comparison of social investment policies in Canada, Australia, Japan, and South Korea;

an international collaborative research project on demography, gender, and care migration; and a comparison of labor market dualization in Europe and East Asia.

JIYEOUN SONG is an assistant professor of political science and international and area studies at the University of Oklahoma. She received her PhD from the Department of Government, Harvard University. Her research interests lie in labor markets, social welfare policies, and the varieties of capitalism in East Asia and Western Europe. She has published articles in several academic journals including *Asian Survey*, *Governance*, and the *Journal of East Asian Studies*.

Preface

In 2006, Jean C. Oi, Jennifer Amyx, and Byung-Kook Kim invited a group of young leading scholars to Stanford University's Walter H. Shorenstein Asia-Pacific Research Center (Shorenstein APARC) as part of their ambitious project to compare and contrast corporate restructuring in three leading global economic powers—China, Japan, and Korea. They wanted to assemble a comprehensive volume that would systematically compare the constraints and challenges of these three dynamic economies, with the aim of making a useful contribution to the growing Varieties of Capitalism literature, which had yet to engage this region in a significant manner. The volume was to allow enough flexibility to identify the distinct challenges faced by each of the three countries, while focusing on the institutions that were critical in enabling (or hindering) corporate restructuring and reform.

The goal was to produce a book that would assemble cutting-edge research that was both theoretically rigorous and rich in empirical analysis, one that would not only bring a new set of countries from the most dynamic region of the world to the Varieties of Capitalism literature, but also remedy the existing literature on the political economy of reform. The latter tended to be static in its analysis, unable to take into account the changing political and economic dynamics in these countries. Thus, the authors were asked to be particularly mindful of the changes that took place in their respective country; to analyze what institutions were critical in the reforms, as well as how, and furthermore to pay attention to the sequence of reforms. This approach would enable the resulting research to highlight the dynamism and sometimes abrupt changes found in these countries.

However, after the authors worked through many revisions and updates, the editors found themselves faced with a difficult decision. The rich collection of papers was adding up to a rather unwieldy comprehensive volume. After much discussion among themselves and the publisher, the editors decided to split the papers into three single-country volumes rather than one comprehensive volume. This would then allow the books to be used as a stand-alone resources for use in courses focused on one country, while preserving the option of using all three volumes in comparative courses. The first volume in this series, *Going Private in China: The Politics of Corporate Restructuring and System Reform*, was published in 2011, and still forthcoming is the third and final volume, *Syncretization: The Politics of Corporate Restructuring and System Reform in Japan*.

Jennifer Amyx regrettably dropped out of the editorship due to health issues, and we hope for her a full and speedy recovery. Byung-Kook Kim was called into government service in 2008—providing him first-hand insight into how the government works—and so Eun Mee Kim was asked to serve as a pinch hitter to Byung-Kook Kim's role as lead editor for this Korea volume. Jean C. Oi played a vital role in this process, from assisting with the book's organization to its final editing and proofing.

The authors in this Korean volume were faced with the challenge of analyzing a Korean political economy that continued to move quite dramatically even while in the course of writing about it. Political leadership changed and new institutions were put in place to deal with corporate restructuring; new social groups sprung up to demand or oppose corporate restructuring, reminders of the dynamic nature of Korean society as well as more challenges for our authors to tackle. Despite continual requests by the editors for revisions and updates to address these newest changes in the Korean political economy, the authors succeeded in their work, and for that we are grateful.

We would like to thank Victoria Tomkinson for her superb management of the editorial process, George Krompacky for his seamless shepherding of the project to its completion, and Jennifer Jung-Kim for her careful editing of the Korea volume. We would like to express our gratitude to Gi-Wook Shin and the Shorenstein APARC staff for their generous support during the conference and completion of the volumes. A very special note of thanks goes to the East Asia Institute, and its chairman Dr. Hong Koo Lee, for their financial and managerial support throughout the conference and in particular for the Korea volume. Hajeong Kim at the East Asia Institute was always there to help us throughout the project.

In the nearly five years since we embarked on this project, much has changed in these three countries. We hope this volume will contribute to the study of this region's dynamism, an area that demands equally dynamic analyses and theories to guide our understanding.

Byung-Kook Kim, Eun Mee Kim, and Jean C. Oi
Seoul, Korea and Stanford, USA

Adapt, Fragment, Transform

1 Introduction

BETWEEN FUNCTIONAL AND POLITICAL EXPLANATIONS[1]

Byung-Kook Kim

The proliferation of developmental state, network, and cultural theories notwithstanding, South Korea[2] remains a great puzzle for political economists. Once thought to be a hopeless case of underdevelopment by U.S. aid officials during the 1950s, South Korea embarked on a path of hypergrowth in the early 1960s. The country's achievement of what World Bank economists celebrated as "growth with equity,"[3] however, meant anything but system stability. Partly driven by internal economic contradictions and partly triggered by external demand or supply shocks, systemic crises have regularly interrupted each of South Korea's long cycles of hypergrowth, entangling its political leadership in intense conflicts over economic priorities, strategies, and institutions. Yet its economy has been resilient, bouncing back from unsettled times through a mixture of shock therapies such as currency devaluation, interest hikes, and wage guidelines—at least until 1997–1998, when Thailand sparked a regionally contagious crisis of capital flight, runs on banks, and corporate failures. During those two years, South Korea was thoroughly humbled, trapped in a destructive liquidity squeeze, which brought down eleven of its top thirty *chaebŏl* groups. Nevertheless, within a year it won back market confidence with speedy and comprehensive attention to its economic problems and by packaging financial, labor market, and corporate restructuring into one integrated reform.[4] However, even

1 This chapter is based on research supported by a Korea University Grant.
2 In this book, South Korea and Korea are used as interchangeable terms.
3 World Bank, *The East Asian Miracle: Economic Growth and Public Policy* (New York: Published for the World Bank by Oxford University Press, 1993), 2–5.
4 Byung-Kook Kim, "The Politics of Financial Reform in Korea, Malaysia, and Thailand: When, Why, and How Democracy Matters?" *Journal of East Asian Studies* 2, no. 1 (February 2002): 185–231.

after this rare moment of system restructuring, the South Korean economy retained many of its original institutions, thus making political economists raise their old questions about the South Korean economic system's stability and its capacity for change, albeit from new perspectives that tried going beyond developmental state, network, and cultural theories.

What kind of economic system was South Korea's original growth machine? Why did it suffer from persistent systemic instability yet prove resilient, recovering its capacity for economic growth precisely when its way of doing business appeared to be collapsing under both endogenously and exogenously originating forces of financial and corporate distress? How could South Korea generate hypergrowth over three and a half decades despite its unstable and perhaps even "dysfunctional" financial, corporate, and labor institutions? Did these institutions have a variable impact on South Korea's pursuit of growth during the 1961–1997 period, working as either an asset or a liability, depending on global and domestic economic conditions as well as political configurations? In what contexts did such institutions become a source of comparative advantage in global competition, and what forces of change unleashed the institutions' dysfunctional proclivities? Who put South Korea on a new track of reform in the early 1990s when it became obvious that the old system of hypergrowth did not conform to the newly emerging environment of democratization and globalization, and why did its scope of reform continuously expand until 1997, when corporate restructuring became system restructuring? What kind of system emerged out of this effort, and what kinds of changes in preferences, capabilities, and roles did it bring for South Korea's state bureaucracy, *chaebŏl* conglomerates, labor unions, and political parties? What remained the same, and what changed?

The insights of Peter A. Hall and David Soskice in their *Varieties of Capitalism* (VoC) are useful in tackling such questions of system stability and change.[5] Their 2001 book, which sparked a lively literature of its own, offers a robust set of conceptual tools with which to analyze South Korea's historical trajectory of economic development in terms of system stability and change. The VoC concept of an economic system as a sum of multiple subsystems governing finance, labor, and product markets with a varying degree of institutional complementarity, as well as its identification of institutional complementarity as a key determinant of the coordination capabilities of any given national economy, encourages us to focus on what is critical: functional or dysfunctional interaction among subsystems. This

---

5 Peter A. Hall and David W. Soskice, eds., *Varieties of Capitalism: The Institutional Foundations of Comparative Advantage* (Oxford: Oxford University Press, 2001).

relational view of political economics enables us to integrate South Korea's reform drives in the realms of finance, labor, and interfirm relations and to grasp their cumulative impact on system performance in global markets. Our use of VoC concepts, however, does not mean that we are adopting Hall and Sockice's ideas wholesale or uncritically. Because *Varieties of Capitalism* grounds its story in the United States' and Western Europe's experiences of system coordination, we are more interested in the authors' underlying relational framework or perspective of analysis than in any of their particular substantive arguments. The system we are conceptualizing has the state as one of its central components, thus distinguishing our research from VoC theories, which see the firm as the pivotal actor. But like VoC theories, our book views the state in relational terms, as supporting and receiving support from multiple other institutions in pursuit of common goals—until exogenously and/or endogenously generated pressures of crisis force the state to search for new ways of interaction with these partly changing, partly continuing other institutions.

Given the privileged role we carve out for the state in our analytic framework, we must confront politics as a force of system stability or change. The VoC literature is aware of both functional and political bases of institutions, which has split its disciples into an "equilibrium-functionalist" approach, as exemplified in Hall and Soskice's original work of 2001, and a "historical-political" school of thought, in which economic institutions are seen as reliant on power relations,[6] politically constituted or codified laws and formal regulatory rules,[7] and compromises on social conflicts.[8] But the chapters in this book take another route. Rather than adopting either an equilibrium-functionalist or a historical-political approach for the sake of logical consistency and parsimony in theory-building, we strive for analytic integration, because institutions are made by both functional and political forces. The South Korean politics of corporate restructuring has consisted of a long history of tension (1988–1997), followed by a brief moment of positive feedback (1997–1999) between functional and political forces of change, which can only be retold by integrating equilibrium-functionalist

6 Kathleen Thelen, *How Institutions Evolve* (New York: Cambridge University Press, 2004).

7 Richard Deeg, "Path Dependency, Institutional Complementarity, and Change in National Business Systems," in *Changing Capitalisms? Internationalization, Institutional Change, and Systems of Economic Organization*, ed. Glenn Morgan, Richard Whitley, and Eli Moen (Oxford: Oxford University Press, 2005), 21–49.

8 Bruno Amable, *The Diversity of Modern Capitalism* (Oxford: Oxford University Press, 2003).

and historical-political insights within one analytic framework. Moreover, by playing off functionalist and political explanations against each other, we intend to show the general ambiguity and inadequacy of some of Hall and Soskice's VoC concepts, as well as examine a series of historical and analytic puzzles in the South Korean path of corporate restructuring.

Institutional Complementarity

As conceptualized by VoC theorists, institutional complementarity exists when two or more sets of institutions experience an increase in performance because of each other's presence. Two or more institutions are said to be complementary when there exists a mutual process of positive feedback or realization of increasing returns between those institutions.[9] The VoC literature posits two types of institutional complementarity, one grounded in competitive market principles, with coordination achieved primarily through formal contract relations, and another based on strategic interaction, with coordination secured by a mutual show of commitment among actors for "information sharing, monitoring, sanctioning, and deliberation."[10] These two types of complementarity respectively make up liberal (LMEs) and co-ordinated market economies (CMEs). The two are said to sharply diverge in coordination style, but strikingly converge in their delivery of positive economic outcomes. At the same time, VoC theories offer a third category of mixed market economies (MMEs), but this category is more a residual one, encompassing a wide range of political economies that are similar primarily in their lack of LME and CME qualities, rather than in their possession of distinctive common institutional characteristics. The concept of MMEs includes virtually all political economies that fall outside Hall and Soskice's typology of LMEs and CMEs. They are categorized as MMEs because they mix market and strategic coordination, and this hybridization is thought to make their subsystems mutually more contradictory and, hence, less capable of high performance.

The South Korean experience, however, does not bear out the VoC literature's dichotomous classification of institutional complementarity into market and strategic coordination types. For Hall and Soskice, who put the firm

---

9 Paul Pierson, "Increasing Returns, Path Dependence, and the Study of Politics," *American Political Science Review* 94, no. 2 (2000): 251–67; and "The Limits of Design: Explaining Institutional Origins and Change," *Governance* 13, no. 4 (2000): 475–99.

10 Peter A. Hall and Daniel W. Gingerich, "Varieties of Capitalism and Institutional Complementarities in the Macroeconomy: An Empirical Analysis," Max-Planck Institute for the Study of Societies, Discussion Paper 04, no. 5 (2004), 8.

on center stage and exclude the state from analysis, coordination is achieved through the autonomous actions of nonstate actors, which can come in either market-based or strategic ways. By contrast, in South Korea, much of the coordination has been achieved by the state, even after the democratic breakthrough of June 1987, which put greater constraints on state capabilities. If state actors are excluded from the analysis, in fact, the South Korean economy looks like a set of dysfunctional subsystems incapable of generating hyper economic growth for any sustained period of time.

Trapped in an intermediate level of organization, fractured into ideologically rival national federations, and caught in dualistic labor market conditions (with the more elite *chaebŏl* workers enjoying better benefits and job security versus irregular contract workers without benefits or job security), South Korea's organized labor movements, Jiyeoun Song argues in Chapter 8, became at the same time too strong to be mere price-takers that accepted market wages, but also too weak to bind major segments of labor and capital into a social contract that set wages, benefits, and job security at economically sustainable levels. The *chaebŏl*'s collective ability to coordinate strategically, Byung-Kook Kim adds in Chapter 2, was also poor. The Federation of Korean Industries, their "summit organization," has been much weaker than Japan's *keidanren*, with neither a sense of camaraderie among its major *chaebŏl* members nor a mechanism for generating credible commitments between *chaebŏl* groups to cooperate on labor issues and industrial policy. As demonstrated by Heon Joo Jung in Chapter 6, South Korea's banking community also failed to develop rules for coordination. Without a capacity for risk assessment, banks became a mere "transmitter" of information provided by their *chaebŏl* clients rather than a monitor of their business activities.

In the absence of an effective mechanism for strategic coordination among business groups, banks, and company unions, the South Korean economy became a world of self-help, where economic actors individually looked after their own interest at the risk of undermining their collective interest. The *chaebŏl* preferred to reduce transaction costs through an expansion of their internal organization, which fueled a more rugged spirit of oligopolistic rivalry rather than a restrained ethos of collaboration in the corporate world (see Chapter 6). In the face of threats of labor unrest, *chaebŏl* groups adopted a "free ride" strategy, urging others to resist labor demands, but individually cutting a separate deal with their own workforce to maintain peace in their worksites. Likewise, in a similar spirit of rugged individualism, South Korea's "rigid but shrinking core" of *chaebŏl* unions fought individually to get workers' wages raised and company welfare programs increased, while their employers shifted soaring costs externally to small- and medium-sized subcontractors and consumers, and internally to unorganized and unprotected irregular workers (Chapters 2 and 8).

The dysfunctional game of self-help also prevailed in South Korea's fragile banking community (Chapter 6). The "principal transactions banks"—later, reorganized into "main creditor banks"—continually rolled over loans not only because they thought they had reduced risks by securing collaterals, but also because their fate had become intertwined with their *chaebŏl* clients' survival. The bankruptcy of a *chaebŏl* threatened its creditors' demise, encouraging those creditors into regulatory forbearance rather than corrective measures. Moreover, because *chaebŏl* groups constituted South Korea's engine of growth, banks were as much in competition with each other to secure *chaebŏl* groups as their clients as *chaebŏl* conglomerates were to obtain bank loans. By playing banks off against each other with threats of switching their main bank, *chaebŏl* groups could defend their privileges. For banks, not to comply with *chaebŏl* wishes was to risk losing their largest customers.

Yet, since instituting a developmental state in 1961, South Korea survived challenges of adjustment in 1972, 1979, and 1986 to grow over 8 percent annually in real terms for three and a half decades. The economy crashed in 1997, but even in this instance of systemic crisis, it worked its way out of severe financial and corporate distress within a year, and went on to an annual economic growth rate of 5.7 percent in 1999–2007. To explain South Korea's history of extended hypergrowth, followed by a short but deep crash and then sustained recovery, despite its *chaebŏl* conglomerates, banks, and company unions' dysfunctional efforts at self-help, we propose to adopt Hall and Soskice's relational perspective, but to emphasize the state as a pivotal force of coordination. Once the state is included as a central actor in the analysis of South Korea, what once looked like a political economy torn apart by coordination failures of individually strong but collectively weak social forces now appears potentially capable of collective endeavors over a sustained period of time. The state's efforts to persuade capital and labor to restrain their instinct to rely only on themselves, to instead cast their lot with the state's program of action, and then to stay with it rather than to defect, should be perceived as a pillar of South Korea's institutional complementarity. The presence of state actors as credible monitors, sanctioners, and deliberators of common interests makes South Korea not an internally contradictory MME but a third type of an internally coherent political economy, which can engage in coordinated endeavors in ways distinct from the methods of the LMEs and CMEs. This third type of institutional complementarity is based on statist interaction, with coordination secured through state actors who determine a division of labor among societal actors and lend their credibility to the implementation of the division of labor either from the top down, in an authoritarian way, or horizontally, through consultation with capital and labor.

The critical analytic task, then, is to decipher specific ways by which state actors endow what would have otherwise been an underperforming MME with, instead, a high level of institutional complementarity. Taking a relational view, Byung-Kook Kim in Chapter 2 zeroes in on the state's reform package of financial, labor, and interfirm relations to trace the potential points of harmony or tension, coherence or incoherence, and complementarity or contradiction of the elements involved. The focus is not on individual policies but on their cumulative sum, which is taken as a window through which to grasp South Korea's relative success, via state coordination, in achieving a high degree of institutional complementarity among its financial, labor, and interfirm subsystems.

During times of economic adjustment, Chapter 2 sums up, South Korea's developmental state (1961–1987) stabilized by means of shock therapy consisting of devaluation, interest hikes, and wage controls, while protecting its microfoundation of hypergrowth—*chaebŏl* groups and their bank subsidizers—from disintegration by assembling a state-brokered, -coordinated, and -subsidized package of mergers and acquisitions (M&As) for ailing *chaebŏl* groups and pursuing a rescue program for failing banks. This combination of "macro" stabilization and "micro" industrial rationalization measures was possible because South Korea's large commercial banks were state-owned and capital markets were state-controlled, because labor unions were repressed by security agencies, and because *chaebŏl* companies could be swapped with only an agreement between their owner-managers on the basis of cross-shareholding.

The 1987–1997 period, by contrast, saw South Korea's traditional adjustment mechanisms of wage freeze, shock therapy, and industrial rationalization challenged by "two forces of megachange," democratization and globalization, to quote Chapter 2. There ensued partial reform—again by the state—to stop, if not reverse, South Korea's loss of institutional complementarity, only to worsen the decline of institutional complementarity and trigger a system collapse in 1997. At the same time, the collapse of its economy in 1997 also became an opportunity to weed out the worst forms of moral hazard from its economic system, when South Korea accepted International Monetary Fund (IMF) conditions in return for an IMF-led rescue operation. Ironically, those terms brought back the state as South

Korea's monitor, sanctioner, and deliberator of common interests, which it now reinterpreted as streamlining *chaebŏl* groups into cost-conscious industrialists, banks into effective risk calculators and risk managers, state agencies into agents of prudential regulation as well as social safety nets for economically depressed sectors, and *chaebŏl* labor unions into partners in tripartite wage determination.

Equilibrium

Just as problematic as Hall and Soskice's exclusion of state actors in their conceptualization of coordination, institutional complementarity, and the dichotomous typology of LMEs and CMEs is their emphasis on system stability. According to Hall and Soskice, the existence of multiple other institutions "X," "Y," and "Z," which depend on an institution "A" for performance, helps make "A" stable through the functional value that "X," "Y," and "Z" gain from "A"'s presence. What is at stake in the event of a change in "A" is how effectively "X," "Y," and "Z" function as an institutional source of national comparative advantage, thus discouraging any disruptive actions toward "A." Such a functionalist understanding of institutions as a self-enforcing equilibrium has become a target of criticism, prompting Hall, among others, to take a more historical-political view, in which institutions are postulated as a historically constituted and variable set of regularized practices, which embodies power relations and serves social goals as much as efficiency gains. As such, institutions are not only a given set of enablers and constraints that shape an actor's range of strategic choices, but also a target of the actor's strategically calculated action, adopted for social purposes as well as efficiency gains albeit within the scope permitted by other institutional arrangements.[11] Even then, however, change is diagnosed as infrequent and equilibrium is seen as more the norm by adherents of the historical-political version of VoC theories.

The problem with both versions of the VoC theories is that, strictly from the perspective of *economics*, South Korea persisted on a path of disequilibrium rather than equilibrium during much of its developmental state era (1961–1988), while *institutionally* its economic system appeared to be stabilized in equilibrium. With state-owned banks de facto socializing business risks by underwriting foreign loans, channeling subsidized policy loans, and providing relief programs for ailing manufacturers, South Korea drove its *chaebŏl* into a seemingly unsustainable strategy of conglomeration and

---

11 Peter A. Hall and Kathleen Thelen, "Institutional Change in Varieties of Capitalism," paper prepared for the Conference of Europeanists, Chicago, March 2006, 1–46.

diversification into unrelated industries on borrowed money. A byproduct of what economists would view as unorthodox bank-subsidized corporate growth was a financial subsystem burdened with colossal nonperforming loans (NPLs). Consequently, the South Korean economy boomed, but also went bust in 1972 and 1979. During its heyday of dirigiste economic growth (1961–1979), in fact, state ministries frequently intervened in the opposite direction of market forces, intentionally distorting prices to get *chaebŏl* groups to invest in what state ministries believed would be South Korea's next frontier of growth, and abruptly adopting shock therapies to correct those market distortions when they seemed to have reached the point of undermining South Korea's growth potential. Economically, disequilibrium was South Korea's norm and equilibrium its deviant moments, achieved only briefly through shock therapy during times of crisis, to prepare for another long cycle of debt-financed hypergrowth.

The unbalanced growth strategy, however, worked because institutionally it was supported by South Korea's resilient developmentalist mechanism of adjustment. At the top of its rationalized yet patrimonial economic bureaucracy sat a newly established Economic Planning Board (EPB, 1961–1994), which acted as South Korea's "coordination hub" by drawing on presidential support and mobilizing internal resources for coordination, from budgetary authorities to licensing and approval powers over foreign loans and foreign direct investment (FDI) to price regulations (see Joo-Youn Jung's Chapter 5). Once the EPB signaled a policy U-turn from hypergrowth to adjustment, line ministries followed with complementary measures of shock therapy. The Ministry of Finance (MoF), presiding over what Heon Joo Jung in Chapter 6 calls South Korea's "loan market–based," "closed," and "relationship-based" financial subsystem, linked its highly subsidized program of debt-rescheduling with the Ministry of Commerce and Industry–brokered industrial rationalization in order to simultaneously rescue state banks and streamline *chaebŏl* groups. Jiyeoun Song writes in Chapter 8 that with South Korea's only labor federation captured by a docile *ŏyŏng* (state-patronized) leadership, industrial workers dispersed into company unions, dissident labor activists kept under close surveillance by security agencies, and ideologically shallow "conservative" political parties consistently failing to develop a social agenda, South Korea's "segmented" labor market ended up supporting debt rescheduling and industrial rationalization with a two-track adjustment process. Within the context of *chaebŏl* groups introducing the practices of permanent employment, seniority-based wage systems, and company welfare programs to stop others from poaching skilled workers, the state focused on restraining wage increases among *chaebŏl* workers. By contrast, for small- and medium-sized enterprises (SMEs), it let market forces determine wages and employment security.

During South Korea's transitional 1988–1997 period, a new pattern of economic and institutional (dis)equilibrium emerged—but in ways contrary to VoC theories. First, economic tensions and contradictions declined sharply as the state learned of the dangers of hypergrowth and attempted stabilization. However, these smaller-scale contradictions cumulatively added up to an imbalance of major proportions over time, making South Korea extremely vulnerable to external shocks after the mid-1990s. Second, unlike its prior developmental state era, South Korea saw its economic disequilibrium gradually deteriorate in tandem with a rising misfit between its subsystems in 1988–1997, which were then undergoing changes under the double pressures of democratization and globalization. Third, the state attempted to adapt to democratization and globalization, but those attempts aggravated rather than alleviated South Korea's problems by failing to link corporate restructuring with parallel reforms in its financial and labor market subsystems. To make a crisis even more likely, most of the state's reform initiatives also failed to reduce economic disequilibrium and institutional misfit at the level of the subsystems by either excluding some of the key components of a subsystem from targets of change, or, when included, altering those components in the opposite direction of functional pressures.

Many of the chapters in this book identify *chaebŏl* groups and *chaebŏl* workers as South Korea's prime drivers of gradually rising economic disequilibrium and drastically widening institutional misfit in 1988–1997. As Eun Mee Kim, Nahee Kang, and Ji Hyun Kim argue in Chapter 7, South Korea's top *chaebŏl* groups, exogenously empowered by U.S. pressures for liberalization, but also transformed into a powerful lobby group after South Korea's 1987 democratic transition, acquired control over myriad nonbank financial institutions (NBFIs) through which they began raising an increasingly large share of capital from overseas. This development profoundly weakened the monetary authorities' ability to control and coordinate the money supply. Moreover, because South Korea's partial reformers retained its internally fragmented supervisory systems, cozy ties with *chaebŏl* supervisees, and lax prudential regulatory rules, NBFIs became a "private cash vault" for *chaebŏl* groups, as Heon Joo Jung describes in Chapter 6. Merchant banks, especially, became a source of instability as they tried to profit from the *chaebŏl* groups' expansionary sprees by channeling relatively inexpensive short-term foreign loans to domestic producers, but without an adequate hedge against foreign exchange risks.

The *chaebŏl* workers' ascent, by contrast, originated solely from South Korea's democratization. Organized into powerful company unions during the Great Workers' Struggle of 1987, *chaebŏl* workers jealously defended their newly won political power and economic privileges by launching their own "summit organization" in 1995, against South Korea's SME-dominant Federation of Korean Trade Unions (FKTU). *Chaebŏl* workers soon transformed into a labor aristocracy, capable of taking the entire South Korean economy hostage in their struggle for higher wages, greater job security, generous company welfare provisions, and even leverage over some of the *chaebŏl* owners' managerial prerogatives. The *chaebŏl* individually opted to make separate economic deals with their company unions rather than follow wage guidelines set either top-down by state authorities or bottom-up by business associations, not only because South Korea's post-1987 "reformist" state and its "fractured" business associations lacked the power to persuade *chaebŏl* unions to accept those wage guidelines, but also because *chaebŏl* groups individually could pursue a three-pronged strategy of self-help: (1) "shift soaring labor costs to SME subcontractors and consumers," (2) "make a swift transition toward high-end product markets," and (3) "hire more nonregular workers," as Jiyeoun Song explains in Chapter 8. The *chaebŏl* employers and employees' alliance behind a group-based strategy of self-help, or "defection" from their broader bourgeois and proletariat classes, respectively, in turn, helped sustain much of South Korea's existing "occupationally segmented social insurance schemes" despite the limited introduction of universal welfare programs in 1988–1997 (see Ito Peng's Chapter 9).

The political empowerment of *chaebŏl* groups and their workers dramatically weakened South Korea's state-led coordination mechanism. As early as 1992, the EPB ceased providing indicative planning. Industrial policy, too, practically disappeared from South Korea's policy discourse after two separate attempts by the Ministry of Finance and the Ministry of Trade, Industry, and Resources (MTIR) to make *chaebŏl* conglomerates regroup around their core competencies through state-brokered business swaps and corporate downsizing failed in 1991 and 1993, respectively (see Chapter 2). The Ministry of Labor (MoL) also saw a series of reform initiatives—from its 1990 "single-digit wage increase policy" and 1991 attempt to cap company welfare expansion by establishing a "total wage system" to its 1992–1996 tripartite strategy of getting *chaebŏl* workers to reduce labor market rigidities in return for a strengthening of their basic political rights—all run into a dead-end because of *chaebŏl* and labor resistance (see Chapter 8). Moreover, failing to introduce internationally "best practices" in prudential regulation and corporate governance in tandem with its top *chaebŏl* conglomerates' establishment of investment firms, securities companies, merchant banks, and insurance companies, South Korea's financial subsystem developed an institutional "void," as explained by Kim, Kang, and Kim in Chapter 7.

The state was aware of the erosion of its capacity to coordinate during 1988–1997, but its two misconceived attempts at recovering these abilities in 1994 and 1996 backfired rather than helped it make the changes needed to become institutionally complementary and economically competitive in its brave new world of globalization and democratization. Having failed to get *chaebŏl* groups to specialize in their core competencies in 1991 and 1993, but internationally committed to capital market liberalization and labor reform as part of its entry in 1996 into the OECD, South Korea de facto fell back on its developmental state paradigm, placing planning, financial, budgetary, fiscal, and monopoly regulatory powers all in one superministry—the Finance and Economy Board (FEB)—through a swift merger of the EPB and the MoF in 1994, which Joo-Youn Jung and Heon Joo Jung diagnose as destroying what had already been a fragile mechanism of checks and balances between advocates of industrial growth and financial stability, export competitiveness and fair trade, and development and distribution within the South Korean economic bureaucracy (see Chapters 5 and 6). The reformers' idea was to recoup the state's power lost to the market and society by centralizing coordination instruments in one agency and to use that superministry to defeat the anticipated opposition to capital market liberalization and labor reform. However, by eliminating the "liberal" EPB— South Korea's prior balancer against the conservative MoF, with vested interests in protecting state banks from bankruptcy—there emerged a state apparatus even more resistant to lifting ceilings on foreign ownership, developing competitive M&A markets, tightening prudential regulations, and restructuring NPLs in tandem with capital market liberalization. The FEB, in fact, saw former MoF bureaucrats triumph over former EPB men in its internal turf wars.

The state's second misconceived attempt at recovering its coordination power, by contrast, focused on restructuring its relationship with society rather than its internal institutional arrangements. From 1992 on, South Korea saw its state expand "tripartite," or "corporatist" experiments from labor to financial issues. With coordination powers housed in one superministry and from what reformers thought was a position of bureaucratic unity and dominance, it instituted a strategy with neo-liberal goals, including a swift removal of labor market rigidities and a strengthening of prudential

regulations, but envisioned achieving those goals through newly established tripartite negotiation channels with capital and labor. The strategy
failed because most of the institutional prerequisites were absent: a hierarchically organized system of interest representation, capable of building
a broad consensus between employers and employees through a dense network of credible bargaining (see Chapter 8), under the guidance of institutionally strong programmatic political parties (Jung Kim's Chapter 4) and
with the support of a "post-developmental" (Chapter 5) regulatory state
(Chapter 6) as well as a universal welfare regime (Chapter 9). The institutional
changes that occurred between 1988 and 1997, in fact, made South Korea
move farther away from those institutional prerequisites. The *chaebŏl* unions'
militancy fractured labor. Big business fragmented too, as its largest members thought they could sustain corporate growth individually by establishing NBFIs and by obtaining foreign loans through South Korea's domestically
and internationally partially liberalized financial subsystem.

The *combination* of these path-dependent institutional changes transformed South Korea's hybrid neo-liberal–corporatist reform into a period
of political and economic instability. First, it created both capital and labor
resistance and triggered a distributive struggle over adjustment costs among
creditors and debtors, as well as among employers and employees—but
without mechanisms for credible bargaining. Second, it increased the danger of a systemic crisis by failing to stop *chaebŏl* groups from relying too
much on loans without adequate risk management and *chaebŏl* unions from
continually raising wages and expanding company welfare programs. The
political and economic instability came at a bad time. The endogenously
driven instability became a systemic crisis far worse than those of 1972 and
1979, because Thailand's economic collapse provoked a massive capital
flight from many of East Asia's new emerging markets, including that of
South Korea. Still, it is important to note that the economic and institutional disequilibria of 1988–1997 were brought about as much by the incremental accumulation of tensions and contradictions within South Korea's
generically weak economy as by the coincidence of its wrongly sequenced,
wrongly timed, and wrongly structured 1988–1997 strategy of institutional
reform with the outbreak of regional financial instability.

It was this systemic crisis that reversed South Korea's trend of falling
institutional complementarity. With more than half of the country's twenty
largest *chaebŏl* groups going bankrupt and many of its banks and NBFIs
faltering in 1997–1998, policymakers accepted IMF conditions and formulated a strategy of system restructuring, which weeded out internal tensions of the economy's subsystems by linking a shock therapy adopted in

one subsystem with those imposed in others in complementary ways. The prime driver of institutional change was a financial restructuring program, which caused a chain reaction of adjustment in labor markets, *chaebŏl* organization, and state functions—albeit in path-dependent directions. That chain reaction, in turn, enabled banks and NBFIs to lay off workers, downscale losses, and tighten prudential regulations. Even then, within each of South Korea's subsystems, there existed "sticky" institutions that resisted or even reversed pressures of organizational change, making the outcome of restructuring diverge from the state's originally intended endpoint. Yet these limitations did not prevent South Korea from instituting a more internally complementary economy. Many of the chapters in this book highlight South Korea's post-1997 success in securing positive results from its system restructuring through the coordination of complementary reform measures among its subsystems.

In Chapter 3, Dukjin Chang, Eun Mee Kim, and Chunwoong Park assess Kim Dae-jung's (Kim Tae-jung, 1998–2003) newly inaugurated reforms as qualitatively altering three traits of South Korea's *chaebŏl* practices: restricted minority shareholder rights, cross-loan guarantees, and excessive debt-financing. By contrast, the attempt at streamlining *chaebŏl* groups along their core competencies through what Kim Dae-jung called "Big Deals"—a revival of South Korea's strategy of business swaps—did not make much progress. The effort at preventing *chaebŏl* owner-managers from wielding unchecked power irrespective of the level of their family members' shares in company stocks fared even more poorly. To make *chaebŏl* owner-managers accountable, the state raised transparency requirements in accounting, legalized hostile takeovers, lifted ceilings on foreign ownership, strengthened insolvency and bankruptcy regimes, prohibited insider trading, and enhanced minority shareholder rights. With these changes, threats of hostile takeovers became real, as Sovereign Global's 2003 acquisition of SK Corp. shares and KCC Group's 2003 attack on Hyundai Elevators demonstrated. However, as appraised by Chang, Kim, and Park, such threats did not necessarily make *chaebŏl* owner-managers legally accountable, let alone develop South Korea's stock markets into an efficient representation of stock values. Still, the changes that were successfully implemented were enough to bring about a new *chaebŏl* more conscious of costs and risks.

The theme of state-initiated but path-dependent changes resulting in a greater functional and political fit among interconnected institutions also frames Heon Joo Jung's analysis of financial regulatory regimes in Chapter 6. After the state's failed attempts at adapting its dirigiste "credit control system" to South Korea's new context of liberalization and democratization solely through a reorganization of supervisory agencies in mid-1997, it made a paradigmatic policy shift, linking its internal organizational issues with South Korea's other root causes of systemic instability that it had hitherto excluded from its reform agenda for fear of political backlash and functional distress: nonperforming loans, legal restrictions on M&As, lax prudential regulations, opaque accounting systems, and weak insolvency and bankruptcy regimes. The state reorganized its internal apparatus swiftly and comprehensively, splitting the FEB into three separate agencies: the Ministry of Finance and Economy (MOFE), Ministry of Planning and Budget (MPB), and Financial Supervisory Commission (FSC). The split provided breathing space for advocates of prudential regulations inside South Korea's still-dirigiste state, whereas Kim Dae-jung's transformation of M&A, accounting, and insolvency and bankruptcy regimes set up more orderly and timely processes of exit for failing banks, NBFIs, and *chaebŏl* groups. These two measures reinforced Kim Dae-jung's corporate governance reform (see Chapter 3) in making *chaebŏl* groups more cost-conscious and risk-averse.

Eun Mee Kim, Nahee Kang, and Ji Hyun Kim in Chapter 7 similarly identify 1997–1998 as a turning point for South Korea's FDI regime, with its key rules and norms changed in ways complementary to its strategy of system restructuring. As Kim Dae-jung and his technocrats perceived, foreign capital constituted an indispensable partner in corporate restructuring, ready to introduce best practices from a position of independence from *chaebŏl* groups. Consequently, the government removed legal ceilings on foreign equity ownership, opened up foreign entries into politically and economically strategic sectors, and streamlined regulatory rules and procedures. The goal was to raise the foreign presence in South Korea to the level of pressuring *chaebŏl* groups and banks into market-driven, arm's length, and rule-based relationships. The size of FDI never hit such a transformative level, but its accelerating growth, especially during 1999–2000, was alarming enough to get *chaebŏl* groups to restructure their businesses under real or imagined threats of foreign takeover.

Jiyeoun Song in Chapter 8 also reports a story of dirigiste attempts at bringing about an institutional breakthrough in labor politics during 1997–1998, in the direction of aiding financial and corporate restructuring. But this chapter diverges from Chapters 3, 6, and 7 by emphasizing a greater level of institutional stickiness in labor markets. As Song analyzes, even during this rare moment of system collapse, shock therapy failed, leaving much of South Korea's dualistic labor markets more or less intact. The internally segmented labor markets—rooted in South Korea's highly concentrated industrial structures, institutionalized through company unions, and prolonged by the rapid spread of irregular contract workers—in fact, further consolidated through 1997–1998. No other subsystem saw such a defeat of state-led restructuring drives. The state's failure in getting newly enacted labor laws to translate into an actual dismantlement of labor market rigidities, however, did not mean that South Korea's labor market subsystem stopped evolving from where it was at the height of its 1997–1998 system crisis. On the contrary, it continually adjusted but in path-dependent ways, with *chaebŏl* groups and *chaebŏl* workers once again falling back on their old formula of labor market segmentation to balance their contradictory requirements of adjustment, industrial peace, and export competitiveness. To prevent strikes, *chaebŏl* groups kept their system of permanent employment, seniority-based wages, and company welfare programs for unionized "regular" workers. To pursue corporate restructuring to strengthen export competitiveness, they also hired additional "irregular" contract workers. This army of irregular workers became second-class citizens within South Korea's workforce, helping *chaebŏl* groups to recover their competitive edge in international marketplaces by getting laid off during hard times and paid less during good times.

By contrast, the state was much more successful in transforming South Korea's "selective" and "occupationally segmented" type of social insurance into a more "universal" kind in the aftermath of the 1997–1998 crisis. As shown by Ito Peng in Chapter 9, from health care to pensions to social welfare, the state moved swiftly to socialize much of its hitherto privately operated welfare and social policy regimes, as well as to universalize the coverage of the population. And these measures bore fruit. The South Korean state, hitherto fiscally conservative, was able to pay for a huge expansion of welfare expenditures. The *chaebŏl*, caught in a liquidity squeeze and facing powerful company unions, welcomed the state's expansion of its welfare roles. The increasing reliance on irregular workers for the restructuring of banks, NBFIs, and *chaebŏl* groups into slimmer organizations, moreover, required the state's provision of a safety net for these workers. Building a welfare state South Korean–style, Peng argues, institutionally complemented South Korea's use of irregular workers in moving to a less rigid labor market.

Regime, International, and State Dynamics

The year 1997 saw South Korea's economy collapse. The puzzle is how, unlike many other East Asian NICs (newly industrializing countries) afflicted by a more or less similar "Thai disease," South Korea used this moment of systemic crisis as a window of opportunity for massive financial and corporate restructuring programs that added up to a system change.[12] The puzzle also has a temporal dimension. Many of South Korea's reform measures that were successfully put in place in 1997–1998 resembled many of its failed reform initiatives of 1996–1997. These episodes of institutional reform were separated by less than a year, but their outcomes were miles apart. The 1997–1998 reform package had most of its measures successfully implemented to trigger path-dependent institutional changes. Consequently, any equilibrium-functionalist or historical-political explanations we give for South Korea's spatial divergence from other East Asian countries in dealing with the crisis also need to fit in logically with our other temporal story of how a similar package of reform could fail in 1996–1997, but succeed in 1997–1998. As shown in the previous sections, the search for an integrated explanation leads to the pivotal role of the state. In every episode of South Korea's reforms, the state decisively shaped the outcome through its choice of national vision, agenda, and strategy. The question is how the state's preferences on these issues were constituted in the first place, which encourages many of the contributors to this book to analyze the actors overlooked by VoC theories until very recently: political regime, international players, and state agencies themselves.

These actors have escaped scrutiny in VoC analyses because much of the original theorizing was empirically based on postwar America and West Germany, whose economies were backed by a stable liberal democracy, enjoyed a position of strength in global financial and maybe even trade sectors, and adjusted through a nonstate coordination mechanism of either LME or CME type. In other words, analysts' choice of empirical cases profoundly shaped their theory-building, in effect obstructing them from considering the impact of political regime changes, international vulnerabilities, and state actors on the patterns of institutional interaction and the choice of institutional complementarity. For these observers, these three actors were "absent" or "invisible" because the U.S. and German cases were alike in having democratically legitimated, societal actor–orchestrated, and relatively autonomous mechanisms of national coordination. Conversely, South Korea's gradual dismantlement of authoritarian politics after 1987, persistent external economic vulnerabilities and weaknesses, and historical legacies of a strong state make it difficult for any analyst to ignore the impact of political regime changes, international players, and state agencies on the dynamics of institutional interaction.

12 See Byung-Kook Kim, "The Politics of Financial Reform in Korea, Malaysia, and Thailand," for South Korea's divergence from Malaysia and Thailand in harnessing its 1997–1998 systemic crisis to launch a comprehensive reform.

In this book we focus on these three variables neglected in the VoC literature to explain the state's preference for and its choice of vision, agenda, and strategy, but we do so within the VoC framework of relational explanation. That is, we seek to explain South Korea's policy choices in terms of how these three variables configure and interact with one another in the reshaping of the state's views on financial, labor, and interfirm subsystems, as well as the subsystems' relationship with the state's two most critical political tasks after 1987: how to legitimize South Korea's newly emerging democratic regime and its directly elected president's administration, and how to accommodate intense U.S. pressures for foreign exchange and capital market liberalization without triggering a systemic crisis. These three variables of regime, international, and state dynamics reinforced each other in encouraging the state's highly destabilizing search for an adaptation strategy precisely when the same variables also made the need for coordination more urgent by causing the financial, labor, and interfirm subsystems to evolve in mutually contradictory directions until 1997.

The most critical actor in the dramas of misconceived reform, policy failure, and system drift during 1988–1997 was the presidency, with its distinctive strengths and weaknesses. As Jung Kim discusses in Chapter 4, because of South Korea's "unstructured" political party system and "programmatically weak" political parties, it was only through presidential leadership that South Korea could attempt to adapt its politically and functionally constrained dirigiste economy to the powerful forces of democratization and globalization. However, because of four institutional arrangements, the president typically saw his public popularity and legislative support undergo a cycle of steep rise and disastrous fall. First, South Korea's adoption of a single five-year nonrenewable presidential term threatened to make the president a lame duck after the middle of his term. Second, however, he could not fight back by opting for a strategy of Latin American–style "delegative democracy," given his lack of power to issue legislative decrees. On the contrary, the president's political fate was closely intertwined with not only his ruling party's share of National Assembly seats but also the loyalty to him from within his party. And that loyalty could only dissipate after his mid-term. Third, he faced an uphill struggle even in securing a stable legislative majority, because National Assembly elections, held every four years in between presidential elections, functioned as a disadvantageous mid-term "vote of confidence" for the president and his party. Losses in National Assembly elections hastened his political eclipse. Fourth, the construction of a legislative majority also became harder because the single-member district plurality voting system had the effect of fragmenting party politics in the context of increased regionalist voting after 1987.

Consequently, Jung Kim explains that the prospect for reform brightened when a *president* backed by a *legislative majority* and enjoying *public popularity* initiated reform during the *early* years of his term. These are extremely stringent conditions for success, because they imply a president must have a programmatic vision, agenda, and strategy at the time of his election. Only then can he initiate a reform package early in his presidential term. But South Korean political parties and electoral contests have been by their nature nonprogrammatic, making such an outcome very unlikely. For Kim Young-sam (Kim Yŏng-sam, 1993–98), in fact, developing a programmatic vision was a task to be tackled after his inauguration, not during his election campaign. Kim Young-sam did come up with a two-pronged reform strategy—but too late in his presidential term. When, after two and a half years of bargaining, his Tripartite Presidential Commission failed to persuade *chaebŏl* workers to accept labor market flexibility measures, including management's right to lay off workers in times of corporate distress, in return for the lifting of tight legal constraints on organized workers' political and civil rights, Kim Young-sam should have deferred labor market reform. Instead, with only a year remaining in his term, he pushed for legislation of a pro-business reform package without political and social provisions in December 1996, as some of his aides had warned he would in the event of labor resistance to the Tripartite Commission's attempt at a class compromise. The unions struck back hard with a "general strike," while opposition parties attacked Kim Young-sam's legislation of reform bills in the opposition parties' absence in the very early morning as thoroughly lacking in procedural legitimacy. The ruling party, with its faction leaders preparing for presidential primaries, in turn, deserted Kim Young-sam and rescinded his pro-business labor laws through a negotiation with the opposition three months later. The party then hoped to save its 1997 election campaign by distancing itself from the politically delegitimized Kim Young-sam.

Incredibly, despite his loss of grip on party politics and state ministries, Kim Young-sam proposed to reorganize South Korea's economic bureaucracy once more in May 1997—this time, in the direction of unifying its financial regulatory authorities and strengthening its central bank's independence. The reorganization proposal, drawn up by a presidential commission in its capacity as an objective third party, free from bureaucratic interests, however, paralyzed South Korea's state apparatus from within, precisely when an exogenously and endogenously driven liquidity-squeeze threatened to force half of its twenty largest *chaebŏl* groups into bankruptcy. The FEB revised bills to recover much of its powers, only to provoke South Korea's central bank and regulators into a strike. The ruling party, fearful of getting entangled in any vote-losing issues during an increasingly volatile election season, opted for a strategy of no-action despite its legislative majority. The opposition also preferred to postpone its legislation until after the electoral contests. Consequently, those bills were shelved for half a year. The election was held in December, but by then South Korea was deep in a systemic crisis. The wrongly timed reorganization program had pushed the country's state agencies into a struggle over regulatory powers and its political parties into inaction when they should have joined forces to combat the contagious regional financial turmoil.

As Jung Kim writes, it was only Kim Dae-jung's reform that was timed correctly, implemented even before his inauguration in February 1998, as thoroughly demoralized Kim Young-sam agreed to de facto hand over power to Kim Dae-jung's transition team. The programmatic vision for which Kim Dae-jung was to use his newly won power, however, was not initially his own. Kim Dae-jung was a rare politician in South Korea's nonprogrammatic party politics, with distinctive policy ideas and visions that he had called *taejung kyŏngjeron* (mass economics) since his 1971 presidential campaign.[13] Those beliefs, however, were progressive ones that did not seem to fit in with South Korea's 1997 situation of systemic crisis and its policy requirement of adjustment. The ideas he now embraced were, in fact, neoliberal shock therapies demanded by U.S. policymakers and IMF representatives. From their programmatic demands, packaged as "IMF conditions," Kim developed ideas on the tasks, strategies, and instruments he believed were needed, and he swiftly translated these into tripartite compromises, laws, policy guidelines, and state reorganization measures before his inauguration. The political parties, *chaebŏl* groups, and labor federations that had vetoed tripartite bargaining only a few months earlier accepted Kim Dae-jung's IMF-driven institutionally complementary package of financial, corporate, and labor market reform measures in 1998 because Kim, with his term just begun, had the power to decisively shape the state bureaucracy's choice of the targets, terms, and processes of restructuring until the middle of his term—or, for the next two and a half more years. Kim Dae-jung was then a politician whose favor was sought most by societal groups and political forces, and whose retaliation was most feared.

The issue of timing, which helps to explain the state's successes and failures in transforming reform ideas into policies, however, leaves many questions of preferences unanswered. Kim Dae-jung not only endorsed the IMF conditions but also went beyond them, adding on top of IMF-demanded

---

13 For an English translation of Kim Dae-jung's ideas, see Kim Dae Jung, *Mass-Participatory Economy: A Democratic Alternative for Korea* (Lanham, MD: University Press of America, 1985).

shock therapies what he termed "*chaebŏl* reform." For Kim Dae-jung, shock therapies were more than a catalyst for economic adjustment; they opened the way to a *system* change. To explain Kim Dae-jung's reinterpretation of IMF conditions, Chapter 2 examines his preferences. As Kim Dae-jung saw it, accepting U.S. and IMF pressure for a drastic financial restructuring program was not only unavoidable, given South Korea's exhaustion of its foreign exchange reserves, but also ideologically desirable and politically advantageous. The partisan map also had transformed in ways that made Kim Dae-jung's preferences coincide even more with system restructuring. The ideological attack on crony capitalism made conservative Yi Hoe-ch'ang's Grand National Party (GNP, Hannaradang) a villain and a culprit rather than a hero responsible for South Korea's glorious history of hypergrowth, but the GNP found itself awkwardly supporting many of Kim Dae-jung's reform measures, because Kim Dae-jung packaged many of them in conservative neo-liberal ideas. The progressives, too, were angered by labor market flexibility measures even though they were countered by an introduction of universal welfare provisions, but they restrained from fully opposing Kim Dae-jung because there existed no viable political force to the left of him in South Korea's ideological terrain to champion their agenda. The destruction of Kim Dae-jung's political authority and credibility would be their loss. On the other hand, as a progressive opposition leader supported by labor union heads and hitherto alienated Chŏlla regional voters, Kim Dae-jung was an outsider, relatively free from the pressure of business interests and without a bureaucratic clientele with a claim on his political support. Thus he could experiment with the idea of system change, owing no debts to *chaebŏl* groups and bureaucratic forces.

By contrast, in Chapter 5 Joo-Youn Jung explains Kim Young-sam's politically and functionally disastrous partial reform in terms of his conservative yet reformist preferences. Kim Young-sam spoke bravely of neoliberal values, but unlike Kim Dae-jung, who gave those ideas progressive twists and turns, Kim Young-sam reinterpreted neo-liberal ideas in essentially dirigiste ways. He considered liberalization the most critical task facing South Korea. The Uruguay Round of trade negotiations was under way, and capital markets gradually but irreversibly opened up under U.S. pressure. Resistance being no option for South Korea's export economy, Kim Young-sam instead opted to go further, deeper, and faster into liberalization than what was being demanded by U.S. policymakers, pledging South Korea's OECD entry within two years. The idea was to pressure banks, NBFIs, *chaebŏl* companies, and labor unions into restructuring by adopting OECD norms in capital markets and labor markets by 1996. To adopt those norms from a position of political strength, free of societal veto players, Kim Young-sam radically centralized state powers in his newly established FEB and made it his pilot agency of liberalization. The *segyehwa* (globalization) strategy had liberalization as its endpoint, but its spirit was anything but liberal. The state was its coordinator, and capital and labor were the targets of top-down mobilization or demobilization. As Joo-Youn Jung writes, Kim Young-sam's dirigiste norms and preferences, packaged in newly imported neo-liberal ideas, enabled South Korea's state bureaucracy, especially its FEB "core institution," to protect its powers from societal encroachments. The FEB used those powers to adopt OECD rules and norms in the hopes that those rules and norms would compel banks, NBFIs, *chaebŏl* groups, and labor unions to restructure according to market signals.

A "New" System?

The greatest puzzle in the post-1997 South Korean politics of system restructuring is what its intended endpoint was and how that resembled or differed from what actually emerged. Confusion on intentions and goals arose because South Korea's top political authorities were extremely eclectic in their pursuit of reform, mixing what looked like unmixable and inappropriate institutional ideas as rationales for the actions they took. There was Kim Dae-jung, who combined a Thatcherite discourse of neo-liberal reform with democratic corporatist and maybe even social democratic ideas, launching a Tripartite Commission but giving it a mission of creating a flexible labor market in parallel with financial restructuring and corporate downsizing at a time when South Korea's internally fragmented *chaebŏl*, organized labor, and financial community lacked the ability to make a credible and autonomous commitment to any comprehensive program of financial and corporate restructuring in corporatist or social democratic fashion (see Chapter 8).

To worsen the confusion, the newly established Financial Supervisory Commission, chosen by Kim Dae-jung as the prime driver of his reforms, spoke of modeling South Korea's financial and corporate restructuring after Great Britain's voluntary, nonjudicial, and autonomous "London Approach," despite the fact that South Korean banks and NBFIs resembled anything but the City of London, which was capable of getting creditors to agree with debtors on a workable distribution of restructuring costs through autonomous deliberation without state intervention (see Chapters 2 and 6). Likewise, after 1999, South Korean regulators included corporate governance structures as a legitimate target of state intervention, because they thought that only with a marked strengthening of corporate transparency and accountability could *chaebŏl* groups be made to shed their old habit of overexpansion (see Chapter 3). This expansion of state role, in turn, prompted many of South Korea's progressive political forces and NGO activists to identify Western Europe's "stakeholder" model, as distinct from the United States' "shareholder" model, as South Korea's endpoint of reform in corporate governance structures.

Such an eclectic mixing of heterogeneous foreign ideas turns the intentions, objectives, and strategies of reformers into a puzzle. Was South Korea's new post-1997 ruling coalition building a CME, as its rhetoric of tripartite bargaining, welfare state, and stakeholder interests implied; or an LME, as its neo-liberal discourse of labor market flexibility, the London Approach, and shareholder interests hinted? Or, could it be neither, since South Korea's badly shaken, and still sticky state-driven financial subsystem, *chaebŏl*-centered corporate subsystem, and company-segmented labor market subsystem hardly fit in with either the LME spirit of autonomous markets or the CME vision of strategic coordination? What were the post-1997 political leadership's intentions, if they had no illusions about building an LME or a CME in South Korea's still statist configuration of economic institutions? The chapters of our volume advise against interpreting South Korea's use of LME or CME ideas as evidence of its economy's rebirth into an LME or a CME. Institutional complementarities in support of such a wholesale remodeling were lacking in South Korea even after its systemic crisis of 1997–1998. The state knew of these institutional limitations, but still stuck with its use of foreign ideas and concepts. To explain such persistence in the use of LME- or CME-style ideas despite the absence of LME- or CME-style institutions, we disaggregate policy discourse into a set of substantive guidelines and a bundle of formal institutional recommendations. The policy set lists of "what to do," whereas its institutional counterpart gave guidelines on "how to do." The two sets of ideas are obviously interrelated, but their interrelationship can be of several mutually distinctive types, not just Hall and Soskice's LME and CME patterns. As will be elaborated in many of our chapters, the South Korean episode of system restructuring during Kim Dae-jung's political rule shows one of the non-LME and non-CME ways of adjustment.

In essence, what South Korea was emulating when it spoke of neo-liberal as well as corporatist ideas was more the ideas' policy guidelines than their institutional underpinnings. The institutional mechanism Kim Dae-jung mobilized to get state policy in tune with those policy guidelines, in fact, was anything but neo-liberal or corporatist, as understood in Hall and Soskice's concept of LMEs and CMEs. The South Korean state bureaucracy constituted an agent of coordination, translating U.S. pressures, IMF conditions, and its newly inaugurated political master Kim Dae-jung's progressive aspirations and partisan interests into a policy package, and getting capital and labor to take mutually complementary actions in support of these policy guidelines through the provision of incentives and disincentives. The state used foreign discourses for setting reformist agendas, goals, and strategies, but for their implementation, it fell back on its own resources because neither capital nor labor had developed capabilities for autonomous market or strategic coordination. The Tripartite Commission could agree, however briefly, on a set of asymmetrical economic bargains only because South Korea's state apparatus sometimes cajoled and other times threatened *chaebŏl* groups into giving their workers a concession and vice versa (see Chapter 8). The supposed "London Approach" likewise was propelled by FSC bureaucrats rather than by an autonomously organized network of creditors and debtors (Chapters 2 and 6). It was also the state that introduced a system of outside directors, institutionalized a more transparent accounting regime, strengthened minority shareholder rights as a check on *chaebŏl* owners in a top-down manner, and created a market for M&As through lifting legal ceilings on foreign ownership (Chapters 3 and 7).

The question is whether such a selective importation of foreign ideas, but not their underlying institutional mechanisms of coordination, worked. The chapters in this volume give complex answers. The South Korean state's capacity for serving as a functional equivalent of the coordinating role Hall and Soskice spoke of for their ideal-type firm in LMEs and CMEs significantly varied across the country's financial, labor, and interfirm subsystems. The greatest barrier to state initiatives was found in South Korea's internally segmented labor movements. The "corporatist" Tripartite Commission, Jiyeoun Song writes in Chapter 8, fell apart only a few days after its February 1998 "grand compromise" amid a revolt of *chaebŏl* unions, thus burying Kim Dae-jung's "neo-liberal" agenda of bringing *chaebŏl* workers more directly under market pressures. The victory of *chaebŏl* employees, however, proved to be more the defeat of other workers, especially new entrants to labor markets, than of the *chaebŏl* employees' victory. When big business could not exercise its dramatically strengthened legal rights to lay off workers in times of distress, it turned to the hiring of irregular workers to break out of wage constraints, as it had done all along—albeit less aggressively— since workers had organized into myopic company unions in 1987. In other words, South Korea managed to achieve the minimum level of labor market flexibility required for its international competitiveness, but this was a product of the *chaebŏl* groups' gradual bifurcation of their own labor force into the privileged regular and underprivileged irregular workers rather than a result of the state's sudden and drastic reform of national labor markets.

The South Korean state's strategy of implementing LME or CME ideas top-down in statist ways had much better luck in financial restructuring. The norms, procedures, and strategies of restructuring, formally modeled after Great Britain's London Approach, helped draw creditors and debtors into FSC-initiated and -brokered negotiation mainly because Kim Dae-jung's tripartite deal of February 1998 obligated *chaebŏl* groups to reduce their debt-equity ratio to 200 percent within two years (see Chapters 2 and 6). Having already seen eight of the top thirty *chaebŏl* groups go under in 1997 alone, and all of South Korea's five largest commercial banks begin negotiating for a foreign takeover of their operations or attempt a thorough restructuring through M&As while sustaining themselves on newly injected public funds in 1998, both creditors and debtors took the FSC guidelines seriously in their major issues of disagreement. The ownership structure of the seven largest banks changed dramatically by 2000; six had foreign banks, financial consortia, or hedge funds as their single largest shareholder. The institutional outcome was slimmer commercial banks and NBFIs, but they became slimmer in ways unintended by Kim Dae-jung's reformers. The newly restructured banks and NBFIs reduced risks, but by zeroing in on collateralized household markets rather than on developing institutional capabilities to properly assess their borrowers' creditworthiness. Moreover, as Heon Joo Jung writes, contrary to Kim Dae-jung's intention to develop a market-driven, arm's length, and rule-based relationship between creditors and borrowers, South Korea ended up with a state-dominated regulatory regime, prone to compromise prudential regulations in the interests of macro political and economic objectives.

Similarly, South Korea's interfirm subsystem showed an intermediate level of institutional stickiness. The most exclusive club of its top thirty *chaebŏl* groups saw seven more of its members either entirely dissolved or dramatically downsized in 1998–2000. The threats of hostile foreign takeover also became real, as Sovereign Global's attack on SK Corp. demonstrated. These two changes ended the *chaebŏl* groups' extremely risky appetite for hypergrowth, but did not make them any more prudential in risk management. Instead those that survived the harsh liquidity squeeze of 1997–1998 swung to the other way, becoming extremely risk averse, because their ownership structure remained unchanged, concentrated in the founders' extended family members. As Dukjin Chang, Eun Mee Kim, and Chunwoong Park report in Chapter 3 and Byung-Kook Kim reports in Chapter 2, the top priority of the survivors became defending their owner-manager family's control of ownership and management, the effect of which was to encourage the *chaebŏl* to stack up piles of retained earnings as insurance against threats of a hostile takeover rather than to take on new large-scale business ventures through a skillful assessment of cash flows.

The state's efforts to translate foreign neo-liberal and corporatist ideas into economic policy on what was institutionally illiberal and noncorporatist South Korean political and economic soil, then, resulted in a novel mix of system change and continuity. On the one hand, the labor market subsystem remained internally segmented with the state prevented from encroaching upon the privileges of *chaebŏl* workers, but at the same time the *chaebŏl* succeeded in securing some labor market flexibility through a greater reliance on irregular workers (see Chapter 8). Likewise, *chaebŏl* groups became slimmer under threats of bankruptcy and hostile takeover, but also continued to be controlled by their owner-managers' extended family. The stock markets also fell below Kim Dae-jung's neo-liberal ambition to develop an efficient market for corporate control because with each *chaebŏl* group still organized as a hierarchical equity network, attempts at hostile takeovers bid up the holding company's stock prices to the value of the entire group rather than to that of the holding company itself, making stock markets extremely volatile (see Chapter 3).

In the financial subsystem, too, foreigners came to control many of South Korea's commercial banks and NBFIs, thus further weakening the state's control over the money supply and, hence, its capacity for industrial policy (see Chapter 7), but at the same time, this change did not lead to the establishment of a "neo-liberal" financial subsystem that made loans on the basis of an objective assessment of the borrowers' cash flows. On the contrary, not only foreign-controlled but also state-owned banks preferred borrowers with collateral rather than making loans on the basis of risk calculation. Making loans on the basis of collateral rather than on an assessment of the borrowers' future streams of cash flow was nothing new in South Korea; this practice had prevailed during the developmental state era (see Chapter 2). The state also found itself between forces of change and continuity. The bureaucracy lost many of its powerful developmentalist resources, first the mechanism of labor control during the Great Workers' Strike of 1987, followed by planning and industrial policy capabilities in the early 1990s, and then nationally controlled financial institutions after 1997, but it still functioned as South Korea's pivotal coordinator not only because it retained influence over a few but crucial policy instruments, such as foreign exchange and interest rates, even after its successive downsizing of role and power after 1988, but also because South Korea lacked other LME- or CME-style mechanisms of coordination. Having grown under state patronage before 1997, and surviving a severe liquidity squeeze through self-help rather than through autonomous collective action since 1997, South Korea's *chaebŏl* groups and financial institutions both failed to develop their own principles, rules, and norms of collaboration (see Chapter 6). The same was true of the labor sector, but for different reasons. South Korean workers were fragmented, first into the "radical" Korean Confederation of Trade Unions and the "conservative" Federation of Korean Trade Unions at the national level, then into myopic company unions at the firm level, and even into regular and irregular workers within the firm. Such an internally fragmented labor organization meant that, if there was to be a mechanism for coordination in labor politics, it had to be the increase of irregular workers. That was possible only when the state acquiesced in South Korea's increasing socioeconomic divide (see Chapter 8), but also provided a social safety net for the losers through a dramatic expansion of welfare expenditures (see Chapter 9).

The critical analytic issue is whether such a mix of change and continuity in South Korea's financial, interfirm, labor market, and state subsystems contributed to the making of a new stable economic system. Many of our contributors think that the restructuring programs of 1997–1998 put the South Korean economy in equilibrium, permanently resolving its historical problem of excessive debt financing. The *chaebŏl* are judged to have lost their appetite for risk taking after witnessing half of the top thirty groups disintegrate during the period 1997–2000. They are described as having turned extremely conservative, preferring to finance investment internally through retained earnings, because they determined that the state's capabilities as a planner of industrial growth, a guarantor of labor peace, and a provider of a financial safety net were all on the decline. These *chaebŏl* groups still relied on additional stock issues, but less frequently because their foremost interest was in defending their control of ownership and management (see Chapter 3). Moreover, South Korea's newly restructured financial subsystem, dominated by foreign capital and still shaken by its late-1990s experience of massive bank failures, was more interested in developing a financially stronger and safer household market than in taking on *chaebŏl* customers. Economically, then, South Korea's new system appeared to be stable, with its financial, interfirm, and labor market subsystems reinforcing each other's influences toward financial conservatism. After three years of massive business failures and layoffs, the South Korean economy finally seemed to have succeeded in weeding out its most dysfunctional trait, corporate overexpansion.

Politically, however, it was not clear that the new system would be stable. The *chaebŏl* groups' achievement of labor market flexibility through the increased use of irregular workers became a target of ideological criticism and a source of political instability (see Chapter 8). Irregular workers, essentially "second-class citizens" in South Korea's segmented labor markets, earning only three-quarters of their more privileged regular coworkers' wages and first to be laid off in times of distress, could readily find political allies, patrons, and supporters in the National Assembly. To be sure, irregular workers were rarely capable of engaging in collective political action on their own, given their dismal level of unionization. Their platform of "equal pay for equal work," however, has had a powerful moral force, making even South Korea's *chaebŏl* workers, a primary beneficiary of the irregulars' low wages and deplorable job insecurity, become supporters of irregular workers and their rights. The South Korean labor federations, to protect the irregular workers without giving up their *chaebŏl* unions' privileges, called for a legally mandatory transformation of irregular workers into regular workers after two years of employment. NGO activists and academic experts also agitated on behalf of unorganized irregular workers. Finally, in a rare bipartisan move, the National Assembly revised labor bills along similar lines in December 2006. The presidential election was then only a year away, making both ruling and opposition political parties compete for the support of irregular workers.

Likewise, Kim Dae-jung's vision of restructuring big business after the shareholder model of corporate governance provoked political opponents to champion the stakeholder model prevailing in CMEs (see Chapter 7). Consensus failed to develop, entangling a series of cross-border M&As in intense political and legal disputes. In such disputes, the arbiter was not state ministries, but the courts, signaling that South Korea had dismantled its developmental state, but had not yet constructed a system of corporate governance that was itself solidly grounded on legal and political consensus.

Unfortunately, however, it is highly unlikely that South Korea's search for an economically *and* politically viable labor market subsystem will end soon. The practice of hiring irregular workers has spread across sectors and within *chaebŏl* groups because it has been only through the hiring of more irregular workers that *chaebŏl* groups have been able to achieve the labor market flexibility needed for international competitiveness. Until South Korea's absence of both LME and CME coordination mechanisms is corrected, any legal initiative to phase out irregular workers, like that of 2006, is bound to fail because it does not resolve the root cause of the *chaebŏl* groups' resort to the hiring of irregular workers—that is, the high wages, generous company welfare benefits, and "iron-rice-bowl" job security enjoyed by regular *chaebŏl* workers, which threaten to erode the *chaebŏl* conglomerates' international competitiveness. Unless this root cause is resolved by the construction of either a LME or a CME mechanism of coordination, which is unlikely given the path dependence of institutional evolution, *chaebŏl* groups will continually engage in self-help, laying off irregular workers before their interim period of two years expires and then rehiring them as irregular workers when they are next needed. The South Korean labor market subsystem still needs to come up with a mechanism of labor market coordination that not only functionally meets the *chaebŏl* conglomerates' requirement of international competitiveness, but also secures the political support of its workforce.

The second set of political tensions and contradictions that calls into question the stability of South Korea's "new" economic system ironically arose from one of its major policy successes since 1997. The *chaebŏl* was made a slimmer organization, but this success came with politically burdensome consequences. As *chaebŏl* groups began generating large retained earnings not only in defense against threats of hostile takeovers but also as a safe source of investment funds, South Korea experienced a precipitous decline in economic growth. The outcome was dissatisfactory for all political forces. For South Korea's burgeoning progressive political forces, *chaebŏl* groups looked irresponsible, sacrificing economic growth and employment for their owner-manager families' interests in management control. To put South Korea back on its path of growth, the progressives thought a further deepening of *chaebŏl* reform was required—this time, toward an effective separation of ownership and management. The *chaebŏl* were also unhappy about the country's decline in economic growth, but for different reasons. The state policy of legally restricting manufacturing firms from acquiring more than a 4 percent share of banks, adopted as part of an effort to weed out threats of moral hazard by basing credit transactions on arm's length principles and sound risk management practices, was criticized as a blatant act of "reverse discrimination" against nationally owned *chaebŏl* groups, as well as an act of sabotage of South Korea's competitiveness in global markets within the new context of open capital markets. The prohibition against any large subsidiary or affiliate firm of South Korea's top *chaebŏl* groups from investing more than 40 percent of its net assets in another affiliate company's stocks has been a hot issue, too. The legal provision was lifted, then reinstituted, and finally repealed again after 1998, attesting to South Korea's lack of national consensus on what should be the goal of *chaebŏl* reform.

Our volume thus has two research objectives: to gain a deeper understanding of South Korea's historical path of financial and corporate restructuring by adopting Hall and Soskice's relational framework of analysis, but also to critically appraise, adapt, and strengthen VoC theories using our evaluations of South Korea's episodes of financial and corporate restructuring since 1997. The chapters strive to improve on the innovative but problematic functionalist concepts of equilibrium and institutional complementarity by focusing on a varying interplay of functional pressures and power relations as the prime driver of system change or continuity. As argued in our chapters, neither functional nor political pressures alone decide system characteristics and their degree of stability and change; rather, it is their patterns of interaction, as South Korea's experience of financial and corporate restructuring teaches us, that shape system characteristics and their evolution. By bringing politics back in as an integral part of South Korea's story of corporate and financial restructuring, we also fill in three missing stories in VoC theories: political regime, international, and bureaucratic dynamics. With the help of these variables, we describe an economic system that denies any easy dichotomous concepts of equilibrium and disequilibrium, functionalism and politics, or stability and instability. The system shows both characteristics, or, rather, has fluctuated between those opposites.

Section I

Patterns and Processes of Change

2 A Search for Institutionally Complementary Reform[1]

Byung-Kook Kim

The year 1997 saw the collapse of the South Korean economy. By September, with an exchange rate that had risen to 915 won per dollar and an interest rate of 11.8 percent driving up South Korea's rate of dishonored bills to a record high level of 0.4 percent,[2] South Koreans spoke of a "crisis." They were in for a great surprise. Within three months, the exchange rate hit 1,415 won per dollar and the interest rate climbed to 15.3 percent, forcing myriad firms into bankruptcy. The rate of dishonored bills quadrupled, which in turn pushed up unemployment from 2.1 percent in October 1997 to 7.6 percent in July 1998. The South Korean stock market was brought to its knees as well, experiencing a freefall of the KOSPI from 677 in September 1997 to 313 by June 1998.

Yet this was not the first time that the South Korean economy became paralyzed under severe financial pressures. In 1972, 1979, and 1986, it had seen supply or demand shocks of external origin trigger a severe increase in nonperforming loans (NPLs) and a foreign exchange shortage, which, if inadequately attended to, could have developed into a crisis of systemic proportions, where corporate failures translated into bank failures and bank failures into corporate failures. The crisis of 1972 was particularly severe, making South Korea freeze payments on *sach'ae* (private curb market loans)

---

1 This chapter is based on research supported by a Korea University Grant.

2 The exchange rate stood at 861 won per dollar only eight months earlier, whereas interest rates had been stable but very high since January 1997—above 11 percent. Once the rate of dishonored bills hit 0.3 percent in March, which was twice the level of normal times, it stabilized—but only until September.

and reschedule bank loans so that the *chaebŏl* would not default on state-guaranteed foreign loans.[3] A similar but less dramatic package of debt rescheduling and subsidies was assembled as part of a rescue operation for the *chaebŏl* in 1979 and 1986.[4]

The word "crisis" was thus as much a part of South Korea's history of modernization as the word "success." After each long cycle of hypergrowth, a brief interlude of corporate and bank distress occurred, imbuing the country's economy with an image of both strength and weakness. This dual image was a natural outcome of its choice of growth strategy. With a per capita GNP of only eighty dollars in 1961, business was a rocky affair in South Korea, facing profound market uncertainty and severely constrained by supply and demand bottlenecks. From this structural condition followed a strikingly risky strategy for economic growth. The state pursued a concerted effort to socialize business risks with the goal of luring the *chaebŏl* into investing in its strategically chosen frontiers of industrial growth.[5] Specifically, for its *chaebŏl* partners tackling strategic industrial projects, the state guaranteed foreign loans, supplied policy loans, encouraged cross-shareholding, relaxed prudential regulations, prohibited hostile corporate takeovers, repressed labor militancy, administratively set extensive wage controls, and permitted insider trading. These measures made up a policy package that cumulatively transformed the *chaebŏl* into aggressive risk-takers in uncertain global markets, diversifying into and conglomerating throughout new frontiers of growth on borrowed money. Accordingly, for South Korea, growth and crisis became inseparable, following one after the other in an inexorable cycle. Loans cleared the way for industrial growth, but by saddling the manufacturing sector with a debt-equity ratio of 300 percent and higher between 1970 and 1997 (see Figure 2.1), they also became a source of systemic vulnerability when the *chaebŏl* could not keep up their payments in times of external demand or supply shock. Corporate distress triggered a crisis throughout the economic system, as it left banks with bad loans and trapped NBFIs in a liquidity squeeze.

3 Eun Mee Kim, "From Dominance to Symbiosis: State and *Chaebol* in Korea," *Pacific Focus* 3, no. 2 (September 1988): 105–21.

4 Chung-in Moon, "Changing Patterns of Business-Government Relations in South Korea," in *Business and Government in Industrialising Asia*, ed. Andrew MacIntyre (Ithaca, NY: Cornell University Press, 1994), 142, 145; and Eun Mee Kim, *Big Business, Strong State: Collusion and Conflict in South Korean Development, 1960–1990* (Albany: State University of New York, 1997), 167–211.

5 Robert Wade, *Governing the Market: Economic Theory and the Role of Government in East Asian Industrialization* (Princeton, NJ: Princeton University Press, 1990), 299–302.

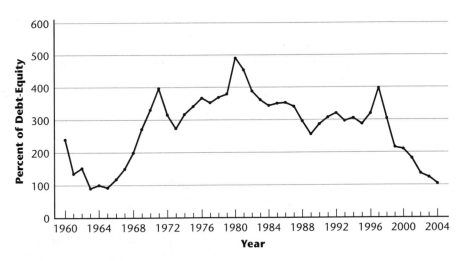

FIGURE 2.1 Average debt-equity ratio of the manufacturing sector, 1960–2004, in percent
Source: Bank of Korea, Economic Statistics System website at http://ecos.bok.or.kr/, as compiled by Jung Kim.

By the late 1970s, with the completion of massive investments in heavy and chemical industrialization (HCI), there lacked easy remedies to the sources of corporate and financial distress. The danger to the over-indebted economic system, in fact, made South Korea even more obsessed with maintaining its rate of hypergrowth, because only then could the overextended *chaebŏl* make payments on their bank loans.[6] And when they were about to fall under external shocks, policymakers consistently chose the option of a state rescue rather than a liquidation of the failing *chaebŏl* groups because the liquidation option was, in the eyes of the *chaebŏl*, a breach of their pact with policymakers to share the risk. The perception of a breach in the pact would damage the credibility of the state as the modernizer of South Korea and, hence, hurt its dirigiste approach to the economy. Additionally, the state believed that it was politically too costly and too risky to let the market do its work of resolving corporate and financial distress through the threats of exit, when banks and NBFIs had become de facto captives of their corporate borrowers. The lenders knew of their loss of leverage over borrowers after decades of providing massive subsidized loans without adequate due diligence and risk management. The colossal size of bad loans made the lenders practice regulatory forbearance, lest a corporate failure threaten the lenders themselves.

6 Yung Chul Park and Dong Won Kim, "Korea: Development and Structural Change of the Banking System," in *The Financial Development of Japan, Korea, and Taiwan: Growth, Repression, and Liberalization*, ed. Hugh T. Patrick and Yung Chul Park (New York: Oxford University Press, 1994), 213–14.

From the perspective of top policymakers, it was not politically possible to go back in time and alter Park Chung Hee's (Pak Chŏng-hŭi, 1961–79) original promise that the state would share the financial risk in return for a conglomerate's entry into uncertain ventures in strategically chosen sectors to aid the economy's growth. But this did not mean that the South Korean state shied away from reform. On the contrary, the pre-1997 period opened up an era of reform—more accurately, *partial* reform—precisely because the political refusal to confront and resolve the root cause of the over-indebted corporate sector by correcting Park's policy legacies forced the state to adopt reform measures to contain the sources of corporate and financial distress from developing into a systemic crisis. Reform was necessary, but the question to be answered by the state was what kind of reform was possible to help contain, and, if possible, gradually resolve the sources of corporate and financial distress rather than magnify the danger of systemic crisis. The South Korean history of economic policy proceeded in three stages: the 1961–1988 period of partial reform that tried to streamline the developmental state by weeding out the more destabilizing elements of its policy package of debt-financed industrialization, the 1988–1997 era of another partial reform that attempted the adaptation of the South Korean economy to the newly emerging historical condition of democratization and globalization, and the post-1997 period that departed from the earlier two stages in striving to bring about a rapid and comprehensive systemic transformation of the South Korean economy into a more neo-liberal type under the pressures of severe corporate and financial distress.

The volatile South Korean history of reform raises a number of questions. Why did partial reform fail in 1996–1997, but not in 1972, 1979, and 1986? Once the South Korean state gave up on partial reform in December 1997 and turned to the unprecedented path of rapid and comprehensive reform in February 1998 under the pressures of financial meltdown, what kind of corporate restructuring program did it embrace? Did the corporate restructuring program of 1998 actually transform the South Korean system of risk management in equilibriuvm-altering or -shifting ways, freeing the economy from overly expansionary tendencies, as its architects claimed? And how did that transformative formula of corporate restructuring arise and become consolidated politically, and with what systemic consequences? To answer these questions, I adopt a modified Varieties of Capitalism (VoC) perspective,[7] identifying finance, interfirm relations, and labor markets as influencing South Korea's choice of corporate restructuring strategy, but, unlike

---

7 Peter A. Hall and David W. Soskice, eds., *Varieties of Capitalism: The Institutional Foundations of Comparative Advantage* (Oxford: Oxford University Press, 2001).

essentially functionalist VoC theories, this process of corporate restructuring is perceived as much a politically driven as a functionally constrained process, with political leaders and state bureaucrats assuming key roles.

Statist Institutional Complementarity, 1961–1988

The "Grow First" strategy of the 1961–1988 period was a package of more or less complementary policy measures, from state guarantees on foreign loans and subsidized policy loans, to cross-shareholding and lax prudential regulations over financial institutions, to prohibition of hostile corporate takeovers, nominal fair trade regulations, and extensive wage control. Put in place by Park and perfected by Chun Doo-hwan (Chŏn Tu-hwan, 1980–88), the Grow First strategy rested on South Korea's bureaucratically driven financial sector (*kwanch'i kŭmyung*), opaque "imperial" corporate governance structure (*ch'ongsu ch'eje*),[8] fragmented company unions (*hoesa nojo*) as opposed to industry-wide corporatist labor federations,[9] and vertically and horizontally integrated interfirm relations (*kyeyŏlhwa*), with the *chaebŏl* serving as the coordinating headquarters.[10] These institutions were functionally complementary under the pre-1988 context of authoritarian rule and heavily protected capital markets, dividing the work to be done in order to support the drive for hypergrowth under the rule of the socialization of business risk. The state banks put industrial growth before their own profit, because they knew their loss would be made up for by public funds in one way or another. The *chaebŏl* responded with their own "can do" spirit of aggressively diversifying into new frontiers of growth, because policy loans and foreign loan guarantees were premised on their entry into strategic sectors. Moreover, their cost of doing so was kept low, as well as made safe without threats on corporate control, by getting affiliate subsidiaries to provide each other some of their equity capital through a system of cross- shareholding and even circular shareholding, which relieved the need to go outside to raise equity capital. In any case, even if the *chaebŏl* were to raise external funds to set up a subsidiary, it was legally protected from

8 See Kim Tong-hun, "Han'guk chaebŏl ŭi chibae kujo" [The corporate governance structure of Korean *chaebŏl*], in *Han'guk chaebŏl kaehyŏkron* [The theory of *chaebŏl* reform], ed. Kim T'ae-hwan and Kim Kyun (Seoul: Nanam Publishing, 1999), 65–104.

9 Song Ho-gŭn, *Han'guk ŭi nodong chŏngch'i wa sijang* [Labor politics and the labor market of Korea] (Seoul: Nanam Publishing, 1991).

10 Byung-Kook Kim (Kim Pyŏng-guk), *Pundan kwa hyŏngmyŏng ŭi tonghak: Han'guk kwa Meksiko ŭi chŏngch'i kyŏngje* [The dynamics of national division and revolution: The political economy of Korea and Mexico] (Seoul: Munhak kwa chisŏngsa, 1994), 322–24.

threats of a hostile takeover, getting their owner-manager families to further underestimate the risks of aggressive debt financing.

Conversely, these acts of financially subsidizing the hypergrowth of *chaebŏl* groups and socializing the risks entailed in the subsidization of corporate growth necessarily prevented South Korea from institutionalizing a well-functioning system of financial safety regulations. On the contrary, the state's underwriting of *chaebŏl* ventures with myriad financial guarantees and colossal policy loans encouraged what prudential regulations would presumably have discouraged. Confident of state support in both good times and bad, each of the privileged *chaebŏl* borrowers, politically chosen as a partner in developing a strategic sector, systematically discounted risks and overestimated the future flows of income, whereas the state banks regularly fell back on regulatory forbearance when the economic situation deteriorated, with an eye to helping their *chaebŏl* clients as well as their own organization weather out the pressures of adjustment and restructuring with the hope that the economy would turn around very soon to enable their *chaebŏl* clients to overcome corporate distress through the resumption of hypergrowth.

To be sure, externally protected from threats of a hostile takeover as well as internally free of checks and balances that might have come from minority shareholders, big business knew that what regulators there were could not but shut their eyes to the state bank's practice of regulatory forbearance, because otherwise some of the *chaebŏl* and state banks could collapse under the weight of massive NPLs. Thus the *chaebŏl* stuck with the strategy of debt financing rather than restructuring bad loans. The extensive practice of cross-shareholding also obstructed prudential regulations, creating an opaque corporate governance structure. The specter of the failure of any one *chaebŏl* company bringing down other affiliate companies through extensive cross-shareholding, moreover, dissuaded the state regulators from implementing even weak financial regulations. In lieu of effective rules, state banks lent only when they secured collateral.[11]

The logic of institutional complementarity worked for labor markets and interfirm relations as well. The financial fragility of *chaebŏl* being a constant, South Korea tried to secure its international competitive edge through the construction of flexible labor markets. As much a product of conscious political engineering by the authoritarian developmental state as a historical legacy of South Korea's bloody war with the North (1950–1953), which

---

11 Hugh T. Patrick, "Comparisons, Contrasts, and Implications," in *The Financial Development of Japan, Korea, and Taiwan: Growth, Repression, and Liberalization*, ed. Patrick and Park, 335, 369.

delegitimized leftist ideologies and crippled labor forces,[12] flexible labor markets helped the *chaebŏl* partly make up for their financial disadvantage through low wages and flexible employment. To keep labor quiescent, the developmental state combined the formally hierarchical, centralized, and all-encompassing "state corporatist" system of political control with the organizationally dispersed Japanese-style "company unions" in nurturing a hybrid strategy of labor control and co-optation.[13] Wary of workers becoming an independent center of power, the state set up a national summit organization—the Federation of Korean Trade Unions (FKTU)—with politically patronized and controlled (*ŏyong*) labor leaders, and legally made this summit organization South Korea's sole representative of worker interests in national political arenas. In fact, the state distrusted even the *ŏyong* FKTU, prohibiting it from establishing industrial federations and meddling in labor disputes at the company level. The state corporatist FKTU was organizationally hollow, with a group of *ŏyong* labor leaders absorbed with internal palace intrigues and factional politics within the FKTU, rather than penetrating and organizing the South Korean working class. In lieu of effective state corporatist organs, much of the task to represent and mediate worker interest fell on fragmented company unions without the resources to resist state policy.

Similarly, once South Korea decided to concentrate scarce productive resources in *chaebŏl* conglomerates in a bid for hypergrowth, the state saw its options become restricted in the issue-area of interfirm relations. Given the state's policy of financially subsidizing hypergrowth as well as allowing extensive cross-shareholding between firms, the option of conglomeration became irresistible for the *chaebŏl*. By getting affiliate companies to provide each other equity capital as well as guarantees on bank loans, each of South Korea's leading *chaebŏl* groups could establish subsidiaries with a minimum level of external equity funds. In other words, they were able to grow and protect the owner-manager family's corporate control at the same time.[14]

12 Byung-Kook Kim, "Ideology, Organization and Democratic Consolidation in Korea," in *Democracy and Communism: Its Ideals and Realities*, ed. Sangyang Chul (Seoul: Korean Political Science Association, 1997), 359–98.

13 Byung-Kook Kim and Hyun-Chin Lim, "Labor against Itself: Structural Dilemmas of State Monism," in *Consolidating Democracy in South Korea*, ed. Larry Diamond and Byung-Kook Kim (Boulder, CO: Lynne Rienner Publishers, 2000), 111–37.

14 Kim Ki-t'ae and Hong Hyŏn-p'yo, "Chaebŏl ŭi t'ŭksŏng kwa ŭiŭi" [The characteristics and meaning of *chaebŏl*], in *Han'guk kyŏngje ŭi kujo* [The structure of Korea's economy], ed. Kim Ki-tae et al. (Seoul: Hanul Academy, 1993); and Securities Exchange Supervisory Commission, "Kukhoe kukchŏng kamsa yogu charyo" [The materials demanded for a National Assembly audit] (September 1989).

Moreover, in the context of the severely underdeveloped markets of finance, labor, technology, and management, transforming economic tasks into an internal exchange within the corporate organization rather than an arms-length market transaction had the additional benefit of helping the *chaebŏl* reduce transaction costs, from search and information costs to bargaining costs, to policing and enforcement costs, as well as exploit opportunities for insider trading and monopoly profits.[15] To get the maximum synergy effect of conglomeration, the *chaebŏl* established an extremely centralized corporate governance structure, with their owner-manager families controlling and coordinating affiliate companies top-down through a large secretariat at headquarters.

The efforts to reduce transaction costs through organizational innovation surfaced even in the *chaebŏl*'s relationship with independent vendors. The *chaebŏl* brought suppliers into a vertically and horizontally integrated multilayer network of production and sought to serve as the coordinator. To be sure, this process of *kyeyŏlhwa*, backed by both the *chaebŏl*'s monopolistic market power and the state's administrative guidance and industrial policy, frequently degenerated into an exploitative relationship, with the coordinator forcing suppliers to take a disproportionate share of the burden in absorbing external demand and supply shocks, but it also went a long way in making possible the state-driven HCI, which required a coordinated effort of price setting, quality control, and investment across forwardly and backwardly linked industries.[16] Given the severe shortage of productive resources, both the state and *chaebŏl* preferred to rely as much on political power and social organization as on market forces in deciding prices, strengthening product quality, and synchronizing investment. For the state to influence firm behavior administratively, it was thought that the market needed to be structured around a few *chaebŏl* and their centrally coordinated network of suppliers. It is obvious that, like conglomeration, the pursuit of *kyeyŏlhwa* de facto prevented the South Korean state from tightening its monopoly and fair trade regulations because the *kyeyŏlhwa* aimed to create monopolistic productive structures.

15 Yu Sŭng-min, "Chaebŏl ŭi kong'kwa: Chaebŏl nonjaeng e taehan pip'an" [The merits and demerits of the *chaebŏl*: A critique of the polemic over the *chaebŏl*], in *Han'guk kyŏngje ŭi chillo wa tae kiŏp chipdan* [The path of the Korean economy and its large business groups], ed. Korean Academic Society of Industrial Organization (Seoul: Kia Economic Institute, 1996), 239–96.

16 Cho Dong-sŏng, *Han'guk chaebŏl yŏn'gu* [A study of Korean *chaebŏl*] (Seoul: Maeil Kyŏngje Sinmunsa, 1990).

That the bureaucratically governed financial sector, opaque corporate governance structure, fragmented company unions, and interfirm relations of *kyeyŏlhwa* made up the institutional complementarities supporting the South Korean developmental state's distinctive strategy of hypergrowth on the basis of the socialization of business risks was visibly demonstrated by three long cycles of hypergrowth (1964–1972, 1974–1979, and 1982–1988).[17] But it was two brief moments of hard times rather than these three long cycles of good times that most clearly showed South Korea's competitive edge arising from its complementary institutions of finance, labor market, and interfirm relations. In the hard times of 1972 and 1979, the state agencies protected the *chaebŏl* from going under by assuming a mutually complementary division of labor in what was called "industrial rationalization."[18] The objective was to stabilize the overheated economy with shock therapy consisting of foreign exchange devaluation, interest hikes, and wage controls,[19] but at the same time to prevent this macroeconomic adjustment from disintegrating its microfoundation of hypergrowth, the *chaebŏl* conglomerates. The vehicle was a state-brokered, -coordinated and -subsidized M&A package, pursued in parallel with a program of bank rescues. And, in the case of 1972, Park Chung Hee also launched debt-financed heavy and chemical industrialization immediately after macroeconomic adjustment and stabilization. To allow *chaebŏl* firms to cut their losses and banks to reduce their NPLs, Park thought he had to rush to expand the economy with the goal of easing the liquidity squeeze as soon as the shock measures drove out the more uncompetitive *chaebŏl* firms from the market.[20]

The rescue of banks was inseparable from the industrial rationalization. On the one hand, policymakers had to back the financial institutions' rescheduling of loans and even their write-offs of bad loans with a fresh injection of public money if they were to keep state banks afloat. On the other hand, the debt rescheduling required a concurrent effort of corporate restructuring, including the dissolution of less-competitive business ventures, if South Korea were to prevent a continuous increase of rescue money and even recover in the future some of the public funds injected to

17 See Alice H. Amsden, *Asia's Next Giant: South Korea and Late Industrialization* (New York: Oxford University Press, 1989).

18 See Kim, *Pundan kwa hyŏngmyŏng ŭi tonghak*.

19 Bela Balassa and John Williamson, *Adjusting to Success: Balance of Payments Policy in the East Asian NICs* (Washington, DC: Institute for International Economics, 1987).

20 Park and Kim, "Korea: Development and Structural Change of the Banking System," 214.

restructure the business firms thought to be experiencing temporary distress under the macroeconomic condition of liquidity squeeze. The question was not whether, but what kind, of corporate restructuring would be chosen in parallel with the bank rescue. South Korea shied away from letting market forces restructure *chaebŏl* groups under the threat of bankruptcy. Instead, it put in place an administratively guided process of industrial rationalization, encouraging stronger *chaebŏl* groups to engage in mergers and acquisitions of weaker ones with a prior pledge from the state that it would support the M&As with financial subsidies. The state-brokered, -coordinated and -subsidized reshuffling of business lines among *chaebŏl* groups was thought of as a substitute for market-led M&As. The goal was to reduce surplus capacity, hold executives accountable for mismanagement, and resolve financial distress, but without a spread of corporate bankruptcy.

Unfortunately, the bureaucratically orchestrated program of industrial rationalization never could serve as a substitute for market-led M&As and bankruptcy, because the mechanisms of state-brokered business swaps and corporate takeovers were designed more as rescue operations than as disciplinary measures. Consequently, industrial rationalization helped big business weather two or three years of hard times, but did not make it financially any stronger. On the contrary, industrial rationalization trapped the *chaebŏl* in deeper moral hazards. Believing that the state would always rescue them in the event of external supply or demand shocks, they pursued a strategy of diversification and conglomeration on the basis of bank loans. And this strategy worked. The *chaebŏl*, supported by the state, got away with their acts of moral hazard without market punishment for a surprisingly long period of time. To be sure, 1986 saw another episode of corporate restructuring—this time, in the South Korea construction industry hit with NPLs in the aftermath of a bust in Middle Eastern markets. But except in this instance of adjustment, the state's strategy of financing the *chaebŏl*'s diversification and conglomeration with bank loans continued without a systemic crisis until 1997. The history of South Korea's economic booms and busts shows how market forces were both weak and strong, readily shaped, distorted, and contained by state power, but also eventually the state was punished for its subversion of market forces and economic rationality.

Democratization and Globalization after 1987–1988

The strategy of risk socialization and its institutional infrastructure of developmental statism might have continued generating hypergrowth, albeit with a regular occurrence of corporate and financial distress, if South Korea's forces of democratization and globalization had been much weaker than they actually were after 1987. These two tidal waves of change struck South Korea simultaneously, with opposition politicians and *chaeya* dissidents forcing a system of direct presidential elections on the unwilling old guards of authoritarian rule in June 1987,[21] and U.S. Treasury officials beginning to press for an opening of the country's capital markets after January 1988.[22] The sequence of events could not have been worse. The conventional wisdom called for a reform of the real sector before an overhaul of the financial system, and a restructuring of domestic industries before an international opening of capital markets,[23] but the pressures of globalization were forcing South Korea to do the reverse. At the same time, the forces of democratization empowered *chaebŏl* workers to challenge management on the issues of job security, wages, and company welfare benefits, while the public increasingly came to demand fair trade and distributive equity. The political dynamics unleashed by each of these two forces inevitably undermined South Korea's developmental statist strategy of hypergrowth. The new ruling elite of South Korea now had to search for a strategy of economic growth *and* institutional reform that would fit in with its new zeitgeist of democratization and globalization.

The most fundamental forces of change unleashed by democratization were ideological. As early as 1987, in the middle of a tumultuous democratic breakthrough, the public let out its hitherto politically silenced outrage against the *chaebŏl*'s way of doing business. The large conglomerates were criticized as living off state subsidies, earning rents from exploiting suppliers and consumers through monopoly market power, indulging in unfair insider trading, and holding down wages without sharing their wealth with society. The state was seen as an accomplice in this illegitimate distribution of risks and profits.[24] This negative appraisal of South Korea's historical legacy inevitably made reform one of the top items on the national agenda after 1988.[25] To be sure, the then-popular "reform" was a foggy idea, used by

21 Hyug Baeg Im, "Politics of Democratic Transition from Authoritarian Rule in South Korea," *Korean Social Science Journal* 21, no. 1 (1995): 144–45.

22 See Securities Exchange Supervisory Commission, *Chabon sijang nyŏnbo* [Capital markets annual] (various issues); and Ministry of Finance and Korea Development Bank, *Han'guk oeja toip samsip-nyŏnsa* [Thirty years of foreign capital imports] (1993).

23 Patrick, "Comparisons, Contrasts, and Implications," 344.

24 Yeon-ho Lee, *The State, Society, and Big Business in South Korea* (London: Routledge, 1997), 29–45.

25 Byung-Kook Kim, "The Politics of *Chaebol* Reform, 1980–1997," in *Economic Crisis and Corporate Restructuring in Korea*, ed. Stephan Haggard, Wonhyuk Lim, and Euysong Kim (New York: Cambridge University Press, 2003), 56–58.

both conservatives and progressives to oppose each other's ideological and political goals. Ironically, however, it was this polysemous character of the public discourse that made reform an extremely threatening idea for both the developmental state and the *chaebŏl* because the term could assemble a broad coalition for change out of ideologically heterogeneous political forces. Moreover, it was an inexhaustible political discourse, capable of giving itself a new political meaning through an articulation of new goals, once its old agendas were realized or as further progress of democratization produced ever higher public expectations.

The ideological impact was most visible in the structural blow that the idea of reform made to labor politics, because of South Korea's extremely weak institutions of political integration and its excessively concentrated economic structure, both of which were outcomes of its strategy of hypergrowth. The developmental state had left the political parties ideologically shallow and organizationally thin,[26] and the "official" labor leaders controlled and patronized (*ŏyong*) by the state so that policymakers could design and implement economic policy with maximum discretionary power without societal forces exercising veto power. The scheme worked, but only until June 1987. Once the democratic breakthrough paralyzed the traditional mechanism of political control, the same political institutions that assured the preponderance of state agencies before 1987—the weak political parties and the fragmented *ŏyong* unions—became an additional cause of the decline of state power. Neither politically integrated by the political parties nor controlled by the *ŏyong* labor leaders, many of the *chaebŏl* workers were initially up for grabs in political struggles between the *chaeya* dissidents and the state, but soon came to be their own masters loyal only to their own interests. They were able to evolve into a powerful political force, separate from the political parties and the official labor federation, because of five structural facilitators. Each of the *chaebŏl* groups: (1) employed a large workforce, (2) integrated forwardly and backwardly linked industrial sectors through both conglomeration and *kyeyŏlhwa*, and (3) geographically concentrated their affiliate companies and suppliers in compact state-constructed industrial complexes with an eye to reducing transaction costs. These big businesses also: (4) earned much of South Korea's foreign exchange, and (5) determined the nation's future growth as an innovator of foreign technology. Consequently, a strike at any of their plants could paralyze production in forwardly and backwardly linked companies and disrupt

26 Byung-Kook Kim, "Party Politics in South Korea's Democracy: The Crisis of Success," in *Consolidating Democracy in South Korea*, ed. Diamond and Kim, 69–80.

the foreign exchange earnings required to generate economic growth, as if the strike had been orchestrated as part of a general strike.[27] Aware of their ability to take the entire economy hostage, *chaebŏl* workers rushed into launching their own trade unions, once the South Korean security forces' political capabilities to repress dissident labor unions began declining precipitously with the democratic transition of June 1987 (see Figure 2.2).

The Great Workers' Strike of 1987, triggered by South Korea's democratization but also profoundly deepening it, resulted in a type of labor politics that undermined South Korea's developmental statist strategy of growth and adjustment. In spite of the spread of democratic corporatist ideas that led workers to transcend the legacies of company unionism to experiment with new forms of labor organization, including regional councils, industry federations, and a national confederation, the South Korean labor market remained dominated by company unions throughout the post-1987 democratic era. However, it is also important to note that with the organization of *chaebŏl* workers into their own company unions during the two month-long Great Workers' Strike, the impact the system of company unions had on the South Korean economy changed dramatically after the democratic transition. Before 1987, the company unions in existence were comprised of workers, hired by small- and medium-size enterprises (SMEs), who lacked resources to challenge the state and capital. Consequently, the company unionism of the pre-1987 developmental era did not stand in the way of the state's efforts to maximize economic growth through the strategy of socializing business risks because the workers that were permitted by the state to organize unions were of the weaker, not the stronger, members of the South Korean working class. By contrast, it was those stronger members of the working class who won the right to organize company unions after 1987, the outcome of which was to increasingly restrain management's prerogatives in the hitherto union-free, *chaebŏl*-dominated strategic industries.

The question was not whether the workers of *chaebŏl* groups would be powerful, but rather how they would flex their muscle. The *chaeya* dissidents and activists, imbued with and empowered by one or another form of progressive ideas, hoped that they would transcend the narrow boundary of company unions in the exercise of their newly found power. In such a hope of getting *chaebŏl* workers to defend the wider class interests of the entire South Korean working class, the *chaeya* worked with *chaebŏl* unions to launch the Korean Confederation of Trade Unions (KCTU) in 1995 as the summit organization of a dissident labor movement in opposition to the

27 Kim and Lim, "Labor against Itself," 121–22.

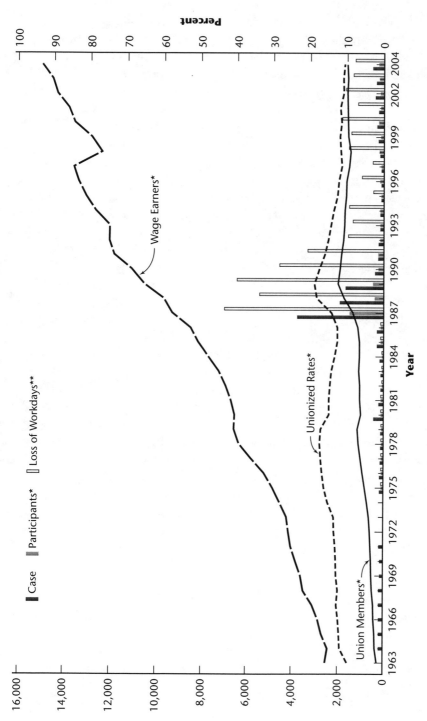

FIGURE 2.2 Trends in unionization and labor disputes, 1963–2004

Sources: Hagen Koo, Korean Workers: The Culture and Politics of Class Formation (Ithaca: Cornell University Press, 2001), 159; Ministry of Labor, Yearbook of Labor Statistics (2005), 467; Ministry of Labor website at http://www.molab.go.kr/; Korea Labor Institute website at http://www.kli.re.kr/; Korean Statistical Information System website at http://kosis.nso.go.kr/, as compiled by Jung Kim.

*Participants, wage earners, and union members in 1,000 persons. **Loss of workdays in 1,000 workdays.

"official" FKTU. Certainly, the KCTU soon became a powerful veto player of many of the state's labor reforms, but it remained essentially a club of the privileged *chaebŏl* workers, failing to acquire an identity, mission, and powerful resources independent of and separate from those of its member *chaebŏl* unions. The KCTU's lack of an esprit de corps left much of the federation's decisionmaking to individual *chaebŏl* unions, which severely weakened South Korea's mechanism of economic coordination and collaboration. Individually too big to be a price-taker that passively and reactively accommodated market pressures, and also collectively lacking any corporatist sense of identity that bred empathy for the less privileged workers in the SMEs, *chaebŏl* unions pushed up wages while guarding their prerogative of life employment, thus causing a serious wage drift.[28]

The disruptive forces of globalization, by contrast, worked primarily through South Korea's underdeveloped financial sector. Under intense U.S. pressure, the state began opening up its weak financial sector, but in partial and risky ways. The problem was that with the banks' holding of massive NPLs and their *chaebŏl* clients' low level of profit, any attempt at reform had to be comprehensive in the sense that the restructuring of bank loans and operations had to be tightly tied in with the measures to strengthen prudential regulations, as well as transparency and accountability in corporate governance structures. Only when these three measures were implemented as an integrated package prior to the opening of financial markets could the South Korean financial system withstand the challenge of stronger foreign financial institutions after the opening of financial markets. However, precisely because of the massive NPLs and the low profit level of the *chaebŏl* that made comprehensive reform that much more necessary, the South Korean economy could also implode in the middle of the three-pronged strategy of comprehensive reform. On the one hand, the restructuring of the banks could spill over into severe corporate distress by prompting the banks to refuse the rollover of loans in the interest of reducing the dangers of loan default in the increasingly uncertain market. On the other hand, the strengthening of prudential regulations and corporate transparency could themselves become a source of financial panic, not only because the size of NPLs was likely to increase in tandem with the strengthening of prudential regulations, but also because the information on NPLs could not be kept away from the public in a more transparent system of corporate governance. In need of pursuing a strategy of comprehensive reform, but also fearing the danger of implosion in the process of comprehensive reform, South Korea

---

28 Ibid.,

ended up pursuing a wrongly sequenced partial reform. Rather than preparing for the opening of financial markets with a prior three-pronged strategy of comprehensive reform, South Korea opened up financial markets to the world while refusing to confront the issues of NPLs, lax prudential regulations, and opaque corporate governance structures. In particular, the country pushed through a foreign exchange deregulation in 1994 and liberalized invisible trade and capital movements in 1996.[29]

To be sure, financial deregulation without a prior strengthening of prudential regulations and corporate transparency was as much a product of political choice as it was an outcome of structural constraints and dilemmas. The *chaebŏl* had by then acquired securities companies, insurance houses, and investment banks in the search for a stable, independent source of capital. Even in the case of South Korea's five largest commercial banks, the top four *chaebŏl* groups came to have a 19.2 percent share of the equity by 1984.[30] This rise of the *chaebŏl* manufacturers' presence and power in the financial sector encouraged partial reform in significant ways. The *chaebŏl* were in favor of financial deregulation and liberalization because they opened new opportunities for financing their ambitious manufacturing ventures, but they were against the strengthening of prudential regulations and corporate transparency because of their financial weakness. By contrast, in the eyes of the policymakers preparing for financial deregulation and liberalization under intense U.S. pressures, the *chaebŏl* constituted South Korea's only actor that could prevent a foreign takeover of banks and NBFIs in open capital markets. Caught between the fear of financial vulnerabilities that could mushroom into a systemic crisis, on the one hand, and the confidence in the *chaebŏl* manufacturers' capabilities to integrate the industry and finance sectors in an internationally competitive manner, if given time, on the other hand, South Korean policymakers of the early 1990s left intact much of the lax prudential regulations and opaque corporate governance structures, while helping the *chaebŏl* grow into a financial powerhouse through a removal of regulatory barriers. Both state and *chaebŏl*, then, preferred keeping many of their old ways of doing business even as they rushed into partial financial deregulation and liberalization.

29 Jin-Young Suh and Byung-Kook Kim, "The Politics of Reform in Korea: Dilemma, Choice, and Crisis," in *The World after the Cold War: Issues and Dilemmas*, ed. Jin-Young Suh and Changrok Soh (Seoul: Graduate School of International Studies, Korea University, 1999), 51–52.

30 Sŏ Chae-jin, *Han'guk ŭi chabon kwa kyegŭp* [The capitalist class of Korea] (Seoul: Nanam Publishing, 1991), 106, 138–39.

Ironically, such a mix of change and continuity profoundly hurt the interests of the state, the architect of the partial reform. In particular, the top four *chaebŏl* groups came to acquire the capabilities to directly raise capital in foreign financial markets, the outcome of which was to irreversibly damage the state's ability to reshape and redirect the behavior of the *chaebŏl*. In fact, having experienced a regular outburst of financial and corporate distress during the developmental state era, big business was by then viewing the state as an obstacle as much as a facilitator of their business ventures, which failed to deliver its promise to channel a stable supply of preferential policy loans through both boom and bust. The myriad NBFIs established by the *chaebŏl* constituted a fallback option that could make up for any shortfalls in policy loans with active fund-raising in foreign financial markets. But it was this hedging effort of the *chaebŏl* that also threatened the state's mechanism of growth and adjustment, because the *chaebŏl*-controlled NBFIs deprived the state of exclusive control over the money supply with which to cool down inflationary pressures before they resulted in a bust.

To undermine state capacity for coordination even more during the 1990s, the state not only failed to prevent the development of a large interest differential between domestic loans and dollar- or yen-denominated foreign loans, but also ended up with an overvaluation of the South Korean currency through the mismanagement of the pegged foreign exchange system. The low-interest rate of foreign loans and the overvalued exchange rate lured the *chaebŏl* and their NBFIs into aggressive foreign borrowing, which made South Korea very vulnerable to an external shock by the mid-1990s. To make the situation worse, much of the foreign loans were borrowed on the short term because the state's financial liberalization program concentrated on the deregulation of short-term but not long-term foreign borrowing with an eye to limiting foreign penetration into financial markets.[31] In other words, the *chaebŏl* and their NBFIs were financing long-term domestic investments with short-term foreign borrowing, precisely when the risk of a steep interest hike at home and a deep devaluation of the won climbed up in the context of macroeconomic mismanagement. Until the risk actualized, corporate borrowing increased geometrically, especially after the financial deregulation and liberalization program began in earnest in 1994 (see Figure 2.3). Supported by the massive injection of foreign loans, the top 22 *chaebŏl* groups newly

31 Steven Radelet and Jeffrey Sachs, "What Have We Learned, So Far, from the Asian Financial Crisis?" Harvard Institute for International Development, CAER Discussion Paper no.37, presented at the annual meeting of the American Economic Association (January 1999), 4–6.

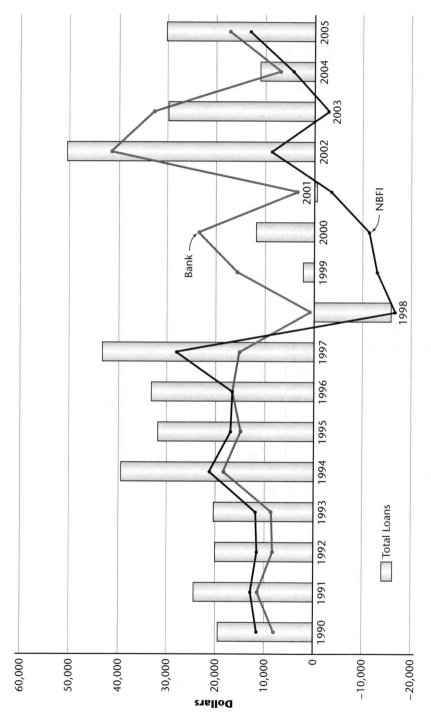

FIGURE 2.3 Trends in corporate borrowing, 1990–2005*

Source: Bank of Korea, at http://ecos.bok.or.kr/, as compiled by Jung Kim.

*Billion won

established a total of 97 affiliate firms in the 1990s. The previous decade had been much more stable, with only 11 new business ventures (see Table 2.1).

To sum up, the South Korean capacity to prevent systemic crisis was limited to begin with, but with the onslaught of democratization and globalization after 1987, it became even more constrained. In effect, these two forces of megachange prevented the South Korean state from using its traditional adjustment mechanisms of wage freeze, shock therapy, and industrial rationalization to put the brakes on overly expansionary economic policy before the forces of interest hikes and devaluation deteriorated to the point of triggering a systemic crisis. Now, the *chaebŏl* and their workers, with their newly enhanced power, were reshaped into a veto player of the traditional adjustment strategy, preventing the state from putting in place a wage freeze, debt restructuring, and industrial rationalization. Ironically, however, the demise of the traditional adjustment strategy also threatened to damage rather than help the interests of the very actors that brought down the strategy and its institutional support mechanisms. In the absence of a new adjustment strategy, there would be no brake to put on the *chaebŏl*'s seemingly insatiable appetite for loan-financed corporate growth, thus making them extremely vulnerable to an increase in foreign interest rates or exchange rates. For *chaebŏl* workers too, the demise of the traditional adjustment mechanism proved to be both a blessing and a curse, letting their unions raise wages and defend lifetime employment in the short run, but also being threatened with wage cuts and layoffs in the long run. The state would be a loser as well, because its traditional option of labor repression no longer worked as a means of crisis prevention

TABLE 2.1

The Patterns of Chaebŏl Expansion[†]

	Related Diversification	Unrelated Diversification	Vertical Integration	Total
1940s	1 (33.3)‡	2 (66.7)	—	3
1950s	8 (23.5)	23 (67.7)	3 (8.8)	34
1960s	21 (23.5)	44 (67.7)	24 (8.8)	89
1970s	83 (36.1)	105 (45.7)	42 (18.3)	230
1980s	106 (23.5)	100 (67.7)	35 (8.8)	241
1990s	175 (51.8)	117 (34.6)	46 (13.6)	338

Source: Wonhyuk Lim, "The Emergence of the *Chaebol* and the Origins of the *Chaebol* Problem," in *Economic Crisis and Corporate Restructuring in Korea: Reforming the* Chaebol, ed. Haggard, Lim, and Kim, 39.

†The dataset includes the twenty-two largest *chaebŏl* groups of 2000, as measured in total asset size. The data indicate the number of newly established companies.

‡Numbers in parenthteses show the percentage of affiliate firms established by related diversification, unrelated diversification, and vertical integration.

or crisis management. The shock was great precisely because it coincided with an equally critical decline of state power in financial markets and over *chaebŏl* groups. The state knew of this systemic danger. The question was, what could it do to prevent the *chaebŏl* and their workers from heating up expansionary pressures to the point of a financial bust?

Partial Reforms and Veto Players, 1990–1997

The 1990s saw a flurry of reformist efforts to prevent the forces of globalization and democratization from worsening South Korea's structural tendency toward economic overexpansion. However, the efforts before the Asian financial crisis of 1997–1998 failed because they were efforts at corporate restructuring by detour, trying to get control of unsustainable hypergrowth by reforming the system's already-collapsing two traditional adjustment mechanisms of industrial rationalization and labor market flexibility in order to fit in with both global financial forces and local political pressures, rather than tackling the root cause of cyclical boom and bust. The state kept much of its Grow First package of foreign loan guarantees, weak prudential regulations, lax fair trade policies, and subsidized policy loans in the belief that any U-turn in these financial and competition policies could make foreign lenders and investors divest in fear of getting stuck with massive NPLs and business losses. Change and innovation were mostly concentrated in the areas of industrial rationalization and labor policy. However, just as South Korea tried reinventing its old remedies of wage freezes and business swaps as vehicles of adjustment, the forces of democratization and globalization were rapidly eroding the state's institutional capacity for labor control and industrial policy.

The state was to learn its lesson the hard way. To prevent *chaebŏl* entry into unprofitable, unrelated ventures, the Ministry of Finance (MoF) came up with a "Main Company Policy" in 1991, whereby each of South Korea's top thirty *chaebŏl* conglomerates would choose two or three affiliate firms as its focus of industrial specialization.[32] For its part, the MoF pledged to lift all restrictive regulations on loans for each of these main companies in return for their restraint in issuing new loan guarantees for the other affiliate firms that fell outside the core areas of specialization. This strategy of making *chaebŏl* groups specialize in two or three core businesses, which the state planned to accomplish through a mix of financial incentives and disincentives, however, flopped. The *chaebŏl* outsmarted the MoF by designating the

---

32 *Chosun Ilbo* (*Chosŏn Ilbo*), September 20, 1991; and *Donga Ilbo* (*Tonga Ilbo*), August 3, October 10, and October 21, 1992.

affiliate firms with large loan guarantees as the core companies, which had the effect of excluding much of the outstanding loan guarantees from the restrictive regulation. The 76 firms designated by the *chaebŏl* as main companies had guaranteed loans worth 38.3 trillion won for affiliate firms before becoming main companies in 1991. To strengthen the pressures for specialization, the MoF considered eliminating all outstanding loan guarantees between all affiliate firms (whether core or non-core companies), but only very briefly. The fear of provoking a run on the banks shelved any idea of shock therapy. Meanwhile, the MoF delivered on its promise of exempting main companies from restrictive regulations, which encouraged the *chaebŏl* to take on even more debt financing.

The 1993 policy of "sectoral specialization" of the Ministry of Trade, Industry, and Resources (MTIR) hardly fared better. In fact, as an architect of South Korea's traditional adjustment strategy of industrial rationalization and as an engineer of administrative guidance during the pre-1987 developmental era, institutionally the MTIR was the opposite of what should have been expected of a watchdog of financial stability. Whereas the pre-1987 MoF reluctantly pursued an easy monetary policy out of systemic needs and under political command, with deep anxiety over the negative repercussions the easy monetary policy had for its organizational mission of financial stability and for the financial health of its client group of state banks, the MTIR believed that South Korea's destiny lay with industrialization and that this destiny would be realized only when the power of the "conservative" MoF was checked. The policy of sectoral specialization revealed the MTIR's expansionist ethos. Whereas the MoF had each of South Korea's top thirty *chaebŏl* groups choose two or three of its affiliate firms as main companies irrespective of industries, the MTIR had each of the *chaebŏl* groups designate two or three "core industrial sectors" for specialization and develop six or seven of its affiliate firms in those core sectors into "leading companies." Again, a generous supply of policy loans was promised to line up the *chaebŏl* behind the state policy. To ensure *chaebŏl* support for sectoral specialization, moreover, the MTIR reclassified the South Korean economy from 73 to 15 industrial sectors.[33] That alone sufficed to exempt the *chaebŏl* from the pressures of specialization, because with such broadly defined boundaries for the core sectors, the *chaebŏl* could claim many of their entries into unrelated businesses to be an instance of horizontal or vertical integration within related industries, thus eligible for policy loans.

33 Ministry of Trade, Industry, and Resources, "Tae kyumo kiŏp chipdan ŭi ŏpjong chŏnmunhwa yudo pangan" [A measure to induce sectoral specialization of large-scale business groups], May 1993.

Despite the rhetoric of policy innovation, then, the specialization policies of both the MoF and MTIR were a revival of South Korea's old recipes
of industrial rationalization,[34] although this time they were pursued as a
preventive measure before the economy's next cyclical round of adjustment
threatened to trigger another systemic crisis.[35] However, even by the two
ministries' pre-1987 lax standards of accountability, the policy initiatives of
1991 and especially 1993 were too soft, including many carrots but no sticks
for reshaping business behavior. The outcome was the opposite of the MoF
and MTIR's intention. The *chaebŏl* selected as their "main" or "leading"
companies those affiliate firms in need of a large dose of new bank loans
rather than those with a proven potential for international competitiveness.
The two ministries' efforts to formulate a policy of specialization that accommodated the vital interests of the *chaebŏl* were essentially the repeat of
the traditional industrial rationalization policy, trying to trigger corporate
restructuring without the threat of hostile takeovers and the pressures of
bank restructuring. It was inevitable that without these threats and pressures, the MoF and MTIR could not force a genuine program of specialization on the *chaebŏl*.

Parallel with the efforts to get big business to specialize through a generous pledge of financial support, South Korea also looked for ways to
recover labor market flexibility. This was because specialization was possible only when big business acquired the capabilities to freely redeploy and
even lay off its surplus workers. Like the cases of specialization policy, the
1990–1997 efforts of labor reform ended up as a fiasco. The historical path
to reform failure, however, could not be more different. Whereas the South
Korean state stopped pursuing the specialization policy after the mid-1990s,
the efforts at labor reform continued into early 1997, when financial and
corporate distress in Thailand began destabilizing many of the East Asian
emerging markets. Moreover, in contrast to the state's accommodation of
chaebŏl interests in the formulation of the specialization policy, its attempt
at labor reform lacked a similar effort to reach out to the main constituency,
organized labor. In the immediate aftermath of the Great Workers' Strike,
the state pursued a strategy of containment. The reform bill of 1990, drawn
up by the Ministry of Trade and Industry (MTI, the immediate predecessor
of the MTIR), proposed to empower management to fight organized labor

34 Ibid.
35 Byung-Kook Kim, "The Politics of Crisis and a Crisis of Politics: The Presidency
of Kim Dae-Jung," in *Korea Briefing, 1997-1999: Challenges and Change at the Turn of
the Century*, ed. Kongdan Oh (Armonk, NY: ME Sharpe, Inc., 2000), 42.

by legally adopting the principle of "no work, no pay," as well as by permitting the employment of irregular "substitute workers" from outside the firm in times of strikes.[36] The idea got nowhere.

Then it became the Ministry of Labor's (MoL) turn to constrain the organized workers' power. By then, wage guidelines had broken down. On the one hand, workers of the *chaebŏl* kept pushing up wages by flexing their newly found organizational power. On the other hand, their employers chose to accommodate rather than fight the militant *chaebŏl* workers, because much of the rising labor costs could readily be passed on to consumers or suppliers of parts and components, given the conglomerates' market power. To appease the militant workers, but without directly breaching the wage guidelines set by the MoL, each of the top *chaebŏl* groups introduced a series of company health care and welfare programs, housing benefits, special allowances, and social programs. In doing so, each of the *chaebŏl* put its own narrow group interests before and above the interests of the *chaebŏl* as a class, individually cutting a deal with organized labor while hoping the others, including the state, would enforce wage guidelines and defend the management's prerogatives. The strategy was basically that of a free ride, urging the state and business federations to confront organized labor even at the expense of work disruptions, but individually cutting a separate deal with their own workforce to maintain industrial peace at their *own* worksites. The strategy undermined the MoL's wage guidelines, prompting the ministry to revise labor laws. In 1991, the MoL tried to recover its influence over wages by legally requiring the consolidation of all payments, including those disbursed in kind, into one yearly stipend.[37] Like the MTI's 1990 attempt at labor reform, however, the MoL saw its proposal of wage consolidation go nowhere under the intense opposition of *chaebŏl* workers.

The failure of "reform from above" brought two lasting changes. From then on, South Korea's top policy circle, whether of conservative or progressive orientation, began thinking in terms of "tripartism," with organized labor directly participating in policymaking processes, in order to make them an owner of labor reform bills and, if that failed, to deprive them of the *myŏngbun* (moral justification) to oppose the outcome of the reform efforts. In 1992, the MoL set up an "inquiry commission" inside the ministry, with half of its members recruited from business and labor federations and the rest from intelligentsia-led "public interest" groups. The idea of tripartism resurfaced in 1996, but this time as a presidential commission. Both the 1992

36 *Donga Ilbo*, March 27, 1990, and *Hankyoreh (Han'gyŏre)*, April 7 and July 5, 1990.
37 *Donga Ilbo*, November 9, 1991.

and the 1996 commissions bravely spoke of bringing about a grand class compromise, with workers accepting labor market flexibility in return for a strengthening of their political and social rights.[38] The outcome was discouraging for the state. The problem lay in the fact that the state was pushing for a corporatist solution without corporatist institutions. A very loose coalition of *chaebŏl* unions, the KCTU could not commit its members to a far-reaching exchange of labor market flexibility measures and political rights. Nor were the political parties interested in engaging in class politics, lest their regionalist bases of electoral support disintegrate under class polarization. The tripartite experiments of 1992 and 1996 were instead conceived and owned by one or another circle of South Korea's reformist intelligentsia, whose influence waxed and waned with changes in presidential priorities. The reformers of 1996 had a particularly tragic journey. After publicly endorsing their corporatist effort at class compromise, Kim Young-sam (Kim Yŏng-sam, 1993–98) opted for a conservative reform-from-above, putting aside the issues of political and social rights to focus only on labor market flexibility, when the representatives of business and labor movements turned down the public representatives' compromise package of exchange in December 1996. The decision destroyed Kim Young-sam and his agenda for labor reform. The KCTU-orchestrated "general strike," coinciding with the outbreak of a corruption scandal that involved one of Kim Young-sam's sons, put the labor reform in shambles within a month.

By mid-1997, partial reform efforts to control unsustainable hypergrowth by innovating the South Korean economy's two traditional adjustment mechanisms of industrial rationalization and labor market flexibility dismally failed. Ironically, however, it was precisely at this moment of failure that Kim Young-sam embarked on a third reform—this time, in the financial sector. While his public support nose-dived to the unprecedented level of below 10 percent and the political parties entered primaries to select their candidate for the presidential election of December 1997, the inner policy circles talked about launching a "big bang" to deal with the root cause of South Korea's corporate and financial distress. Included in the initial talks of a big bang were the strengthening of prudential regulations over financial institutions, the independence of the central bank from the Finance and Economy Board (FEB, a super-ministry established by the merger of

---

38 Ch'oe Yŏng-gi, Chŏn Kwang-sŏk, Yi Ch'ŏl-su, and Yu Pŏm-sang, *Han'guk ŭi nodong pŏp kaejŏng kwa nosa kwan'gye: 1987-nyŏn ihu nodong pŏp kaejŏngsa rŭl chungsim ŭro* [Labor law revisions and industrial relations in Korea: The history of labor law change since 1987] (Seoul: Korea Labor Institute, 2000), 117–206.

the MoF and the Economic Planning Board in 1994), the legalization of market-driven M&As of banks and NBFIs, the lifting of restrictions on foreign ownership of financial institutions, and the resolution of NPLs.[39] Like Kim Young-sam's other reform efforts, this talk of a big bang quickly disappeared in the realization that NPLs, estimated as 14.3 percent of all outstanding loans, could implode in the middle of a big bang, with the effect of entrapping both *chaebŏl* and banks in a severe liquidity squeeze. The financial reform instead became an entrenched bureaucratic turf war, with the central bank and FEB fighting over licensing and approval powers, supervisory authority, and monetary policymaking.

The bureaucratic turf war ended with the FEB retaining much of its licensing and approval powers in reform bills. These bills of bureaucratic reorganization, however, went nowhere until the country's extremely volatile presidential race of December 1997 ended. Until the election was over, both ruling and opposition political parties refused to bring the bills to a vote in the National Assembly, in the fear of losing popular support. The dodging of the issue might have helped their presidential campaign, but did not alleviate the internal and external pressures of economic crisis. On the contrary, the National Assembly's inability to vote on the financial bills came to symbolize the lack of the political will to meet the challenge of the Asian financial crisis, thus only driving the market deeper into panic. By the time the election was held in December 1997, eight of South Korea's top thirty *chaebŏl* groups, including Kia (the eighth largest *chaebŏl*), Halla (twelfth), and Hanbo Group (fourteenth), had failed under the weight of massive NPLs, making foreign investors and lenders divest in fear of the spread of corporate and bank distress. The fear was extremely contagious, because these corporate failures coincided with the regional spread of capital flight and exchange speculation after Thailand sought an International Monetary Fund (IMF) bailout in June 1997. The regional financial turmoil made it appear that many countries of East Asia, including South Korea, had engaged in "crony capitalism," where the privileged few captured state agencies to pillage banks and sabotage market forces in pursuit of rents.[40] The loss of confidence in the fundamentals of South Korea's political economy turned domestic corporate and financial distress into an external crisis that threatened default on foreign loans, as foreign investors sold South Korean stocks

---

39 *Joongang Ilbo (Chungang Ilbo)*, January 10 and March 15, 1997.

40 Byung-Kook Kim and Hyug Baeg Im, "'Crony Capitalism' in South Korea, Thailand, and Taiwan: Myth and Reality," *Journal of East Asian Studies* 1, no. 1 (February 2001): 5–7.

and stopped rolling over loans as part of their efforts at risk management. The threat of massive business failure, which the critics of big bang theories had warned, became real—even without the actualization of a big bang.

System Restructuring, 1997–

The year 1997 contained two surprises. First, despite a series of clear and consistent signals of crisis given by market forces, including the stunning failures of Hanbo and Kia Group, South Korea thought its troubles would somehow go away if it put in place the usual rescue policy package. Unlike the previous quarter-century, however, corporate and financial distress continued to deteriorate even with persistent state intervention in foreign exchange markets. Relief loans did not work this time. Second, for the first time in postwar South Korean electoral politics, the 1997 presidential elections resulted in the victory of an outsider with progressive political inclinations, Kim Dae-jung (1998–2003), which, coupled with the financial crisis, put the economy on a path-breaking and equilibrium-shifting experiment of corporate and system restructuring. The policy issues that had thus far been kept off the reform agenda, including loan guarantees, prudential regulations, corporate governance structures, fair trade, and NPLs, were all put on the table for the first time in the history of South Korea's modernization.[41] That change of agenda enabled policymakers to reshape *chaebŏl* behavior more effectively than the previous attempts at partial reform by adding sticks to their traditionally carrot-based adjustment policies.

The comprehensive assembling of financial, corporate, and labor reform had multiple causes. Structurally, with the financial markets fully liberalized under U.S. and IMF pressures, South Korea could not but embark on a widening of the scope of reform. Once corporate distress triggered bank distress, a vicious circle set in to sharply restrict the state's range of policy choices. The two pressures of corporate and financial distress not only fed on each other to increase the size of NPLs, but also jointly set off a foreign exchange crisis by causing massive capital flight. The foreign investors' loss of confidence, visibly shown in the rapidly falling rollover rate of foreign loans, in turn, dramatically drove up interest rates and foreign exchange rates, thus increasing corporate and financial distress even further. Consequently, with much of the foreign exchange reserves wasted in defending its overvalued currency during 1997, South Korea accepted IMF conditionalities in return for an IMF-led ftinancial rescue operation. The

41 Kim, "The Politics of Financial Reform in Korea, Malaysia, and Thailand," 185–231.

country's leaders had to face the issue of resolving the NPLs, because only then could banks resume new lending and roll over existing loans, investors could regain trust in local markets and reverse capital flight, and the state could build momentum for recovery.[42] The agreement with the IMF consisted of five shock therapy measures: to allow a flexible layoff of workers in times of corporate distress, accelerate M&As of insolvent financial institutions with the help of a massive infusion of public funds, lift protectionist barriers and regulatory controls in capital markets to permit foreign takeover of financial agencies and *chaebŏl* groups, institutionalize robust prudential regulations, and keep up fiscal austerity.[43] The IMF was thus forcing South Korea to put in place what its 1990s partial reformers had refused to do for fear of systemic breakdown.

These structural pressures, however, translated into concrete programmatic action only because there existed a political force that saw its interests as coinciding with an overhaul of the South Korean economic system. Only with such a political force in power could South Korea embrace reform of a very broad scope with great speed, as it did within two months of the financial collapse. Elected president only sixteen days after South Korea's acceptance of the IMF conditionalities,[44] Kim Dae-jung was the right man for the job of system restructuring. As a nationalist with a strong track record of supporting a dialogue with North Korea, he could open up capital markets without getting accused of selling out to the U.S.-led international finance. As a charismatic leader of the progressive political forces, having sided with distributive justice over economic growth, mass welfare over fiscal balance, and labor rights over employer prerogatives throughout his fiery career as a political rebel since the early 1970s, Kim Dae-jung was capable of fighting ideological challenges from both the right and the left more effectively than any other South Korean leader as he now pushed for socially costly reform policies. The lack of any credible alternative political leaders to the left of Kim Dae-jung on South Korea's historically constrained ideological spectrum

---

42 Carl-Johan Lindgren, Tomas J. T. Baliño, Charles Enoch, Anne-Marie Gulde, Marc Quintyn, and Leslie Teo, "Financial Sector Crisis and Restructuring: Lessons from Asia," IMF Occasional Paper, no.188 (2000), 17.

43 Jack Boorman, Timothy Lane, Marianne Schulze-Ghattas, Aleš Bulíř, Atish R. Ghosh, Javier Hamann, Alexandros Mourmouras, and Steven Phillips, "Managing Financial Crisis: The Experience in East Asia," IMF Working Paper, WP/oo/107 (June 2000), 5-15. See also Stephan Haggard, *The Political Economy of the Asian Financial Crisis* (Washington, DC: Institute for International Economics, 2000), 87–125.

44 Byung-Kook Kim, "Electoral Politics and Economic Crisis, 1997–1998," in *Consolidating Democracy in South Korea*, ed. Diamond and Kim, 173–201.

restrained both the KCTU and the FKTU from sabotaging his leadership even during massive layoffs and wage reductions, lest they lose their only spokesperson in the national arena. The *chaebŏl* too were prevented from overtly challenging Kim Dae-jung, because many of his reform programs were written in their preferred language of market-friendly neo-liberalism.

Moreover, in Kim Dae-jung's eyes, neo-liberal ideas, which had originated as a conservative programmatic vision of dismantling bloated welfare states in Western democracies, could become an instrument of progressive reform in South Korea's historical context of bureaucratically driven finance, opaque corporate governance structures, regulatory forbearance, hierarchically organized interfirm relations, rampant insider trading, and rising wage differentials between *chaebŏl* and SME workers. Many of the IMF conditionalities, if implemented thoroughly over a sustained period of time, would prevent the *chaebŏl* from many abuses of their monopolistic market power. The paradoxically progressive potential of conservative neo-liberal ideas encouraged Kim Dae-jung to talk of going beyond the IMF conditionalities after his election. As the president-elect, even before his inauguration in February 1998, he took charge of managing the financial crisis and got South Korea's top four *chaebŏl* groups to sign on to his "Five Principles of *Chaebŏl* Reform" that appealed for transparency in corporate governance structures, reduction of cross loan guarantees, improvement of financial structures, specialization around core business lines, and accountability of majority shareholders and executive managers. In August 2000, Kim added three more principles and goals: separation of industrial capital from financial capital, prohibition of circular shareholding as well as insider trading, and rigorous prevention of irregular inheritances.[45]

To be sure, many of Kim Dae-jung's "five-plus-three principles" of *chaebŏl* reform were not new to the South Korean discourse of reform. On the contrary, they had been much discussed during the 1990s episodes of partial reform. But his way of economic reform was new in two decisive manners. First, whereas his predecessors chose targets of reform in a very selective way, embracing only a few of these much-talked principles of policy change, Kim Dae-jung saw the five-plus-three principles about to make up an integrated policy package, in which the likelihood of effectively implementing any one of the five-plus-three principles depended on the presence of efforts to reshape institutions along the other principles. That is, the success

---

45 *Chosun Ilbo*, January 13, 1998; and August 15 and 20, 2000. See also Jongryn Mo and Chung-in Moon, "Business-Government Relations under Kim Dae-jung," in *Economic Crisis and Corporate Restructuring* in Korea, ed. Haggard, Lim, and Kim, 128-33.

of an institutional reform along the lines of any one of the five-plus-three principles was posited to depend on the coexistence of institutional reforms along the other principles. Second, again unlike his predecessors, who back-pedaled even on partial reform when faced with signs of political resistance, Kim Dae-jung stuck with his comprehensive approach for change, in fact adding the three principles on top of the original five principles in order to weed out the systemic sources of financial and corporate vulnerability. These two differences arose because Kim Dae-jung saw *chaebŏl* reform as a prerequisite for what he envisioned as South Korea's double transformation into both a democracy and a market economy, whereas for his predecessors, reforms had been largely an effort to strengthen South Korea's developmental state model by getting rid of its systemic bias for hyper-corporate expansion. In addition to advancing Kim Dae-jung's progressive ideological vision, *chaebŏl* reform also served the partisan interests of his new ruling coalition. The president had long accused the *chaebŏl* of causing social inequity and moral decay. Now, armed with neo-liberal ideas, Kim Dae-jung even questioned the *chaebŏl*'s capacity to deliver economic growth and stability. By extension, the double critique of the *chaebŏl* as unethical and inefficient dealt a great blow to the political patrons, clients, and allies of the *chaebŏl*, the conservative Grand National Party (Hannaradang).

The question for Kim Dae-jung was not whether but how to pursue a comprehensive path to *chaebŏl* reform. The choice of strategy was heavily influenced by South Korea's institutional setting. Because the pre-1988 developmental state had for three and a half decades consciously chosen to reduce threats of bankruptcy in the development of strategic industrial sectors with an eye to tempting the *chaebŏl* to invest in high-risk but also high-payoff business ventures, the South Korean economy of 1997–1998 was without effective insolvency and bankruptcy regimes to support corporate and financial restructuring without setting off a market panic that could drive even fundamentally viable, but temporarily distressed companies into liquidation.[46] There were two ways South Korea's lack of sound insolvency and bankruptcy regimes could raise the costs of corporate and financial restructuring to an unnecessarily high level. First, without adequate expertise, know-how, and experience in corporate restructuring, South Korea could mistakenly close down temporarily distressed, but viable companies when, as in the case of 1997–1998, interest rates and foreign exchange rates shut up, putting even solvent business companies at the brink of bankruptcy. Second,

46 Danny M. Leipziger, "Industrial Restructuring in Korea," *World Development* 16, no.1 (1988): 124.

even if it was to succeed in sorting out business companies temporarily in distress from those insolvent and put each in restructuring or liquidation processes, respectively, costs would not be minimized unless those temporarily distressed, but viable companies were compelled to downsize and restructure businesses under credible threats of bankruptcy. But that depended on sound insolvency and bankruptcy regimes, which South Korea did not have. The South Korean court lacked the authority, power, and expertise to supervise corporate restructuring.[47] To be sure, Kim Dae-jung began revising the laws on bankruptcy, corporate taxes, M&As, and foreign ownership after 1997, which could make market exit a real threat, but these revisions came too late to help in the most critical 1997–1998 phase of corporate debt restructuring.

Lacking sound insolvency and bankruptcy regimes, South Korea inevitably ended up choosing the strategy of restructuring corporate debt outside the courts. The authorities claimed that their alternative strategy of corporate and financial restructuring was modeled after Great Britain's "London Approach," but this claim too hid rather than revealed the nature of South Korea's path to systemic restructuring. The London Approach strives to bring a nonjudicial resolution of financial distress by getting all key creditors and debtors, in collaboration with and under guidance of the central bank, agree on a long-term financial support package of maturity extensions, interest holidays, debt-equity conversions, and new money for those companies that the creditors collectively identify as financially viable, provided they put in place a comprehensive restructuring program of management changes, asset sales, layoffs, and even M&As.[48] Such a voluntary, nonjudicial, and autonomous exchange of financial support and corporate restructuring was possible in Great Britain because its financial institutions constituted a community with common principles, rules, and norms that enabled members to collectively work out a solution to challenging issues of restructuring, including asset revaluation, debt prioritization and rescheduling, injection of new working capital, and management change, with a keen sense of mutual trust and under the informal guidance of what was recognized as an impartial and independent central bank. In the case of South

47 Youngjae Lim, "The Corporate Bankruptcy System and the Economic Crisis," in *Economic Crisis and Corporate Restructuring in Korea*, ed. Haggard, Lim, and Kim, 207–30.

48 Gerald E. Meyerman, "The London Approach and Corporate Debt Restructuring in East Asia," in *Managing Financial and Corporate Distress: Lessons from Asia*, ed. Charles Adams, Robert E. Litan, and Michael Pomerleano (Washington, DC: Brookings Institution Press, 2000), 300–3.

Korea, however, the three and one-half decades of statist development had deprived it of any such organizational infrastructures. Having served as a channel for subsidized policy loans, South Korean financial institutions were not only individually very low in asset valuation and risk-management capabilities, but were also saddled with massive NPLs, which discouraged them from seriously negotiating debt restructuring with debtors at least in the short run, for fear of their own bankruptcy.[49] The South Korean financial institutions made up a house divided, without institutional mechanisms of coordination and always looking to the state for a signal in lending policy.[50]

Unfortunately for South Korea, moreover, its lack of sound insolvency and bankruptcy regimes, which forced it into adopting a strategy of nonjudicial resolution after the model of the London Approach, paradoxically obstructed the implementation of its chosen nonjudicial strategy. The problem was that the London Approach of getting creditors and debtors nonjudicially and voluntarily engaged in debt restructuring works only when there exists a working legal framework of bankruptcy. That is, the threat of falling back on the legal procedures of bankruptcy and court receivership was what provided British creditors and debtors with an incentive both to restrain their temptation to get a free ride and to agree voluntarily and nonjudicially on a coordinated program of corporate restructuring outside of court procedures. South Korea was, then, emulating Great Britain's London Approach in an institutional setting devoid of many of its preconditions, inevitably making it pursue nonjudicial debt restructuring in most un-British ways. Formally, the South Korean creditors and debtors set up ad-hoc coordinating committees for deliberation on debt restructuring, as happened in Great Britain. The real driver, however, that pushed the ad-hoc coordinating committees to a creditor-debtor agreement on maturity extensions, interest holidays, and debt-equity conversions in exchange for a comprehensive corporate restructuring program of management changes, asset sales, layoffs, and M&As, was the Financial Supervisory Commission (FSC), a newly established state organ with the trust of Kim Dae-jung.[51] The commission's visible hand worked in a typically dirigiste South Korean way on the issues

49 Kyung Suh Park, "Bank-led Corporate Restructuring," in *Economic Crisis and Corporate Restructuring in Korea*, ed. Haggard, Lim, and Kim, 181–202.

50 Gregory Root, Paul Grela, Mark Jones, and Anand Adiga, "Financial Sector Restructuring in East Asia," in *Managing Financial and Corporate Distress: Lessons from Asia*, ed. Adams, Litan, and Pomerleano, 150–72.

51 Masahiro Kawai, Ira Lieberman, and William P. Mako, "Financial Stabilization and Initial Restructuring of East Asian Corporations: Approaches, Results, and Lessons," in *Managing Financial and Corporate Distress: Lessons from Asia*, ed. Adams, Litan, and Pomerleano, 106–12, 129–34.

of asset revaluation, debt prioritization and rescheduling, injections of new working capital, and management and ownership change.[52] First, the FSC resorted to administrative guidelines, setting a 200-percent upper limit on the debt-equity ratio for *chaebŏl* groups across industries in February 1998 to force both *chaebŏl* and financial institutions to downsize. In the case of South Korea's top five *chaebŏl* groups, which dwarfed other conglomerates, Kim Dae-jung even had the FSC attempt to mediate a "Big Deal." Essentially a program of business swaps, it tried to revive South Korea's obsolete tradition of industrial rationalization.[53] Second, a massive injection of public money empowered the FSC to move forward on corporate and financial restructuring. In 1997–1998 the state disbursed a total of sixty billion dollars of public money to finance the cost of debt restructuring.

The Big Deal failed to take place, and the "London Approach" degenerated into a top-down dirigiste program of corporate restructuring. Nonetheless, Kim Dae-jung's strategy of getting the powerful state bureaucracy to tackle the urgent tasks of bank and corporate restructuring and to construct a sounder mechanism for insolvency and bankruptcy, not only in the interest of facilitating on-going restructuring processes but also for the goal of preempting future financial and corporate distress, "worked" in the sense that, in spite of the still looming shadow of moral hazards, regulatory forbearance, and preferential treatment of the bigger conglomerates, the bureaucratically formulated rules like the 200-percent upper limit on the debt-equity ratio set into motion programs of corporate restructuring, albeit in crude bureaucratic ways.[54] Consequently, in 1999, South Korea was engulfed in another round of major reshuffling in the corporate world, with seven *chaebŏl* groups dropping from the ranks of the top thirty. The remaining twenty-three conglomerates boasted of an atverage debt-equity ratio of 164.1 percent by 1999, a reduction of 199.1 percentage points in a

52 Financial Team, Korea Development Institute, *1998-nyŏn kŭmyung pumun chŏngch'aek yŏn'gu charyo moŭm chip* [A 1990 collection of policy study materials on the financial sector] (Seoul: Korea Development Institute, 1998), 3–14.

53 The Big Deal aimed to induce South Korea's top five *chaebŏl* conglomerates to concentrate on their respective "core" industries through engineering multiple, interlinked business swaps across the aircraft, automobile, oil refining, petrochemicals, power generation, rolling stock, semiconductors, and ship engines industries, with the FSC playing the role of a neutral facilitator. The idea first appeared in early 1998, but produced discouraging results. See International Monetary Fund, "Republic of Korea: Economic and Policy Developments," IMF Staff Country Report, no. 00/11, (February 2000): 104.

54 See Paola Bongini, Stijn Claessens, and Giovanni Ferri, "The Political Economy of Distress in East Asian Financial Institutions," World Bank Policy Research Working Paper, no. 2265 (January 2000), 1–3, 11–14.

year, mostly through issuing new shares and revaluing assets.[55] The financial system was shaken up even more dramatically. By July 1999, nineteen of South Korea's original thirty merchant banks were shut down, twenty-six commercial banks had been consolidated into twelve through M&As and liquidations, and eighteen investment trust companies were streamlined into four with a massive injection of public money, while a flurry of legislative activism developed market exit mechanisms, including the establishment of a public asset management company, legislation of dramatically strengthened bankruptcy laws, fostering of M&A markets, tightening of prudential regulations, and lifting of legal upper ceilings on foreign ownership in equity, bond, and money markets.[56] These legislative efforts helped the FSC-driven dirigiste corporate restructuring by enabling the FSC to threaten bankruptcy with credibility so that the *chaebŏl* would settle for the second-worst option of cooperating with the FSC. The threat looked credible also because the newly amended laws and regulations drew in an army of foreign investors looking for bargain sales.

The gap between rhetoric and reality was even greater in labor reform. Because bank and corporate restructuring required labor market flexibility, Kim Dae-jung included labor reform as an integral part of the "class compromise" he sought when launching a Tripartite Commission of labor, capital, and state representatives a week before his presidential inauguration in February 1998. The tripartite framework was in a sense a revival of Kim Young-sam's failed 1996 labor reform program, envisaging an exchange of worker concessions on labor market flexibility measures in return for state concessions on labor rights in social and political spheres. This time, however, pursued by South Korea's progressive political forces with Kim Dae-jung at the forefront and initiated in the unusual context of a systemic crisis, tripartite deliberations brought a crucial political deal. The state-initiated and -brokered Tripartite Commission had its representatives from labor and capital agree on the simultaneous strengthening of workers' social and political rights and flexibility of labor markets.[57] Unfortunately, the pact lasted only few days because the KCTU voted down its leadership's appeal to

55 Yi Wŏn-hŭm, Yi Han-dŭk, and Pak Sang-su, "Tae kiŏp chipdan ŭi puch'ae piyul chojŏng sokdo e kwanhan yŏn'gu: IMF oehwan wigi sijŏm ŭl chŏnhu han chagŭm chodal haengt'ae ŭi pyŏnhwan pigyo" [A study of the leverage adjustment speed hypothesis in large business groups: A comparison of financing behavior changes between the pre- and post-currency crisis period], *Asia-Pacific Journal of Financial Studies* 28 (2001): 89.

56 International Monetary Fund, "Republic of Korea: Economic and Policy Developments," 96, 101.

57 Jongryn Mo and Chung-in Moon, "Korea after the Crash," *Journal of Democracy* 10, no. 3 (1999): 154–58.

endorse the tripartite agreement, but the revolt of the KCTU rank-and-file members did not stand in the way of the South Korean National Assembly's drive to legislate a series of labor reform bills based on the tripartite accord. The signing of the tripartite agreement was enough to get both conservative and progressive political parties to endorse the principle of labor market flexibility and jointly push through the labor bills.

In sum, South Korea's newly revived discourse of tripartism proved to be more critical in clearing the way for legislative activism than in actually forcing labor market flexibility on privileged *chaebŏl* workers. Even before the new labor bills were legislated, the Tripartite Commission de facto collapsed, because the South Korean labor organization was not amenable to any tripartite solution. The workers were internally splintered, with their loyalty focused on company unions. The summit organization also was fragmented, with the KCTU representing *chaebŏl* workers and the FKTU speaking for SME workers. The ideology of social democracy, which integrates workers into one cohesive class in both ideology and organization in Western European corporatist societies, thus making pact-making and deal-making possible not only between heterogeneous forces in the labor movements, but also between the summit organizations of labor and capital, was also absent in South Korea. The outcome was a politically destabilizing intermediate level of labor organization, which could not prevent the strong (*chaebŏl* unions) from individually advancing their interests at the expense of the weak (SME unions) on the basis of their market power. The *chaebŏl* unions were too powerful and too big to become mere price-takers that accepted wages and benefits as set by the market, but they were also too fragmented among themselves to collectively formulate an economically sustainable national wage agreement and to negotiate with capital for a grand compromise on the basis of that collective labor agreement.[58]

On the other hand, the breakdown of tripartism did not mean that South Korea's search for labor market flexibility ended there. On the contrary, because the state could not but push forward its dirigiste program of corporate and financial restructuring if South Korea was to exit from the systemic crisis of 1997–1998, the search for labor market flexibility had to continue. In the absence of corporatist ideology, institutions, and policy traditions, it came to be *chaebŏl* companies, with the implicit consent of their company unions, that consolidated a system of "irregular workers" to give their

---

58 For a similar argument on the relationship between organizational concentration and political instability, see Samuel H. Beer, *Britain Against Itself: The Political Contradictions of Collectivism* (New York: Norton, 1982).

internal labor market the minimum flexibility required to exit from financial distress and recover international competitiveness. The employment of irregular workers was nothing new in South Korea. The corporate community had been recruiting irregular workers in greater numbers since the outburst of industrial conflict in 1987. The collapse of Kim Dae-jung's effort to build institutions of tripartism in 1998 simply made the *chaebŏl* do what they had been doing all along, but in a more systematic, persistent, and strategic way.

The outcome of the *chaebŏl* groups' greater resort to the employment of irregular workers was the strengthening of labor market dualism in South Korea. Whereas the national labor market remained segmented into the privileged *chaebŏl* workers and underprivileged SME workers, the internal labor market of the *chaebŏl* came to pit regular workers against irregular workers.[59] By the time Kim Dae-jung proudly announced South Korea's graduation from IMF rescue operations in 1999, the country was to possess a labor market that triggered ideological polarization, partisan conflict, and moral tensions. At its shrinking core stood the "labor aristocracy" of *chaebŏl* workers, still capable of defending their job security, wages, and company welfare prerogatives through their implicit approval of their management's practice of meeting a sizable part of its new labor requirements through the employment of irregular workers. These irregular workers, hired through an outside supplier of contract labor, bore a disproportionate share of the country's labor adjustment and restructuring costs by accepting low wages and getting laid off first in times of corporate distress, thus protecting regular workers from job insecurity and wage instability. They constituted second-class citizens within the *chaebŏl* workforce, joining service-sector workers and SME employees to make up the political periphery in South Korea's dualistic labor market.[60]

What occurred after 1998 was, then, a change of degree. The core of regular *chaebŏl* workers shrank in its relative size, but nonetheless survived as the privileged few. The rising wage difference between the core and periphery

59 Yu Kyŏng-jun, "Pijŏng'gyujik munje wa koyong ch'angch'ul" [The problem of temporary workers and job creation], in *Han'guk kyŏngje kujo pyŏnhwa wa koyong ch'angch'ul* [Changes in the Korean economic structure and the creation of employment], ed. Yu Kyŏng-jun (Seoul: Korea Development Institute, 2004), 464–518.

60 Yu Kyŏng-jun and Yi Hŭi-suk, "IMF ihu nodong sijang ŭi pyŏnhwa mit chŏnmang" [The change and forecast of the Korean labor market after the crisis], Research Paper 99–02, Korea Development Institute (1999); and Ch'oe Kyŏng-su, "Nodong sijang yuyŏnhwa ŭi koyong hyogwa punsŏk: Kohyŏng poho kyuje wanhwa rŭl chungsim ŭro" [An analysis of the employment impact of flexible labor market measures: A focus on the relaxing of employment security regulations], Research Paper 01–09, Korea Development Institute (2001), 56–57.

became a major political issue, but stopped short of triggering generalized social unrest partly because irregular workers were not unionized, and partly because labor market flexibility was strengthened in parallel with progressive political measures. First, the Tripartite Commission's pact of February 1998 promised an expansion of social welfare expenditures in return for the labor representatives' acceptance of labor market flexibility. Second, it also elaborated the five principles of *chaebŏl* reform as the *chaebŏl*'s share of the burden in corporate and financial restructuring. Kim Dae-jung's new ruling political coalition even spoke of "dismantling" the *chaebŏl* in its braver moments of experimentation.[61] The president, too, made clear in his inaugural address his turn to progressivism by identifying the simultaneous construction of democracy and a market economy as the trademark of his presidency.[62] And he was intent on putting his words into action. At the height of systemic crisis, the state dissolved Daewoo (Taeu, 1999) and split Hyundai (Hyŏndae) Group into multiple conglomerates (2000), thereby burying for good the myth of *taema pulsa* (the big never die, or too big to fail) that the pre-1988 developmental state had created through the policy of risk socialization.[63] The failure of South Korea's two largest *chaebŏl* groups shook up big business and reinforced market pressures for a change in corporate behavior.

This is not to say that the post-1997 flurry of bank and corporate restructuring brought the dismantlement of the *chaebŏl*. To be sure, corporate governance became more transparent and accountable with the reform of laws and regulations on accounting, foreign ownership, bankruptcy, M&As, minority shareholder rights, and insider trading, but those *chaebŏl* groups that survived the shock therapy of *chaebŏl* reform still retained much of their earlier imperial (*ch'ongsu*) corporate governance structure, with the owner-manager family in control of daily business operations and the myriad subsidiaries controlled through a maze of cross-shareholding.[64] The outcome of Kim Dae-jung's financial, corporate, and labor restructuring was a new type of *chaebŏl* rather than their dismantlement. Having seen the weaker

---

61 Yu Sŭng-min, *Chaebŏl, kwayŏn wigi ŭi chubŏm in'ga: Wigi ihu chaebŏl chŏngch'aek ŭi p'yŏngga wa kwaje* [Is the *chaebŏl* the villain behind the crisis?: An evaluation of the post-crisis *chaebŏl* policy and its agendas] (Seoul: Korea Development Institute, 2000), 44–50.

62 Chung-in Moon and Song-min Kim, "Democracy and Economic Performance in South Korea," in *Consolidating Democracy in South Korea*, ed. Diamond and Kim, 164–65.

63 See Dong Gull Lee, "The Restructuring of Daewoo," in *Economic Crisis and Corporate Restructuring in Korea*, ed. Haggard, Lim, and Kim, 150–77.

64 Myeong-Hyeon Cho, "Reform of Corporate Governance," in *Economic Crisis and Corporate Restructuring in Korea*, ed. Haggard, Lim, and Kim, 286–305.

ones of their breed collapse under massive NPLs, the survivors came to understand that South Korea had entered a brave new era, in which they could not fall back on the state's rescue operation in times of corporate distress. The lesson profoundly changed the survivors' business behavior even when they retained many of the *chaebŏl* organizational characteristics. The new *chaebŏl* were more concerned with cash flow than with sales growth, less prepared for bold risk-taking, and more wary of threats of hostile takeovers. The breakdown of the myth of *taema pulsa* meant that the new *chaebŏl* was slimmer in structure, more conservative in finance, more cautious in market entry, but still organizationally centered on the owner-manager families and tied to affiliate companies through the system of cross-shareholding. The change of behavior was nowhere more visible than in the new *chaebŏl*'s massive accumulation of retained earnings.[65]

Precisely as South Korea's *chaebŏl* survivors shed their expansionist "gene," the banks also turned conservative. The massive injection of public money, coupled with the radical lifting of legal barriers and obstacles against foreign ownership, in effect, resulted in a dualistic financial system, where the state and foreign capital took over many of the insolvent private financial institutions and competed side by side for a greater market share.[66] Although the state became an owner of some of South Korea's major commercial banks, thus reversing the policy of privatization launched since the early 1980s, the financial sector did not return to the old practice of subsidizing the manufacturing sector because the state-owned banks of the post-1997 period were under the pressures of competition with foreign-owned financial institutions. The presence of foreigners influenced the state banks' calculation of benefits and costs, making many of their directors silently resist administrative guidance on loan policy, lest foreign competitors penetrate deeper into South Korea's profoundly shaken credit markets. In other words, Kim Dae-jung's financial and corporate restructuring succeeded in its negative goal of preventing banks from once again becoming subsidizers of *chaebŏl* groups. By contrast, there was much less progress on the reformers' positively defined agenda of transforming banks into genuine

---

65 Korea Chamber of Commerce, "Kiŏp yuboyul hyŏnhwang kwa sisajŏm" [The current situation of corporate retained earnings and its implications], July 4, 2007.

66 Kim Hyŏn-uk, "Oeguk chabon ŭi ŭnhaeng sansŏp chinip hwakdae e taehan ihae wa kyuje" [An understanding of and regulation of the expansion of entry into the banking industry by foreign capital], in *Kiŏp kyŏngyŏngkwŏn e taehan yŏn'gu: Siljŭng punsŏk kwa chedo chŏngbi pangan ŭl chungsim ŭro* [Studies on corporate management control in Korea: An empirical analysis and a measure of institutional modification], ed. Yŏn T'ae-hun, Research Paper no.05-07, Korea Development Institute (2005), 185–258.

financiers that provided loans on the basis of an objective assessment of the borrowers' future streams of cash flow. Like the new *chaebŏl*, the newly restructured banks were outright risk-averse rather than carefully risk-calculating creditors. Once they recovered financial solvency after a massive injection of public money, the banks focused on South Korea's relatively safe domestic housing market, with real estate serving as collateral, because having disbursed loans mainly on the basis of state directives and guidelines throughout their years of operation, they lacked the expertise in risk management that was required for making loans on the basis of the borrowers' future stream of cash flow.[67]

The power of "path dependence" was, then, much more formidable than Kim Dae-jung's new ruling coalition had expected. On the one hand, Kim Dae-jung did break away from his conservative predecessors' strategy of partial reform. On the other hand, his comprehensive reform set into motion financial and corporate restructuring, but within the institutional context of business concentration, labor market dualism, weak financial institutions, and state dominance, it did not mean that South Korea became another "neo-liberal" economy. The *chaebŏl*, for one, did not fade away as a way of organizing business. On the contrary, they emerged stronger, by shedding much of the structural excesses responsible for their overly aggressive risk taking. In fact, as shown by their great increase in retained earnings, the *chaebŏl* went too far in the other direction, toward an aversion rather than a management of business risks. The structurally transformed financial system displayed a similar spirit of risk aversion, continuing its practice of preferring borrowers with collateral, this time in the household real estate market.

To enter a virtuous cycle of growth and to capture niche markets in global markets, then, South Korea had more learning to do. In its restructuring program of 1997–1998, South Korea came only half-way in the long march toward *chaebŏl* reform. The remainder of this journey looked as challenging as the first half. This time, its success would depend more on the *chaebŏl* and the financial community's capacity to learn risk management and less on the state apparatus, whose capabilities to coordinate the economy and influence the *chaebŏl* ironically declined even more with the state-driven restructuring program of 1998.

---

67 Son Uk and Yi Sang-jae, "Kŭmyung sŏbisŭ sŏnjinhwa rŭl wihan kwaje" [Agendas for the advancement of financial services], in *Sŏbisŭ pumun ŭi sŏnjinhwa rŭl wihan chŏngch'aek kwaje* [The policy agendas for advancing the service sector], ed. Kim Ju-hun and Ch'a Mun-jung, Policy Paper no no. 07-04, Korea Development Institute (2007), 288, 293–97, 300.

3 Continuity and Change in South Korea's *Chaebŏl* Reform since the Asian Financial Crisis[1]

Dukjin Chang, Eun Mee Kim, and Chunwoong Park

By the early 2000s, the Asian financial crisis (AFC), which swept through Asia in 1997–1998, seemed all but over. There were some pockets of slow growth among Asian nations, but these appeared more to be caused by economic downturns in their major trading partners—i.e., the U.S. and Japan—as many of these economies were dependent on trade. South Korea was an exemplary case even among the hardest-hit countries. It paid off its structural adjustment loan from the International Monetary Fund (IMF) in 2001, three years ahead of schedule. In South Korea the average annual growth rate of gross domestic product (GDP) reached 7.2 percent in 2002, after recording a negative growth rate of −6.9 percent in 1998.[2] The unemployment rate was reduced to 3.3 percent in 2002 from a high of 7.0 percent in 1998, current account balances showed a surplus of $6 billion, and exports reached a high of $162 billion by 2002.[3]

Although the South Korean government seemed to have successfully resuscitated its economy with the IMF restructuring program, the vortex had a huge impact on both the South Korean state and corporate sectors in the country, in particular on the state-*chaebŏl* relationship.[4] Along with the

1 This chapter is based on research supported by a Korea University Grant.

2 National Statistical Office, 1998; National Statistical Office, 2002. https://www.index.go.kr/egams/stts/jsp/potal/stts/PO_STTS_IdxMain.jsp?idx_cd=2736&bbs=INDX_001.

3 Bank of Korea, 1998; Bank of Korea, 2002; National Statistical Office, 2002. https://www.index.go.kr/egams/stts/jsp/potal/stts/PO_STTS_IdxMain.jsp?idx_cd=1063&bbs=INDX_001; http://www.bok.or.kr/.

4 Family-owned and to a large extent still family-managed business groups in South Korea. They are basically networks of hierarchically organized equity ties. In this chapter, *chaebŏl* may either indicate a single business group or refer to a collectivity of business groups in South Korea.

restructuring packages by the IMF, two consecutive liberal-progressive regimes in South Korea, under Kim Dae-jung (Kim Tae-jung, 1998–2003) and Roh Moo-hyun (No Mu-hyŏn, 2003–8), attempted to establish a new relationship between the state and *chaebŏl*, accelerating movement away from the developmental state. Although the Kim Dae-jung administration, which was inaugurated in 1998 along with the IMF restructuring programs, inevitably had to carry out some strong market-reform policies, the Roh Moo-hyun administration tried to reduce state intervention in corporate sectors compared to previous regimes.

Chaebŏl reform was the main target by both the state and the IMF restructuring programs. *Chaebŏl* were seen by the IMF, the South Korean government, and the public, as a key culprit that caused, or at least precipitated, the crisis, leading to intensive and extensive restructuring measures. The results a decade after the AFC, however, show a mixed picture about whether corporate restructuring led to major systemic changes in the corporate sector. *Chaebŏl*, to be sure, reformed some of their outdated practices in order to survive, but their inter-firm network structure in large part seems unchanged even after undergoing intensive restructuring. In particular, most of the *chaebŏl* founder families still took advantage of the inter-firm network structure of their *chaebŏl* in order to strengthen their control over the whole business group despite their relatively small equity shares.[5] The resilience in their corporate governance, however, turned out to be a double-edged sword which could hurt the holder (the *chaebŏl* founder family), when the effects of the systemic restructuring began to appear, as will be explained in more detail later in this chapter.

The AFC and the ensuing IMF restructuring programs were a momentous event in that they more greatly contrasted the divergent paths that the state and *chaebŏl* have taken. On the one hand, the IMF programs pushed the state to expedite its transition from the developmental state that had already started in the early 1980s, constrained the interventions of the South Korean government into the domestic market, accelerated market opening to foreign capital, and dismantled both the barriers and the regulations imposed on the economic subjects. Nonetheless, the South Korean state had yet to set any specific regulatory model to replace its old developmental state. On the other, the IMF programs which assumed *chaebŏl* to be a simple collectivity of firms did not reach the core of the *chaebŏl* governance structure.

---

5 This has been called a "nested hierarchy." See Eun Mee Kim (Kim Ŭn-mi), Dukjin Chang (Chang Tŏk-jin), and Mark Granovetter, *Kyŏngje wigi ŭi sahoehak: Kaebal kukka ŭi chŏnhwan kwa kiŏp chipdan yŏn'gyŏl mang* [Sociology of the economic crisis: Transformation of the developmental state and business group networks] (Seoul: Seoul National University Press, 2005).

That is, although many reforms were implemented, *chaebŏl* governance has continued since the AFC.

Thus, this chapter's goal is two-fold: *changes* and *continuities*. We view that while changes surpassed continuities in the state sector, continuities outstripped changes in the *chaebŏl* sector despite a number of reforms. First, we show three takeover episodes that occurred in top *chaebŏl*, such as Hyundai (Hyŏndae) Group, SK Group, and Samsung (Samsŏng) Group. We examine this resilience by introducing a specific equity-holding structure we call the "nested hierarchy."[6] This chapter also describes the changes brought on by corporate restructuring measures before and after the AFC, discussing what has changed in the environment and in the corporate sector in terms of restructuring. By examining the changes, we are able to understand to what extent corporate restructuring has brought systemic changes in South Korea's corporate sector. After mapping out the paths that both the South Korean state and *chaebŏl* have taken since the 1980s, we proceed to examine the 30 largest *chaebŏl* as a whole with respect to their ownership structure. Along with an analysis of their inter-firm network structure and the centrality of the founder families, we argue that families of larger *chaebŏl* tend to hold smaller equity and that the three episodes could be extended to the other 27 *chaebŏl* as well. We point out that *chaebŏl* confront a dilemma about how to proceed. In conclusion, we propose that the South Korean state and the AFC restructuring measures created an institutional void and provided institutional complementarities.

Three Episodes Regarding *Chaebŏl* Governance Structure

Hyundai's Familial Conflict

On August 4, 2003, Chŏng Mong-hŏn, the chairman of Hyundai Group,[7] was found dead in a flowerbed located in the group's headquarters in Seoul. Investigation concluded that he had committed suicide by jumping out of his 12th floor office window. On August 21, Chŏng Sang-yŏng, chairman of KCC Group and uncle of the late Chŏng Mong-hŏn, declared that he would be the regent for Hyundai Group to help continue the decedent's corporate vision. Normally, it should have been the board of directors that decided

6 Dukjin Chang, "Privately Owned Social Structures: Institutionalization-Network Contingency in the Korean *Chaebol*" (PhD diss., Department of Sociology, University of Chicago, 1999).

7 After the death of its founder Chŏng Chu-yŏng (Chung Ju-yung) in 2001, the Hyundai Group divided into five independent groups: Hyundai Group, Hyundai Motors Group, Hyundai Department Store Group, Hyundai Heavy Machinery Group, and Hyundai Development Company Group.

who would be the next chairperson. But kinship ties suddenly became paramount in this emergency situation, signaling that the *chaebŏl* is a mixed construct of economic and social forces.

Few believed that Chŏng Sang-yŏng's real intention was to help his nephew's business group. The true reason, people suspected, was the potential conflict between the Chŏng and Hyŏn families, to which family the huge Hyundai Group belonged. Chŏng Mong-hŏn was married to Hyŏn Chŏng-ŭn and they had had a daughter and a son. If he had not committed suicide, there would have been no such conflict because normally his son, an offspring of the Chŏng family, would have succeeded the chairman's position. Because of the unexpected death, matters became very complicated as Chŏng Mong-hŏn's son was only a high school student. Moreover, Kim Mun-hŭi, Chŏng Mong-hŏn's mother-in-law, was the second largest shareholder of Hyundai Elevator, right after the deceased. Hyundai Elevator was a de facto holding company of Hyundai Group. If someone from the Chŏng family did not succeed the chairman's position, it was likely that control over Hyundai Group could go to the Hyŏn family.

Despite Chŏng Sang-yŏng's declaration, Hyŏn Chŏng-ŭn was inaugurated as the new chairperson of Hyundai Group on October 21, with the approval of the board of directors. Since Hyŏn had not had a previous role in the group, it was a big surprise. Although it was obvious that the members of the Chŏng family were very uneasy, they could not oppose the decision publicly because Hyŏn's inauguration was perfectly legal. Right after the surprising event, a rumor was circulated in the Korean stock market that someone was gathering shares of Hyundai Elevator. On November 14, three weeks after Hyŏn's inauguration, Chŏng Sang-yŏng declared that he had acquired the Hyundai Group. It turned out that he used a private equity fund through which he collected 20.63 percent of Hyundai Elevator's shares between October 22 and November 4, giving him a 31.2 percent stake. It looked like the short-lived dispute was over. But three days later on November 17, Hyŏn announced that she would make the company a *kungmin kiŏp* (a company owned by the people of Korea) with a capital increase of ten million shares. The official account was to make it a completely dispersed ownership company that would never need to worry about monopoly control by an individual. The plan was to issue ten million new shares, 20 percent of which would be assigned to the employee stock ownership association. To ensure ownership dispersion, any single investor would only be allowed to purchase up to 200 shares. The catch was that two million shares were to be assigned to the employee stock ownership association, which was already favorable to Hyŏn. If the plan succeeded, Hyŏn would easily recover the largest shareholder's position, while Chŏng Sang-yŏng's 31.2 percent would be diluted down to 11.2 percent. Chŏng Sang-yŏng instantly filed a petition to the courts for an injunction against the capital increase.

On December 12, the court decided that the issuing of ten million new shares would not to be allowed, brightening Chŏng Sang-yŏng's prospects for acquiring Hyundai Group. Moreover, on the last day of 2003, Chŏng announced that he had finally acquired 50.1 percent of Hyundai Elevator's shares. This time it definitely looked like the game was over. But Chŏng Sang-yŏng was charged with violating the "5 percent rule," which requires that anyone who acquires more than 5 percent of a company's shares must publicly announce the fact within five days of acquisition. On February 11, 2004, the Securities and Futures Commission (SFC) decided that Chŏng Sang-yŏng had to sell off 20.78 percent of Hyundai Elevator shares by May 20. Hyŏn Chŏng-ŭn once again became the largest shareholder of Hyundai Group and remained as the chairperson.

Two years later in April 2006, Chŏng Mong-jun, the chairman of Hyundai Heavy Machinery Group and the younger brother of the late Chŏng Mong-hŏn, acquired 26.68 percent of Hyundai Merchant Marine, another de facto holding company of Hyundai Group. Hyŏn instantly declared that it was another attempt at a hostile takeover, although Chŏng Mong-jun denied it and announced that it was just a portfolio investment. Hyŏn also said, in an emotional email to the employees of Hyundai Group, that she was still a member of the Chŏng family although her husband was no longer there. Meanwhile, she continued to collect more shares of Hyundai Merchant Marine. In June 2006, a group of well-known women's organizations declared that it would support Hyŏn and asked Chŏng Mong-jun to stop the immoral attempt to take over his sister-in-law's business group.[8]

This episode shows that *chaebŏl* in South Korea are more than an economic phenomenon in which social forces are immersed. After Chŏng Mong-hŏn's unexpected suicide, patrilineal familism was used to legitimate Chŏng Sang-yŏng's takeover attempt. Hyŏn countered it with another form of familism placing herself as a member of the Chŏng family, and used nationalism as an excuse for her planned capital increase of ten million shares. In the second attempt by Chŏng Mong-jun in 2006, women's organizations in South Korea voiced out in favor of Hyundai Group and its chairperson Hyŏn. In addition, the two takeover attempts raised the question of family boundaries in the South Korean *chaebŏl* context. Is Hyŏn Chŏng-ŭn a member of the Chŏng family even after the death of her husband? Chŏng Sang-yŏng's takeover attempt implied that the Chŏng family was not sure. Much

8 http://www.kncw.or.kr/

less explicitly, another attempt by Chŏng Mong-jun also nuanced that Hyŏn Chŏng-ŭn was not a part of the family. The question, however, became more vivid in 2006 as Hyŏn Chŏng-ŭn declared that she was still a member of the Chŏng family.

In 2010, Hyŏn's power within the Hyundai Group seemed robust. Even though her brother-in-law, Chŏng Mong-jun, could still be a potential threat, holding a considerable number of shares of Hyundai Merchant Marine, few believed that he would wage another showdown against his sister-in-law. She doubled the total assets of the Hyundai Group since her inauguration. Besides group management, she put much effort in businesses with North Korea, which were initiated by her father-in-law and husband. By visiting North Korea and meeting Kim Jong Il (Kim Chŏng-il) in August 2009, she played a role in thawing the frozen inter-Korea relationship. What is interesting for our discussion is the rise of her daughter, Chŏng Chi-i, within the Hyundai Group. In 2009, at the age of 32, she was promoted to executive director and some observers expect her to eventually succeed her mother at Hyundai Group. For women, the chairperson position of South Korean *chaebŏl* has largely been off-limits. With few exceptions (e.g., Shinsegae Group), women of each *chaebŏl* have thus far taken roles unrelated to their group business or have only been occasionally in charge of peripheral firms. If there is no male successor, then a son-in-law or an adopted son is expected to be the next candidate for the throne. Since many *chaebŏl* still retain patrilinealism, the rise of Chŏng Chi-i along with a few other women executives who are daughters of chairpersons can be interpreted as a significant signal challenging the patrilineal tradition of South Korean *chaebŏl*.

Another intriguing aspect of the intra-family dispute over the control of the Hyundai Group was the movement of stock prices of related companies. In April 2003, four months before Chŏng Mong-hŏn's death, Hyundai Elevator stocks traded at about 4,300 won. On the day of his death, the price was slightly over 10,000 won. The price began to rise as Chŏng Sang-yŏng declared regency on August 21 and fluctuated between 20,000 and 30,000 won until October 21. Right after Hyŏn Chŏng-ŭn was inaugurated as the new chairperson on October 21, the stock price began to skyrocket. It hit the ceiling at 99,700 won on November 6 and then crashed down to below 40,000 won as Chŏng Sang-yŏng declared his acquisition of the Hyundai Group on November 14. But Hyŏn Chŏng-ŭn's announcement of a ten million share increase on November 17 once again reversed the direction of the price movement up to above 90,000 won within only a month. As Chŏng Sang-yŏng declared his acquisition for the second time of a majority 50.1 percent on December 31, the stock price began to ebb. The mandatory sale-off decision by the SFC accelerated the downward movement to between 30,000 and 40,000 won. The stock price of KCC, the de facto holding company of Chŏng Sang-yŏng's KCC Group, also took a roller coaster ride, but exactly in the opposite direction of Hyundai Elevator.

Significant in this long and recurring dispute are three points. One is the broad band of stock price fluctuation. At its peak, the price of Hyundai Elevator shares was nearly 19 times that in April 2003. Although proxy fights usually entail a price increase, a gap as large as 19 times is not easily explained without taking into account the control premium that the firm's position in the equity network of Hyundai Group brings. Investors know that since acquiring Hyundai Elevator means acquiring the whole group in the context of a hierarchical equity network such as *chaebŏl,* the two parties in the proxy fight theoretically are willing to pay up to the value of the whole group regardless of the value of the target firm. That it was still happening in 2003–2004 suggests that the fundamental logic of *chaebŏl* organization had not changed at all despite the AFC and ensuing reform measures. Second, there is the fact that minority shareholder rights have been almost completely neglected. The stock price movement had nothing to do with the fundamental value of the related companies. Except for a tiny fraction of extremely lucky investors, most minority holders lost money because they did not have insider information on what was next to reverse the trend in the stock price movement. Third, and perhaps most interestingly, it signaled the very first serious takeover attempt at one of the largest *chaebŏl* business groups. *Chaebŏl,* especially large *chaebŏl,* were once considered invincible, unless disbanded by a strong state, as had happened to Kukje Group in the early 1980s. A hostile takeover attempt in the stock market had not seemed feasible. As can be seen below, however, the case of Hyundai Group was not an isolated episode.

SK versus Sovereign Global

On April 11, 2003, Sovereign Global, a multinational investment company founded by two New Zealanders, acquired 14.99 percent of SK Corp., the de facto holding company of SK Group, the third largest *chaebŏl* in South Korea at the time. With its acquisition, Sovereign Global became the second largest shareholder of SK Corp. A year later in March 2004, however, it turned out that Sovereign's shares, including friendly shares, amounted to 32 percent, while Chairman Ch'oe T'ae-wŏn's total shares, also including friendly shares, amounted to 37.62 percent. Once again, a proxy fight ensued. Because there was only a 5.52 percent gap between the two parties, the crucial issue was how many minority holders each party could co-opt. The situation was not favorable to Ch'oe T'ae-wŏn because in February 2003 he had been charged with an accounting fraud that amounted to 1.5 trillion won. Sovereign Global effectively focused on this weak link—problems of transparency and governance caused by the chairman—to persuade minority holders to side with Sovereign Global. In a series of four full-page ads in major newspapers, Sovereign Global consistently emphasized small shareholders' rights, transparency, expertise, global competitiveness, cooperation between South Korean business and foreign capital, and even patriotism. The last of the four ads appeared on March 10, 2005, the day before the general meeting of the shareholders, and said:

> If you want to smile together, see the big picture. Think of tomorrow. Show your existence, and what you can do. The real rights of shareholders. You are the owner. Exercise your right to appoint a talented and ethical manager, to bring change, and to make a world of happiness. Show people's power to make our company more profitable and our country flourish further, with transparent and expert management. It is only then that our company can be at the center of change. It is only then that people of Korea can put on a big smile. Stand up, Korea![9]

Although the attempt eventually proved to be unsuccessful, many observers thought that Sovereign Global had good potential. The fact that shares of foreign holders had increased significantly after the AFC could work favorably for Sovereign Global. In addition, civil society, which had argued strongly for enhancing transparency in corporate governance and minority holders' rights, could not speak out against Sovereign Global. In fact, Chang Ha-sŏng, the most famous minority holders' rights activist, stated that Sovereign Global did within a month what the South Korean government could not do for five years, pointing out the further positive effect on corporate governance that Sovereign Global's takeover attempt could bring. Compared to Sovereign Global, Ch'oe T'ae-wŏn did not have much to say. He could only indirectly imply the contributions to the South Korean economy that SK Group had made under his family's management and timidly try to ignite South Korean nationalism. Compare Sovereign Global's above ad with SK Corp.'s newspaper ad, which appeared only once:

> The dream of 48 million people. Because it was the desperate dream of all Koreans, and because someone had to do it, SK Corp. is doing it. SK Corp. is producing petroleum in 19 petroleum fields located in 11 foreign countries. We are making the dream of being an oil-producing country come true in places

9 Sovereign Global's full-page newspaper ad appeared in major newspapers, including *Chosun-Ilbo*, *Joongang Ilbo*, *Dong-A Ilbo*, *Hankyoreh*, *Maeil Business Newspaper*, and *Korea Economic Daily*, on March 10, 2005.

outside our country. But we can't be satisfied yet. In order to make Korea an energy-independent country, SK Corp. won't stop stepping forward even in the hot seas of the equator or in the deep forests of the Amazon. Precious things that others can't do. SK Corp. is doing those things. We are producing energy for Korea. SK Corp.[10]

Fortunately for Ch'oe, he won the proxy fight on March 11, 2005, by an unexpectedly large margin of 60.63 to 38.17 percent, mostly because foreign shareholders supported Ch'oe contrary to common expectations. Theoretically, it did not matter to ordinary investors whether Ch'oe or Sovereign Global was the controlling shareholder. However, in practice, it does matter. Given the problems of corporate governance that allows amplification of the largest shareholder's control, it might be better to have Ch'oe, who is unavoidably pressured by public opinion, remain in South Korea's legal jurisdiction and has vested interests in South Korean society, rather than Sovereign Global. Although Ch'oe won the fight, the possibility of losing South Korea's third-largest business group to foreign hands was very real. In order to persuade small shareholders, Ch'oe had to promise that he would separate ownership and control and also improve SK Corp.'s governance taking GE's board of directors as a model.

In addition, we suggest that it should be made clear that it was not Sovereign Global but the possibility of a hostile takeover that might have exercised some positive influence on corporate governance in South Korea. Sovereign Global spent 178 billion won to acquire its 14.99 percent of SK Corp. shares. If successful, the takeover could have brought Sovereign Global unlimited control over some fifty trillion won value of SK Group's assets—an amount 300 times as large as the initial investment. The governance problem lies in the very structure that enables the largest shareholder to amplify his or her control up to 300 times, using the hierarchically organized equity network across member firms in the business group, but not in who is at the top. In this sense, we suggest that South Korea civil society's initial support for Sovereign Global was misdirected, more or less misidentifying the problem.

Samsung and Its Succession Drama

Another episode that reveals the core dimensions of the corporate governance structure of South Korean *chaebŏl* happened at South Korea's best-known and largest business group, Samsung Group, as the chairman bequeathed his fortune to his offspring. In retrospect, the seeds were planted

---

10 SK Corp.'s full-page newspaper ad, which appeared in major newspapers on March 2, 2005.

in 1995 when then-chairman Yi Kŏn-hŭi (Lee Kun-hee) gave six billion won to his son, Yi Chae-yong, who then paid 1.6 billion won in taxes on the gift. Upon receiving this seed money, Yi Chae-yong spent 2.3 billion won to acquire 121,000 shares of S-One, a subsidiary of Samsung Group. After the company's IPO in early 1997, he sold the shares at 37 billion won. Yi also spent 1.9 billion won in 1995 to acquire 470,000 shares of Samsung Engineering, which later were worth 23 billion won in 1997 after listing the company. He also purchased in March 1996 1.8 billion won worth of Cheil Communications' convertible bonds (CBs), which brought him 16 billion won in two years. A rough calculation tells us that through a series of buying and selling of shares of Samsung Group subsidiary firms, the 4.4 billion won he initially received from his father became about 76 billion won in less than three years. This series of miraculous trading did not stop there. The most critical ones were yet to come. In December 1996, Yi purchased 9.6 billion won's worth of Samsung Everland's CBs.[11] In three months he converted these into shares, which amounted to 25.1 percent or 4 trillion won. At the same time in March 1997, he also purchased Samsung Electronics's CBs valued at 45 billion won, which he later converted into shares in August 2004. This was about 0.65 percent of Samsung Electronics shares, worth 5.6 trillion won. In February 1999, Yi also spent 4.7 billion won to purchase Samsung SDS's bonds with warrants, which he exercised in eight months to acquire 9.1 percent of the company's shares amounting to 36 billion won. In this series of trading, he not only snowballed his money but also took control over Samsung Group because of his ownership in Samsung Everland and Samsung Electronics, which were at the top of the hierarchically organized equity ties of the business group. No one would have believed this had been purely a run of luck. One cannot say, however, that this was illegal in the absence of hard evidence. It was technically legal because he paid 1.6 billion won in taxes on receiving the seed money from his father. There was no evidence to say that what happened after the receipt of the seed money was illegal. People's Solidarity for Participatory Democracy, a non-governmental organization (NGO) best known for a minority holders' rights movement, brought this case to court. After a long debate, the court ruled in 2009 that Yi Kŏn-hŭi was only partially guilty of financial wrongdoing.

It was in this context that the issue of revising the Financial Industry Structure Improvement Act (FISIA) surfaced. First enacted in 1997, the

11 Yi Chae-yong and his three younger sisters purchased 1.25 million CBs of Samsung Everland at 7,700 won per share in 1996. But when Samsung Card, a subsidiary firm of Samsung Group, purchased the shares of Samsung Everland from *Joongang Ilbo* (*Chungang Ilbo*) in 1998, the price per share was approximately 100,000 won.

law stipulated that a financial institution has to obtain approval from the Financial Supervisory Commission when it acquires more than 20 percent of the shares of a company belonging to the same business group or when it owns more than 5 percent and at the same time exercises effective control over the company. The spirit of the law was to prevent *chaebŏl* from using depositors' money to maintain family control over a business group. Despite the stipulation, however, it turned out that Samsung Card acquired 25.64 percent of Samsung Everland's shares without FSC approval. Samsung Life Insurance was also a 6.9 percent shareholder of Samsung Electronics. The two cases were slightly different because the latter acquisition had been made before the enactment of the law. The loophole was that the law as enacted in 1997 simply stated the regulations but did not specify what the sanctions would be in case of a violation. Reform bills were submitted separately by the Ministry of Finance and Economy and by the ruling Uri Party. Of the two reform bills, the stronger was the one by the ruling party, because it mandated a sell-off of shares in case of violation.

On the surface, the problem might look relatively simple, but in fact it is not. Samsung Electronics is highest in the hierarchical equity network of the business group. Samsung Everland is also right next to Samsung Electronics in its role maintaining the ownership structure of the group. Moreover, Samsung Everland is critical in the inheritance of the group's control from Yi Kŏn-hŭi to Yi Chae-yong. Unlike the other large *chaebŏl* (Hyundai Motors, LG, and SK), in Samsung Group the role of financial companies in buttressing the ownership structure of the founder family is essential. If the equity links from the two financial companies—Samsung Life Insurance and Samsung Card Corporation—to other core subsidiary firms in Samsung Group were nullified or severely restricted, as the proposed bill dictated, the controlling power of the founder family over the whole group would have shrunk considerably.

Samsung Group started defending itself by arguing that the reform bill might result in the handing over of the group's control to foreign hands. Given Samsung Group's position in the South Korean economy, with its exports amounting to roughly 25 percent of the country's total exports, it was plausible to question whether it was acceptable to turn over the group's control to foreign shareholders. And it was a question no expert could definitively answer. It was true that the reform bill, if passed, would result in a much weaker control by the Yi family. But would it be weak enough for a hostile takeover to be realized? No one knew. Those favorable to Samsung tended to estimate the probability of such a scenario to be higher, while critics argued that there would be no such possibility even after the reform bill. No matter which side of the debate was correct, from our point of view, what is significant is that the scenario of Samsung's hostile takeover sounded at least partially realistic. Voting for this reform bill at the National Assembly was postponed several times, which would not have happened if there was no possibility of a hostile takeover.

The recent verdicts associated with Samsung Group's succession and the enactment of the bill (FISIA) in December 2006 legally finalized the disputes and conflicts regarding Samsung Group. First, the Supreme Court ruled in May 2009 that there was no evidence that the executives of Samsung Everland intentionally engaged in assigning the CBs at a lower price to Yi Chae-yong and his sisters, annulling the original decisions and returning the case to the local court. Second, the Supreme Court ruled in May 2009 that chairman Yi was innocent in the CB assigning, confirming the two local courts' verdicts.[12] Third, the enactment of the FISIA in December 2006 restricts the voting rights of shareholders who hold more than 5 percent in the financial companies of Samsung Group, and the bill mandates the selling of excess shares within five years from the enactment date.

Each episode represents the traits illustrated by Granovetter's well-known discussion of South Korean business groups.[13] First, the *Hyundai Group v. KCC Group* case shows that familism is still prevalent in South Korean *chaebŏl* and that the rights of minor shareholders are largely ignored in important decisions like M&A attempts. Likewise, in the Samsung Group case, shareholders other than the Yi family and their allying executives were excluded from the CB assignment.[14] In both *chaebŏl*, the idea that family members have to inherit group leadership was the main concern of those involved. It is remarkably notable that even Hyŏn took advantage of a different form of familism against her uncle-in-law's patrilinealism. In contrast to a single firm, thus, there is virtually no typical principal-agent problem between the largest shareholder and the manager in South Korean *chaebŏl*, because they are often the same person or members of the same family. Rather, the most serious agency problem lies in the relationship between the alliance of owner-managers and minor shareholders.

12 The main reason the court acquitted the executives and chairman Yi of charges came from the fact that all subsidiary firms in *chaebŏl* are legally independent, and therefore assumes that executives might make independent decisions in the assignment of CBs.

13 Mark Granovetter, "Business Groups and Social Organization" in *The Handbook of Economic Sociology*, ed. Neil J. Smelser and Richard Swedberg (Princeton, NJ: Princeton University Press, 2005).

14 It is notable that the public prosecutor originally accused the executives of dereliction of duty.

The SK Group case not only shares the agency problem with the two other cases, but also implies that relatively small equity of the founder family results in challenges from outside. The hierarchical equity network, which once worked favorably only for the founder family to amplify its control, has now proven that it can become a double-edged sword when there is a takeover attempt from the outside. A double-edged sword can hurt not only the minority holders but also the founder family.

By contrast, the South Korean state, once famous for micro-managing the everyday activities of *chaebŏl*, could do nothing but rely on legal judgments by the court or the Securities and Futures Commission (SFC). In addition, the period in which all three cases took place is indicative of the relationship between the state and *chaebŏl*. The next section deals with the political economy of corporate restructuring in South Korea from the 1980s to 2000s, accounting for why and how the South Korean state stood inactively in the three cases. We will then examine the overall characteristics of the 30 largest *chaebŏl*.

The Political Economy of Corporate Restructuring: Changes

Under what circumstances could the three episodes regarding *chaebŏl* ownership take place? Of interest is the fact that all three coincidently occurred from the late 1990s to the mid-2000s, when the South Korean government steered away from being a developmental state. The two takeover attempts—*Hyundai v. KCC* and *SK v. Sovereign Global*—and the Samsung succession drama would not have taken place if the South Korean state had been a strong developmental state. Acknowledging that the IMF restructuring package created both changes and continuities in the South Korean economy, we view that the mixture of changes and continuities caused an institutional void, and an appropriate regulatory system for corporate behavior has yet to be established. By contrast, the *chaebŏl* have still retained their old ways to control their governance despite some changes in their business practices. This section scrutinizes the external and internal backgrounds of restructuring. It deals specifically with how and what aspects of the political backgrounds have been changed by investigating IMF programs, globalization and market liberalization, and democratization in South Korea.

Globalization, Democratization, and the Developmental State before the Asian Financial Crisis

To properly understand how outside forces influence corporate restructuring, it is necessary to see attempts to adjust the domestic political economy to external environments. In South Korea, since the state-led globalization, democratization, and market liberalization took place together, or at least occurred very close together, the three occasionally overlapped. We present how globalization and the movement of foreign capital changed the dynamics of global and domestic capital and precipitated the AFC. We also discuss how democratization and economic liberalization in South Korea led to the deterioration of the developmental state's influence in the economy and enhanced the power of various interest groups including labor and NGOs.

Globalization and Foreign Capital

The advent of globalization since the 1990s has brought about huge movements of capital, goods, and people around the world. South Korea was no exception to this increasingly globalized world. In fact, in order to make sure that South Korea does not miss out on this great opportunity, the Kim Young-sam administration (Kim Yŏng-sam, 1993-98) announced the *segyehwa* (globalization) policy in 1994, signaling a state-supported globalization in South Korea. Prior to this change, South Korea was notorious for its high entry barrier to the domestic capital market, with the percentage of shares owned by foreigners hovering around only 3 percent. However, since the *segyehwa* policy announcement and greater market openness, the value of shares in the South Korean stock market owned by foreigners jumped to around 10 percent just one year later.

One could argue that South Korea still had relatively high barriers to entry even after the *segyehwa* policy, because there remained many restrictions such as foreign ownership caps on corporate equities. In fact, South Korea was still very slow at opening the financial market, especially when compared to countries such as Mexico and Turkey.[15] There was also evidence that some parties within the South Korean state did not want rapid liberalization, fearing a loss of control over the domestic market and the corporate sector.[16] Nevertheless, the *segyehwa* policy signaled an important policy shift because the partial opening of the financial market entailed many related changes, such as the easing of foreign borrowing by South Korean firms, which later proved critical to South Korea's vulnerability to the AFC, and eventually, the lifting of barriers to exit. The value of foreign-owned shares in the South Korean stock

15 Arvid Lukauskas and Susan Minushkin, "Explaining Styles of Financial Market Opening in Chile, Mexico, South Korea, and Turkey," *International Studies Quarterly* 44. no. 4 (2000): 695–723.

16 Jung-en Woo, *Race to the Swift: State and Finance in Korean Industrialization* (New York: Columbia University Press, 1991); Deena Khatkhate and Ismail Dalla, "Regulated Deregulation of the Financial System in Korea," World Bank Discussion Paper, no. 292 (1995).

market remained between 10 and 15 percent during 1992-97, but it increased to around 30 percent, equivalent to 300 trillion won, by 2010.[17]

This policy shift was very significant for the corporate sector. First, it signaled that the *chaebŏl* could more readily borrow from foreign financial institutions. Second, it allowed the *chaebŏl* to actively acquire or establish firms overseas, which often required access to foreign capital from foreign financial institutions. Finally, this meant that the *chaebŏl* could also be vulnerable to foreign investors. The threat of potential acquirers armed with enough capital to attack vulnerable but huge *chaebŏl* became a reality.

The vulnerability of the South Korean market to foreign investors and foreign capital in general was realized through the AFC. The AFC started from a foreign exchange flight followed by a domestic credit crunch. Thus, an immediate solution to this problem appeared to be attracting more foreign capital, which in turn required changes in the restrictive policies on foreign capital. Many barriers to entry, such as ceilings on equity holdings by foreigners, permission for foreigners' equity acquisitions by the head of the Ministry of Finance and Economy (MOFE), and approval of foreigners' equity acquisitions by the board of directors, have been abolished. In addition, foreign capital was exempted from regulations on a financial institution's acquisition of shares of non-financials. As a result, the share of foreign capital in South Korea's major businesses skyrocketed. Three of the eight nationwide banks became foreign-owned in the immediate aftermath of the AFC.

Figure 3.1 shows how quickly foreign shares increased in the South Korean equity market and that the increase of foreign influence accelerated since the AFC. As of 2003, foreigners accounted for about 40 percent of the value of all listed stocks and about 50 percent in the top ten listed companies. Despite this rapid expansion of influence, the problem lies in the fact that it has not produced the originally expected positive consequences, such as corporate governance. An event-history analysis of mergers and acquisitions involving South Korean firms for the 1997–2000 period reveals that foreign acquisitions of South Korean firms were not affected by the price-to-book ratio but rather were affected by variables usually unassociated with acquisitions, suggesting that foreign capital largely responded to cheap shopping opportunities rather than solid investment opportunities.[18]

17 Foreign Investments in Domestic Securities in October 2010 of the Financial Supervisory Service in Korea. http://english.fss.or.kr/fsseng/emdc/prs/fss_v.jsp?menuName= PRESS+RELEASE&menuIndex=0&fssIndex=10761.

18 Joon Han and Dukjin Chang. "Changing Corporate Governance in Korea: Rise of a Market for Corporate Control or the Strategic Adaptation of *Chaebol*?" *Development and Society* 32, no. 2 (2003): 253–70.

FIGURE 3.1 Percentages of foreign-owned shares in Korean companies, 1991–2003
Source: Data obtained from the Korea Exchange (http://www.krx.co.kr).

The advent of globalization and the rapid influx of foreign capital presented an important condition in which corporate restructuring must take place. Foreign investors in the stock market, foreign-owned financial institutions, and M&A attempts by foreign investors on major *chaebŏl* suggest that corporate restructuring must also be understood within this broader global political economy. It is in this broader context that the IMF entered and began to request changes in the corporate sector.

Democratization, Economic Liberalization, and the Developmental State

In South Korea, important changes were taking place along with changes in the global political economy. Economic liberalization began as early as the mid-1980s. Although the South Korean economy as a whole and the *chaebŏl* in particular continued their rapid expansion through the 1980s, South Korea's flagship industrial policy of the developmental state era—i.e., the heavy and chemical industrialization policy—officially ended in 1979, together with the assassination of its inventor, President Park Chung-hee (Pak Chŏng-hŭi, 1961–79). The Chun Doo-hwan (Chŏn Tu-hwan, 1979–88) regime strived to find a new direction for its economic policies, but the Second Oil Crisis shook the world in 1979. Thus, the Chun regime shifted its economic policy from "developmental" and "industrial policies" focusing on economic expansion, to one that was more focused on stabilization of prices and economic liberalization. As a result, bank privatization began in 1980, and the government declared that real interest rates were to remain above zero.

On the political front, by the mid- to late 1980s, forces for democratization gained momentum, and the authoritarian, military-backed Chun had to acquiesce to public pressure. His handpicked successor, Roh Tae-woo (No T'ae-u, 1988–93), declared on June 29, 1987, that South Korea should move forward with democratization, promising direct presidential elections, which millions of protestors had demanded. However, due to the split among the opposition, Roh won the presidential election in 1987 without a majority vote. Roh was a former military general, but he could no longer continue with authoritarian rule. Democratic transition had taken place in South Korea, and many interest groups including labor and NGOs increasingly voiced their opinions and would no longer tolerate authoritarian policies in all sectors of society. These changes meant that the developmental state, which had directed and controlled the corporate sector, was also subject to challenges from civil society. In particular, labor was no longer acquiescent to repressive policies that favored the *chaebŏl*, and the *chaebŏl* were also voicing their objections to excessive control by the developmental state. The latter was seen by the developmental state with great alarm, since the *chaebŏl* were the largest beneficiaries of the developmental state, in contrast to labor, which had been oppressed by the state. The *chaebŏl* began to demand economic liberalization, although this also meant that they would no longer be dependent on the state for capital. It appeared that the *chaebŏl* no longer had to rely solely on the state for capital. Some of the key characteristics of the developmental state eroded with democratization and economic liberalization.[19] There was no longer a flagship government agency—e.g., Japan's Ministry of International Trade and Industry or the South Korean Economic Planning Board—to aggressively and extensively intervene in the market; financial institutions, which provided the means for economic intervention, were no longer under state ownership and control; there was greater access to foreign capital without the state as an intermediary; and market opening meant that the developmental state was no longer functioning.[20]

19 Chalmers Johnson, *MITI and the Japanese Miracle: The Growth of Industrial Policy, 1925–1975* (Stanford, CA: Stanford University Press, 1982); Eun Mee Kim, *Big Business, Strong State: Collusion and Conflict in South Korean Development, 1960–1990* (Albany: State University of New York Press, 1997).
20 Kim, *Big Business, Strong State.*

Institutions that were once dependent on the state for their survival began to challenge the state. For example, the *chaebŏl*, which expanded greatly in the 1970s due to the state's heavy and chemical industrialization policy, were now opposing and challenging the state.[21] The *chaebŏl* were not only challenging the state's interventionist industrial policies, but they were opposing the state in the political arena as well. In the 1992 presidential election, the founder of the Hyundai Group, Chŏng Ju-yŏng, ran for president. Although Chŏng did not win the presidency, it was one more example that the *chaebŏl* were no longer willing to be in the passenger's seat of the South Korean developmental vehicle.

The *chaebŏl* were also finding alternative sources of funding to the state-controlled domestic banks. The *chaebŏl* acquired and established many NBFIs (nonbank financial institutions) whose market share went above 50 percent by the mid-1980s. The *chaebŏl*'s NBFIs became an important source of their much-needed capital, and thus the *chaebŏl* were becoming less dependent on domestic banks and the state. In addition, the *chaebŏl* were aggressively diversifying their businesses into unrelated business sectors during the 1980s, which led to greater independence from the state.[22]

The South Korean government, on the other hand, began to distance itself from the *chaebŏl*. Sometimes characterized as a transition from dominance to symbiosis,[23] the state now realized that the *chaebŏl* could be its potential competitor and the state announced many regulatory policies from the late 1980s. It is notable that the South Korean state began to strengthen the Monopoly Regulation and Fair Trade Act (MRFTA) and banking laws from the late 1980s as a means to control the unwielding *chaebŏl*.

However, something analogous to an institutional void was silently finding its place in the South Korean developmental state. We suggest the concept of a post-developmental state to characterize this institutional void. The South Korean state began to withdraw from its developmental role, but had yet to reorganize itself into an effective "regulatory state." The state has to be able to intensively use competition policy and financial supervision to become a regulatory state. The South Korean state had not made this transformation. The Fair Trade Commission's role continued to

---

21 Ibid.

22 Hong Chae-bŏm and Hwang Kyu-sŭng, "Han'guk kiŏp ŭi tagakhwa wa kyŏngje chŏk sŏnggwa e kwanhan yŏn'gu" [A study on the diversification and economic performance of Korean firms], *Kyŏngyŏnghak yŏn'gu* [Research in business administration] 26 (1997): 493–511; Kim, *Big Business, Strong State*.

23 Kim, *Big Business, Strong State*.

be maintaining regulations on the *chaebŏl*'s cross-shareholdings instead of setting the rules for market competition. Financial supervision was still lax, as was painfully revealed during the AFC.

Corporate Restructuring after the Asian Financial Crisis[24]

Leading economists provided two divergent explanations for the causes of the AFC.[25] Economists who prioritized endogenous factors argued that the financial excess and the subsequent financial collapses were the main cause of the AFC.[26] Financial intermediaries, who believed that they had implicit government guarantees on their loans, were subject to moral hazard problems, which caused overpricing of assets, and, in turn, contributed to making the financial conditions of these intermediaries look sounder than they actually were. Scholars favoring endogenous explanations recommended implementing a better regulatory scheme for domestic financial institutions and eliminating widespread moral hazards among economic subjects in the domestic market. By contrast, another group of economists pointed out the weakness in the fundamentals of Asian economies from the mid-1990s. Unlike the endogenous explanation, scholars in this group stressed the external environments which led the Asian economies to the financial crunch.[27] Creditor

24 The discussion in this section borrows heavily from Chapter 7 of Kim, Chang, and Granovetter, *Kyŏngje wigi ŭi sohoehak.*

25 Our discussion here is limited to economic explanations because they are the ones that provided the rationale for the post-crisis reform policy implemented by the South Korean government. For political explanations see Bruce Cumings, "The Asian Crisis, Democracy, and the End of Late Development," in The Politics of the Asian Economic Crisis, ed. T.J. Pempel (Ithaca, NY: Cornell University Press, 1999); Chalmers Johnson, "The Developmental State: Odyssey of a Concept" in *The Developmental State,* ed. Meredith Woo-Cumings (Ithaca, NY: Cornell University Press, 1999); Robert Wade and Frank Veneroso, "The Asian Crisis: The High Debt Model versus the Wall Street Treasury-IMF Complex," *New Left Review* I, no. 228 (March-April 1998): 3–24; and for sociological explanations see Gary G. Hamilton, *Cosmopolitan Capitalists: Hong Kong and the Chinese Diaspora at the End of the 20th Century* (Seattle: University of Washington Press, 1999).

26 Tomãs J.T. Baliño and Angel J. Ubide, "The Korean Financial Crisis of 1997: A Strategy of Financial Sector Reform" IMF Working Paper, no. 99/28 (March 1999).

27 Stephen Radelet and Jeffrey Sachs, "The East Asian Financial Crisis: Diagnosis, Remedies, Prospects," *Brookings Papers on Economic Activity,* no. 1 (1998): 1–74; Steven Radelet and Jeffrey Sachs, "What Have We Learned, So Far, from the Asian Financial Crisis?" Harvard Institute for International Development, CAER Discussion Paper no. 27, presented at the annual meeting of the American Economics Association, January 1999.

panic and weakness in international capital markets were seen as the main causes of the crisis. Although they acknowledged the excessive short-term foreign liabilities many Asian economies had maintained, they were more inclined to provide prescriptions for better regulation of the international capital market. The scholars who advocated the exogenous explanation suggested that the state should regulate the flow of foreign capital. Admitting that the Asian countries were in part responsible for the financial crunch because they had maintained a high level of short-term foreign liabilities, they warned that rapid market liberalization in developing countries might make things worse.[28]

Of interest was the fact that, although the two groups were opposed to each other in explaining the cause of the AFC and the remedies, they had a similar effect on the organizational environments of the *chaebŏl*. A better regulatory scheme for financial institutions and subsequent elimination of moral hazard was the solution proposed by the first explanation. This meant that the *chaebŏl* would now need higher profitability rather than government support for continued supply of capital. However, the *chaebŏl*'s return-on-investment (ROI) was notoriously lower than that of their independent counterparts.[29] This can be understood given the context of the developmental era when growth, not efficiency, mattered. In other words, for the *chaebŏl*, none of the usual economic variables—age, debt ratio, financial cost, and industry effect—could explain their ROI, although the efficiency of asset growth could be explained.[30] As widely recognized for decades, the South Korean *chaebŏl* exemplified a development trajectory led by the state's supply of cheap credit.[31] Throughout the 1970s and up to the mid-1980s, the *chaebŏl* were heavily dependent on domestic bank credit given

28 Alejandro Diaz, ed., *Trade, Development and the World Economy: Selected Essays of Carlos F. Díaz-Alejandro* (Oxford: Basil Blackwell, 1988); Ronald I. McKinnon and Huw Pill, "Credible Liberalizations and International Capital Flows: 'Overborrowing Syndrome'," in *Financial Deregulation and Integration in East Asia*, ed. Takatoshi Ito and Anne O. Krueger (Chicago: University of Chicago Press, 1996), 42.

29 Dong-sŏng Cho, *Hankuk chaebŏl yŏng'gu* [A study of Korean *chaebŏl*] (Seoul: Maeilkyŏngjesinmunsa, 1990).

30 Chang, "Privately Owned Social Structures."

31 Jeff Frieden, "Third World Indebted Industrialization: International Finance and State Capitalism in Mexico, Brazil, Argentina, and South Korea," *International Organization* 35, no. 3 (1981): 407–31; Stephan Haggard, *Pathways from the Periphery* (Ithaca, NY: Cornell University Press, 1990); Chalmers Johnson, "Political Institutions and Economic Performance: The Government-Business Relationship in Japan, South Korea, and Taiwan," in *The Political Economy of the New Asian Industrialism*, ed. Frederic C. Deyo (Ithaca, NY: Cornell University Press, 1987), 136–64; Robert Wade, *Governing the Market* (Princeton, NJ: Princeton University Press, 1990).

at cheaper-than-market rates through export finance programs and special-purpose financial institutions. Domestic banks—state-owned until the early 1980s and state-controlled since then—did not have the autonomy to set their own rates. Since the mid-1980s, as financial liberalization proceeded, emphasis began to shift toward NBFIs owned by the *chaebŏl*. These NBFIs, which were themselves subsidiaries of the *chaebŏl*, lent at favorable rates to the same *chaebŏl*'s member firms.

The second exogenous explanation proposes to eliminate the asymmetry between short-term foreign debt and short-term foreign assets to prevent the possibility of multiple equilibriums. As painfully revealed during the initial stage of structural adjustment, much of the short-term foreign debt had been borrowed by *chaebŏl*-owned NBFIs—especially merchant banks—once again confirming that these NBFIs were an important source of capital for the business groups to which they belonged. Close monitoring of cross-border movements of short-term capital shut down this important pipeline. Even worse for the *chaebŏl*, the first IMF program, which was accepted by the South Korean government, included maintenance of fiscal and monetary austerity, high interest rates, and closure of many banks and NBFIs. To summarize, regardless of which explanation for the causes of the AFC we follow, the domestic effects on the organizational environment of the *chaebŏl* are similar: *increasing hardship in capital mobilization* and *continued demand for corporate restructuring*.

This observation is confirmed in an evaluation by the IMF of its programs in crisis countries, in which the authors state that, "financial sector restructuring stood at the top of the structural restructuring agenda and formed the centerpiece of all three programs;"[32] "[a]s the process of financial sector restructuring advanced, the importance of complementary measures to address weaknesses in the corporate sector became increasingly evident";[33] and "[r]eforms to promote governance and competition in the program countries included . . . restructuring and dismantling corporate networks such as *chaebŏl* in Korea."[34] These assessments imply that financial sector restructuring was somewhat mistakenly seen by the IMF as the key to corporate restructuring, while in fact persistent corporate ownership patterns in the *chaebŏl* made the financial sector–led restructuring only partially successful.

32 The three programs refer to IMF-supported programs in Indonesia, South Korea, and Thailand. See Timothy Lane, et al., *IMF-Supported Programs in Indonesia, Korea, and Thailand: A Preliminary Assessment* (Washington, DC: International Monetary Fund, 1999).

33 Ibid., 71.

34 Ibid., 71.

The two progressive regimes played a relatively minor role when the *chaebŏl* were faced with great challenges in the aftermath of the AFC. During the Hyundai Group takeover attempts, the state intervened only twice. One was the court ruling on December 12, 2003 that the capital increase of ten million shares was illegal. The other was the decision by the SFC on February 11, 2004 that required Chŏng Sang-yŏng to sell off 20.78 percent of Hyundai Elevator shares within three months. Both were minimal interventions in the sense that the state intervened only when a petition was filed. Even then, the state's role was confined to providing an interpretation of the law. If we recall the South Korean state's fame for micro-managing business group activities, and also consider the importance of Hyundai Group in the South Korean economy, these minimal interventions were a surprising change from the past. In the case of the M&A attempt by Sovereign Global over SK Group, the state did absolutely nothing to help out the country's third-largest business group. Rather, the state's hands might have been tied because of two things: Ch'oe T'ae-wŏn's accounting fraud in the previous year and the government's gradual shift to a weaker state model.

As for Samsung Group, the state's stance was most ambiguous. It was the ruling Uri Party that submitted the tougher reform bill, while the proposal by the MOFE was more modest. When the reform bill was actually presented to the National Assembly, the voting was postponed several times despite the fact that the Uri Party had the majority position. The government refused to admit that there was a possibility of a hostile takeover, but it acted as if the possibility were there. Finally, in November 2005 the ruling party decided that it would adopt separate solutions for the two cases of Samsung Group's violations of the law. A separate solution meant that the shares of Samsung Electronics owned by Samsung Life Insurance would not have to be sold off, but the voting rights for shareholders of more than five percent would be confined. Although this would sting Samsung Group, it was also a compromise with the reality of the business group's position in the South Korean economy. The Uri Party had to announce a lengthy explanation for this somewhat self-contradictory decision. Its explanation was that it was a decision to respect the spirit of *chaebŏl* reform, while minimizing the damage to private business and at the same time avoiding the possible debate surrounding violation of the Constitution. On the same day, People's Solidarity for Participatory Democracy (PSPD), one of the most influential NGOs in South Korea, also made a public announcement in which it argued that "from now on, the Uri Party shouldn't even think of mentioning reform."[35]

---

35 PSPD's public announcement on November 24, 2005 (http://blog.peoplepower21 .org/Economy/15230).

The two progressive regimes under Kim Dae-jung and Roh Moo-hyun tried to differentiate themselves from their previous authoritarian regimes in various aspects. Indeed, for the ten years of their terms, South Korean society progressed toward a more democratic and liberal society than ever before. But, when it came to economic regulations, the democratic and liberal progress resulted in a dismantling of authoritarianism without proper government regulation.

South Korean *Chaebŏl* since the AFC: Continuities

The AFC and the ensuing corporate restructuring measures brought about significant changes in the *chaebŏl*. Before and after the AFC, several *chaebŏl* went bankrupt and disaggregated. But the *chaebŏl* that survived the tsunami of the AFC expanded their business more than ever before. On the surface, the *chaebŏl* accepted the various measures recommended by the IMF and enforced by the South Korean government. However, as mentioned earlier, the governance structure of the *chaebŏl* features hierarchically organized inter-firm networks. Hence, the other governance issues are peripheral because problems such as accounting transparency, mandatory appointment of outside directors, and streamlining of subsidiaries all derive from the ownership structure. Although 99 percent of *chaebŏl* subsidiaries appointed outside directors to comply with the reform measure, the rate of approval by those outside directors of proposals submitted by the incumbent management was reported to have reached 99 percent. The Big Deals, the representative reform policy for business streamlining, proved not to be a big deal because many of the business swaps simply led to oligopolistic market domination by the largest *chaebŏl* rather than to streamlining of their businesses. Furthermore, the fact that the chairperson of a *chaebŏl* group is entitled to agree upon a business-to-business swap with the chairperson of another *chaebŏl* strongly implies that the fundamental problem lies in the ownership structure. This next section looks at the changes and continuities in the South Korean *chaebŏl*, and analyzes why they did not, or could not, change their governance structure.

Changes

The South Korean state announced five goals of corporate restructuring. They were transparency in management, elimination of cross-debt guarantees, improvement of the financial structure, better corporate governance, and streamlining of business activities. Considering that transparency is an abstract concept that needs to be quantified, a consolidated financial statement was proposed as an indicator. Prior to this measure only individual firms' financial statements (and not of the *chaebŏl* as a whole) were produced. There were many intra-group transactions and cross-investments within the *chaebŏl*, which led to over-counting of sales and assets. So by simply adding the financial statements of the *chaebŏl* member firms could not give an accurate account of the financial status of a *chaebŏl*, which the *chaebŏl* could then abuse to receive unfair bank loans, and/or unfairly favorable interest rates from domestic banks. Thus, a consolidated financial statement was seen as a first step toward corporate transparency.

Second, cross-debt guarantees among member firms within a *chaebŏl* led to unfair access to bank loans for decades. Thus, new cross-debt guarantees were immediately banned and pre-existing ones were to be resolved by March 2000. The third goal was improvement of the financial structure. There was a vicious cycle of high debt and the developmental state's bailout of insolvent *chaebŏl* firms. In other words, the *chaebŏl* firms accrued high debt to expand their businesses from the state-controlled (earlier, state-owned) domestic banks, and the developmental state provided bailout funds if a *chaebŏl*-affiliate firm showed signs of insolvency. The *chaebŏl* and the developmental state were co-conspirators in the myth of "too big to fail." Hence, it was critical to lower the debt-to-equity ratio of the *chaebŏl* in order to improve their financial structure, and to also prohibit the developmental state from bailing out *chaebŏl* firms. The *chaebŏl* were required to lower their debt-to-equity ratio to or below 2 by March 2000, from a high of 4–5 during the 1980s and 1990s.

The fourth goal was to introduce better corporate governance to meet global standards. Despite the fact that the chairman and his family's share was only a small fraction of the total shares, protection of shareholder interest through corporate governance had been virtually absent, i.e., the *chaebŏl* chairman and his family were able to wield unchecked power in managerial decisions irrespective of their actual shares in company stocks. This was due to the ownership structure of the *chaebŏl*, which we discussed earlier with the three *chaebŏl* cases. Thus, the minimum share threshold for small shareholders' collective action was to be lowered significantly in order to provide small shareholders their due right to challenge the *chaebŏl* owner's control of the *chaebŏl* so as to exceed his/her ownership share. The last goal was streamlining business activities. One of the major criticisms about *chaebŏl* was that they pursued aggressive diversification in unrelated businesses, which resulted in crowding out small- and medium-size enterprises (SMEs), and excessive competition and over-investment among *chaebŏl* in many markets. Thus, the *chaebŏl* were required to declare their core businesses and abandon non-core firms either through selling or by means of the "Big Deals."[36]

36 The Big Deals were a government-mediated (or government-pressured) program to swap businesses among the *chaebŏl*.

In terms of observation of the five goals, those measures were successfully institutionalized. First, transparency in management has been enhanced through the consolidated statements, the opening of the M&A market, alleviation of restrictions on voting rights of institutional investors, stronger company monitoring through the financial market, and greater transparency in the decision-making process in the board of directors through a mandatory appointment of outside directors. In addition, the cross-debts had been eliminated altogether as of March 2000 and the issuance of new cross-debts has been prohibited by law.[37] The role of the chief executive officer (CEO) also has been legalized. Third, the financial structure has improved. The *chaebŏl*'s high debt-to-capital ratio was a grave concern before and after the AFC. The average ratio of the top 30 *chaebŏl* peaked at 4.68 in 1997 when the AFC occurred, but the ratio dramatically plummeted to 1.67 in 2000.[38] As of 2006, the ratio still remained around 1.87. Intriguing were the outsider directors of larger firms which belonged to the *chaebŏl*. In order to attain the fourth goal, better corporate governance, the designation of outside directors became mandatory for all listed companies, and the board of directors held the ultimate decision-making power. Last, the Big Deals, which were aggressively promoted by the Kim Dae-jung government, dictated business swaps across *chaebŏl*. These restructuring measures have contributed to recuperating the South Korean economy and the *chaebŏl*. Figure 3.2 illustrates how well the four largest *chaebŏl* have been expanding their group size since the AFC, even though Hyundai Group was divided into five groups through a series of group divisions in the 2000s and LG Group was also partitioned into three groups in 2003 and 2006.

Of the top four *chaebŏl* which boosted their total assets between 1997 and 2006, the most prominent is Samsung Group. Samsung Group nearly doubled its total assets from 63 trillion to 113 trillion won during the period. In spite of a series of divisions since 1999, the members of Hyundai Group are still robust.[39] In particular, Hyundai Motors Group, which inherited Hyundai Group's motor parts division in 2001, became the second largest *chaebŏl* in 2006 by increasing its assets from 36 trillion to 64 trillion won.[40] While undergoing two group divisions, in 2003 and in 2006, respectively, LG Group raised its assets from 51 trillion to 54 trillion won. The sum of the three LG Group

37 Yu Sŏng-min, *Chaebŏl wigi ŭi chubŏm in'ga* [Are *chaebŏl* the culprit of the crisis] (Seoul: Pibong ch'ulp'ansa, 2000).

38 We only calculated the ratio of *chaebŏl* that survived. If the collapsed *chaebŏl* were included, the ratio in 1997 should have been much higher than 4.68.

39 For the rest of Hyundai Group, refer to Table 3.1.

40 Hyundai Motors Group started to report its assets from 2001.

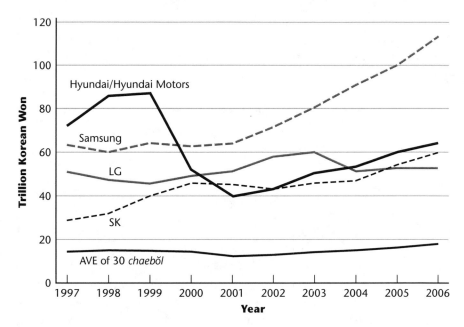

FIGURE 3.2 Group total asset changes from 1997 to 2006
Note: Each line does not consider recent group divisions.
Source: 2001 Hyundai Motors Group.

families—LG, GS, and LS—became even larger: 81 trillion won.[41] SK Group was not an exception from the rally as it drastically increased its assets from 29 trillion to 60 trillion won. However, the benefits were not even. Even within *chaebŏl*, the disparity between larger *chaebŏl* and the rest has become wider since 2000.

In spite of these reforms and the consequent changes, however, the corporate governance of the largest *chaebŏl* appeared to be intact. The corporate restructuring measures, which were largely designed to deal with the economic causes of the crisis, appeared to have missed the target. Corporate governance in the context of business groups, as illustrated in the three cases discussed earlier, can take on a form very different from that of a single firm. A Korean *chaebŏl* consists of a network of firms, which are legally independent from one another but share a common identity such as a firm name (e.g., Samsung). And without exception, a *chaebŏl* network is made up of complicated yet hierarchically organized equity ties. We have previously explained at length the differences between a single firm and *chaebŏl*, but let

41 LG Group was divided into three: LG, GS, and LS; 81 trillion won is the aggregation of the three groups' assets.

us reiterate it for the upcoming analysis. The biggest difference between a single firm and *chaebŏl* comes from the fact that there is virtually no typical principal-agent problem between the largest shareholder and the manager because they are often the same person or members of the same family. If KCC Group had been run and dominated by professional managers who were disinterested in familial concerns, the proxy fight with Hyundai Group in 2003 between the two groups would not have happened. Moreover, the owner-manager of one subsidiary is often the same person, or a family member of the owner-manager of another subsidiary, forming an alliance of owner-managers. As observed in the case of the Samsung inheritance above, since the subsidiaries are legally independent of one another, the practices by Samsung Everland executives to designate chairman Yi's offspring as a beneficiary of the company's CBs was not illegal.

This kind of problem is most serious for business groups characterized by hierarchical equity ties such as South Korean *chaebŏl*, because the owner-manager at the top of the hierarchy can mobilize and transfer resources in the subsidiaries to do almost anything at his or her command.[42]

Figures 3.3 and 3.4 show the inter-firm network of Samsung Group, reflecting the firms' assets with circle sizes. Made up of 62 subsidiary firms, Figure 3.3 provides a nearly illegible map of the Samsung inter-firm network. But it depicts a cluster at the center, marginalizing relatively small subsidiary firms. Figure 3.4, a simplified map of the Samsung inter-firm network with its 19 larger subsidiary firms, zooms in on the cluster and shows how the network at the core is actually formed.[43] In the figure, the equity investments from the owner-family go to several larger member firms such as Samsung Electronics, Samsung Corporation, Samsung Life Insurance, and Samsung Everland. In turn, these core subsidiaries invest in other member firms to fortify both the membership across firms and the owner family's

---

42 For a detailed discussion of the existence of a hierarchical equity network, see Chang, "Privately Owned Social Structures."; Dukjin Chang, "Financial Crisis and Network Response: Changes in the Ownership Structure of *Chaebol* Business Groups Since the Asian Crisis," paper presented at the Georgetown Conference on Korean Society, December 1999. Blockmodel analyses of the equity holding networks of Korea's top *chaebŏl* as of 1989 revealed that they can be summarized into an isomorphic structure termed "nested hierarchy," where the chairman's family amplifies the control by means of multiple indirect ties. See Granovetter, "Business Groups and Social Organization" for more theoretical discussion and comparison with business groups in other countries.

43 The Yi family directly invests in thirtteen subsidiary firms out of sixty-two. We sort out only nineteen in order to provide a clearer figure, and as a result, only six subsidiaries appear to have a link with the Yi family.

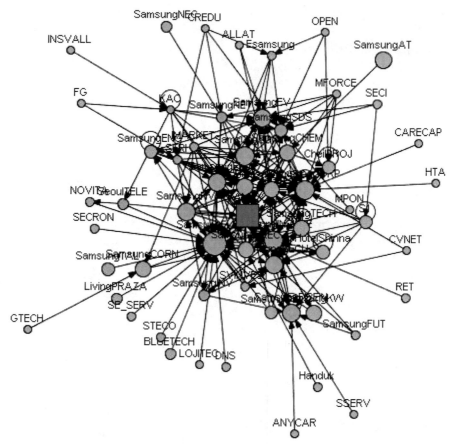

FIGURE 3.3 Inter-firm network of the Samsung Group as of 2003

Source: Rendered by the authors based on data from the Financial
Supervisory Service of Korea (http://dart.fss.or.kr/).

entrepreneurship with the aid of the subsidiary firms. For example, Samsung
Electronics, the largest company in the group and in the country, has 30 equity links with other subsidiary firms. Samsung Life Insurance also holds 16
links, Samsung Everland holds 12 links, and Samsung Corporation holds 17
links with other subsidiaries. In addition, these web-like investment links
are organized hierarchically so that the founder family can govern the whole
business group with relatively smaller equity stakes.[44]

Table 3.1 shows the total amount of equity that the founder family of each
chaebŏl held as of 2006. Although the amount of equity holding by founder

44 Chang, "Privately Owned Social Structures"; Chang, "Financial Crisis and Network Response."

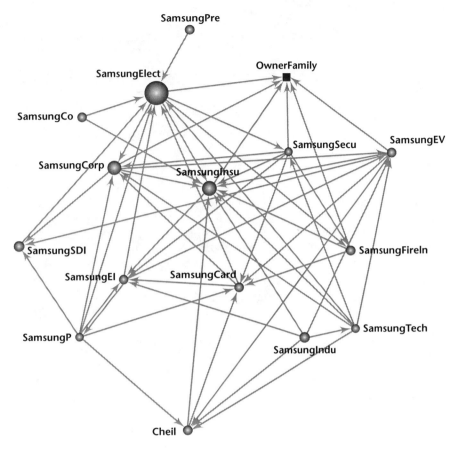

FIGURE 3.4 Simplified map of Samsung inter-firm network
Source: DART (Data Analysis, Retrieval and Transfer System) of the Korean Financial Supervisory Service (http://dart.fss.or.kr/), and Korea Information Service, Inc. (www.kisline.com/).

families varies from *chaebŏl* to *chaebŏl*, most of the 30 largest Korean *chaebŏl* founder families, in particular, the largest 4 (Samsung, Hyundai Motors, SK, and LG), show their relatively smaller equity portion of the totals. This result accounts for why Hyundai Group and SK Group suffered from M&A threats by outsiders. The founder family of SK Group owns only 2.41 percent of the total equity of the whole business group. As for Hyundai Group, its founder family owns 4.11 percent of the total, slightly more than the SK founder family. This means that theoretically anyone who holds more than 2.41 percent of the total equity in SK Group and more than 4.11 percent of Hyundai Group could take over the whole business network. Moreover, this is not particular to SK Group and Hyundai Group, but is observed in several other *chaebŏl*

TABLE 3.1

Founder Family Equity Holding Percentages of the 30 Largest Chaebŏl *as of 2006*

Rank	Group	Equity Holding (percent)	Rank	Group	Equity Holding (percent)
1	Samsung	3.06	16	Daelim	14.54
2	Hyundai Motors	5.75	17	Hyundai	4.11
3	SK	2.41	18	Dongkuk Steel	19.84
4	LG	6.68	19	Hyundai Department Store	16.74
5	Lotte	13.46	20	KCC	41.21
6	GS	17.16	21	Koron	7.97
7	Kumho	9.87	22	Hyosung	27.80
8	Hanjin	9.66	23	Hyundai Development	12.99
9	Hyundai Heavy Industries	7.36	24	Dongyang	2.38
10	Doosan	2.77	25	Taekwang	34.16
11	Hanhwa	4.33	26	Dongyang Chemical	30.55
12	Shinsegae	25.40	27	Hansol	5.9
13	LS	21.42	28	Orion	10.93
14	CJ	11.03	29	Hankuk Steel	28.84
15	Dongbu	17.97	30	Daesang	27.84

Source: The authors' calculation based on DART (Data Analysis, Retrieval and Transfer System) of the Korean Financial Supervisory Service (http://dart.fss.or.kr/).

Notes: In order to figure out how much a founder family owns within a *chaebŏl*, we multiplied its shares by the equity capital that each member firm in the *chaebŏl* reports annually. Assets of financial subsidiaries in *chaebŏl* were excluded in ordering the ranks.

such as Doosan Group (2.77 percent), Dongyang Group (2.38 percent), and even Samsung Group (3.06 percent).

Then, how is the equity holding related to *chaebŏl* expansion? Instead of using the equity holding percentages suggested in the table above, we employ Bonacichi's status centrality in calculating the founder families' centrality in their *chaebŏl* firm network.[45] Because cross-holding and circular investments are commonly observed in *chaebŏl* inter-firm networks, the Bonacich index is suitable for measuring centralities in a given network.[46] By putting founder fam-

45 Phillip Bonacich, "Power and Centrality: A Family of Measures," *American Journal of Sociology* 92, no. 5 (1987): 1170–82; Phillip Bonacich and Paulette Lloyd, "Eigenvector-like Measures of Centrality for Asymmetric Relations," *Social Networks* 23, no. 3 (2001): 191–201.

46 It should be noted that measuring an agent's status in a network usually calls for at least two considerations. One consideration involves his/her status with reference to others in the network. The assumption of equality of every player in a clique is mostly invalid in real situations, since status and popularity vary from person to person. That is to say, status in a cluster is not due only to how many choose, but also who chooses whom.

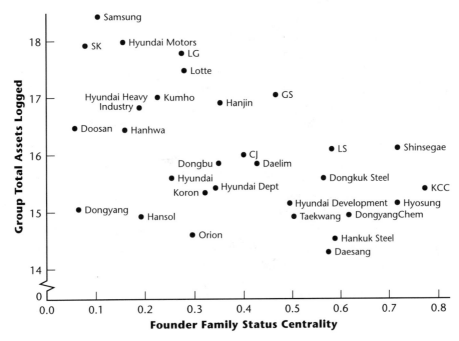

FIGURE 3.5 Scatter plot of group size as of 2006 based on founder family centrality

Source: DART (Data Analysis, Retrieval and Transfer System) of the Korean Financial Supervisory Service (http://dart. fss.or.kr), and Korea Information Service, Inc. (www.kisline.com).

ily centrality over the sum of all centralities in a network, we standardized them and made them comparable to one another. Based on how much an owner family holds out of the total shares of a whole business group,[47] this index approaches 1 as an owner family holds all, whereas 0 when an owner family holds nothing. Thus, the more shares an owner family possesses and therefore the more powerful it is in a business group, the index becomes closer to 1.[48]

Paired with their group size, represented as logged group total assets, the index displays a negative correlation (−.50) in Figure 3.5. This negative

---

See Bonacich, "Power and Centrality," 1170–82; Leo Katz, "A New Status Index Derived from Sociometric Analysis," *Psychometrica* 18, no. 1 (1953):39-43. The other consideration relates to the distance of transmitting a command, supposing a person maintains a number of direct and indirect relationships. See Stanley Wasserman and Katherine Faust, *Social Network Analysis: Methods and Applications* (Cambridge: Cambridge University Press, 1994).

47 Katz, "A New Status Index Derived from Sociometric Analysis," 39–43; Wasserman and Faust, *Social Network Analysis*.

48 To standardize each centrality of each *chaebŏl*, we divided the centrality of owner families by the aggregate of every centrality all member firms possibly have.

correlation between the two variables indicates that the founder family of larger *chaebŏl* tends to have less equity. In fact, the founder's share becomes diluted as outside capital flows in. Market liberalization since the 1990s has facilitated capital inflows from foreign investors and enabled *chaebŏl* to expand their business faster, while lowering the equity proportion the founder family holds. In addition, privatization of public corporations and acquisition of other *chaebŏl*'s firms throughout the Big Deal during the restructuring period have rapidly dwindled family equity proportions. It was not such a concern when the Korean state was a Big Brother that dictated everything but at the same time protected everything. As Big Brother dwarfed, however, that became a big concern for the *chaebŏl*. In relation to group growth, this tendency presents a dilemma for the *chaebŏl*: whether to change their governance structure to be competitive or to retain what they have done thus far. The former guarantees higher growth and profits than other competitors, but asks the family to step down from its current position. The latter warrants its positions, but demands the family have slower growth and lower profits.

Conclusion

The Asian financial crisis and its ensuing measures had a huge impact on both the state and corporate sectors of South Korea. However, the effects on the two realms differed. On the one hand, the AFC led the South Korean government to accelerate its transition from a developmental state, a process that had already begun in the 1980s. Coupled with political democratization in the country, departure from being an authoritarian developmental state and heading toward liberalization was unavoidable. As a result of the transition, barriers to the South Korean domestic market were dismantled. On the other hand, for corporate sectors, in particular the *chaebŏl*, the AFC was Janus-like. The restructuring measures relieved a series of regulations over them, but at the same time, they lost overarching regulations that implicitly or explicitly shielded them.

We have argued throughout this chapter that the AFC and its restructuring programs served as a momentum which made the state change its old manner but let the *chaebŏl* still keep things the old way. We have contended that an institutional void has been created by the ebb of the state. We believe that the three instances of ownership contests among *chaebŏl* from the early 2000s are due to this institutional void. Although the two democratic regimes since the AFC pushed South Korean society as a whole to be more democratic than ever before, they have not drawn any specific state model which properly regulates corporate sectors. In the midst of the void, by contrast, the governance structure of South Korean *chaebŏl* surged. The *chaebŏl* have obediently or even actively followed the recommended measures by the IMF and the South Korean state and therefore have renovated many of their old-fashioned practices. At the same time, however, they have succeeded in preserving the core of their governance structure. Our analysis of their equity holding and ownership structure has proved that a hierarchically organized inter-firm network is still prevalent in the *chaebŏl* governance structure, though the amounts of equity holdings vary from *chaebŏl* to *chaebŏl*.

The globalized, liberal, and expanded market environments for South Korean *chaebŏl* raise a bifurcated challenge. For the small- and medium-sized *chaebŏl*, in which many founder families hold relatively stable amounts of equities, they have to choose whether to pursue faster or more gradual growth. If they choose to rapidly enlarge their enterprises, their equities will quickly be diluted. However, as far as they pursue gradual growth of their business, their enterprises will not easily fall or be broken by external threats. For larger *chaebŏl*, what matters is how to protect their business group from outside threats such as M&As because their old ownership structure was revealed to be vulnerable, as the state ebbed away from developmentalism.

Thus, as for the institutional complementarities, the South Korean *chaebŏl* situation offers three lessons. First, the legacy from the past growth era trajectory is much stronger than had been assumed. The older *chaebŏl* ownership structure constitutes the core of their governance structure. Since those sitting at the top of the hierarchical ownership structure have little incentive to give up, they tend to mobilize every means to resist change. Second, there is no guarantee that globalization or increasing interconnectedness across borders will lead the less-developed countries to converge their business practices with those of the more advanced countries. In spite of a number of reforms, the core of the *chaebŏl* governance structure is still intact. Third, the departure of the state does not warrant an order in the corporate sector, but it leaves a void of institutions and regulations. The inactive, or in a sense reluctant, interventions of the South Korean state in the corporate sector resulted in abrupt stock price fluctuations and granted privileged favors to a few *chaebŏl*.

The lessons suggest that the South Korean *chaebŏl* are not a pure economic phenomenon, but rather a socio-politically constructed structure. Thus, any approach that does not take into account the dynamics between the state and the corporate sector will fail to understand the complexities. The experiences South Korea has undergone in the last ten years show that the relation between the state and the corporate sector is pivotal for economic coordination, while the pattern of the relationship can change as time passes. In addition, the lessons imply that what fundamentally matters for institutional restructuring is to reform the relation between the state and the corporate sector, not to reform either or both of them. The co-existence of continuity and discontinuity observed in both sectors of South Korea exemplifies that importing foreign institutions does not guarantee planned changes, but rather creates an institutional void.

Section II

Forces of Change in Corporate Restructuring

4 Presidential Powers, Political Parties, and Corporate Restructuring in South Korea

Jung Kim[1]

If a group of political scientists tried to identify the most unpredictable configuration of party politics on the global stage during the 1990s, they would be hard pressed to point out a configuration other than that of South Korea. Between 1988 and 2000, the average lifespan of political parties in Korea was 31.5 months or little more than two and a half years. While thirteen parties with different names existed during the period, none sent candidates into the presidential or legislative elections more than once.[2] To the extent that parties greatly varied from election to election, they were unable to provide predictable policy choices to the electorates. As a result, voters suffered from ill-defined and fluctuating policy preferences since they had little opportunity to establish a stable party identification based on policy platforms.

Few would question that such an unstable party system would impose great difficulties on presidents in implementing reform policies. Likewise, it seems unlikely that political parties without a tradition of programmatic competition would play a constructive role in processes of economic renewal. In scholarship on party politics and political economy, unstructured

1 The author gratefully acknowledges insightful comments from Byung-Kook Kim, Eun Mee Kim, Jean Oi, and Frances Rosenbluth. He is also indebted to Jai Kwan Jung, Sun Lee, Dean Ouellette, Jiyeoun Song, and participants at the "System Restructuring in East Asia" conference at Stanford University in June 2006 for their cogent remarks on an earlier version of this chapter. Financial support from the MacMillan Center for International and Area Studies at Yale, the Council on East Asian Studies at Yale, and the Institute for Far Eastern Studies at Kyungnam University in Seoul made this research possible.

2 Aurel Croissant, "Electoral Politics in South Korea," in *Electoral Politics in Southeast and East Asia*, ed. Croissant, Gabriele Bruns, and Marei John (Singapore: Friedrich Ebert Stiftung, 2002), 233–75.

TABLE 4.1

Outcomes of Corporate Restructuring in Eight Countries

Share of Nonperforming Loans of the Corporate Sector

	Indonesia	Korea	Malaysia	Thailand	Czech R.	Turkey	Mexico	Brazil
1998 (1999)	48.6	(19.7)	15.0	(40.5)	20.7	6.7	11.3	5.3
2002 (2001)	42.0	(9.9)	9.6	(22.3)	9.6	17.0	4.8	6.1
Change	−6.6	−9.8	−5.4	−18.2	−11.1	+10.3	−6.5	+0.8
Ranking	4	3	6	1	2	8	5	7

Corporate Leverage (ratio of debt to assets)

	Indonesia	Korea	Malaysia	Thailand	Czech R.	Turkey	Mexico	Brazil
1998	0.74	0.70	0.67	0.56	0.27	0.32	0.34	0.43
2002	0.57	0.40	0.67	0.66	0.14	0.48	0.30	0.59
Change	−0.17	−0.30	0	+0.10	−0.13	+0.16	−0.04	+0.16
Ranking	2	1	5	6	3	7	4	7

Profitability of Corporations (dollar return on assets)

	Indonesia	Korea	Malaysia	Thailand	Czech R.	Turkety	Mexico	Brazil
1998	−10.4	−8.3	−8.3	1.7	−1.0	9.9	1.7	−0.4
2002	9.7	5.9	−7.1	6.6	3.0	2.9	1.0	−7.6
Change	+20.1	+14.2	+1.2	+4.9	+4.0	−7.0	−0.7	−7.2
Ranking	1	2	5	3	4	7	6	8

Note: Author's calculation based on data from the source.

Source: Stijn Claessens, "Policy Approaches to Corporate Restructuring around the World: What Worked, What Failed?" in *Corporate Restructuring: Lessons from Experience*, ed. Michael Pomerleano and William Shaw (Washington DC: World Bank, 2005), 42, 44, and 48.

party systems and programmatically weak parties are usually considered to be a redoubtable hindrance to economic reform.[3]

However, the outcomes of the corporate restructuring of Korea in the post-1997 economic crisis turned conventional wisdom upside down. A recent study of the World Bank reports that Korea's restructuring performance generally outstripped those of other crisis-affected economies of the late 1990s–Indonesia, Malaysia, Thailand, the Czech Republic, Turkey,

---

3 Anna Grzymała-Busse, *Rebuilding Leviathan: Party Competition and State Exploitation in Post-Communist Democracies* (New York: Cambridge University Press, 2007); Andres Rius and Nicolas van de Walle, "Political Institutions and Economic Policy Reform," in *Understanding Market Reforms*, vol. 1, *Philosophy, Politics, and Stakeholders*, ed. José Maria Fanelli and Gary McMahon (New York: Palgrave Macmillan, 2005), 176–202; Susan C. Stokes, "What Do Policy Switches Tell Us About Democracy?" in *Democracy, Accountability, and Representation*, ed. Adam Przeworski, Stokes, and Bernard Manin (New York: Cambridge University Press, 1999), 98–130; and Stephan Haggard and Robert R. Kaufman, *The Political Economy of Democratic Transitions* (Princeton, NJ: Princeton University Press, 1995).

Mexico, and Brazil–in its scope and speed. Tellingly, as shown in Table 4.1, the improvement of the quality and intensity of restructuring in the country stand out: the share of nonperforming loans of the corporate sector sharply decreased to 9.9 percent in 2001 from 19.7 percent in 1999 (the third-best performance among the eight countries); corporate leverage significantly declined to 0.4 in 2002 from 0.7 in 1998 (the best performance); and the profitability of corporations remarkably increased to 5.9 in 2002 from −8.3 in 1998 (the second-best performance). Of the eight economies, only three–Indonesia, Korea, and the Czech Republic–consistently showed positive progress in every dimension of corporate restructuring. Korea was the front-runner for overall restructuring outputs.

Here exists a puzzling incongruity between theoretical expectations and empirical evidence. Why has corporate restructuring in Korea, which suffered from one of the most chaotic, unstructured, and volatile patterns of party politics around the world, proceeded faster, deeper, and wider than that in other crisis-affected countries? Why has party competition, which largely deviated from programmatic concerns, not undermined the effectiveness of reform programs? And why have political parties that maintained only tenuous linkages between society and the state not imperiled the implementation of a reform agenda?

This chapter suggests that the answer to the questions lies at the essential feature of party politics in Korea: *underinstitutionalization of political parties*. An institutionalized party corresponds to what is usually referred to as a programmatic party that has a long-term relationship with a certain group in the electorate characterized by a common set of interests.[4] Forming programmatic linkages with a party, the interest group influences the policy platform and the selection of leaders in exchange for contributions and other resources that are critical for the production of public policies. Thus the degree of institutionalization of a party is directly related to the degree to which the interest group can control the leader, or inversely related to the degree of the leader's discretion over policy. In other words, the degree of party institutionalization is a function of the relative power of the leader and interest group.[5]

It is evident that the traits of Korean political parties are the exact opposite of the notion of an institutionalized party. They are defined by the relationship with regionalist leaders whose discretion over party activities

4 Herbert Kitschelt and Steven I. Wilkinson, "Citizen-Politician Linkages: An Introduction," in *Patrons, Clients, and Policies: Patterns of Democratic Accountability and Political Competition*, ed. Kitschelt and Wilkinson (New York: Cambridge University Press, 2007), 1–49.

5 Torben Iversen, *Capitalism, Democracy, and Welfare* (New York: Cambridge University Press, 2005), 122–79.

is extremely large. To the extent that they are loyal agents of their leaders rather than interest-based constituencies, it is not surprising that parties could not carry out expected functions such as societal representation, interest aggregation, and political integration.[6]

At the same time, however, the *institutional weakness* also made it difficult for parties to organize a coherent and credible opposition to reforms. Lacking a tenable connection with distinct interest-based constituencies, they were unable to express and channel the voice of antireform interest groups onto the political decision-making process. As a result, they allowed the chief executive to undertake drastic corporate restructuring measures, insulating her or him from social pressures. If they were deeply rooted in societal interests, both opposition and ruling parties could have acted as a most formidable stumbling block for the president in the corporate restructuring process by mobilizing constituencies who were penalized by the reform. Presumably such a sweeping corporate reform would have been hard to envision with well-institutionalized political parties.[7] In other words, only the parties that were weakly institutionalized actually facilitated president-initiated corporate reform in Korea.

This counterintuitive argument does not mean that underinstitutionalized parties are always good for economic reform. Their responses to economic reform vary depending on the strength of *presidential powers*.[8] In this chapter, I argue that only a president who secures *both* a majority support in the legislature *and* maintains a high public popularity is capable of executing sweeping economic reform policies. If the president lacks either numerical power in the legislature or leadership power over the public, he will have a hard time dealing with political parties in carrying out economic reform. In the second section, I elaborate on the argument with regard to the relationships between underinstitutionalized parties and presidential powers, focusing on economic reform legislation. The third section substantiates the insights derived from the second section and examines three different cases of economic reform legislation in Korea since 1987. The final section gives conclusions.

---

6 David C. Kang, "The Institutional Foundations of Korean Politics," in *Understanding Korean Politics: An Introduction*, ed. Soong Hoom Kil and Chung-in Moon (Albany: State University of New York Press, 2001), 71–105.

7 Conor O'Dwyer and Branislav Kovalčík, "And the Last Shall be First: Party System Institutionalization and Second-Generation Economic Reform in Postcommunist Europe," *Studies in Comparative International Development* 41, no. 4 (2007): 3–26.

8 Javier Corrales, "Presidents, Ruling Parties, and Party Rules: A Theory on the Politics of Economic Reform in Latin America," *Comparative Politics* 32, no. 2 (2000): 127–49.

Presidential Powers and Economic Reform Legislation

Even though a president usually plays the leading role in formulating an economic reform agenda in presidential democracies, he or she still must have legal authorization of the legislature to make public policies. To the extent that extensive institutional renewal and corporate restructuring require corresponding legislative change, the legislature becomes a gatekeeper for president-initiated economic reform policies. Because most decisions are made by majority rule in the legislature, the enactment of economic reform policies necessitates collective action among a large number of legislators.[9]

Determinants of Presidential Powers

As in most democratic legislatures, the National Assembly of Korea is organized along party lines, which implies that political parties are the near-universal means of coordinating any action. Hence, the support of political parties that control a majority of the National Assembly is the sine qua non of economic reform legislation.[10] This is especially true for Korean presidential democracy where the president does not have strong constitutional legislative powers to circumvent the legislature.[11] Unlike his Latin American counterparts, the Korean president is not permitted to issue legislative decrees that enable the executive to implement important economic reform policies without the formal consent of the legislature. The lack of decree authority forces him to depend exclusively on his partisan power in the legislature to enact economic reform policies. The partisan power of a president is largely contingent

9 Gary W. Cox, "The Organization of Democratic Legislatures," in *The Oxford Handbook of Political Economy*, ed. Barry R. Weingast and Donald A. Wittman (New York: Oxford University Press, 2006), 141–61.

10 As I defined the term earlier in this chapter, "institutional weakness of parties" indicates the low degree of programmatic connections between party leaders and interest groups. Due to the dominance of regionalist party leaders over party members in the assembly, "strong party discipline" in the legislative arena coexists with "weak party institutionalization" in the electoral arena. See John Carey and Andrew Reynolds, "Parties and Accountable Government in New Democracies," *Party Politics* 13, no. 2 (2007): 255–74.

11 I use the term presidential power as the ability to enact legislative agenda. There are usually two aspects of presidential legislative power; one is *constitutional* and another *partisan*. The constitutional legislative power of the Korean president is *exogenous* to the party composition of the assembly and relatively weaker in comparative perspective so I mainly focus on the partisan legislative power that is *endogenous* to the legislative party composition. See David J. Samuels and Matthew Søberg Shugart, "Presidentialism, Elections and Representation," *Journal of Theoretical Politics* 15, no. 1 (2003): 33–60.

upon: 1) the number of seats that the presidential party controls in the legislature—the numerical power, and 2) the degree of loyalty that the presidential party members devote to presidential leadership—the leadership power.[12]

Several institutional features of the Korean democratic polity make it less likely that the president will be equipped with a stable legislative majority. First, presidential elections in Korea after the democratic transition of 1987 are held every five years, while elections for the National Assembly since 1988 are held every four years. In such a nonconcurrent electoral format, legislative elections function like midterm elections in which the fortunes of the president's party tend to fade. Second, a single-member district plurality (SMDP) voting system is applied to elect legislative members. Since a SMDP works mostly in favor of the largest party at the district level, it tends to intensify the regional fragmentation of legislative seats, unsettling the legislative ground of the president. In fact, no presidential party has won a majority of seats in the legislative elections except Roh Moo-hyun's (No Mu-hyŏn's, 2003–08) Uri Party in 2004.[13]

However, the initial seat distributions that conferred a majority status to opposition parties in the National Assembly had repeatedly been reversed by presidents in favor of the ruling parties. President Roh Tae-woo (No T'ae-u, 1988–93) overturned the opposition-dominated legislature originating from the 1988 election, striking a three-party merger with Kim Young-sam's (Kim Yŏng-sam, 1993–98) and Kim Jong-pil's (Kim Chong-p'il's) parties in 1990. Facing 1996 electoral results where opposition parties commanded a majority of seats in the legislature, President Kim Young-sam invalidated the popular verdict with predatory recruitment of opposition legislators immediately after the election, as Roh had done in 1992. President Kim Dae-jung (Kim Tae-jung, 1998–2003) tipped the balance of power in the legislature within six months of his inauguration by resorting to judiciary investigations of opposition politicians.[14]

To recap, institutional effects at the level of the electoral system that made it difficult for the president to win a legislative majority have been offset by institutional effects at the level of the party system that allowed the president to reverse popular verdicts. The recurring pattern of majority

12 Tun-jen Cheng, "Political Institutions and the Malaise of East Asian New Democracies," *Journal of East Asian Studies* 3, no.1 (2003): 1–41.

13 Uk Heo and Hans Stockton, "The Impact of Democratic Transition on Elections and Parties in South Korea," *Party Politics* 11, no. 6 (2005): 674–88.

14 Yong-Ho Kim, "Korea," in *Political Party Systems and Democratic Development in East and Southeast Asia*, vol. 2, *East Asia*, ed. Wolfgang Sachsenröder and Ulrike E. Frings (Aldershot, England: Ashgate, 1998), 132–78.

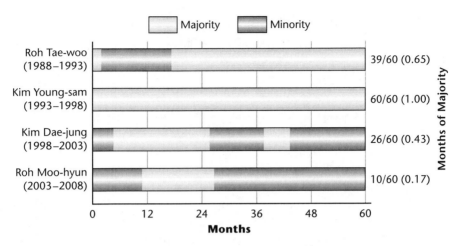

FIGURE 4.1 Status of presidential parties in the National Assembly
Note: Author's calculation based on data from the source.
Source: National Assembly of the Republic of Korea, Knowledge Management System, http://likms.assembly.go.kr/record/index.html.

shifts through massive defection from the opposition to the ruling coalition clearly bears out the underinstitutionalization of political parties in Korea.[15] Such frequent party fusion and fission are unthinkable in a system of institutionalized parties since the constituency will sanction and deselect transient politicians. The lack of strong connections with interest-based constituencies made political parties highly fluid institutions that increased uncertainty and disorder in legislative politics. However, at the same time, the very fluidity generated by weakly institutionalized party structures actually facilitated the consolidation of the president's partisan power in the legislature, permitting recurrent party-switching of opposition legislators.[16] The status of presidential parties in the assembly since 1987 is illustrated in Figure 4.1.

15 Due to the tenuous programmatic linkages between politicians and citizens, legislators primarily use parties to maximize individual pork and short-term electoral success in Korea. Thus their affiliation decisions are mainly affected by the electability of their leaders in approaching the presidential race and then their resource availability to fulfill their purposes during tenure. For discussions on party switching in Korea, see Kuniaki Nemoto, "Mixed Incentives for Legislative Behaviors: Party Label, Office Benefits, and Party Discipline in Korea," paper prepared for the annual meeting of the Midwest Political Science Association, April 2009.

16 Steven Levitsky and María Victoria Murillo, "Conclusion: Theorizing About Weak Institutions: Lessons from the Argentine Case," in *Argentine Democracy: The Politics of Institutional Weakness*, ed. Levitsky and Murillo (University Park: Pennsylvania State University Press, 2005), 269–89.

Presidential Numerical Power and Legislative Performance

To corroborate the association between the numerical power of the president in the legislature and the success of the executive-initiated economic reform legislation, I conducted content analysis of the summaries of 2,846 executive-initiated bills that were introduced in the National Assembly between 1988 and 2006 in order to sort out legislation that was intended to affect corporate reform in Korea. First, of 2,257 executive-initiated bills that passed in the assembly, I identified 61 corporate reform bills that were considered to directly impact corporate behavior. Second, I classified 94 financial reform bills and 32 labor market reform bills that were likely to influence corporate reform, assuming that there existed strong institutional interdependence among corporate, financial, and labor market reforms in Korea.[17] Combining the three subsets of bills, I identified them as 187 bills that were expected to impact corporate restructuring. For the sake of convenience, I will hereafter call them "economic reform bills," as they were expected to effect corporate reform.

Seemingly, variations in presidential performance to enact economic reform bills largely reflected their respective numerical power in the legislature. As shown in Table 4.2, the approval rates of the executive-initiated economic reform bills varied, ranging from the highest of 90 percent during the Kim Young-sam (Kim Yŏng-sam, 1993–98) government to the lowest of 53 percent during the Roh Moo-hyun government. It is not surprising that President Kim Young-sam, who enjoyed a stable majority in the legislature during his entire term, was the most successful in controlling an economic reform legislative agenda. President Roh Moo-hyun's poor legislative performance in passing economic reform bills is not difficult to understand once we see that he had majority control of the legislature for only ten months.[18] Considering that both Presidents Roh Tae-woo (1988–93) and Kim Dae-jung (1998–2003) experienced a minority situation in the National Assembly for a certain period during their presidencies,

17 On institutional complementarities among corporate, financial, and labor market reforms in Korea, see Chung H. Lee, "The Political Economy of Institutional Reform in Korea," *Journal of the Asia Pacific Economy* 10, no. 3 (2005): 257–77 and Byung-Kook Kim, "The Politics of *Chaebol* Reform, 1980–1997," in *Economic Crisis and Corporate Restructuring in Korea: Reforming the Chaebol*, ed. Stephan Haggard, Wonhyuk Lim, and Euysung Kim (New York: Cambridge University Press, 2003), 53–78.

18 It is an interesting question why party-switching ceased to be rampant under the Roh Moo-hyun presidency. While I suspect that it could be a symptom of gradual party institutionalization so that politician-citizen linkages have been—however slightly— strengthened, the substantiation requires systematic research.

TABLE 4.2

Approval Rates of Executive-Initiated Economic Reform Bills

	1988–1992		1993–1997		1998–2002		2003–2006	
	I	A	I	A	I	A	I	A
Corporate Reform	7	4 (.57)	21	19 (.90)	39	33 (.85)	12	5 (.42)
Financial Reform	11	11 (1.00)	34	30 (.88)	56	47 (.84)	9	6 (.67)
Labor Reform	2	1 (.50)	13	12 (.92)	15	10 (.67)	17	9 (.53)
Total	20	16 (.80)	68	61 (.90)	110	90 (.82)	38	20 (.53)
Legislation at Large	368	321 (.87)	879	807 (.92)	902	717 (.80)	695	412 (.59)

Notes: I: the number of introduced bills; A: the number of approved bills. Author's classification based on content analysis of each bill's summary (a complete list is available from the author).

Source: National Assembly of the Republic of Korea, Knowledge Management System, http://likms.assembly.go.kr/bill/jsp/StatFinishBill.jsp.

it is understandable that their legislative impact on economic reform—although still impressive—fell short of Kim Young-sam's.

Presidential Leadership Power and Legislative Performance

In order to understand the partisan power of the president in the legislature, however, analysis of the quantitative aspect must be complemented by that of the qualitative: the degree of loyalty that the presidential party members devote to presidential leadership. Outwardly, it seems less problematic for a president to secure the loyalty of the ruling party members. With the near-absolute control over candidate selection and party finance, the president can effectively discipline the legislative behavior of the ruling party members. The deep penetration of presidential influence into legislative action of the political parties' co-partisans in the legislature is another testimony to the parties' underinstitutionalization. The low degree of party institutionalization easily permits the president to concentrate and personalize partisan power in the legislature and consequently take strong initiatives in economic reform. At the same time, however, it also implies that the president does not have the effective coalition-building apparatus to align programmatically with interest-based constituencies. Lacking an institutionalized conduit to organize a sustainable pro-reform alliance with interest groups, presidential leadership on economic reform tends to rely heavily on the president's personal public appeal. Thus the intensity of the ruling party members' loyalty to the president is likely to mirror the trends in his popularity with the public.[19]

19 Guillermo O'Donnell, "Delegative Democracy," in *The Global Resurgence of Democracy,* 2nd ed., ed. Larry Diamond and Marc F. Plattner (Baltimore, MD: Johns Hopkins University Press, 1996), 94–108.

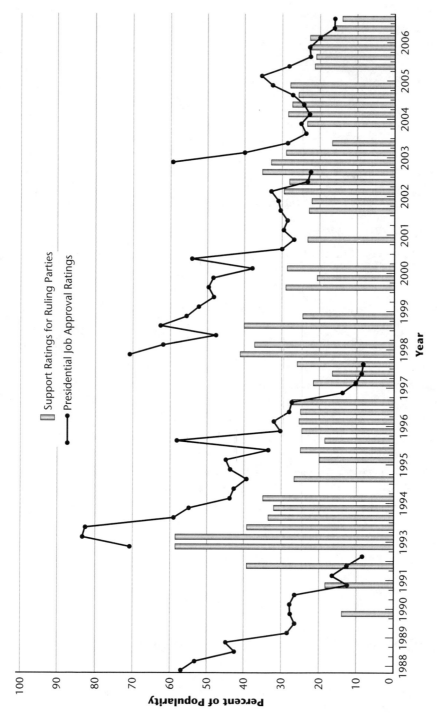

FIGURE 4.2 Presidential and ruling parties' popularity
Source: Gallup Korea Database, www.gallup.co.kr/gallupdb/gallupdb.asp.

It seems that one of the most significant institutional determinants of the presidential popularity is the proviso that "the term of office of the President is five years, and the President cannot be reelected" as stated in Article 70 of the Constitution.[20] The constitutional stipulation makes presidents temporarily popular but with wide swings in popularity during their five-year tenure. Figure 4.2 illustrates presidential job approval ratings in Korea—a proximal indicator of presidential popularity, revealing a general pattern: 1) presidents began their job with relatively high popularity that lasted for the first one or two years of their term, 2) their popularity declined with some fluctuation in the third and fourth years, and 3) their popularity plummeted to and remained at the bottom during the final year of their term. On the other hand, the rate of support for ruling parties generally followed the trends in presidential popularity, but there was an exception: it tended to increase during the fifth year of a presidential term. This temporal rise reflected the popularity of newly selected presidential candidates. To the extent that the fate of ruling parties depended on electoral success in the approaching presidential race, the loyalty of ruling party members shifted away from the incumbent president toward the prospective president. In other words, an incumbent president no longer became the principal of the ruling party members. The nonrenewable single-term presidency thus deprived the officeholders of their leadership power in the fifth year of their term. Once incumbent presidents became unpopular with the public and impotent in the legislature, they were nothing but political liabilities for the ruling party members. In fact, every president has withdrawn from his party in the fifth year of his term since 1987.[21]

It is possible to depict presidential leadership power in the legislature as a continuum in which an outgoing president's power lies at the lowest extreme whereas an incoming president's power lies at the highest extreme. The implication is that the likelihood of initiating economic reform legislation decreases with the lapse of presidential tenure. Thus even when a president controls the majority of the legislature, he will be unable to initiate economic reform policies as his term approaches the end. If a president ignores the decreasing function of leadership power and introduces a large number of economic reform bills in his fifth year of the term, then his initiatives are likely to fail. As shown in Figure 4.3, this happened in 1997.

20 The Constitution of Korea is available at http://confinder.richmond.edu/country.php.

21 Aurel Croissant, "Legislative Powers, Veto Players, and the Emergence of Delegative Democracy: A Comparison of Presidentialism in the Philippines and South Korea," *Democratization* 10, no. 3 (2003): 68–98.

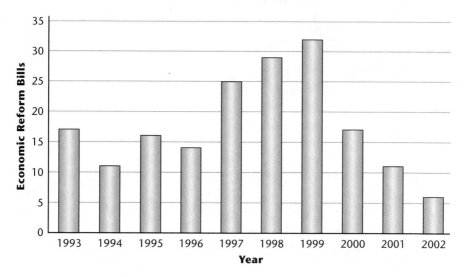

FIGURE 4.3 Number of executive-initiated economic reform bills by year
Source: See Table 4.3.

Although Kim Young-sam entered his final year of the term, he introduced the largest number of economic reform bills of his presidency. Predictably, thirteen financial reform bills introduced in August could not be enacted until December.[22] In contrast, the legislative strategy of Kim Dae-jung generally conformed to the declining function of presidential leadership power: he introduced the largest number of economic reform bills during his first two years of the term when he maintained reasonably high public popularity and then adjusted the number downward during his presidency.

To encapsulate the discussion of presidential powers in the legislature, four possible combinations of components form a two-by-two matrix, as shown as Table 4.3. At the top left is the configuration of a dominant president and a subservient ruling party. When a president enjoys high public popularity as well as majority support in the legislature, he has a ruling party that meekly acquiesces to most of his economic reform policies. President Kim Dae-jung in 1998–1999 succeeded in enacting a comprehensive corporate restructuring agenda under such a partisan condition. At the bottom

22 Kim Young-sam was overly ambitious in launching the Presidential Commission for Financial Reform during the winter of 1997 when he had already entered the last year of his term. It was extremely unfortunate to see the Asian financial crisis hit the region during the summer when the executive's financial reform package was completed, and he was too helpless to legislate the reform bills in the legislature during the fall once his party's presidential candidate had been selected.

TABLE 4.3

Variants of Presidential Powers and Party Strategies

		Leadership Power	
		High	Low
Numerical Power	Majority	Dominant president Subservient ruling party *President Kim Dae-jung (1998–1999)* Sweeping corporate reform	Ineffective president Opportunistic ruling party *President Kim Young-sam (1996–1997)* Partial corporate reform
	Minority	Indecisive president Opportunistic opposition party *President Roh Tae-woo (1988–1989)* Partial corporate reform	Impotent president Recalcitrant opposition party *President Roh Moo-hyun (2003–2004)* Meager corporate reform

Note: Author's classification.

right is the arrangement in which a president does not have a majority of the legislature and suffers from low public popularity. In this case, a recalcitrant opposition party that controls the legislature makes him an impotent president, rejecting his reform proposals or refusing to compromise. This partisan setting is very close to the early years of the Roh Moo-hyun presidency during 2003–2004 when little corporate reform was accomplished.[23] When an outgoing president who holds a majority of the legislature tries to enact economic reform legislation, the ruling party responds to him opportunistically. The ruling party will reluctantly shore up the president to the extent that the support does not harm the electoral prospects of the party. Otherwise, presidential action will be ineffective since the ruling party will withdraw legislative support for the president. It was the partisan configuration of corporate reform that President Kim Young-sam tried carrying out during the last years of his term in 1996–1997 that delayed legislation. In the opposite situation, when an incoming president does not have a majority of seats in the legislature, the opposition party's response to his reform policies is opportunistic as well. The opposition party will challenge the president to the extent that the confrontation does not backfire. Presidential action tends to be indecisive because the president must calculate the subtle responses of the opposition party in order to initiate economic reform in the legislature. The first two years of the Roh Tae-woo presidency in 1988–1989 were

23 Thus I do not examine the corporate reform episode during the Roh Moo-hyun presidency in this chapter.

characterized by such a partisan arrangement whereby he mostly preferred the status quo to any legislative change in terms of corporate reform. In the following section, I flesh out the arguments by analytically narrating three historical cases of economic reform legislation.

Three Case Studies on Economic Reform Legislation

The history of institutional reform in Korea since 1987 provides three distinctive episodes of economic reform legislation that are highly relevant for the purpose of this chapter.[24] The first encompasses attempts at economic reform legislation triggered by democratization between 1987 and 1989 when President Roh Tae-woo's ruling party did not command the legislature. During the period, the majority opposition parties took the legislative initiative, exploiting the demands of interest groups that were unleashed from authoritarian political control. Thus this case will explain the fate of economic reform legislation when the president lacks numerical power in the assembly at an early stage of tenure.[25]

The opposite situation is found during the economic reform legislation of 1996-1997 when President Kim Young-sam's ruling party controlled the legislature. Although he entered a later stage of his term at that time, the president took advantage of globalization to enhance national competitiveness and initiated corresponding legislative action to adjust the economic system to international standards. This case is therefore pertinent to understanding the relationship between economic reform legislation and a majority president who has lost his leadership power in the legislature.[26]

The third effort at economic reform legislation resulted from an economic crisis between 1998 and 1999 when, except for a brief period, President Kim Dae-jung's ruling coalition secured a majority of seats in the legislature. Due to the unprecedented magnitude of economic distress, the president was considered to have a mandate from the public to pursue

24 Larry Diamond and Doh Chull Shin, "Introduction: Institutional Reform and Democratic Consolidation in Korea," in *Institutional Reform and Democratic Consolidation in Korea*, ed. Diamond and Shin (Stanford, CA: Hoover Institution Press, 2000), 1–41.

25 Robert E. Bedeski, *The Transformation of South Korea: Reform and Reconstruction in the Sixth Republic under Roh Tae Woo, 1987–1992* (New York: Routledge, 1994), 78–93.

26 Stephan Haggard and David Kang, "The Kim Young Sam Presidency in Comparative Perspective," in *Democratization and Globalization in Korea: Assessments and Prospects*, ed. Chung-in Moon and Jongryn Mo (Seoul: Yonsei University Press, 1999), 111–31.

drastic reform during his first two years in office. This case will show us the outcomes of economic reform legislation when the president held both numerical and leadership power in the legislature.[27]

Democratization and Economic Reform Legislation, 1987–1989

On August 1, 1987, the entire staff of the Bank of Korea (BOK) issued a statement demanding the independence of the central bank from the government. On the same day, the Federation of Korean Industries (FKI) representing corporate interests also published an official opinion paper, arguing that the autonomy of the BOK must be enhanced to establish a prudent financial regulatory system and to reduce the uncertainty of corporate activities resulting from unjustifiable political pressure. Two weeks later, however, Minister of Finance Sagong Il explicitly opposed the idea, insisting that BOK monetary policies should operate within the general policy framework of the government, which has the final authority on economic policies. Since then, the revision of the BOK Act has become one of the most controversial issues between the BOK and the Ministry of Finance (MoF).[28]

Surfing on the wave of democratization, three opposition parties—Kim Dae-jung's Party for Peace and Democracy (PPD), Kim Young-sam's Unification Democratic Party (UDP), and Kim Jong-pil's New Democratic Republic Party (NDRP)–pledged during the 1988 legislative election to revise the BOK Act to guarantee independence from the government and made a joint reform bill after securing a majority of seats in the legislature.[29] Despite the anticipated reaction of President Roh Tae-woo and the MoF, opposition leaders seemed determined to introduce the bill in the legislature, expecting that the president could not oppose them against democratization pressure. On August 9, 1988, however, when members of the Monetary Policy Committee (MPC) opened to the public an opinion paper in favor of the MoF on the issue, their determination proved shaky. Responding to the

27 Yeonho Lee, "Participatory Democracy and Chaebol Regulation in Korea: State-Market Relations under the MDP Governments, 1997–2003," *Asian Survey* 45, no. 2 (2005): 279–301.

28 Chŏn Hong-t'aek, "Kŭmnyung kaehyŏk: Chungang ŭnhaeng mit kŭmnyung kamdok chedo kaep'yŏn sarye [Financial reform: The case of the central bank and the reorganization of financial supervisory institutions], in *Han'guk kyŏngje kaehyŏk sarye yŏn'gu* [Case studies on economic reform in Korea], ed. Mo Chong-nin, Chŏn Hong-t'aek, and Yi Su-hǔi (Seoul: Orǔm, 2002), 485–500.

29 The Bank of Korea Act, established in 1950, stipulated the primary purposes of the Bank of Korea to perform the typical functions of a central bank in consultation with the government.

MPC's view, the opposition parties hurriedly changed the substance of the joint bill to embrace the MoF's position. As this unprincipled policy swing invoked strong resistance from the staff and the union of the BOK, they swiftly withdrew the revised bill and changed their stance once again for the BOK. In the end, the PPD and UDP submitted their respective re-revised bill to the legislature on December while the NDRP ceased to commit to the issue. With the dissolution of unified efforts by opposition parties to revise the BOK Act, the impetus for financial reform also dwindled away.

While the bills introduced by the PPD and UDP drifted in the legislature for almost a year, the MoF drafted its own bill in consultation with the ruling Democratic Justice Party (DJP) and made a request for advice to the MPC in October 1989. Considering the predictable confrontation between BOK and the MoF, the MPC recommended that the revision of the BOK Act be reserved for a long-term policy matter. The DJP accepted the recommendation and decided not to submit the MoF bill. Following suit, the Finance Committee of the National Assembly decided to put aside the opposition party–initiated bills in December. Consequently, the two-and-one-half-year legislative battle to revise the BOK Act had changed nothing.[30]

Financial reform was concerned with the extent to which the central bank should decide its monetary and financial regulatory policies independently from the government. Thus it constituted one of the essential tasks in transforming a state-led developmental economic system into a liberal market economic system. In particular, the financial reform legislation was supposed to change the regulatory authority of the credit allocation system from the MoF to the to BOK, which could have facilitated corporate reform to enhance the transparency of corporate financial structures. It took another ten years to see such a salutary impact of financial reform on corporate restructuring, however. Since President Roh Tae-woo could not control a majority of the legislature, he let events take their own course until it became clear that he had to act. He either vetoed reform bills in the legislature by the majority opposition coalition or he did not actively implement his own reform policies. As a result, in his first two years of tenure, the president inadvertently avoided decisive actions on economic reform issues. Given institutional complementarities among corporate, financial, and labor market reforms, it is not surprising that little progress toward corporate restructuring was witnessed during this period.

30 Kang Man-su, *Hyŏnjang esŏ pon Han'guk kyŏngje 30-nyŏn* [Thirty years of the Korean economy from a first-hand view] (Seoul: Samsŏng kyŏngje yŏn'guso, 2005), 231–49.

Globalization and Economic Reform Legislation, 1996–1997

LABOR REFORM LEGISLATION: Fallaciously equating joining the Organisation for Economic Co-operation and Development (OECD) with becoming an advanced industrial nation, President Kim Young-sam orchestrated economic agencies to carry out extensive institutional reform to meet the OECD's requirement by November 1996.[31] As a target of institutional renewals, he announced the New Industrial Relations Plan in April 1996 and one month later launched the Presidential Commission on Industrial Relations Reform. In exchange for lifting the old legal framework that prohibited political participation of unions, intervention of third parties, and recognition of plural unions (three prohibitions against unions), the commission sought to establish a new legal structure that would authorize management's right to lay off workers in business emergencies, flexible allocation of working hours, and temporal redeployment of nonregular workers (three authorizations for employers). The attitudes of participants in the commission were too intransigent to work out a compromise, however. The Korean Confederation of Trade Unions (KCTU), established by dissident union activists in 1995, and the Federation of Korean Trade Unions (FKTU) were not anxious to make any concessions to employers in order to abolish the three prohibitions. Likewise, the FKI and the Korea Employers Federation (KEF) were barely conciliatory in bargaining with unions in order to introduce the three authorizations. Not surprisingly, the commission could not strike a consensus between stakeholders on vital issues and hence handed over the task to the inter-ministerial committee that would draft labor reform bills in November.[32]

On December 10, the president approved the committee's labor reform bills, including abolition of the three prohibitions and the introduction of the three authorizations except for the temporal redeployment of nonregular workers. When the government introduced the bills to the National Assembly on the next day, however, no stakeholders welcomed the reform policies. While the KCTU and FKTU insisted that the bills were in favor of employers, the FKI and KEF argued that they would only benefit the unions. Predictably, the opposition parties—Kim Dae-jung's National Congress

31 C. S. Eliot Kang, "*Segyehwa* Reform of the South Korean Developmental State," in *Korea's Globalization*, ed. Samuel S. Kim (New York: Cambridge University Press, 2000), 76–101.

32 Byung-Kook Kim and Hyun-Chin Lim, "Labor Against Itself: Structural Dilemmas of State Monism," in *Consolidating Democracy in South Korea*, ed. Larry Diamond and Byung-Kook (Boulder, CO: Lynne Rienner Publishers), 111–37.

for New Politics (NCNP) and Kim Jong-pil's United Liberal Democrats (ULD)—shirked their job to deliberate the bills, claiming that such a controversial matter should be discussed with sufficient time. They were not necessarily opposing the reform policy per se, but opportunistically trying not to engage in the subject in anticipation of an uncertain repercussion. Although within the ruling New Korea Party (NKP) several legislators also urged leaders to cautiously deal with the issue that the stakeholders had not yet reached an agreement, the NKP's Supreme Representative Yi Hong-gu and other frontbenchers entrusted by the president strictly disciplined the backbenchers and even amended the bills in favor of employers to postpone permitting plural unions at the national level for three years. They finally drove the ruling party members to pass the bills in the legislature at dawn on December 26 when no opposition party members appeared at the plenary session.

The ruling party's unilateral passage of the reform bills took only seven minutes and brought about unprecedented nationwide union strikes. The political turmoil lasted for a month, and the president decided to reconsider the passed bills and told the ruling party to recommence legislative bargaining on the labor reform bills with the opposition parties on January 21, 1997. Although the final outcomes of the three-party negotiations were actually to return to the original bills submitted by the government, it seemed undeniable that the president's leadership in reform policy implementation was severely damaged through the legislation process.[33] The labor reform legislation established a new institutional framework in regulating labor relations. It enabled employers to enhance the flexibility of employment practices and also gave unions the ability to increase the availability of legal protection in labor disputes, which might further promote corporate reform suitable for a functioning market economic system.

Financial Reform Legislation

In January 1997, President Kim commenced the Presidential Commission for Financial Reform to deal with the independence of the central bank and the reorganization of financial regulatory authorities. In particular, the consolidation of the existing four financial supervisory offices—the Office of Bank Supervision, the Securities Supervisory Board, the Insurance Supervisory Board, and the Nonbank Supervisory Authority—into a unified regulatory agency became one of the most contentious issues between

33 Young Cheol Kim, "Industrial Reform and Labor Backlash in South Korea: Genesis, Escalation, and Termination of the 1997 General Strike," *Asian Survey* 38, no. 12 (1998): 1142–60.

the Finance and Economy Board (FEB), established in 1994 as a result of the merger of the MoF and the Economic Planning Board, and the BOK. While the FEB preferred the establishment of a unified financial supervisory authority under its jurisdiction, the BOK opposed the idea because it took bank supervisory functions away from its control.[34]

The recommendation presented by the commission in June was generally considered to be a reasonable compromise between the FEB and the BOK. In exchange for the integration of separate financial regulatory functions into a unified authority, the commission sought to enhance the autonomy of the monetary policies of the central bank. However, this compromise proved ephemeral as the minister of the FEB, the governor of the BOK, the senior secretary to the president on Economic Policy, and the chairperson of the commission agreed to modify the commission's recommendation to leave the BOK's policy independence as it was.[35]

In August when the government submitted thirteen financial reform bills to the National Assembly, the unions representing the BOK and the four agencies targeted for elimination threatened to strike. In principle, the ruling NKP with the majority of the legislature could have passed the bills. However, the loyalty of NKP legislators had shifted away from President Kim toward the presidential candidate Yi Hoe-ch'ang (Lee Hoe-chang) when he captured the nomination in July. Since President Kim had already been critically discredited due to the mismanagement of the chain reaction bankruptcies of *chaebŏl* at that time, it was a rather a rational response of Yi and his aides in the NKP to differ from the unpopular incumbent president. Consequently, in order to avoid any adverse repercussion on the approaching presidential election, they quickly promised that they would not dispose of the reform bills without the consent of the opposition parties. For the same reason, however, the opposition parties had few incentives to cooperate. The NCNP and ULD did not want to associate with the controversial financial reform that might potentially damage their prospects in the presidential election. Although the Minister of the FEB Kang Kyŏng-sik strongly urged the leaders of political parties to expedite the legislation, they were extremely reluctant to process the bills and finally agreed to postpone the legislation until after the election in December.[36]

34 Kim Young-sam, *Kim Yŏng-sam taet'ongnyŏng hoegorok, ha-gwŏn* [Memoirs of President Kim Young-sam, vol. 2] (Seoul: Chosŏn ilbosa, 2001), 283–87.

35 Kang Kyŏng-sik, *Hwallan ilgi* [A diary of the financial crisis] (Seoul: Munyedang, 1999), 147–75.

36 Stephan Haggard and Jongryn Mo, "The Political Economy of the Korean Financial Crisis," *Review of International Political Economy* 7, no. 2 (2000): 210–15.

During the last year of the Kim Young-sam presidency, the central mode of party activity was a wait-and-see approach on economic reform legislation. To avoid taking any risky positions on economic reform issues, the party opportunistically reacted to the president-initiated reform policies. Once the loyalty of the majority ruling party to the president flagged, the fate of important economic reform legislation was doomed. Even when the president had a ruling party that controlled the majority of the legislature, he still could not carry out economic reform policies without leadership power.

Economic Crisis and Economic Reform Legislation, 1998–1999

In the middle of the economic crisis, Kim Dae-jung won against the ruling Grand National Party (the GNP was renamed from the NKP in November 1997) candidate Yi Hoe-ch'ang by a margin of 1.6 percent of the valid votes in the December 18 presidential election. The crisis and the subsequent bailout inescapably brought international financial institutions such as the International Monetary Fund (IMF) and the World Bank into the policymaking process. The presence of the IMF in effect reduced the political costs of economic reform and provided a convenient shield for the president-elect since any unpopular policy and outcome could be blamed on external pressure.[37] Still, the policy-making drift that characterized the second half of the year loomed large because the president-elect would not assume his office until February 1998. Thus, management of the economic crisis at that time largely depended on management of the political transition for the next two months since any conflict between the incoming and outgoing presidents would have had devastating consequences.

The potential danger of a power vacuum, however, proved groundless. Two days after the election, Kim Dae-jung and Kim Young-sam met and agreed to form a 12-member Joint Presidential Committee on Economic Policies in which six members of the incoming ruling coalition of the NCNP and ULD worked with six ministerial-level officials of the outgoing government economic agencies. The committee served as the de facto crisis-management cabinet under the president-elect's control. The economic crisis enabled Kim Dae-jung to secure bipartisan legislative support as well. The GNP and the president-elect's coalition of the NCNP and ULD agreed to convene a special session of the National Assembly to deal with the economic reform bills required under the IMF program. With the cooperation of the GNP, the

---

37 Meredith Woo-Cumings, "Miracle as Prologue: The State and the Reform of the Corporate Sector in Korea," in *Rethinking the East Asia Miracle*, ed. Joseph E. Stiglitz and Shahid Yusuf (New York: Oxford University Press, 2001), 363–69.

legislative power of the president-elect during the power transition period was actually much stronger than that of any incumbent president.[38]

In hindsight, the solid foundation of Kim Dae-jung in the legislature was of particular importance for the course of Korea's economic reform in general and corporate restructuring in particular since major reform legislation was enacted at that time. On November 29, thirteen financial reform bills that had been stalled for 130 days since August sailed through the legislature. The legislation laid the blueprint for financial reform of the incoming government, creating the Financial Supervisory Commission to which Kim Dae-jung delegated substantial power for restructuring financial industries.

Once the financial reform legislation was set in motion, the president-elect commenced informal meetings with the heads of the top five *chaebŏl* on January 13, 1998 and with the heads of 30 others on February 6 to lay the groundwork for corporate reform legislation. Early on, Kim Dae-jung and the heads of the top five *chaebŏl* agreed on five principles of corporate restructuring to enhance transparency of corporate governance, to resolve cross-debt guarantees, to improve the financial structure, to streamline business activities, and to strengthen the accountability of corporate management. Meanwhile the president-elect set up a Tripartite Commission to strike a binding industrial contract between employers and workers on January 15. Through the commission in which the FKTU and KCTU participated, Kim Dae-jung could extract labor concessions on the issue of layoffs in exchange for political and economic compensation.

As Kim Dae-jung had already secured the agreements of the major stakeholders for economic reform with consultative mechanisms, it became difficult for the GNP to oppose the reform legislation. Consequently, the National Assembly transformed ten reform bills to restructure the corporate sector and to increase labor market flexibility into binding laws on February 14. Before the formal inauguration of his presidency, Kim Dae-jung had already completed the essential reform legislation for corporate restructuring.[39]

However, it also meant that the crisis-driven armistice of party politics that temporarily stopped partisan bickering came to an end. When Kim Dae-jung officially began his term on February 25, party politics as usual resumed, creating political gridlock. Above all, the president had to realize that his ruling NCNP-ULD coalition did not secure a majority of the

38 Kim Yonghwan, *Imja, Chane ka saryŏnggwan anin'ga* [You are the commander] (Seoul: Maeil kyŏngje sinmunsa, 2002), 313–50.

39 Stephan Haggard, *The Political Economy of the Asian Financial Crisis* (Washington DC: Institute for International Economics, 2000), 139–215.

legislature. Immediately, a deadlocked and divided government emerged as the GNP declined to confirm Kim Chong-p'il as prime minister. Although the president appointed him as acting prime minister on March 3, the confirmation issue produced unproductive partisan squabbling for almost six months, delaying a number of legislative reforms in the legislature. The legislative drift forced the president to dare to unify the executive and legislative branches under his control. Starting with absorbing independents and legislators of minor parties, he seduced several opposition GNP politicians and even wielded prosecutorial powers to threaten them to defect from their party. The highly fluid nature of political parties enabled the president to manufacture a stable lawmaking foundation in the legislature even through such questionable political manipulation. As a result, the ruling NCNP-ULD coalition finally succeeded in realigning the distribution of seats in the legislature to control the majority in September. The majority status of the presidential coalition in the legislature lasted until June 2000 when the legislative election produced another round of divided government.[40]

During the twenty months of unified government, public support for the president was relatively high and stable. Actually, Kim Dae-jung was the only president whose average job approval rating during the second year of the term went beyond 50 percent (51.6 percent). Roh Tae-woo's approval rating was 33.3 percent, Kim Young-sam's 45.3 percent, and Roh Moo-hyun's 24.9 percent. According to a Korea Barometer survey that was conducted in November 1999, 95 percent of respondents strongly or somewhat believed that the Korean economic system would need fundamental changes.[41] The near-universal national consensus on economic reform boosted the president into an unswerving leadership position in the course of corporate restructuring.

Facing a president who was largely considered to have a clear mandate to pursue public reform, the opposition GNP was hard pressed to block reform legislation in the legislature. While the GNP temporally delayed the enactment of a number of corporate reform bills to extract partisan concessions from the government, it neither directly opposed the substance of presidential reform policies nor organized interest groups that were adversely affected by the reform measures. Rather, the GNP demanded that the government take more decisively market-oriented reform measures in addressing problems in the corporate sector. Although the opposition party tried to discredit the government by exploiting a series of corruption scandals

40 O Sŭngyong, *Punjŭm chŏngbu wa Han'guk chŏngch'i* [Divided government and Korean politics] (Seoul: Han'guk haksul chŏngbo, 2005), 282–309.

41 Bernd Hayo, "Mass Attitudes toward Financial Crisis and Economic Reform in Korea," *Socio-Economic Review* 3, no. 3 (2005): 500.

at that time, its position on corporate restructuring did not sharply diverge from that of the ruling coalition. Despite the contentious appearance of the legislature that resulted from inter-party conflicts over noneconomic reform issues, the efficiency of the legislative process in dealing with corporate reform legislation during the period remained high.[42]

In sum, Kim Dae-jung succeeded in implementing drastic corporate reform measures with strong presidential powers. During the two months of the transition period, the president-elect commanded a de facto a grand coalition government in which vital economic reform legislation was swiftly enacted by extraordinary bipartisan legislative support. Although Kim Dae-jung temporally suffered from a divided government situation, the high fluidity of political parties permitted him to reconstruct a legislative majority while persuading opposition legislators en masse to defect. In addition, the unprecedented magnitude of the economic crisis at that time gave him a popular mandate to play the leading role in corporate restructuring and other economic reforms. He never hesitated to combine the numerical power in the legislature and the leadership power in the public in order to carry out swift economic reforms. The opposition party, lacking strong connections with societal interest groups inflicted by economic reform, was incapable of organizing a viable anti-reform alliance. The characteristics of underinstitutionalized political parties thus became a facilitating condition for the president-initiated economic reforms.

Conclusion

This chapter started with a puzzle of why corporate restructuring in Korea, which had had one of the most unpredictable patterns of party politics around the world, has proceeded further than in any other crisis-affected country. Turning conventional wisdom upside down, I suggested a counterintuitive argument that the persistent underdevelopment of political parties actually facilitated government economic reform. The underinstitutionalization of Korean political parties inadvertently insulated the reform-minded president and other policymakers from potentially tenacious political opposition, allowing them to undertake radical corporate restructuring and other economic reforms. Lacking tenable institutional linkages with an interest-based constituency, the parties could not translate what might be substantial anti-reform social resistance into an organized political opposition to the president.

42 Jongryn Mo and Chung-in Moon, "Business-Government Relations under Kim Dae-jung," in *Economic Crisis and Corporate Restructuring in Korea*, ed. Haggard, Lim, and Kim, 127–49.

However, there is a critical caveat. The function of underinstitutionalized parties is conditional on the strength of presidential powers. Specifically, I identified two components of presidential powers to enact economic reform legislation. The first element is the majority seats that the presidential party controls in the legislature and the second is the strong loyalty that the presidential party members devote to presidential leadership. Only when the president succeeds in combining both ingredients of partisan power, can he launch major economic reform policies with stable legislative support.

Seizing the reform opportunity is not easy, however. On the one hand, while key institutional features of the electoral system in Korea made it difficult for presidential parties to secure a majority of the legislature, the highly fluid nature of the party system permitted the president to manipulate popular verdicts. On the other hand, whereas the president acquired the allegiance of ruling party members in the early stage of his presidency, the devotion was destined to dwindle along with the lapse of his tenure, due to the nonrenewable single-term presidency. Considering these delicate institutional conditions that affected the strength of presidential powers, it becomes clear that temporally there have been very limited chances that enabled the president to implement far-reaching corporate and other economic reforms in Korea. To be precise, underinstitutionalized Korean parties will become one of the facilitating conditions for sweeping economic reform only if the president initiates comprehensive economic reform legislation at the earlier stage of his term with the support of a majority of the legislature.

The case studies of three episodes of economic reform legislation that occurred with different combinations of presidential powers offer empirical support for the arguments. During the early stage of his presidency between 1987 and 1989, Roh Tae-woo did not control the legislature. Surfing on the wave of democratization, the majority opposition parties took the initiative to enact financial and labor reform policies. However, since the programmatic underpinning of the reform proposals was extremely shallow, their commitment to economic reform was highly contingent on the response of the stakeholders. Once the proposed economic reform intensified conflicts of interest between the stakeholders, the opposition parties were incapable of mediating, opportunistically oscillating between them. Without a legislative foundation, the president could not act decisively. Accordingly, no major economic reform bills sailed through the legislature.

Whereas the case of democratization-triggered economic reform legislation showed the weight of the numerical power of the president, the outcomes of the economic reform drive of Kim Young-sam between 1996 and 1997 testified to the significance of presidential leadership power. When he initiated financial reform legislation, he had entered a lame-duck period in his term. The majority ruling party had already shifted their political concerns away from the incumbent president's reform projects toward the approaching presidential election. Consequently, the president was unable to obtain the necessary legislative support from his ruling party members. Without coherent loyalty among the ruling party members, the majority power of the party in the legislature was useless for the president. As a result, major economic reform bills were stalled until after the presidential election.

Thanks to the unparalleled magnitude of the economic crisis, Kim Dae-jung could acquire a legitimate mandate to pursue wide-ranging economic reform even before he assumed the presidency and maintained it for the first two years of office. In addition to bipartisan legislative support during the transition period, he could manufacture a stable majoritty of the legislature partly due to the organizational fluidity of underinstitutionalized parties at the earlier stage of his tenure. Combining numerical power with leadership power, he succeeded in swiftly implementing corporate and other economic reform policies.[43] The opposition party that had few institutional connections with interest-based constituencies was largely ineffective in converting anti-reform social groups into viable political forces to the government. In other words, underinstitutionalized political parties were indispensable political assets for the president to consolidate partisan power in the legislature and to defuse government reform opposition in society.

43 In accounting for the relative success of Korea in corporate restructuring, I do not rule out alternative explanations—for example, the impact of the Asian financial crisis. In this chapter, however, my analytic focus is exclusively on the lawmaking ability of the president and its relationships with political parties in the context of the Korean polity.

5 State Coordination in Transition and Corporate Restructuring in South Korea

Joo-Youn Jung

If the Asian financial crisis in the late 1990s was a major turning point in scholarly discussions on the benefits of state interventionism in economic development, the South Korean economy's big stumble during the crisis was a fatal blow to the "myth" of state-led economic development.[1] The state, once regarded as an engine of Korea's economic success, has lost its raison d'être and faced demands for retreat. Neo-liberal market institutional reforms, which have allegedly transformed the Korean state-led economy closer to the Anglo-American neo-liberal model, have become new *causes célèbres*. Corporate restructuring, especially of *chaebŏl*, has become one of the central *causes* during the post-crisis period.[2]

However, such a sudden shift of attention away from the state to market institutions neglects a critical point, that a national economic system is a web of complementary institutions in diverse issue areas. One cannot have a comprehensive and accurate understanding of institutional changes in one issue area, e.g., the corporate sector, without investigating changes in other key issue areas closely interconnected with it in the context of the entire national economic system. Institutional interdependence and

[1] The rise of the East Asian economies has drawn scholarly attention to successful state-led industrialization and diverse "pathways from the periphery." State-centric theories, such as developmental state theories, challenged the conventional laissez-faire belief in the efficacy of a self-adjusting market coordination mechanism by arguing that the state's "market-conforming" intervention in the economy was the engine of East Asian late-development.

[2] As will be shown in this chapter, corporate restructuring in Korea focuses on *chaebŏl*.

interconnectedness between complementary institutions suggest that institutions within a national economic system, subordinated to the logic of the national institutional matrix, can be resilient, and changes in one subsystem would be limited without changes in the key institutions that define the national economic system.

This chapter zeroes in on *state coordination*. State coordination had been the defining characteristic of the Korean economic system in the pre-crisis period, and institutional continuity and discontinuity in state coordination can significantly confine or enable off-path institutional transformation in the subsystems, including the corporate sector. The core institution of Korea's state coordination was the bureaucracy. By analyzing the evolution of the top coordination agency within the Korean state bureaucracy since the early 1990s, this chapter attempts to shed light on the possibilities of off-path neo-liberal reform in the corporate sector.

On the surface, major institutional changes in the top coordination agencies since the 1990s seem to testify to the retreat of the Korean interventionist state from the market. Facing endogenous and exogenous pressure to redefine the state's economic roles, i.e., political democratization and financial liberalization, the bureaucratic coordination system that had been led since 1961 by one powerful coordination agency, the Economic Planning Board (EPB), began to walk an off-equilibrium path in 1994 and was considerably weakened in the post-crisis period. The decline of the bureaucratic coordination center appears to signify the loosening of the tight institutional ensemble in the Korean state-coordinated economic system and neoliberal institutional reform in the corporate sector breaking away from the state-coordinated system.

However, this chapter, by analyzing the politics of bureaucratic restructuring, shows that waning bureaucratic coordination does not necessarily mean the weakening of state coordination or the decline of state intervention in the Korean economic system. Despite the dominant rhetoric of neo-liberal economic reform and the state retreat from the economy, a series of unprecedented coordination agency restructurings in the post-crisis decade neither intended nor resulted in the weakening of state coordination in the Korean economic system. Reformist presidents utilized the new exogenous and endogenous crisis and challenges as opportunities to strengthen their reform initiatives and attempted to build their power bases in the bureaucracy by restructuring the top coordination agencies.

A major consequence of top coordination agency restructurings since the 1990s, was not the end of the Korean interventionist state's coordination but a shift in the redistribution of coordination power *within* the state. While policy coordination within the bureaucracy has been considerably weakened and decentralized, presidents have taken back the coordination power previously delegated to the economic bureaucracy and have intervened in the coordination process more directly than before. Persistence of state coordination suggests that continuity rather than discontinuity prevails in the Korean state-coordinated economic system in transition, and that path dependency in the corporate sector is likely to persist.

The Korean State-Coordinated Economic System

State Bureaucracy as the Coordinator

Institutional analyses of economic action have emphasized the institutional mechanisms by which economic activities are coordinated. According to neoclassical theories, most economic coordination can be achieved through the market mechanism, and when markets alone are insufficient, other private-sector organizations such as intra-firm coordination suffice. The broadly defined "Varieties of Capitalism" (VoC) literature has produced intriguing studies of diverse capitalist economic systems by paying attention to alternative coordination mechanisms to the market, and defined coordinated or non-liberal market economies (CMEs) against liberal market economies (LMEs), especially of an Anglo-American model. Yet the VoC literature, which focuses on the micro-economy of firms as the center of comparative studies of national capitalism, tends not to pay much attention to the state as an important non-market coordinator.

What distinguishes pre-crisis Korea from other CMEs, such as Germany, was the high level of state involvement in the economic actors' transactions, especially through credit allocation.[3] Here, the state economic bureaucracy played an essential role. The economic bureaucracy's control over the economy was strongly dependent on its regulation of capital markets[4] that served

---

3 John Zysman, *Governments, Markets, and Growth: Financial Systems and the Politics of Industrial Change* (Ithaca, NY: Cornell University Press, 1983).

4 Robert Wade and Frank Veneroso, "The Asian Crisis: The High Debt Model Versus the Wall Street-Treasury-IMF Complex," *New Left Review* I, no. 228 (1998): 3–23 and Kanishka Jayasuriya, "Authoritarian Liberalism, Governance and the Emergence of the Regulatory State in Post-crisis East Asia," in *Politics and Markets in the Wake of the Asian Crisis*, ed. Mark Beeson, Kanishka Jayasuriya, Hyuk-Rae Kim, and Richard Robison (New York: Routledge, 2000).

targeted industrial expansion. A considerable amount of indirect or direct intervention by the state bureaucracy and close intertwining between business and the state, while turning the financial sector into an extension of the finance ministry and the central bank for the purposes of developmental economic policies,[5] constituted a common trait of the state-coordinated market economy in Korea.

The state economic bureaucracy designated strategic industries and chose firms to undertake the task of building them up. Then banks, whose lending decisions were subordinated to the economic bureaucracy, provided "patient" money to those firms to support state industrial policy.[6] The economic bureaucracy also provided the selected firms with subsidies, new entry-restrictions, and tax breaks, while forcing labor to accept tight wage control in return for lifetime employment. This is how the highly bank-debt dependent and highly diversified large industrial conglomerates, *chaebŏl*, were created. The "problematic" *chaebŏl* corporate governance and feeble financial monitoring were the children of these interlocking subsystems orchestrated by the state economic bureaucracy[7] and the consequential institutionalization of a "state-bank-*chaebŏl* nexus."[8]

In other words, Korea's developmental economic system was a tightly woven web of interdependent institutions coordinated by the state economic bureaucracy. Being the planner, executor, monitor, and coordinator of state-led economic development, the economic bureaucracy operated a policy regime composed of closely interrelated issue areas, such as corporate, financial, and labor sectors. Industrial policies, therefore, were not formulated in isolation or for the benefit of the corporate sector alone. They were made and implemented in coordination with financial and labor policies, to best serve the ultimate goal of the system—economic growth.

5 Wolfgang Streeck, "Introduction: Explorations in the Origins of Nonliberal Capitalism in Germany and Japan," in *The Origins of Nonliberal Capitalism: Germany and Japan in Comparison*, ed. Wolfgang Streeck and Kozo Yamamura (Ithaca, NY: Cornell University Press, 2001).

6 Even in 1993, policy loans in Korea constituted more than 40 percent of total domestic loans. See World Bank, *The East Asian Miracle: Economic Growth and Public Policy* (New York: Published for the World Bank by Oxford University Press, 1993), 309.

7 For more discussions on the *chaebŏl* issues, see Stephen Haggard, Wonhyuk Lim, and Euysong Kim, eds., *Economic Crisis and Corporate Restructuring in Korea: Reforming the Chaebol* (New York: Cambridge University Press, 2003).

8 See Jang-Sup Shin and Ha-Joon Chang, *Restructuring "Korea Inc."* (New York: RoutledgeCurzon, 2003) for more in-depth discussions on this nexus.

A concept that is useful in portraying such a tight institutional interconnectedness in the Korean developmental economic system is "institutional complementarities."[9] Institutions are interconnected or tightly coupled as part of a system, creating "ensembles" that link institutions in one area within a system to those in the other areas.[10] Therefore, individual organizations and institutional subsystems within one nation are subordinated to its national institutional logic.[11] In addition, the changes in one subsystem would be limited without the systemic changes in the interrelated institutions. A successful reform in one sector requires successful reforms in other closely related areas.

In the Korean developmental economic system, changes in the state economic bureaucracy, the coordinator of this institutional ensemble, not only facilitate or hamper reforms in a particular sector but also transform the nature of the entire system. This chapter zeroes in on the economic bureaucracy as the core institution, of which change is critical to corporate restructuring. More specifically, it focuses on the top coordination agency in charge of coordination within the Korean developmental bureaucracy. For about thirty years from the early 1960s up until the early 1990s, the EPB had been that top coordination agency.

9 The concept starts with the idea that institutions, organizations, and social values in an economic system tend to cohere with each other, though the degree of coupling among them varies. This concept carries a heavy micro-economic nuance: certain efficiencies are achieved by the synergy effect of complementary institutions that make up for the deficiencies of one another and provide missing ingredients to one another. Such a complementarity gives particular economies comparative institutional advantages. See J. Rogers Hollingsworth and Robert Boyer, "Coordination of Economic Actors and Social Systems of Production," in *Contemporary Capitalism: The Embeddedness of Institutions*, ed. J. Rogers Hollingsworth and Robert Boyer (New York: Cambridge University Press, 1997); Colin Crouch, "Complementarity and Fit in the Study of Comparative Capitalisms," in *Changing Capitalisms?: Internationalization, Institutional Change, and Systems of Economic Organization*, ed. Glenn Morgan, Richard Whitley, and Eli Moen (New York: Oxford University Press, 2005); Richard Deeg, "National Business Systems," in *Changing Capitalisms? Internationalization, Institutional Change, and Systems of Economic Organization*, ed. Morgan, Whitley, and Moen; and Peter A. Hall and David W. Soskice, eds., *Varieties of Capitalism: The Institutional Foundations of Comparative Advantage* (New York: Oxford University Press, 2001).

10 Crouch, "Complementarity and Fit in the Study of Comparative Capitalisms."
11 Deeg, "National Business Systems."

The EPB: Top Coordinator within the Bureaucracy

The EPB was established on July 22, 1961. In charge of economic planning and the budget, the EPB functioned as the "coordination hub" of the Korean developmental economic system. Industrial policies were implemented according to the EPB's coordination between ministries in charge of their respective issue areas.

To begin with, the EPB drew up industrial policies based on the annual review procedure that it had established in its five-year plans. Then fiscal incentives, entry permits, trade protection, foreign participation, technological R&D support, and credit and foreign exchange allocation were all organized into coherent packages.[12] The EPB secured budgetary funds and foreign commercial loans for industrial projects; the Ministry of Commerce and Industry (MCI) regulated market entry and terms of domestic competition, selecting firms with a proven track record of past performance and giving them a monopoly on production; and the Ministry of Finance (MoF) provided the selected firms with tax cuts, tariff protection, and bank subsidies. Other line ministries also joined this web of policy coordination. The Ministry of Labor (MoL) illegalized labor unions and suppressed labor disputes while the Ministry of Home Affairs (MHA) and security forces put work places under close surveillance.[13]

What was the source of the EPB's intra-bureaucracy coordination power? One important source of the EPB's intra-bureaucratic coordination power was its official status within the bureaucracy. The EPB was placed at least a "half step" higher than other ministries within the bureaucratic hierarchy. The minister of the EPB concurrently held the position of deputy prime minister with the legal right to "control and coordinate relevant ministries regarding economic planning and administration." In addition, in the process of long-term and short-term economic policy planning and implementation, especially the Five Year Economic Development Plans, the EPB was in the position of assigning tasks and resources to other economic ministries and could institutionalize their participation in the EPB-centered policymaking and implementation.[14] It also exerted initiatives in

12 Tun-Jen Cheng, Stephan Haggard, and David Kang, "Institutions and Growth in Korea and Taiwan: The Bureaucracy," *Journal of Development Studies* 34, no. 6 (1998): 87–111.

13 Byung-Kook Kim, "The Leviathan: Economic Bureaucracy under Park Chung-Hee," paper presented at the annual meeting of the American Political Science Association, Boston, 2002.

14 Jin-Wook Choi, "Regulatory Forbearance and Financial Crisis in South Korea," *Asian Survey* 42, no. 2 (2002): 251–75.

the policy-making process by presiding over key decision-making organizations within the economic bureaucracy, such as the Conference of Economic Ministers and the Council of Economic Ministers.[15] The agenda control power of the EPB at these meetings was critical. The EPB could present to the president the policy issues that it was interested in, educate him about them, and secure his support for them.

Another essential tool of the EPB's effective intra-bureaucratic policy coordination was its budgetary control. Budget allocation means setting priorities among competing national agendas and thus among bureaucracies in charge of different issue areas. With the EPB controlling the "wallet," it was hard for other ministries to openly rebel against the EPB's frequent intervention in diverse policy issues in the name of policy coordination. With its control over the fiscal agenda and budget expenditures, the EPB could bring ministries with conflicting interests to concessions and agreements. Its role as the long-term national agenda-setter and resource-allocator enabled the EPB to influence not only economic policies but also other issue areas that, in the end, were interconnected to economic policies.

Yet there was an even more decisive factor than such institutional factors to EPB's predomination and coordination power within the bureaucracy— the support of the president. The role of the EPB as the top coordination agency and its relationship with the development-oriented authoritarian president are particularly important to understand not only the role of the EPB in Korea's developmental economic system but also the transformation of the top coordination agencies since the early 1990s.

The EPB and the President

Korea's developmental economic bureaucracy was built under the Park Chung-hee (Pak Chŏng-hŭi) regime (1961–79). This is when the key institutional characteristics of the Korean economic bureaucracy as well as its relationship with the president were formulated.

Like in the cases of many authoritarian rulers, economic development was an indispensable ingredient of political legitimacy to Park, who seized power through a military coup. Economic growth also meant achieving

---

15 The Conference of Economic Ministers was a formal meeting that reviewed and determined the economic policies before being presented to the State Council. The Council of Economic Ministers was an informal and irregular meeting where a few relevant ministers discussed and determined important economic policies. The conference in particular served as the most important decision-making mechanism, where different opinions of economic ministers and other relevant ministers were discussed and coordinated.

supremacy over North Korea and building the foundation for national security. President Park chose the state bureaucracy rather than a political party as an institutional basis to effectively achieve economic growth and consolidate his political power, and bestowed the bureaucracy almost exclusive policy-making and implementation power. The best among newly recruited high-level bureaucrats were assigned to economic ministries, especially the EPB and the MoF. The EPB's elite bureaucrats had particularly distinguished careers, frequently penetrating other line ministries and seconding ministerial or bureau director posts in the name of policy coherence and efficiency.[16] Given that the institutional power of the coordination agency and advantageous career paths of its elite members were dependent on the president's patronage and support, members of the coordination agency had a strong incentive to identify their organizational and personal interests with the success of Park's and his successors' visions for state-led economic development.

Such a tight interest alignment between the president and the economic bureaucracy began to loosen in the early 1990s with different political incentives from those of their predecessors. Rising to power at a time of surging demands for political democratization, they began to see the developmental bureaucracy from the authoritarian past not as an asset but as a liability. The dependency of the Korean economic bureaucracy on the president enabled reformist presidents to execute dramatic restructurings of the top coordination agencies when windows of opportunity were created. The following section analyzes why and how top coordination agency reforms were pushed through under the Kim Young-sam (Kim Yŏng-sam) government (1993–98) and Kim Dae-jung (Kim Tae-jung) government (1998–2003).

The Politics of Top Coordination Agency Restructuring Since the 1990s

The EPB-centric institutional equilibrium of Korea's developmental economic bureaucracy began to go through major changes in late 1994, when the Kim Young-sam government suddenly announced the merger of the EPB and the MoF. As a result, a new gigantic supra-agency, the Finance and Economy

---

16 For more details, see Byung-Kook Kim, "Bringing and Managing Socioeconomic Change: The State in Korea and Mexico" (PhD diss., Harvard University, 1987) and Byung-Kook Kim, "The Park Era: Agent, Structures, and Legacies," paper presented at the annual meeting of the American Political Science Association, Boston, 2002.

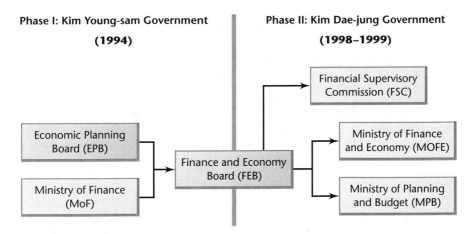

FIGURE 5.1 Restructurings of the top Korean coordination
economic agencies in the 1990s
Source: Author.

Board (FEB), was created.[17] Yet, before long, the FEB also went through dismemberment with the outbreak of the financial crisis in 1997. Between 1998 and 1999, two rounds of FEB restructuring were initiated by the newly inaugurated Kim Dae-jung government, creating the Ministry of Planning and Budget (MPB) out of the FEB. By May 1999, the EPB was dismembered into three agencies—the Ministry of Finance and Economy (MOFE), the MPB, and the Financial Supervisory Commission (FSC)[18] (Figure 5.1).

17 The Korean name of this new agency was "Chaejŏng kyŏngje wŏn," i.e., the Finance and Economy "Board," when it was established in 1994. Its Korean name then changed to "Chaejŏng kyŏngje pu," i.e., the "Ministry" of Finance and Economy, as the result of the 1998 restructuring. Regardless of the changes in its Korean names, the official English name of the agency remained the same between 1994 and 2008: the "Ministry" of Finance and Economy. However, observing the editorial guidelines of this volume, I call the 1994–1998 MOFE the "FEB" in this chapter.

18 Existing studies on Korea's post-crisis economic bureaucracy mostly discuss the FSC, the financial regulatory agency that played a key role in the post-crisis financial reform. However, this chapter chooses not to. This chapter focuses on the evolution of the coordination within the Korean economic bureaucracy since the EPB. The evolution of financial supervision, originally under the MoF jurisdiction, is an issue that is closely related to but goes beyond this chapter's domain. In addition, the FSC establishment, initiated in January 1997 and concluded in December 1997, was a separate reform process from the MPB establishment that is the focus of this chapter. For a detailed analysis of the FSC, see Heon Joo Jung's chapter in this volume.

The impetus for state institutional reform can be both exogenous and endogenous. Exogenous shock can stimulate or force widespread changes across all key domestic institutional systems. And change in a given system may also occur as a result of factors endogenous to that system.[19] Korea is an intriguing case since major bureaucratic restructurings of the coordination agencies in the 1990s were carried out under exogenous pressure from economic liberalization and financial crisis as well as endogenous pressure from political democratization. Political democratization, rapidly progressing in Korea since 1987, increasingly challenged the legitimacy of the state-coordinated economic system that was formulated and nurtured under the development-oriented authoritarian regimes. The Asian financial crisis in 1997 created a decisive juncture by dramatically exposing the weakness of the existing system and presenting the urgent need for comprehensive institutional reform in Korea.

There is no doubt that such pressure for reform created a critical momentum for major bureaucratic institutional changes. Without the needs and popular demands for redefining the role of the interventionist state and enhancing bureaucratic efficiency generated by such pressure, restructuring a powerful state agency would have been extremely difficult. However, needs for reform do not guarantee reform.[20] They do not explain why a particular reform policy was chosen, either. While the exogenous and endogenous preconditions tell us why a change of institutional equilibrium was deemed necessary, they do not tell us why institutional reform did take place and why particular institutional alternatives were chosen. Looking into the process of the top coordination agency's institutional transformation, this section shows that the top coordination agencies' fates were determined not merely as solutions to the given problems and challenges.

President Kim Young-sam and the Closure of the EPB

Financial liberalization, pursued in Korea since the 1980s and accelerated in the early 1990s, began to loosen the tight institutional ensemble in the Korean state-coordinated economic system. This was mainly because bureaucratic coordination in the Korean developmental economic system was possible thanks to the limited capital mobility and the regulated domestic

19 Masahiko Aoki, *Toward a Comparative Institutional Analysis* (Cambridge, MA: MIT Press, 2001) and Deeg, "National Business Systems."

20 For an excellent study on this point, see Barbara Geddes, *Politician's Dilemma: Building State Capacity in Latin America* (Berkeley: University of California Press, 1994).

TABLE 5.1
Corporate Financing in South Korea (%)

Source	1970	1975	1980	1985	1990	1993
Indirect Finance	39.7	27.7	36.0	56.2	40.9	32.8
• From banks	30.2	19.1	20.8	35.4	16.8	13.7
• From NBFIs	9.5	8.6	15.2	20.8	24.1	19.0
Direct Finance	15.1	26.1	22.9	30.3	45.2	53.3
Foreign Borrowing	29.6	29.8	16.6	0.8	6.8	−2.3
Others	15.6	16.4	24.5	12.7	7.1	16.2

Source: Joon-Ho Hahm, "The Government, the Chaebol and Financial Institutions before the Economic Crisis," in *Economic Crisis and Corporate Restructuring in Korea: Reforming the Chaebol*, ed. Stephan Haggard, Wonhyuk Lim, and Euysung Kim (New York: Cambridge University Press, 2003), 86.

financial sector, and maintained by the effective monitoring of the corporate debt by the state bureaucracy and restrictions on external borrowing.[21]

Increasing financial liberalization since the 1980s enabled the *chaebŏl* to secure their own alternative capital sources, and thus gain more and more independence from the influence of the state bureaucracy. As Table 5.1 shows, corporate borrowings from nonbank financial institutions (NBFIs)[22] and direct financing through commercial paper, corporate bonds, and stocks have significantly increased since the 1980s, undermining the MoF's supervision over loan decisions and direct and indirect control over the corporate sector. Rising labor unrest with the progress of democratization since 1987 started to threaten the cheap and stable supply of labor and further weakened industrial policy coordination by the state economic bureaucracy. The need to rethink the old roles of the developmental economic bureaucracy began to surface. Rapid political liberalization also brought the legitimacy of the developmental economic bureaucracy that had represented the authoritarian developmental era into serious question. With the election of Kim Young-sam as president in 1992, the EPB became a target of reform.

On November 17, 1994, President Kim Young-sam unveiled his ideas about *segyehwa* (globalization, or internationalization in Korean), which became a representative catchphrase of his government. Declaring that it was time for "*segyehwa*," he began to reveal various reform plans to "globalize" Korea. On December 3, 1994, the president surprised both the public

21 Jayasuriya, "Authoritarian Liberalism, Governance and the Emergence of the Regulatory State in Post-crisis East Asia."

22 Under the tight control of bank credits by the government, the NBFIs were an important source of alternative financing for the *chaebŏl*.

and the bureaucracy by announcing a plan to abolish the EPB, which had been secretly prepared by his close advisors. The abolition was explained as an essential part of the reform drive for *segyehwa* to improve government productivity, stimulate the competitiveness and autonomy of the private sector, and realize the idea of *segyehwa* throughout the government.[23] The abolition was swiftly executed. Soon after the announcement, the "Government Organization Law Amendment Bill" was submitted to the National Assembly on December 6 and passed by the National Assembly on December 23. The closure of the EPB had a significant symbolic meaning. On the surface, it seemed to put an official end to Korea's state-led "developmental era" and clearly signal the retreat of the interventionist state that became inevitable in the time of economic globalization and political democratization.

However, questions remain. The particular institutional choice is puzzling because it went directly against the major rationales of the EPB abolition, i.e., reducing power concentration within the bureaucracy as well as bureaucratic intervention in the economy. Combining the budget, planning, and policy coordination functions of the EPB and the tax, financial, and fiscal functions of the MoF, the reform created an even more gigantic and powerful agency than the EPB—the FEB—that other ministries could hardly check or oppose. With the FEB as the new coordinator, power concentration within the bureaucracy was aggravated. In addition, ironically, the EPB, a brain agency with no policy constituency of its own, was the biggest pro-liberalization voice within the bureaucracy. The merger of the liberal EPB and the conservative MoF considerably weakened the institutional support for economic liberalization and deregulation inside the bureaucracy.

The propagated political rhetoric of reform, therefore, is misleading. One needs to understand the political utility of the EPB closure to President Kim Young-sam, who was celebrated as the first "civilian" president in Korea since the 1961 military coup. Just as economic development was the raison d'être of the authoritarian presidents, "reform" was a keyword for

23 See Kongboch'ŏ [Government Information Agency], *Munmin chŏngbu 5-nyŏn kyehoek paeksŏ* [A comprehensive report on the five years of reform during the Kim Young-sam administration] (Seoul: Kongboch'ŏ, 1997), 103–7; Kim Yŏngmin, "Munmin chŏngbu chŏngbu chojik kaep'yŏn ŭi naeyong kwa munje chŏm" [Issues regarding government reorganization during the Kim Young-sam administration], *Inha taehakkyo sahoe kwahak yŏn'guso nonmun chip* [Social science treatise, Inha University],17 (1999): 329–48; and Chŏng Yong-dŏk, "Han'guk ŭi chŏngbu chojik ŭi kaep'yŏn" [Korean government reorganization]," *Han'guk chŏngch'aek hak'oebo* [Korean policy studies review] 4, no. 1 (1995): 58–84.

President Kim's political legitimacy. Despite the ups and downs of its organizational power in competition with other ministries, the EPB had been the most trusted and favored advisor to the previous authoritarian presidents since 1961. President Kim Young-sam, rather than inheriting the "remnant" of the past from which he strived to differentiate himself, had a strong incentive to use it as a reform target to show his unyielding will for reform. The interest alignment between the EPB and the president, a key to the EPB's institutional power, was broken.

In addition, by late 1994, the Kim Young-sam government had set 1996 as the target year to enter the Organisation for Economic Co-operation and Development (OECD), which was to be one of President Kim's major achievements. Critical changes in the international economic environment, such as negotiations for the Uruguay Round (UR) agreements,[24] were also under way, heralding a further opening up of the Korean economy in the near future. It was under these circumstances that President Kim Young-sam began to actively promote "*segyehwa*" as the catchphrase for his government's reform drive. If bureaucratic reform was to be implemented, the particular institutional choice needed to be powerful enough to highlight the reformist nature of the government and effectively demonstrate the president's will and capacity to pursue even extremely difficult reforms. The closure of the EPB, the top coordinator of the bureaucracy, was an effective "shock therapy."[25]

Despite its close association with the neo-liberal ideas of economic reform and liberalization, the EPB closure did not primarily aim at bureaucratic deregulation or state retreat from the market. To begin with, unlike common misunderstanding, these were not the main goals of the *segyehwa* drive. *Segyehwa* was a top-down reform drive that saw the redefined yet persistent role of the state as the key to enhancing Korea's international competitiveness. It attempted to address core problems in comprehensive issue areas of Korean society, ranging from education to the legal system,

---

24 The UR was the 8th multilateral trade negotiation of the General Agreement on Tariffs and Trade (GATT). Lasting from September 1986 to April 1994, it transformed the GATT into the World Trade Organization (WTO). The UR was launched in Punta del Este in Uruguay (hence the name).

25 Author's interview with Park Dong-Suh (Pak Tong-sǒ). Park was then the chairman of the Administrative Innovation Commission, a presidential advisory commission that made recommendations on administrative reforms directly to the president. Upon the request of President Kim Young-sam, he prepared proposals for bureaucratic reform in utmost secrecy. Chǒng, "Han'guk ǔi chǒngbu chojik ǔi kaep'yǒn," 73–74 also shares this view.

paying no primary attention to economic issues. Active state intervention was deemed particularly essential for welfare and education reform, which were the top priority issue areas.[26]

This shows that President Kim Young-sam actively reinterpreted neoliberal economic globalization as a challenge that required the persistent role of the state, and utilized the challenge as a powerful rationale to solidify his political leadership. The institutional transformation of Korea's bureaucratic coordination system was initiated in this context, playing an essential part in the president's reform drive. The main purpose behind the top coordination agency restructuring was not to weaken the bureaucracy or transform the nature of state coordination in the economic system. There was a clear discrepancy between the political rhetoric and the actual intentions of the EPB reform, which characterizes the subsequent top coordination agency restructurings and explains why, despite dramatic institutional changes, continuity dominates the Korean state-coordinated economic system.

President Kim Dae-jung and the Establishment of the MPB[27]

The FEB did not last long. Soon after the outbreak of the financial crisis in late 1997, the FEB went through a series of dismemberments under the Kim Dae-jung government. In February 1998, the FEB was first split into three agencies. The Planning and Budget Commission (PBC) and the National Budget Office (NBO) were created out of the FEB, and the remaining FEB was downgraded from a board to a ministry level and renamed as the Ministry of Finance and Economy (MOFE). Then in May 1999, another round of reform was implemented. The Ministry of Planning and Budget (MPB) was created by the merger of the PBC and the NBO. Figure 5.2 summarizes this FEB restructuring process between 1998 and 1999.

The single most dominant explanation for FEB restructuring, initiated only a few years after the powerful agency's creation, was the Asian financial

26 Author's interviews with Park Se-il (Pak Se-il), the first senior secretary to the president for policy planning, and Suh Jin-Young (Sŏ Chin-yŏng), the chairman of the Presidential Commission on Policy Planning at that time. Also see Kongboch'ŏ, *Munmin chŏngbu 5-nyŏn kyehoek paeksŏ*; Segyehwa ch'ujin wiwŏnhoe [The Globalization Promotion Committee], *Segyehwa ŭi bijyŏn-kwa chŏllyak* [Globalization: Visions and strategies] (Seoul: Segyehwa ch'ujin wiwŏnhoe, 1995); and Segyehwa ch'ujin wiwŏnhoe [The Globalization Promotion Committee], *Segyehwa paeksŏ* [White paper on globalization] (Seoul: Segyehwa ch'ujin wiwŏnhoe, 1998).

27 More detailed analysis on the MOFE reform discussed in this section can be found in Joo-Youn Jung, "Reinventing the Interventionist State: The Korean Economic Bureaucracy Reform under the Economic Crisis," *Pacific Focus* 23, no. 1 (April 2008): 121–38.

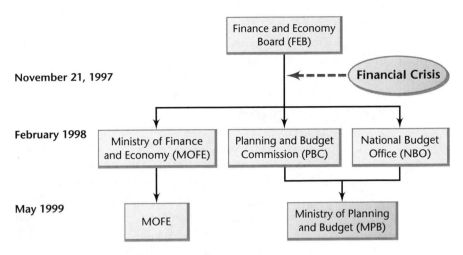

FIGURE 5.2 Restructuring of the Finance and Economy Board, 1998–1999
Source: Author.

crisis. Considering its devastating impact on the national economy and the magnitude of bureaucratic failure in preventing such a disaster, [28] it was not surprising that the FEB, then the top coordination agency, was blamed and targeted for reform. The dismemberment of the FEB seemed to exemplify the dramatic failure and inevitable end of state interventionism in the era of financial globalization. However, a closer look into the FEB dismemberment process exposes a puzzling fact. As the names of the three new agencies created in the process of FEB dismemberment—the Planning and *Budget* Commission, the National *Budget* Office, and the Ministry of Planning and *Budget*—suggest, the central issue in both rounds of reform was taking the budgetary function out of the FEB. Why was the budgetary function at the

28 After all, Korea was on the verge of national insolvency. Prior to the crisis, short-term debt in Korea amounted to US$70.18 billion, which was twice as much as the country's total international reserves. A net inflow of borrowing from commercial banks amounted to US$13.1 billion between January and September 1997, but was quickly reversed to a net outflow of US$8.8 billion between October and November 1997. With only a few days of foreign reserves left and a massive outstanding short-term debt denominated in dollars, Korea had no choice but to accept the US$57 billion in the IMF rescue package and a long list of conditionalities. The impact on the economy was severe. On December 23 1997, the exchange rate hit 1,960 won per dollar, which was a 85.6 percent devaluation since November 21, 1997. Between June and December 1997 alone, the stock market collapsed by 50 percent. Real GDP growth rate in 1998 was negative 5.8 percent, compared to 9 percent in 1995, 7 percent in 1996, and 5 percent in 1997. The unemployment rate, which was 2.6 percent in December 1997, reached 8.7 percent by February 1999.

center of a major bureaucratic restructuring in the middle of a national emergency? To answer this puzzle, one needs to understand the logic of a political battle over bureaucratic reform under the façade of crisis management.

With the outbreak of the national crisis, then President-elect Kim Dae-jung began to work on bureaucratic reform plans before the inauguration of his new government. Despite the grave situation, dismembering the FEB was a politically difficult task, particularly due to the fragmented decision-making structure. In late 1994, the ruling Democratic Liberal Party (DLP) was holding over the half of the seats (55.2 percent) in the National Assembly, and President Kim Young-sam had a strong grip over the ruling party as its "party boss." With the ruling party and the president practically sharing a policy preference, the decision-making structure was highly cohesive. But the structure in 1998 was a lot more fragmented. Kim Dae-jung's National Congress for New Politics (NCNP), a long-time opposition party, created a coalition with the United Liberal Democrats (ULD) before the presidential election, introducing a powerful veto player in the policy-making process. The NCNP also had to face a strong opposition party, the GNP. The GNP held over the half of the seats in the National Assembly (53.8 percent) from February 1998 to August 1998, and had yet to lose the majority to the coalition in August 1998.

Even from the early stage of discussing the FEB reform, there were serious conflicts regarding the contents of the reform bill between the two coalition government parties and the opposition GNP. The central issue of contention was where to place the budgetary function of the FEB. The president wanted to create a separate coordination agency with budgetary functions so that it could support and execute his economic reform agenda, especially of the government and public sectors. As mentioned earlier, control over the budget is an essential intra-bureaucratic coordination tool. Especially when the reform can potentially generate resistance within the bureaucracy, whether or not the coordination agency has the power to allocate the budget becomes a critical factor for the success of the reform.[29] The president's plan was to create a vehicle that could engage in policy planning and coordination, drive other ministries toward reform, and lead comprehensive public sector reforms targeting the government, state-owned enterprises, and government-affiliated organizations.[30]

29 Kihoek yesanch'ŏ (MPB), *Chŏngbu kaehyŏk paeksŏ* [White paper on government reform] (Seoul: Kihoek yesanch'ŏ, 2000).

30 Author's interview with Jin Nyum (Chin Nyŏm), the first chairman of the PBC.

Thus the ruling NCNP insisted on creating a new agency with budgetary control and keeping it under the president's direct control. Since the prime ministership was to be allocated to the ULD according to the coalition agreement, the ULD wanted to place the new agency under the direct control of the prime minister. On the other hand, the GNP, which in 1998 was holding the majority in the National Assembly and thus had veto power, opposed both and argued for keeping the budgetary function in the FEB. Dividing the budgetary function among three agencies was the compromise among these three parties to break the gridlock. The PBC, placed directly under the president, was to make guidelines for budget allocations, while the NBO, kept under the MOFE's jurisdiction, was placed in charge of actual budget allocation and management. The MOFE was in charge of accounting.

Not quite achieving the original goal of establishing an independent budgetary agency under his control, President Kim Dae-jung initiated another round of government reorganization in November 1998. What he proposed was merging the PBC and the NBO into one agency directly under the control of the president. As expected, the ULD opposed this proposal. After a long negotiation process, the two coalition parties compromised on creating the MPB under the prime minister. The GNP resisted this idea, but, this time, the coalition parties were holding the majority in the National Assembly and could pass the bill without the agreement of the GNP. The bill was finalized and implemented in May 1999.[31]

As this brief overview of the FEB dismemberment process indicates, the primary goal of the top coordination agency restructuring in the middle of a national financial crisis was not to weaken the FEB or diminish state coordination of the economy. Government documents on the FEB restructuring process show that, at the early stage of discussion, excessive state intervention indeed was criticized as the major cause of the financial crisis,

31 For good details on the entire process, see Na Chung-sik, "Han'guk chungang chaejŏng kigu pyŏnch'ŏn ŭi yŏksa chŏk punsŏk—Pak Chŏng-hŭi, Kim Yŏng-sam, Kim Tae-jung chŏngbu ŭi chaemu haengjŏng chojik kaep'yŏn e kwanhan sarye punsŏk ŭl chungsim ŭro" [A historical analysis of Korean national financial institutions' transformation under the Park Chung-hee, Kim Young-sam, and Kim Dae-jung administrations], Han'guk haengjŏngron chip [Korean public administration quarterly] 11, no. 3 (1999): 541–61 and Pak Tae-sik, "Chŏngbu chojik kaep'yŏn e taehan chedo sŏnt'aek chŏk punsŏk: Kungmin ŭi chŏngbu chojik kaep'yŏn ŭl chungsim ŭro" [An institutional choice analysis of government reorganization: Government reform under the Kim Dae-jung administration], Han'guk haengjŏng hakpo [Korean review of public administration] 35, no. 3 (2001): 1–19.

and "neo-liberalism,"[32] market principles, and democratic values[33] were upheld as ideals for the government reorganization. But soon the needs to strengthen the president's leadership by granting him budgetary control began to be emphasized.[34] In the following battles over budgetary power, the three parties involved were fighting for a new bureaucratic institutional alignment that could best enhance their political power, or at least prevent other parties' gain. Their major concern behind the new institutional choice, therefore, was a far cry from reducing state intervention in the economic sphere and enhancing market autonomy as a remedy to the crisis. On the contrary, the focal point was the redistribution of coordination power, which was contested under the financial crisis.

Once again, the driving force behind the coordination agency restructuring was the reformist president. The financial crisis in 1997 was unquestionably an ordeal for the Korean economy, but it was not merely a harsh constraint on President Kim Dae-jung. The crisis opened a rare window of opportunity for him to consolidate his leadership despite his weak political power base and to pursue reform measures that would have been extremely difficult in the absence of the crisis. President Kim Dae-jung actively utilized the crisis as a political asset and interpreted the nature of the crisis as one that needed strong presidential leadership. He regarded a new coordination agency equipped with budgetary power as a necessary tool for that purpose. His goal was strengthening, not weakening, state coordination of the economy.

Transformation of the State Coordination System and Corporate Restructuring

The EPB-centric coordination system that had characterized the Korean state-led economic development for three decades has experienced important institutional transformation since the early 1990s. Table 5.2 summarizes how the coordination system within the economic bureaucracy has evolved since the early 1990s as a result of a series of bureaucratic restructurings.

A key characteristic of the coordination within the Korean developmental economic bureaucracy up until 1994 was the prominent role of the EPB. Three key economic ministries—the EPB, MoF, and, to a lesser extent, the MCI—had created a certain power balance, while the EPB functioned as

32 Kihoek yesan wiwŏnhoe (PBC), *Chŏngbu chojik kaep'yŏn paeksŏ* [White paper on government reorganization] (Seoul: Kihoek yesan wiwŏnhoe, 1998).

33 Kihoek yesanch'ŏ (MPB), *Chŏngbu kaehyŏk paeksŏ* and Korea Development Institute (KDI), *DJnomics* (Seoul: Korea Development Institute, 1999).

34 Kihoek yesan wiwŏnhoe (PBC), *Chŏngbu chojik kaep'yŏn paeksŏ*.

TABLE 5.2

Evolution of the Coordination System Within the Economic Bureaucracy

	1961–1994 Developmental System	1994–1997 Interim System	1999–2008 Post-crisis System
	Balanced power, strong coordination	*Centralized power, weak coordination*	*Dispersed power, politicized coordination*
Coordination Center	EPB	FEB	President (Blue House)
Intra-bureaucratic Power	Concentrated on the EPB with a power balance (EPB-MoF-MCI triangle)	Highly concentrated on the FEB (MOFE dominance)	Dispersed (MOFE-FSC-MPB)

Source: Author.

the strong, effective coordinator and long-term policy planner, utilizing its higher institutional status and budgetary power.

The merger of the MoF and the EPB in December 1994 put a drastic end to this long EPB dominance and created a gigantic new super coordinator, the FEB. Incorporating the EPB's responsibilities over the budget and long-term planning and the MoF's extensive portfolios on finance, the treasury, and tax, the FEB generated a very high level of power and resource concentration within the bureaucracy. The increased power concentration in the top coordination agency, however, did not result in stronger, more effective coordination. On the contrary, the interim period between 1994 and 1997 is marked by dramatically weakened bureaucratic coordination. The merger in 1994, which was secretly prepared, abruptly announced, and swiftly implemented, created a lacuna in the functions that the EPB used to be in charge of. First of all, the creation of the FEB removed the checks and balances that the EPB had provided within the bureaucracy, especially to the MoF. Through macroeconomic policy coordination, the EPB had checked the MoF's power and advocated institutional reforms regarding finance and taxation. Within the FEB, the policy coordination and reform-oriented functions of the EPB became subordinate to the financial and fiscal functions of the MoF. The chance to pursue comprehensive structural reforms against the interests of the financial sector, a policy constituent of the MoF, had declined.[35]

The merger also considerably weakened the information gathering, long-term planning, and macroeconomic monitoring by the EPB and intensified fragmentation within the top coordination agency. In the gigantic FEB, the financial and fiscal issues that needed daily attention became

35 Author's interviews.

an organizational priority, while longer-term tasks such as monitoring the bigger picture of the economy and gathering macroeconomic data were set aside.[36] The FEB suffered information-sharing and communication problems as well. It was partly due to the large size of the organization that made intra-coordination tough and partly due to the old rivalry between the EPB and the MoF. These problems provide hints regarding why the FEB, supposedly a powerful coordination economic agency, had not promptly detected and responded to the signs of crisis in 1997. The abolishment of the EPB and creation of a new top coordination agency at the end of 1994 resulted in the sudden and significant weakening of the system coordination and monitoring capacity of the economic bureaucracy. [37]

By 1999, the dismemberment of the FEB, the super-ministry during the short interim period, created three new agencies—the MOFE, MPB, and FSC. In terms of the division of labor within the economic bureaucracy, this measure made the post-crisis decade from 1999 to 2008 partly a return to the pre-1994 model. The MPB, in charge of the budget and planning, was a revival of the EPB in a weaker version, and the MOFE was a revival of the MoF, although the financial supervisory function was taken over by the FSC. In terms of coordination, however, the post-crisis system shows clear differences from any of the two pre-crisis systems. Policy coordination by one top agency had broken down, and the power relationship between economic agencies had become more horizontal than before. The organization and personnel of the Policy Coordination Bureau that used to be in charge of coordination still remained in the MOFE, but without an effective coordination tool such as budget, the bureau's coordination function

36 Interview with a former top-level officer at the EPB and then the FEB. The fact that official government figures on foreign debts emerged only in March 1998, more than three months after the peak of the crisis, underscores the gravity of government failures in information collection after the merger. Chung in Moon and Sang-young Rhyu, "The State, Structural Rigidity, and the End of Asian Capitalism: A Comparative Study of Japan and South Korea," in *Politics and Markets in the Wake of the Asian Crisis*, ed. Mark Beeson, Kanishka Jayasuriya, Hyuk-Rae Kim, and Richard Robison (New York: Routledge, 2000).

37 The weakening of state coordination and the institutional void generated as a result are often regarded as one of the major causes of the financial crisis, or at least why the earlier signs of the crisis could not be better monitored and handled by the once-so-efficient Korean economic bureaucracy. For example, see Jang-Sup Shin and Ha-Joon Chang, *Restructuring "Korea Inc."* and Eun Mee Kim (Kim Ŭn-mi), Dukjin Chang (Chang Tŏk-jin) and Mark Granovetter, *Kyŏngje wigi ŭi sahoehak: Kaebal kukka ŭi chŏnhwan kwa kiŏpchiptan yŏn'gyŏlmang* [The sociology of economic crisis: The transformation of the developmental state and business group networks] (Seoul: Seoul National University Press, 2005).

became nominal. The MPB had budgetary power, but neither was in charge of economic policy coordination nor restored the organizational power and prestige of the EPB. With no one agency having enough power or authority to sway the other agencies, the bureaucratic policy coordination among agencies and thus different issue areas had been considerably weakened.

However, the weakening of bureaucratic coordination does not automatically mean the weakening of state coordination in the Korean economic system. An important phenomenon that had developed in the post-crisis period is that, in the absence of a bureaucratic coordination hub and effective bureaucratic coordination, political coordination by the president began to play a more prominent role than before. This does not mean that the president's role in policymaking and coordination was feeble in the past; the president had always been a key actor in economic policymaking and implementation, and as discussed earlier, presidential support had always been a major source of power for top coordination agencies. However, in the pre-1994 system, the president delegated policy coordination to the EPB, and the EPB performed its role in cooperation with the Blue House. The Blue House's policy inputs and coordination in the pre-1994 system were made *through* the EPB. Now the Blue House itself had become the coordination center, collecting policy inputs and assigning tasks to relevant agencies.[38]

As shown in the cases of the *chaebŏl* "Big Deals" and "Workout" programs,[39] the post-crisis corporate restructuring under the Kim Dae-jung government was not left to market logic but led by the state, especially with the direct intervention of the president supported by newly created or strengthened agencies such as the MPB, the Fair Trade Commission (FTC), and the Financial Supervisory Commission (FSC). For corporate restructuring, the role of the FSC became particularly important. In place of the traditional industrial policy coordinated by the EPB, the FSC began to enforce corporate restructuring on *chaebŏl* through its financial supervisory power. Despite the prevalent rhetoric of neo-liberal market-oriented economic reform, the president put direct pressure on *chaebŏl* to follow the government-orchestrated corporate restructuring programs such as the Big Deals. The FSC also directly intervened in *chaebŏl* Workout programs through its influence over commercial banks.[40]

With industrial policy no longer coordinated by one strong top agency and the passing of the economic emergency that had required vanguard

38 Author's interview.
39 Big Deals were business swaps among the top five *chaebŏl* and Workout was a bank-sponsored restructuring program for the sixth to thirtieth *chaebŏl*.
40 Shin and Chang, *Restructuring "Korea Inc.,"* ch. 4.

agencies to stand at the forefront of reform, policy coordination at the top government leadership level had become routinized. The declining coordination power of the bureaucracy and the growing coordination role at the top political leadership level continued under the Roh Moo-hyun (No Mu-hyŏn) government (2003–8). During Roh's presidency, the coordination role of the Office of the Prime Minister (OPM) increased considerably, which was possible by the president's decision to delegate more policy coordination power to the prime minister.

Conclusion: Implications for Corporate Restructuring in the Future

By tracing the institutional reform process of the top coordination agencies since the early 1990s, this chapter attempted to illuminate the transformation of the Korean state-coordinated economic system and the possibilities for off-path institutional reform in the corporate sector. It showed that top coordination agencies of the Korean economic bureaucracy had undergone important institutional transformation since the early 1990s, which resulted in considerably loosened and weakened bureaucratic coordination in the Korean economic system in the post–financial crisis period. Does the waning of bureaucratic coordination indicate the weakening of state coordination in the Korean economic system and the decoupling of the tightly interlocked institutions that enables off-path evolution of a subsystem? In other words, are we observing the process of the Korean interventionist state's retreat from the position of coordinator and progress toward market-driven corporate restructuring where the state only plays the role of a facilitator?

On the surface, the answer to the above question seems to be positive. This chapter showed that the centralized bureaucratic coordination that had characterized the pre-1994 developmental economic system has indeed broken down. The time of industrial policy, orchestrated and monitored by one top economic bureaucracy, has also ended. However, this chapter also highlighted that such changes in the bureaucratic coordination center do not necessarily imply the end of state coordination.

An important characteristic of the top coordination agency restructurings in Korea since the early 1990s was the discrepancy between the façade of neo-liberal reform and the underlying political intention. Although economic globalization and political democratization had provided powerful exogenous and endogenous pressures and rationales to redefine the role of the interventionist state since the 1990s, a series of bureaucratic institutional reforms, presented as key measures to achieve such a goal, was neither a passive reaction to such pressures, nor intended for the withdrawal of the state from economy. While emphasizing the irresistible tide of economic globalization and the needs for neo-liberal market reform, reformist presidents reinterpreted the new political and economic challenges as conditions that required redefined yet still active state intervention, guided by strong top political leadership. As a result, the top coordination agencies were restructured in a way to strengthen or justify the president's reform policy initiatives and support strong top-down state-led reform measures.

What we observe in this process has been the shift and redistribution of coordination power *within* the state. A series of bureaucratic restructurings has moved the center of system coordination away from the bureaucracy to the president. Unlike their predecessors who delegated control over economic policymaking and daily policy coordination to their trusted technocrats, presidents of democratized Korea seem to want much more direct say in the process of reform policymaking and implementation, put distinct personal marks on the policies, and actively claim credit for a particular reform policy outcome. While the bureaucratic coordination power has considerably declined, presidents have become the center of economic policy coordination in the post-crisis period.

Such a shift, not a decline, of state coordination power suggests that continuity rather than discontinuity prevails in the Korean state-coordinated economy, fundamentally limiting the chance of off-path institutional reform in the corporate sector. Just as in the cases of top coordination agency restructuring, a discrepancy between the political rhetoric and intention has been a key characteristic of the corporate restructuring process. Under the façade of neo-liberal principles in corporate restructuring measures, the political will of the presidents to maintain control over the course of corporate restructuring has persisted. Furthermore, coordination directly exposed to frequent and direct penetration of short-term political interests harms the consistency and effectiveness of reform. In the absence of an institutionalized coordination hub, conflicts of interests among bureaucratic agencies with different policy preferences and constituents are intensified, and the policy-making process can become overly politicized when agencies seek external political support or moderation. These problems explain why corporate restructuring policies in post-crisis Korea have been largely inconsistent and slow, showing no clear sign of a long-term strategy or a consensus on the general direction of reform, and why rapid progress in market-driven restructuring of the Korean corporate sector is not likely to take place in the near future.

6 Financial Regulation and Corporate Restructuring in Korea[1]

Heon Joo Jung

Korea's financial reform since 1997 has been regarded as one of the most successful reform cases in terms of its speed and scope by most observers, notably the International Monetary Fund (IMF) and the World Bank, especially when compared to other reform projects initiated at the same time—i.e., corporate, labor, and public sector reforms.[2] Conventional wisdom says that globalization and financial deregulation provide a strong incentive for government and business alike to upgrade their financial system and corporate governance toward a more market-oriented system with enhanced prudential regulation and transparency. In particular, economic crises have been frequently regarded as catalysts that break deadlock over changes and speed up economic reforms in which international actors such as the IMF and rating firms play a significant role. Korea's experience since 1997 confirms that institutional reform of financial regulation was accelerated to cope with the unprecedented crisis, and positive market response to this reform was taken as an indicator of reform success.

A closer look at the reform process, however, shows that this initial success might not have been possible without what had been regarded as something that should have been reformed previously. Korea's institutional

1 I would like to thank Byung-Kook Kim, Jennifer Amyx, Alicia Ogawa, Eun Mee Kim, and Jean Oi for their greatly helpful comments on the earlier versions of this chapter.

2 Michel Camdessus, "Crisis, Restructuring, and Recovery in Korea," remarks at the Conference on Economic Crisis and Restructuring, IMF 99/27 (December 2, 1999); Scott Roger, "The Asian Crisis Four Years On," *Finance and Development* 38, no. 1 (March 2001).

legacies—dominance of the Ministry of Finance (MoF)[3] in financial regulation through its resources and personnel networks, state interventionism in the financial sector, and the significant role of financial institutions in corporate financing—that once were regarded as being partly responsible for the crisis, in fact became an engine for initiating corporate restructuring and reinvigorating the Korean economy in the crisis situation (see Chapter 5 by Joo Youn Jung). When top policymakers were required to execute narrowly defined reform programs, they were able to successfully exploit these resources and capacities to design reform programs and implement them in the acute phase of the crisis. Nevertheless, the challenges policymakers faced immediately after the crisis were different from those of later years. Faced with competing policy goals, policymakers found themselves incapable of pursuing reform programs with only limited time, resources, and capacities, leaving little choice but to advance their own policy agendas.

This observation raises questions about the roles of financial regulation and financial institutions in corporate restructuring in Korea. Did the financial crisis and reform transform institutional characteristics in financial regulation and their relationship with the corporate sector? If these institutional legacies had helped Korea recover from the crisis, were they still conducive to corporate restructuring and further reforming the Korean economic system a few years after the crisis? A central question this chapter addresses is how Korea's financial restructuring contributed to corporate restructuring. This question is complicated because the role of financial institutions in corporate governance showed significant variation in its relationship with diverse corporate clients as well as in its relationship with state actors. The answers to these questions will help us better understand key characteristics of post-crisis Korea's financial regulatory reform and its impact on corporate restructuring.

These questions are closely linked to the growing literature on how and to what extent various institutional arrangements of a national political economy are able to adapt themselves to new challenges, resulting in

3 South Korea's MoF, like other governmental agencies, was frequently renamed and reorganized especially after democratization as newly elected presidents attempted to change the governmental structure to better serve their policy goals. The MoF became the Finance and Economy Board (FEB) as it merged with the Economic Planning Board (EPB) in 1994 during the Kim Young-sam administration. Later, the FEB was reorganized into the Ministry of Finance and Economy (MOFE) in 1998 as a part of bureaucratic reorganization under the Kim Dae-jung administration. In 2008, the Lee Myung-bak administration renamed it the Ministry of Strategy and Finance (MOSF).

different economic performance and post-hoc institutional arrangements.[4] In this literature, institutional fitness or complementarities are a key to understanding institutional changes and outcomes (see Chapter 1 by Byung-Kook Kim). The interconnectedness among various institutions and reform agendas, moreover, often poses serious dilemmas and tradeoffs for policymakers whose policy options are sometimes competing. In this regard, South Korea's comprehensive economic reform efforts provide a great opportunity to examine the ways in which institutional arrangements surrounding financial and corporate restructuring develop.

This chapter finds both recurrent patterns and changes in the relationship among financial institutions, firms, and the state. On the one hand, Korea's financial reform, part of which was externally imposed by IMF conditionalities, reshuffled the traditional relationship among key actors with the introduction of new rules, regulations, and actors such as international investors and new regulatory agencies. Newly established supervisory agencies adopted prudential regulatory measures that had not been taken seriously in the pre-crisis period. Financial institutions with increasing foreign participation began to focus more on profitability and efficiencies than on market share. They also found that the crisis and restructuring strengthened their influence on firms, especially large firms without *chaebŏl* affiliation and small- and medium-sized enterprises (SMEs).

On the other hand, despite, or because of, the collapse of the myth of "too big to fail" (TBTF), the relationship among financial institutions, the state, and *chaebŏl* largely survived reform efforts intact. As bankruptcy of *chaebŏl* became a real possibility, *chaebŏl* restructuring was regarded as something that could lead to a series of failures of financial institutions which already had accumulated massive nonperforming loans (NPLs). Although the myth of "too big to fail" collapsed with the failure of the second largest *chaebŏl*, Daewoo (Taeu), its failure ironically strengthened the bargaining power of the remaining *chaebŏl* on reform programs.[5] The possible negative externalities of another *chaebŏl* collapse on the banking sector and the possibility of the whole Korean economy derailing rapid recovery were politically unacceptable once the acute phase of the crisis was over. As

4 Masahiko Aoki, *Toward a Comparative Institutional Analysis* (Cambridge, MA: MIT Press, 2001); Peter A. Hall and David W. Soskice, eds., *Varieties of Capitalism: The Institutional Foundations of Comparative Advantage* (New York: Oxford University Press, 2001).

5 Although Daewoo was the third or fourth largest *chaebŏl* during most of the 1990s, it became the second largest one on the eve of its collapse in terms of total assets according to the Fair Trade Commission.

a result, bank-led, or de facto state-led, corporate restructuring turned out to be less effective in changing *chaebŏl* behavior.

This analysis of continuity and change shows that although post-crisis financial and corporate restructuring was not merely scratching the surface, it could not achieve what had been initially expected: a market-oriented financial system with arm's length and rule-based financial regulation, prudent lending, and improved corporate monitoring. Despite the initial reform success, old practices in financial regulation and bank lending survived the reform efforts, as shown in a new crisis in 2002–2003 that created millions of credit delinquents. It indicates that we need to ask whether formal institutional changes and departure from the past accompanied changes in informal practices and incentive structures of relevant actors and, therefore, behaviors and policy choices—a question that has not been asked because of the early success of reform. A careful examination of how and the extent to which financial restructuring impacted corporate restructuring will help us better understand the forces for stability and change in the South Korean financial system.

Disaggregating the Institutional Arrangements of the Financial System

A deeper understanding of the financial system and its variations requires a systemic analysis of the ties among financial institutions, firms, and government and their changes.[6] Even though institutional arrangements of financial systems are similar at a higher level of analysis, they may be comprised, at a lower level, by dissimilar components with profound consequences on longer-term systemic changes. This chapter focuses primarily on: 1) the relationship between financial institutions and firms, 2) the relationship between government and financial institutions, and 3) financial openness and foreign participation (see Figure 6.1).

Once the three components of institutional arrangements of the Korean financial system are analyzed, it is very important to determine how these components can be aggregated into a specific financial system in different periods and institutional contexts. Korea's financial system during developmental periods had combined loan market-based corporate financing and excessive state intervention—i.e., nationalization—in a closed financial market. This chapter examines if the Korean financial system had been transformed into a new system with capital market-based corporate financing

---

6 John Zysman, *Governments, Markets, and Growth: Financial Systems and the Politics of Industrial Change* (Ithaca, NY: Cornell University Press, 1983).

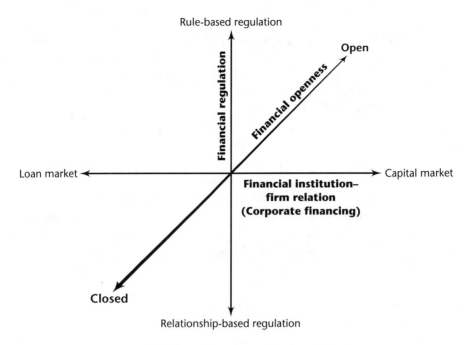

FIGURE 6.1   Three dimensions of the financial system
Source: Author.

with rule-based regulation in an open financial market. Also, it investigates if these changes had any impact on corporate restructuring. Disaggregating the financial system into its components helps us identify the sources of changes and continuities between the pre-crisis and post-crisis periods.

First, the relationship between financial institutions and firms is of great significance especially when the major financial sources for investment come from loan markets (indirect financing), not from capital markets (direct financing). Financial institutions have a great incentive to engage in firms' investment decisions because they share investment risks with the firms. However, the monitoring role of financial institutions over firms is not automatically warranted. Rather, monitoring can be effectively performed only when financial institutions have incentives and capacities. Moreover, when financial institutions rely heavily on a small number of major corporate clients, potential risks of corporate bankruptcy would prohibit financial institutions from actively engaging in corporate restructuring. In this regard, the lopsided relationship of financial institutions with *chaebŏl* should be differentiated from that of non-*chaebŏl* enterprises.

To systematically analyze variations in this relationship, this chapter takes a closer look at the initiation and development of the "principal transactions bank" (PTB) system that was adopted to use banks to monitor corporate behavior. As for empirical data, I examine (a) changing shares of the capital and loan markets in financing firms, (b) shares of banks and nonbanking financial institutions (NBFIs)[7] in financing firms, (c) share of collateralized loans in total loans, and (d) share of NPLs.

First, as Zysman clarifies, a capital market-based system in which firms can raise funds from active stock and bond markets would witness less dependence of firms on bank loans which in turn would discourage banks from investing in monitoring corporate behaviors and building monitoring capacities.[8] Otherwise, financial institutions would have strong incentives to be involved in corporate decision-making, especially regarding long-term and risky investments. Therefore, by looking at corporate financing and its changes over time, we can examine the incentive structure of financial institutions and their potential role in corporate governance. Second, given much looser restrictions on the ownership structures of the NBFIs in the Korean financial system that permitted firms to own NBFIs, the increasing share of NBFIs in financing firms could undermine effective corporate monitoring by banks. By contrast, stricter restrictions on bank ownership that inhibited the influence of *chaebŏl* on banks indicate that the large share of banks in corporate financing could strengthen corporate monitoring. Third, although any lending involves risks, the ways in which financial institutions hedge against risks would be a significant indicator in assessing the capacity and incentive of financial institutions. In this sense, the reliance on collaterals reflects the lack of capacity to properly assess the creditworthiness of borrowers as well as a reluctance to engage in corporate decision-making. Finally, more NPLs in total loans generally indicate imprudence in loan decisions and the lack of incentives and capacities of financial institutions to examine the soundness and profitability of firms' investment decisions.

This relationship between firms and financial institutions can be understood properly in the context of the Korean political economy only when the second component is taken into account: the relationship between financial institutions and government. Not only had the Korean government actively used interest rate and credit policies to influence capital flows but it also engaged in the operations of financial institutions in various informal ways such as "parachute appointments" (*nakhasan insa,* or the re-employment of ex-regulators in private financial institutions). This relationship has significant

---

7 In Korea, NBFIs include most nondepository financial institutions such as securities firms, insurance companies, merchant banks, investment trust companies, credit card companies, and so forth.

8 Zysman, *Governments, Markets, and Growth,* ch. 2.

implications for corporate monitoring because financial institutions would not have strong incentives to monitor firms if lending decisions were not independently made. Moreover, the corporate governance structure of financial institutions is another crucial issue because the cozy relationship between supervisors and supervisees can cause favoritism, regulatory forbearance, and failure. Although this relationship can reduce transaction costs to a certain extent, it can also encourage financial institutions to conceal their problems and postpone timely corrective action. Finally, the intra-governmental relationship among various regulatory agencies—the MoF and the Bank of Korea (BOK)—can influence the way in which financial institutions are regulated.

This relationship can be more specifically analyzed by examining (a) regulation of credit policies, (b) ownership structure of financial institutions, (c) informal ties between government and financial institutions, and (d) relationship among various financial regulatory agencies and their incentives and capacities to regulate financial institutions. First, when interest rates and credit allocations are determined by governmental decisions, there is little incentive for financial institutions to investigate lenders' creditworthiness. Otherwise, financial institutions would invest in building their monitoring capacities. Second, the ownership structure of financial institutions is of great significance in understanding their influence on corporate financing. Owned either by the state or by firms, financial institutions would not properly monitor corporate behaviors. Third, the close relationship between government and financial institutions through parachute appointment practices would not strengthen corporate monitoring because financial institutions would rely more on the relationship itself than on their profitability for survival. This practice, however, can be instrumental in financial and corporate restructuring by securing private compliance and functioning as information conduits. Therefore, the roles ex-regulators play in their post-retirement positions should be investigated to see if this practice would positively contribute to financial and corporate restructuring. Fourth, financial institutions are more likely to take risks in lending if regulatory agencies lack regulatory capacities and higher coordination costs exist among them. Therefore, we need to examine whether and to what extent financial reform influenced incentives, the capacities of regulatory agencies, and their coordination.

The final component is the international dimension given the increasing financial openness since the 1980s and its growing impact on the domestic financial system. The potential influence of foreign participation in the financial market may be multi-directional. First, foreign financial institutions with advanced skills might be interested in changing corporate governance by utilizing their monitoring capacities. Whether or not increasing foreign participation in the Korean financial system positively contributed to corporate monitoring, however, should not be taken for granted, but needs an empirical analysis. Also, their participation and exit option can threaten regulatory authorities to adopt more market-oriented regulatory measures and practices. The role of foreign participation in the financial system and corporate restructuring, however, can considerably vary depending on whether its primary loan target is households or firms. Therefore, international factors include (a) the level of financial openness, (b) foreign participation and performance in financial markets, and (c) the role of foreign participation in corporate financing.

An analysis of the three dimensions of Korea's financial system in the changing contexts of economic development, democratization, economic crisis, and reform will shed light on the ways in which financial institutions and regulation influenced corporate behaviors and vice versa.

Pre-crisis Financial Regulation Under the Developmental Regime in Korea

It had been widely acknowledged that intervention by the Korean government in the financial sector was an essential element not only in the development of the financial system but also in broader developmental policies.[9] Tight control over all internal and cross-border capital flows laid the foundation for Korea's financial system and regulatory framework as well as the developmental state. Nationwide commercial banks (NCBs) were nationalized in 1961 by the government until the early 1980s and allocated credit under direct state control. Economic development being a top priority, Park Chung-hee (Pak Chŏng-hŭi, 1961–79) in the early 1960s used nationalized banks to channel policy loans to finance export-oriented corporate investments and heavy and chemical industrialization (HCI), providing explicit repayment guarantees to foreign financial institutions on loans borrowed by Korean firms. As corporate actors, especially *chaebŏl*, became increasingly independent from the state and banks in their investment decisions and financing options, however, the credit control system became less effective in securing compliance from the *chaebŏl*. Banks, even after privatization in the early 1980s, had little incentive and limited capacity to improve the capital structure of the *chaebŏl* as long as the myth of "too big to fail" persisted.

9 Alice H. Amsden, *Asia's Next Giant: South Korea and Late Industrialization* (Oxford: Oxford University Press, 1989).

Financing Firms: Credit Control, PTBs, and NBFIs

The nationalization of NCBs in 1961 and its consequences are the key to understanding financial development and its relationship with the corporate sector. This is because state control of credit allocation through nationalized banks fundamentally changed the incentive structures of corporate and financial sector actors. Due to nationalization, the expectation of a state guarantee on corporate borrowing—especially long-term foreign loans—that met certain criteria was shared widely enough for firms to borrow more than they needed. The resulting investment boom in the late 1960s funded by foreign borrowing became a huge burden on corporations, especially after the currency devaluation of 18 percent in 1971 and an additional 7 percent in 1972.[10] Fear of systemic risk and contagious effects resulted in the August 3 Measure in 1972 which bailed out ailing firms.[11] With increasing concerns over the concentration of bank loans in a few firms and lack of proper monitoring of the corporate sector by banks, Park introduced a "credit control system" (yŏsin kwalli chedo), the May 29 Measure, in 1974. The system placed a ceiling on bank credits to top businesses to reduce excessive loans to the same businesses by coordinating among banks and improving the capital structure of companies.[12]

Coordination among banks in Korea, however, was one of the challenges policymakers had to face to achieve their policy goals. It was neither the Anglo-Saxon market way of coordination nor the German way of coordination based on networks among banks. On the one hand, the financial market was too underdeveloped to import an Anglo-Saxon model. Networks among banks, on the other hand, were too weak to effectively enforce bank compliance and they lacked the capacity to implement this credit control system. Two primary institutional arrangements for coordination in Korea were

10 See Byung-Sun Choi, "Financial Policy and Big Business in Korea: The Perils of Financial Regulation," in *The Politics of Finance in Developing Countries,* ed. Stephan Haggard, Chung H. Lee, and Sylvia Maxfield (Ithaca, NY: Cornell University Press, 1993), 29–30. According to Choi (p. 30, fn. 17), the debt/equity ratio increased by 229.7 percent from 83.7 percent in 1965 to 313.4 percent in 1972.

11 Wonhyuk Lim, "The Emergence of the *Chaebol* and the Origins of the *Chaebol* Problem," in *Economic Crisis and Corporate Restructuring in Korea: Reforming the Chaebol,* ed. Stephan Haggard, Wonhyuk Lim, and Euysung Kim (Cambridge: Cambridge University Press, 2003), 45.

12 Sang-Woo Nam and Dong-Won Kim, "The Principal Transactions Bank System in Korea and Its Comparison with the Japanese Main Bank System," World Bank, Economic Development Institute (1994).

the Seoul Bankers' Club, which became the Korean Banker's Association in 1975, and the Financial Association (*kŭmyungdan*). However, both lacked competence, internal cohesiveness, and autonomy from the government. For instance, the Financial Association Agreement (*kŭmyungdan h'yŏpjŏng*), which set guidelines for everyday operations of banks from 1964 to 1984, was honored primarily because noncompliance was punished directly by the regulatory authorities.

In the absence of an effective coordination mechanism among banks, this credit control system required a more institutionalized relationship between banks and *chaebŏl*, especially because the level of corporate governance transparency was very low and therefore the cost to evaluate the capital structure and financial situation of *chaebŏl* firms was high. In July 1974, PTBs, modeled after the Japanese "main bank" system, were introduced to implement the credit control system.[13] A bank that had a major business relationship with the core company of a business group became the PTB for all companies of the group and controlled credit supply to them on behalf of the state. It also gathered and sent information on the financial and credit situation of the firms to the regulatory authority—the Office of Banking Supervision and Examination (OBSE) of the BOK.[14] When selected as a "top" business group, the group had to obtain approval from its PTB before making real estate purchases or portfolio investments in other companies.

The original purpose of efficient credit allocation and constraints on excessive loans to top business groups, however, became frequently compromised by higher policy goals such as the catch-up industrial policy. This was inevitable when all PTBs were directly controlled by the developmental regime. First, although Park and top economic bureaucrats wanted to reduce the possible risks involved in "excessive" loans to *chaebŏl,* they did not want to discourage the *chaebŏl* from making sometimes risky investments. Therefore, when the *chaebŏl* complained of a lack of investment capital, policy loans were extended directly to their affiliate companies, bypassing the PTBs. Second, combining the credit control and PTB systems turned out

13 See Sang-Woo Nam and Dong-Won Kim, "The Principal Transactions Bank System in Korea," in *The Japanese Main Bank System: Its Relevance for Developing and Transforming Economies,* ed. Masahiko Aoki and Hugh Patrick (Oxford: Oxford University Press, 1994) for the differences between the principal transactions bank system in Korea and the main bank system in Japan.

14 Although companies that did not belong to the "top" business groups also should have had banks with which they maintained a closer business relationship than other banks, the banks were simply money-lenders.

to be much less effective in exploiting banks to change corporate behavior. Because the credit control system was supposed to put a ceiling on loans to *chaebŏl*, there was little incentive for *chaebŏl* to follow what was suggested by the PTBs that could not supply credit on their own.[15] As a result, the PTBs also became less interested in developing their monitoring capacities and evaluating business groups' investment plans.[16] Moreover, the rescue of conglomerates in 1972 and the lack of clear responsibilities of PTBs made both PTBs and corporations dependent on state decisions and bureaucratic discretions. PTBs merely played the role of *transmitters* of the information provided by *chaebŏl*. There were few that could say no to the government-led HCI drive and overexpansion of *chaebŏl* to unproductive businesses. Although the Park regime and the MoF adopted the PTB system to solve the coordination problem and to change *chaebŏl* investment behavior, it failed for several reasons: a lack of cohesive networks among banks, the nationalization of NCBs, the overwhelming power of the MoF, and the role of *chaebŏl* in developmental policy goals.

Unlike banks, NBFIs were allowed to be owned by *chaebŏl* and became the favorite source of corporate finance, especially for *chaebŏl*. Entry barriers to NBFIs were lowered in 1972 and interest rates were set higher to mobilize resources in informal curb markets and put them under state control.[17] For the Park regime, this policy choice was also purported to strengthen financial markets that had suffered financial repression and distortions during the 1960s and to prevent financial disasters. Although strengthening the credit control system to restrain *chaebŏl* behavior and to mobilize resources through NBFIs were legitimate concerns of the Park regime, the *chaebŏl's* freer access to credit through NBFIs undermined Park's efforts to influence *chaebŏl* investment behavior.

It was under Chun Doo-hwan (Chŏn Tu-hwan, 1979–88) when steps toward more liberal policies were taken to deal with the negative consequences of developmental policies under Park, such as the overcapacity of *chaebŏl* and financial underdevelopment in the context of the second oil shock, social unrest after Park's assassination, and liberalizing pressure from the United States. The privatization of the NCBs during 1981–1983 and the amendment of the Banking Act in December 1982 to separate the financial

15 Nam and Kim, "The Principal Transactions Bank System."

16 Choi Doo-Yull, *Pidaech'ingjŏk kiŏp kŭmyung kyuje wa oehwan wigi* [Asymmetric corporate financial regulation and Korea's 1997 currency crisis] (Seoul: Korea Economic Research Institute, 2002).

17 Choi, "Financial Policy."

TABLE 6.1

Structure of Corporate Financing, 1970–1996 (Inflow, %)

	1970	1975	1980	1985	1988	1990	1991	1992	1993	1994	1995	1996
Indirect Finance	**39.7**	**27.7**	**36**	**56.2**	**27.4**	**40.9**	**41.8**	**36.3**	**31.4**	**44.5**	**31.8**	**28**
Borrowing from Banks	30.2	19.1	20.8	35.4	19.4	16.8	19.8	15.1	13.1	20.7	14.9	14
Borrowing from NBFIs	9.5	8.6	15.2	20.8	8	24.1	22	21.1	18.3	23.8	17	13.9
Direct Finance	**15.1**	**26.1**	**22.9**	**30.3**	**59.5**	**45.2**	**37.9**	**41.4**	**52.9**	**38.1**	**48.1**	**47.2**
Commercial Papers	0	1.6	5	0.4	6.1	4	-3.8	7.6	13.9	4.9	16.1	17.5
Corporate Bonds	1.1	1.1	6.1	16.1	7.5	23	24.2	12.1	14.5	14.2	15.3	17.9
Stocks	13.9	22.6	10.9	13	40.6	14.2	15.1	13.1	14.7	14.8	14.4	10.9
Foreign Borrowing	**29.6**	**29.8**	**16.6**	**0.8**	**6.4**	**6.8**	**4.4**	**4.6**	**-2.2**	**4.9**	**8.4**	**10.4**
Others*	**15.6**	**16.4**	**24.5**	**12.7**	**6.7**	**7.1**	**15.9**	**17.7**	**18**	**12.4**	**11.7**	**14.4**

Source: Data from 1970 to 1991 (Joon-Ho Hahm, "The Government, the *Chaebŏl* and Financing Institutions before the Economic Crisis," in *Economic Crisis and Corporate Restructuring in Korea*, ed. Haggard, Lim, and Kim); For data after 1992, *BOK Quarterly Bulletin* (various years). In cases where there is a conflict in terms of the data, the latter data in the latter bulletin are employed.

Note: * Includes commercial trade credits, borrowing from government, bill payables, reserves for retirement allowance, etc.

and corporate sectors,[18] however, did not necessarily result in changes in the nature of the bank-firm relationship.

First, the credit control system continued in the 1980s as one of the main regulatory measures for *chaebŏl* but failed to achieve its primary goals of solving coordination problems and changing corporate behaviors.[19] While the main purpose of the credit control system under Park was to improve the capital structure of *chaebŏl*, the credit control system under Chun emphasized restrictions on the concentration of economic power.[20] With the adoption of "basket control of credit" in 1984 that limited the share of large business groups in the banks' total credit, the state hoped to reduce the concentration of bank loans to *chaebŏl*, provide more bank credit to SMEs, and restrain *chaebŏl* from risky overexpansion.[21] As a result, the share of loans to *chaebŏl* in total bank loans declined substantially.[22] This decline, however, was accompanied by an increase of direct financing and capital flows from NBFIs (also see Table 6.1).[23] More importantly, this change in the pattern of corporate financing implied that banks had less leverage over *chaebŏl* and became more reliant on *chaebŏl* investments and performance. Despite the decreasing share of new loans to *chaebŏl*, a large share of total bank loans had been extended to *chaebŏl* that could utilize nonbank funding options. It meant that banks had to share investment risks of *chaebŏl* but could not strongly influence *chaebŏl* investment decisions. This lopsided relationship between financial institutions and *chaebŏl* is crucial in understanding *chaebŏl* restructuring after the financial crisis.

Moreover, the increasing role of NBFIs in corporate financing was not followed by prudential regulation over them. The MoF, without sufficient supervisory capacities and inspectors, delegated its authority over NBFIs to several supervisory agencies. These agencies were also without supervisory capacities and coordination among them was ineffective. Finally, even after privatization, the relationship between PTBs and *chaebŏl* was not stabilized

18 The Act stipulated that no individual or corporation could possess more than 8 percent of the total shares of commercial banks.

19 Joon-Ho Hahm, "The Government, the *Chaebol* and Financial Institutions before the Economic Crisis," in *Economic Crisis and Corporate Restructuring in Korea*, ed. Haggard, Lim, and Kim, 81–83.

20 Nam and Kim, "The Principal Transactions Bank System"; Choi, *Pidaech'ingjŏk kiŏp kŭmyung kyuje wa oehwan wigi*, 38–39.

21 Joon-Ho Hahm, "The Government," 82.

22 Cho Yoon Je and Kim Joon Kyung, "Credit Policies and the Industrialization of Korea," *Korea Development Institute Research Monograph* 9701 (December 1997), 46.

23 Byung-Kook Kim, "The Politics of *Chaebol* Reform, 1980–1997," in *Economic Crisis and Corporate Restructuring in Korea*, ed. Haggard, Lim, and Kim; Hahm, "The Government."

due to frequent changes in criteria for selecting corporations to be subject to credit control. During the period of 1974–1987, financial regulatory authorities employed five different criteria to select business groups that would be put under the credit control system. Frequent changes of selection criteria also caused business groups to find more stable sources of corporate financing other than banks. The consequence was a rapid increase in non-performing loans (NPLs) beginning in the early 1980s. While the level of NPLs in bank loans was virtually zero until the end of the 1970s, the share of NPLs increased rapidly in the 1980s when NCBs were privatized. For instance, while the share of NPLs in total loans by NCBs was 1.08 percent in 1978, it increased to 8.57 percent in 1983 and 10.85 percent in 1984.[24]

In sum, the pattern of corporate financing since the 1970s showed: 1) the significance of state-guaranteed foreign loans—primarily, long-term borrowing in the 1970s, 2) the increasing role of the NBFIs, and 3) the increasing share of direct financing. The credit control system was initially adopted to constrain excessive loans to a small number of *chaebŏl* and to exercise corporate control through the PTBs. The implementation of the credit control system, however, was frequently interrupted by the pursuit of rapid economic growth. Moreover, risk-taking investments by *chaebŏl* were encouraged. This conflict of policy goals—constraints on loans to *chaebŏl* and promotion of *chaebŏl* investments—resulted in ineffective corporate control by the financial institutions, and contributed to the rapid increase in NPLs in the early 1980s.

Government-Financial Institutions Relationship: Fragmented Regulatory System

Although state intervention per se in the financial sector is extremely important for financial stability and development, the implementation of financial regulation in Korea was detrimental. Overlapping power among supervisory authorities and the rotation system of bureaucrats encouraged regulatory forbearance and undermined effective financial supervision.[25] From licensing to developing new financial products and opening new branches, most activities of financial institutions were subject to financial

24 Pyung Joo Kim, "Financial Institutions," in *Korea's Political Economy: An Institutional Perspective*, ed. Lee-Jay Cho and Yoon Hyung Kim (Boulder, CO: Westview Press, 1994), 305.

25 Yung Chul Park and Dong Won Kim, "Korea: Development and Structural Change of the Banking System," in *The Financial Development of Japan, Korea, and Taiwan*, ed. Hugh T. Patrick and Yung Chul Park (Oxford: Oxford University Press, 1994), 189.

regulation, which was dispersed among the MoF and the BOK. The BOK assumed supervisory authority over the banking sector until the sixth revision of the BOK Act in December 1997.[26] The MoF exercised supervisory authority over NBFIs through agencies such as the Securities Supervisory Board (SSB), the Insurance Supervisory Board (ISB), and the Non-bank Insurance Corporation (NBIC), for mutual savings and finance companies and merchant banks.

This multiplicity of the financial supervisory system had a significant negative impact on the development of the financial system. First, this dispersion of authority resulted in a lack of consistency in supervisory practices and high coordination costs among regulatory bodies. Only in 1994 could supervisory agencies request information on financial institutions under other supervisory agencies.[27] Moreover, the discrepancy between the authorities and the responsibilities of the MoF and BOK over financial supervision undermined its effectiveness.[28] For example, while the OBSE supervised commercial banks, the trust business of these banks was supervised by the MoF, which also had the authority to grant and revoke bank licenses.[29] In cases of regulatory failure, however, this overlap and opacity in the boundaries of supervisory authorities encouraged each authority to shift the focus of blame to the other.[30] Second, an informal and close relationship between the regulators and the regulatees was maintained through "parachute appointments" of retired ex-regulators in top executive positions of financial institutions. This practice—similar to *amakudari* ("descent from heaven") in Japan—was especially pervasive and entrenched

26 When the original BOK Act was passed in May 1950, the financial supervisory authority was the Bureau of Bank Supervision in the BOK. It was renamed the Office of Bank Supervision and Examination when the BOK Act was first revised in May 1962 (BOK Act on May 5, 1950; revised May 24, 1962).

27 *Chosun Ilbo* (*Chosŏn Ilbo*), "Ŭnhaeng-jŭngkwŏn-pohŏmsa kamsa wihae" [For inspection of banks, securities firms, and insurance firms], August 7, 1994.

28 Board of Audit and Inspection of Korea (BAI), *Kongjŏk chagŭm kamsa paeksŏ* [White paper for public fund inspection], 2003.

29 Donghyun Ji and Jaeha Park, "The Korean Banking Sector: Current Issues and Future Direction," in *Rising to the Challenge in Asia: A Study of Financial Markets: Vol. 7, Republic of Korea* (Manila: Asian Development Bank, 1999), 38.

30 One of the primary examples was the regulatory failure and subsequent interagency conflicts between the OBSE and ISB over responsibility for a fraudulent 47.3 billion won sale of the Military Intelligence Command site in southern Seoul in 1992. This case was called the biggest financial incident during the Roh Tae-woo administration. See *Donga Ilbo* (*Tonga Ilbo*), "Sonpal anmatnŭn ŭnkamwŏn pokamwŏn chosa" [Investigations by the OBSE and ISB do not match well], July 10, 1992.

among NBFIs and government-related financial institutions.[31] This was because financial institutions whose activities had been under the control of regulatory authorities needed ex-regulators in order to maintain a good relationship with them. Moreover, financial expertise was much less important than the personal ties of ex-regulators since interest and credit policies were under state control and most loans were extended on the basis of the value of collaterals. Many high-ranking ex-officials from the military and police services were appointed to crucial positions in financial institutions and related governmental agencies, such as the Korea Asset Management Corporation (KAMCO, Sŏngŏp kongsa).[32] Given that many NBFIs had been affiliated with chaebŏl, the "parachute appointment" practice facilitated the cozy relationship between chaebŏl and financial regulators.

Finally, the rotation system in the Korean bureaucracy made supervisory bureaucrats more susceptible to regulatory forbearance.[33] Because those bureaucrats were motivated to protect their careers by maintaining the status quo, they were likely to delay potential failures until they moved to other bureaus. In addition, this rotation system made it hard for supervisors to have sufficient capacity and information to effectively supervise the financial system.[34]

This fragmented regulatory system and close relationship between supervisors and supervisees discouraged banks and other financial institutions from enhancing their monitoring capacities and influencing corporate behavior. Rather, when supervisory authorities were fragmented and lacked capacity for prudential regulation, financial institutions relied on employing

31 Yoon-Shik Park, "Financial and Corporate Restructuring Lessons from Korea to Latin America and the Caribbean," paper prepared for the Inter-American Development Bank, April 2003, 8–9; Ji and Park, "The Korean Banking Sector," 38.

32 For example, as of November 1992, many top positions in most important government-owned financial institutions were filled by those who had no training in the financial sectors: the Credit Management Fund by an ex-police official; the Korea Development Bank by an ex-military official; the Industrial Bank of Korea by an ex-police official; the Korea Minting and Security Printing Corporation by an ex-military official; and the Housing and Commercial Bank by a former minister of justice. See Donga Ilbo, "Kŭmyungkye nakhasan insa yŏch'ŏn" [Parachute appointment practice still continues in the financial sector], November 18, 1992.

33 For different reasons of regulatory forbearance, see Jin-Wook Choi, "Regulatory Forbearance and Financial Crisis in South Korea," Asian Survey 42, no. 2 (March/April 2002), 252–55.

34 On average, Korean career bureaucrats stayed in their current positions for 3.33 years in 1989 and for 2.61 years in 1993. Those at the level of director-general (grade 2) stayed in their current positions for 4.33 years in 1989, but for 1.847 years in 1993. See Ministry of Government Administration, Kongmuwŏn t'ongkye [Statistics on public officials], 1989; 1993.

ex-regulators for market share and growth rather than on making prudent loan decisions that could change corporate behavior. This was especially evident among the NBFIs owned by *chaebŏl*.

New Challenges: Financial Liberalization and Democratization

Following gradual privatization of the NCBs in the early 1980s, there was a series of efforts toward financial liberalization, including reducing entry barriers to NBFIs and freeing interest rates in the early 1990s.[35] Although the tripartite relationship among the powerful MoF, banks with coordination and monitoring problems, and *chaebŏl* intermittently required adjustment, the state was able to distribute adjustment costs evenly across society thanks to its authoritarian regime and relatively closed financial system.

Democratization in 1987–1988 and partial capital account liberalization, however, made it increasingly difficult for the state to implement adjustments. During the early 1980s, Korea experienced continued current account deficits although their size was declining. In order to make up for the deficit, the Chun regime partially liberalized capital inflows while maintaining tight regulations on capital outflows.[36] Also, restrictions on short-term foreign borrowing were relaxed while those on long-term borrowing were maintained, later contributing to the financial crisis.[37] Capital account liberalization enabled *chaebŏl,* especially the largest ones, to raise funds independent from commercial banks and the state through their affiliate NBFIs (see Table 6.2).[38] As a consequence, the share of the 30 largest *chaebŏl* in bank loans decreased from 28.6 percent in 1986 to 18.9 percent in 1991, while their share in credit by NBFIs amounted to 43.6 percent in 1990.[39] Similarly,

35 The MoF announced its plan for a four-stage interest rate liberalization in August 1991 and implemented the first stage of the plan on November 21, 1991, the second stage in October 1993, the third stage from July 18, 1996 to November 20, 1995, and the final stage on July 7, 1997 (MoF/FEB, Press Release, various issues).

36 Wang Yunjong, "Capital Account Liberalization: The Case of Korea," unpublished manuscript, 2002.

37 Especially in 1995 government regulations on foreign borrowing were substantially reduced and the result was quick growth of foreign debt, which nearly tripled from US$44 billion in 1993 to US$120 billion in September 1997 (BOK, *Economic Statistics*). See Tomás J.T. Baliño and Angel J. Ubide, "The Korean Financial Crisis of 1997: Strategy of Financial Sector Reform," IMF Working Paper, no. 99/28 (March 1999), 22.

38 Eun Mee Kim, *Big Business, Strong State: Collusion and Conflict in South Korean Development, 1960–1990* (Albany, NY: State University of New York Press, 1997), 189; Edward M. Graham, *Reforming Korea's Industrial Conglomerates* (Washington DC: Institute for International Economics, 2003), 62–63.

39 Nam and Kim, "The Principal Transactions Bank System," 32.

TABLE 6.2

Chaebŏl *Ownership of NBFIs in Korea, 1990 (%)*

Type of Institutions	Share of Top 5	Share of Top 10	Share of Top 30
Life Insurance Companies	36.5	36.5	38.4
Marine and Casualty Insurance Companies	28.0	41.4	44.5
Securities Companies	26.3	36.5	63.1
Merchant Banks	12.8	23.3	23.3
Short-term Finance Firms (Investment Trust Companies)	7.2	10.1	29.9
Mutual Credit and Savings Banks	1.2	1.6	4.7

Source: Seong Min Yoo, "Evolution of Government-Business Interface in Korea: Progress to Date and Reform Agenda Ahead," Korea Development Institute Working Paper (November 1997), 70.

preferential finance as a proportion of total domestic credit was reduced from 47.4 to 28.1 percent between 1980–4 and 1990, showing the decreasing influence of the government on *chaebŏl*.[40] Problematic was that the NBFIs were much less interested in improving the capital structure of *chaebŏl*, not just because many of them were owned by *chaebŏl* and taken as the "private cash vaults" of the *chaebŏl*, but also because they were not adequately regulated by the supervisory authorities.[41] For instance, such operations as leasing operations and short-term lending were not subject to prudential regulation and supervision by the BOK and other supervisory authorities.

Moreover, the Roh Tae-woo (No T'ae-u, 1998–93) administration began to loosen the credit control system in 1991 to encourage specialization and streamlining of business activities by exempting major companies—up to three—of each top business group from the credit control system. This reduced the influence of banks on *chaebŏl* business activities even further. Especially in the absence of strict regulation of financial transactions among *chaebŏl* affiliate companies, this relaxation of the credit control system implied that *chaebŏl* restructuring was a mere slogan. Furthermore, as *chaebŏl* could raise funds abroad more easily due to their improved credit ratings and financial liberalization, the policy effectiveness of the credit control system dwindled. This policy shift under Roh was a clear indication of the strong influence of *chaebŏl* on financial institutions and regulatory decisions.

40 Tat Yan Kong, *The Politics of Economic Reform in South Korea: A Fragile Miracle* (London and New York: Routledge, 2000), 78.

41 Hahm, "The Government," 87; Kim, "The Politics of *Chaebol* Reform," 62.

In this context, the PTB system, originally designed to exercise corporate control, evolved into a system that consolidated banks' reliance on their business with *chaebŏl*. As *chaebŏl* enjoyed more flexibility in corporate financing, banks were increasingly concerned that their monitoring and involvement in corporate decisions would encourage *chaebŏl* to raise new funds from sources other than banks. Therefore, even if banks found *chaebŏl* activities risky, they had little choice but to finance risky projects so as not to lose their major clients. Korean banks had relied primarily on collateral to hedge against these risks. This lending practice revealed the reluctance of financial institutions to engage in corporate investment decisions. Data on banks' lending behavior indicate that Korean banks continued to rely on collateral despite increased risks and a series of financial liberalization measures in the early 1990s that required more prudence in lending.

In terms of the relationship between government and financial institutions, old practices continued even after democratization. Unlike during the military regimes under which military and police officials were the main beneficiaries of parachute appointments, the parachute appointments in financial institutions were dominated by ex-MoF (later, ex-FEB) officials. As a result, the media criticized this practice by stressing that the whole financial system had been placed under the trusteeship of the so-called Mofia (a coinage combining MoF and Mafia). For instance, the most important positions, including the governors of the BOK and supervisory agencies, were filled by ex-FEB bureaucrats. Also, as of December 1995, around 390 former FEB (including MoF) officials were re-employed at the level of the board of directors of financial institutions.[42]

The MoF (FEB) actually suggested a unified regulatory system in 1987 and introduced a bill for an integrated supervisory agency in 1995. Both efforts, however, attempted to fend off increasing pressure for BOK independence since the separation of the OBSE from the BOK would negatively impact the BOK's organizational interests and, therefore, discourage the BOK from insisting on its independence. Failing to take seriously the problems resulting from partial liberalization and short-term private loans from abroad, the rise of NBFIs, unbridled *chaebŏl* expansion, and the poor regulatory system, the MoF's suggestions could not help the Korean financial system cope with the new challenges.

---

42 *Chosun Ilbo*, "Nakhasan insaro kŭmyungkye sint'ak t'ongch'i" [Trusteeship over the financial sector by means of parachute appointments], May 1, 1996.

Aborted Financial Reform on the Eve of Crisis

During the Kim Young-sam (Kim Yŏng-sam, 1993–98) administration, the scope of the credit control system became even more limited and, consequently, the 30 largest business groups in 1993 and the 10 largest business groups in 1996 were put under the credit control system. In addition, admission to the OECD in 1996 required Korea to open up its financial market and to relax its tight regulation over capital movements in line with the OECD's Code of Liberalization of Capital Movements and Current Invisible Operations. While this opening up of the financial market made it easier for domestic firms to access cheaper capital from abroad, it also meant that domestic financial institutions had to compete with foreign institutions with less protection. This required a more enhanced financial supervisory system that could effectively reduce financial market volatility. It was in this context that Yi Sŏk-ch'ae (Lee Suk-chae), a former EPB bureaucrat and then Senior secretary to the president on economic affairs, suggested improved financial and administrative services to the corporate sector and financial reform to restore economic vitality.[43] The financial reform effort in the last year of Kim Young-sam's presidency was a crucial test of the willingness and capacity to break old practices and transform institutional arrangements among firms, financial institutions, and the state.

When Kim Young-sam announced that a financial reform committee would be created to plan sweeping reform, this plan was viewed as a Korean-style financial "Big Bang." Therefore, the Presidential Commission for Financial Reform (PCFR) was established on January 22, 1997 as an advisory committee to discuss financial reform programs.[44] Despite its pledge to plan sweeping financial reform, the PCFR was unable to see how finan-

---

43 Pak T'ae-gyun, *Kwallyo mangguk ron kwa chaebŏl sinhwa ŭi Bungkwoi* [National ruin by the bureaucracy and the collapse of the *chaebŏl* myth] (Seoul: Sallim Publishing, 1997), 157.

44 The PCFR consisted of 31 members (13 businesspersons, 9 financiers, and 9 financial specialists and professors) as well as 15 full-time economists (Joon-Ho Hahm, "Financial System Restructuring in Korea: The Crisis and its Resolution," in *East Asia's Financial Systems: Evolution and Crisis*, ed. Seiichi Masuyama, Donna Vandenbrink, and Chia Siow Yue [Tokyo and Singapore: Nomura Research Institute and Institute of Southeast Asian Studies, 1999], 109–10). Despite the effort to preempt MoF bureaucrats from exerting influence on the PCFR's decision-making, it was reported that those who had maintained a good relationship with the FEB made up a majority. See *Chosun Ilbo*, "Kŭmyung kaehyŏk wiwŏn 31 myŏng t'ŭkching" [Characteristics of 31 PCFR members], January 21, 1997, 11; *News Plus*, "Hanpo chal t'ŏjyŏtta, kwanch'i kŭmyung k'alchil" [Hanbo incident to get rid of bureaucracy-controlled finance], no. 71, February 13, 1997.

cial reform should be linked to other critical reform agendas such as M&As among banks, resolution of the NPL problem, and foreign participation in the domestic financial market. For instance, although there had been some debate on how to promote M&As among banks to change their ownership structure, including participation of *chaebŏl* in bank ownership, the M&A issue was excluded from the agenda because it was hard to predict its consequences on the financial system and the corporate sector and because there was increasing concern about the negative repercussions of M&As, such as labor unrest, on the upcoming presidential election in December.

Without tackling potentially explosive issues, the commission presented three sets of recommendations for financial reform to the president for consideration and approval.[45] In the second set of recommendations, reported to the president on June 3, 1997, the PCFR suggested the independence of the central bank and restructuring of the supervisory system. More specifically, the PCFR's main recommendations were: 1) to establish a financial watchdog committee under the direct control of the prime minister, 2) to strengthen the Monetary Board as the BOK's top policy-making body in order to enhance central bank independence, and 3) to unify supervisory authorities under the new financial watchdog. When critical issues were excluded from the reform agenda, the focus of financial reform was placed on governmental reorganization, not on more fundamental changes in the financial system. Even changes within the system proposed by PCFR, however, provoked intense debates and bureaucratic turf battles, especially between the FEB and the BOK.

In early June after a series of behind-the-scenes meetings among four top decision-makers—the finance minister, BOK governor, the senior secretary to the president on economic affairs, and PCFR chairman—financial reform bills with quite different content from the original recommendations were introduced. The final version of the bills approved by the president was regarded as being heavily influenced by the policy preferences and organizational interests of the FEB.[46] For example, according to the bills, the BOK's role would be reduced to issuing bank notes, minting coins, and some managerial functions, while the Financial Policy Office of the FEB would lose only less than one-third of its organizational resources and most of them would

45 The first and final sets of recommendations were not contentious, partly because they were too basic and vague.

46 Kim Hong-bŏm, *Han'guk kŭmyung kaep'yŏn ron* [Reforming the institutional structure of financial supervision in Korea] (Seoul: Seoul National University Press, 2006).

be transferred intact to the new supervisory agency. Furthermore, the FEB would retain authority for licensing and sanctioning as well. Despite strong resistance from the BOK and other supervisory agencies, the government decided to present the reform bills to the National Assembly, placing them in the hands of lawmakers.

The legislation process of the financial reform bills in the latter half of 1997 clearly demonstrated the inability of lawmakers to acknowledge the significance of these reforms and their reluctance to change the status quo, especially in the context of the lame-duck presidency and upcoming presidential election. While the biggest opposition party—the National Congress for New Politics (NCNP), led by Kim Dae-jung (Kim Tae-jung)—expressed its opposition to these reforms, the ruling party—the New Korea Party (NKP), led by Kim Young-sam and later Yi Hoe-ch'ang (Lee Hoi-chang)—though able to make a winning coalition with the Democratic Party, was reluctant to push forward. When the 13 financial reform bills were submitted to the 185th regular session of the National Assembly in September 1997, the opposition parties—the NCNP and ULD (United Liberal Democrats), led by Kim Chong-p'il—stood united against the idea of unifying existing supervisory bodies into a single agency. This was primarily because they feared the predictable loss of popularity in the face of fierce opposition from the BOK and other supervisory agencies. Alternatively, they proposed a consultative council to coordinate among these supervisory agencies.

Before being sent to the plenary session of the National Assembly, the financial reform bills should have been passed by the Finance and Economy Committee.[47] The role of the Finance and Economy Committee was of tremendous significance given that the decisions by the standing committees usually pass the plenary session without critical changes. One significant change made at this stage of policymaking was that the committee tried to place the new supervisory agency *under* the *FEB*, not under the Office of the Prime Minister (OPM) as proposed. The primary reason was the political interest of the individual lawmakers on this committee. If the supervisory agency were to be put under the OPM, it would be under the influence of the Government Administration Committee which has the authority to inspect the OPM and its subordinate organizations. The lawmakers of the Finance and Economy Committee made this change to continue their influence on the new supervisory agency and therefore most financial institutions. This

---

47 Among 30 committee members, those who supported the government-drafted reform bills were 17 members—from the NKP (14), Democratic Party (2), and NPP (New Party by the People) (1) and those who opposed the bills were 13 members—from the NCNP and ULD.

was not a trivial issue for lawmakers whose political power draws from the ministries they supervise in the Korean bureaucratic polity. Moreover, given the weakening party discipline and increasing uncertainty about the presidential election, the individual lawmakers' effort to secure benefits at hand seemed to be the driving force behind this decision.

As the issues became more contentious and election day approached, all political parties tried to avoid further involvement in these bills because they could potentially run counter to their election strategies. The NCNP-ULD coalition, which agreed to select a single presidential candidate, strongly opposed the bills, especially the idea of placing the new supervisory agency under the already-powerful FEB. It decided not to participate in the full session of the committee and not to vote on the bills. Forced to choose either to pass the bills unilaterally or to shelve the bills, the NKP chose not to pass the bills in fear of negative repercussions on the presidential election.[48] In addition, given the president's departure from the party, the NKP had little incentive to undertake burdensome legislative programs handed over from the lame- duck administration. Especially when the gap between the two presidential contenders was becoming narrower in most public opinion polls, it might have been politically costly to change policy positions and endorse the bills only one month before the election. Although the FEB urged the passage of the bills and argued that if they could not be passed, the FEB would be forced to ask for an IMF bailout program, the warning fell on deaf ears. No political actors dared to play for high stakes in the presidential election. On November 18, 1997 the regular session of the National Assembly closed with the passage of only three financial reform bills that were much less contentious, and the remaining bills were shelved until the next session scheduled for January 1998.

In sum, the financial reform efforts in Korea until the end of the regular session of the National Assembly were far from successful. State reorganization became *the* issue in financial reform programs while other key issues—M&As, NPL problems, and opening up of the financial market—were not on the table. Although financial reform was promoted in order to help corporate revitalization, the linkage between financial and corporate restructuring was not seriously discussed. The upcoming presidential election overwhelmed other issues, forcing key actors to view the issue of financial and corporate restructuring as electoral gains or losses.

---

48 The NKP and Democratic Party officially formed the Grand National Party (GNP) at their joint convention on November 21, 1997 and nominated Yi Hoe-ch'ang of the NKP as the presidential candidate of the new party. With the merger of the NKP and Democratic Party (DP) and joining of some independent lawmakers, the GNP became an absolute majority party, with 161 lawmakers out of 299.

Politics of Financial Reform and Corporate Restructuring

It was only after Korea officially applied for the IMF bailout program on November 21 and the new president was elected on December 18, that the three major parties—GNP, NCNP, and ULD—agreed to pass the financial reform bills by the end of 1997. Although lawmakers on the Finance and Economy Committee, especially those from the GNP, refused to compromise, they had little choice but to reluctantly accept the proposal by President-elect Kim Dae-jung (1998–2003) to place the new supervisory agency, the Financial Supervisory Commission (FSC), under the OPM. The IMF supported this proposal as well. The deadlock over the financial reform bills was finally broken with the emergence of the new presidential leadership and the growing sense of crisis and national emergency.

The need for financial reform had been recognized well before the financial crisis. However, the PCFR could not predict the extent to which this issue might become contentious and what political factors might impede putting ideas into action. More importantly, the PCFR did not understand how financial reform could be implemented in the broader institutional context. The crisis and the IMF's comprehensive plans, in this sense, made it possible, though with pains, for top policymakers to pursue financial reform in tandem with other reforms, especially corporate restructuring, and to take seriously institutional complementarities.

Corporate Restructuring: Bank-led or Not?

At the beginning of the crisis, Kim Dae-jung realized that the resolution of the corporate debt problem would be a prerequisite for the recovery of the economy. On January 13, 1998, Kim Dae-jung met top *chaebŏl* leaders and agreed upon five principles of corporate restructuring (see Table 6.3). In addition, in August 1999, he proposed three more principles that directly tackled *chaebŏl* problems, reflecting his progressive ideas. In addressing both the financial and corporate problems, Kim Dae-jung and key economic bureaucrats restructured banks and NBFIs before restructuring corporate debts. This was not only because policymakers believed that once banks could restore soundness, they would be in a position to lead corporate restructuring but also because major banks were effectively nationalized and the government could easily exploit its largest shareholder status in these banks for corporate restructuring.

With this overall plan for financial and corporate restructuring in mind, Kim Dae-jung initiated changes in the issue areas that had not been discussed seriously. On January 21, 1998, two large commercial banks—Korea First Bank and Seoul Bank—were taken over by the government. In June 1998, five

TABLE 6.3

"5 plus 3" Corporate Restructuring Principles

Five Principles (February 1998)	To improve corporate governance and enhance transparency
	To eliminate cross guarantees among affiliates
	To improve capital structures and reduce debt levels
	To concentrate on core businesses
	To strengthen the accountability of controlling shareholders and management
Three Additional Principles (August 1999)	To reduce circuitous equity ownership and unfair transactions among affiliated companies
	To sever the control of *chaebŏl* over the financial sector through the improvement of corporate governance of NBFIs
	To strengthen gift and inheritance taxation

Source: Adapted from *Joongang Ilbo*, May 16, 2001, 3.

nonviable banks—Daedong, Dongnam, Dongwha, Kyungki, and Chungchong Banks—were liquidated and merged into other NCBs.[49] M&As were no longer taboo when a merger between two major banks—Korea Commercial Bank and Hanil Bank—was announced in July 1998. NPL problems were dealt with squarely to prevent further deepening of the financial crisis. Bad assets were separated from good assets and then were transferred to KAMCO. Massive layoffs and reductions in the number of branches of financial institutions followed. These new developments demonstrated the effectiveness of financial regulation, especially when regulatory authorities had clear mandates and goals and were fully backed by strong presidential leadership.

More important was the fact that financial restructuring was pursued in the context of institutional changes in related areas: prudential regulation, insolvency reform, accounting reform, asset management corporation (KAMCO) reform, and so forth.[50] Unlike pre-crisis financial reform efforts in 1997, institutional complementarities were taken seriously. For instance, KAMCO reorganized it as a "bad bank" to purchase and liquidate NPLs from financial

49 Doowon Lee, "South Korea's Financial Crisis and Economic Restructuring," in *Korea Briefing 1997–1999: Challenges and Change at the Turn of the Century*, ed. Kongdan Oh (Armonk, NY: ME Sharpe, 2000).

50 Wonhyuk Lim and Joon-Ho Hahm, "Turning a Crisis into an Opportunity: The Political Economy of Korea's Financial Sector Reform," in *From Crisis to Opportunity: Financial Globalization and East Asian Capitalism*, ed. Jongryn Mo and Daniel I. Okimoto (Stanford, CA: Walter H. Shorenstein Asia-Pacific Research Center, 2006), 114–16; International Monetary Fund, "Republic of Korea: Economic and Policy Developments," IMF Staff Country Report, no. 00/11 (February 2000), 101; Lee Suk-jun, "Accounting Reform Gathers Momentum in Korea," *Korea's Economy 2004* (Seoul: Korea Economic Institute and Korea Institute of International Economic Policy, vol. 20, 2004).

institutions. Purchasing and liquidating NPLs properly required stricter rules on NPL classification and provisioning. Stricter NPL criteria were introduced in July 1998 while a forward-looking approach to asset classification (FLC) was adopted later in 2000 to better reflect the future performance of borrowers. Meanwhile, it would not have been possible to properly assess the financial situation of borrowers if there had not been accounting reform in May 1998, such as the establishment of accounting standards and combined financial statements. These complementary institutional changes began to be recognized as integral parts of successful financial and corporate restructuring.

Concerning corporate restructuring, corporations were divided into three groups: top five *chaebŏl,* mid-sized *chaebŏl* (6th to 64th largest *chaebŏl*), and SMEs. The top five *chaebŏl,* too large for creditor banks alone to lead restructuring, were subject to "Big Deal" and voluntary restructuring, while an out-of-court Workout program, modeled after the London Approach by the Bank of England, was used primarily for mid-sized *chaebŏl* and some large non-*chaebŏl* firms.[51] The Workout program, however, was "more intrusive than the London Approach in that the supervisory authorities played a decisive role in setting the direction of the Workout programs for individual firms."[52]

To implement the Workout programs, the Corporate Restructuring Accords (CRAs) were signed by more than 200 banks and NBFIs and expected to play a key role in corporate restructuring. Financial regulatory authorities introduced the "main creditor bank (MCB) system" based on the PTB system and adopted new selection criteria for the credit control system in order to encourage MCBs to negotiate financial restructuring agreements with their major debtor groups. However, MCBs were reluctant to take a tough approach to Workout firms for fear of endangering their prospects for meeting the requirement of the BIS ratio set by regulatory authorities. In this event, the FSC intervened and threatened Workout firms with direct inspection and credit supply on behalf of the MCBs. Despite the pledge for bank-led corporate restructuring, it was the state that resolved coordination problems and accelerated corporate restructuring.

The top five *chaebŏl* initially resisted pressure for voluntary restructuring because they had access to external funds other than from banks and

51 International Monetary Fund, "Republic of Korea"; For detailed explanation of the Workout program, see Kyung Suh Park, "Bank-led Corporate Restructuring," in *Economic Crisis and Corporate Restructuring in Korea,* ed. Haggard, Lim, and Kim.

52 Kyung Suh Park, "Bank-led Corporate Restructuring," 183; also see Eun Mee Kim (Kim Ŭn-mi), Dukjin Chang (Chang Tŏk-jin), and Mark Granovetter, *Kyŏngje wigi ŭi sahoe hak: Kaebal kukka ŭi chŏnhwan kwa kiŏp chipdan yŏngyŏl mang* [Sociology of economic crisis: Transformation of developmental state and business group networks] (Seoul: Seoul National University Press, 2005), ch. 5.

NBFIs and they delayed submitting their "Capital Structure Improvement Plans (CSIPs)." When multi-directional pressures were imposed by the government—from direct instructions to reinforcement of bank monitoring of compliance with the CSIPs and accounting guidelines—the top five *chaebŏl* started to take the CSIPs seriously. More importantly, unlike previous ineffective efforts, *chaebŏl* reform under the Kim Dae-jung administration was implemented under very different circumstances. The government had little choice but to allow even top-tier *chaebŏl* to go bankrupt. In addition, *chaebŏl* reform programs were designed to be comprehensive so that *chaebŏl* would be unable to bypass reform efforts as the "5 plus 3" corporate restructuring principles indicated.[53] By mid-1999, four top *chaebŏl* were out of serious trouble while Daewoo, the second largest *chaebŏl*, failed to implement restructuring programs, and became bankrupt in August 1999.

Mid-sized *chaebŏl*, without enough resources or access to external funds, were more responsive to bank-led corporate restructuring. There had been three approaches to restructuring: 1) restructuring under the Workout programs, 2) restructuring on the *chaebŏl's* own terms outside the Workout framework, and 3) restructuring under court protection. First, the initial Workout plans were not successful as only about 10 percent of the CSIPs signed between the MCBs and the Workout companies were implemented.[54] The FSC, therefore, decided to actively use its supervisory and regulatory power to force the MCBs to closely monitor the Workout plans and to sanction non-compliance. Second, approximately 60 affiliate companies of 13 mid-sized *chaebŏl* that were bankrupt were under court receivership. The progress of companies that had filed for court receivership was initially slow since 85 percent of these firms were still under court protection as of 1999, although *chaebŏl* such as Kia Motors was sold early and normalized their operations.[55] In general, however, corporate restructuring showed considerable progress in 2000 as debt-equity and debt-asset ratios were lowered to the level of the United States and other developed countries.[56] A comprehensive approach with enhanced prudential regulation,

53 Jongryn Mo and Chung-in Moon, "Business-Government Relations under Kim Dae-jung," in *Economic Crisis and Corporate Restructuring in Korea,* ed. Haggard, Lim, and Kim; Kim, Chang, and Granovetter, "Kyŏngje wigi ŭi sahoe hak."

54 Lee, "South Korea's Financial Crisis."

55 International Monetary Fund, "Republic of Korea," 112.

56 For example, the debt ratio (the ratio of liabilities to stockholders' equity) in the manufacturing sector was 135.4 as of the end of 2002, down from 396.3 percent in 1997, well below the level of 167.4 percent in the United States during the same period. See Bank of Korea, *Quarterly Bulletin* 35, no. 2 (June 2003): 52, table 1.

TABLE 6.4

MCBs and Selection Criteria for Major Debtor Groups, 1998–2009

	1998	1999	2000	2001	2002	2003	2004	2005	2006	2007	2008	2009
Selection Criteria	Corporations Belonging to Large Business Groups[a]		Corporations Belonging to 60 Largest Business Groups[b]		Business Groups with Debt in Excess of 0.1 percent of Total Outstanding Credits[c]							
					440 billion won	510.2 billion won	625.8 billion won	665.5 billion won	688.5 billion won	742.8 billion won	918.2 billion won	1,210.7 billion won
# of Major Debtor Groups	62[d]	57	60	60	35	29	25	29	36	42	43	45
# of Affiliate Companies	2196	2091	1834	1830	1306	1296	1340	1534	1849	2188	2562	3050
# of MCBs	11	10	9	9	8	6	6	6	6	6	6	6

Source: Financial Supervisory Service, *Podocharyo: Juch'aemugyeyŏl Sŏnchŏngkyŏlkwa* [Selection result of the major debtor groups] (annual press releases, 2000–2009).

Notes: [a] Those that have 250 billion won or more of total credit; [b] Selected on the basis of loans from banking institutions; [c] Over the previous year, but because the actual selection takes place at the end of the previous year, the "previous year" actually means two years before; [d] While 66 groups were selected, 4 groups were excluded due to the decline of total credit.

bankruptcy reform for accelerated reorganization, new accounting standards, and strengthened financial disclosure turned out to be effective in corporate restructuring.

The relationship between MCBs and firms, however, revealed the limits of bank-led corporate restructuring. As for top-tier *chaebŏl*, bank-led corporate restructuring was much less effective in the context of economic recovery than during the crisis because bankruptcies of the top *chaebŏl* would lead to bankruptcies of MCBs and derail rapid economic recovery. This was politically unacceptable. The MCBs found it suicidal to pursue aggressive *chaebŏl* restructuring. Rather, MCBs were motivated to do everything possible to save these largest *chaebŏl* from financial difficulties and bankruptcy. More importantly, not only MCBs but also state actors—the top leadership and financial regulatory agencies—realized that more bankruptcies of top-tier *chaebŏl* would be catastrophic as the whole national economy became more reliant on the top *chaebŏl* in the aftermath of the crisis. For instance, the top 30 *chaebŏl* accounted for 43.3 percent of total sales in 1998, increasing from 39.3 percent in 1996.[57] Furthermore, among the top 30 *chaebŏl*, the contribution of the top five *chaebŏl* to the national economy grew faster than that of the remaining top 25 *chaebŏl*.[58] As a result, the role of financial institutions in restructuring the top *chaebŏl* was very limited.

In addition, bank-led corporate restructuring for medium-sized *chaebŏl* had another problem with implementation. Despite the Korean government's efforts to adopt the London Approach and to strengthen the monitoring role of financial institutions in corporate governance, frequent changes in the selection criteria for the credit control system since 1998 implied that the relationship between MCBs and debtor groups had not been institutionalized enough for banks to accumulate information and develop proper risk assessment capacity. Since the financial crisis, there had been three major changes in the selection criteria, in 1998, 2000, and 2002. Because these changes did not provide stable expectations for mid-sized *chaebŏl*, the relationship between MCBs and debtor groups became unstable. A stable expectation was very important for mid-sized *chaebŏl* because groups excluded from the main debtor groups would no longer be prohibited from making mutual payment guarantees under the terms of the CSIPs. The Improvement Plan also included stipulations calling for reduced debt-for-equity ratios, restructuring of all affiliate companies, and improvements in corporate governance (see Table 6.4).

57 Mo and Moon, "Business-Government Relations."
58 Yi Yun-ho, *Chaebŏl ŭi chaemu kujo wa chagŭm chodal* [The capital structure and financing of Korean *chaebŏl*] (Seoul: Nanam Publishing, 2005), ch. 9.

Moreover, there were no clear restrictions on changes for the MCBs for debtor groups and their affiliate companies. As a result, *chaebŏl* switched their MCBs in pursuit of preferential treatment such as lower interest rates. Banks competed with one another to secure *chaebŏl* as their major clients. This lack of an institutionalized relationship combined with frequent changes of selection criteria weakened the monitoring functions of banks. More importantly, changes of MCBs and competition among them strengthened the influence of *chaebŏl* on banks.

This situation seemed to repeat past experiences in that the PTBs had been ineffective in changing corporate behavior during developmental periods. The key difference, however, was the institutional context in which corporate restructuring took place. The post-1997 corporate restructuring was facilitated by complementary reform initiatives: financial restructuring and prudential regulation, bankruptcy law reform, accounting reform, and so forth. These reform initiatives and success in the initial stage of reform, in turn, were indebted to institutional legacies that had been put in place since the developmental periods: the role of the presidency, financial regulation as a tool for achieving policy goals, and the significance of financial institutions in corporate governance. Despite these favorable conditions, bank-led, or de facto state-led, *chaebŏl* restructuring was only partially successful, and was unable to make meaningful changes in the corporate behavior of the top *chaebŏl*. On the one hand, *chaebŏl* reduced the level of the debt-to-equity ratio, adopted more transparent consolidated financial statements, discontinued inter-subsidiary debt payment guarantees, reduced cross-shareholding among affiliate companies, and so forth. On the other hand, *chaebŏl*, especially top-tier *chaebŏl*, that survived the economic crisis continued to be unaffected by financial institutions and regulatory authorities in their key corporate decisions.

Corporate Financing: Continuity and Change

To better understand the longer-term prospects for the relationship between financial institutions and firms, we need to take a look at changes and continuities in corporate financing. After the financial crisis and collapse of the TBTF myth, banks started to consider carefully the risks of loan concentration and reduced their loans to *chaebŏl*. When the banks themselves were under pressure in 1998, loans were almost zero as banks demanded that firms repay debt without providing new loans. NBFIs, once one of the primary funding sources for *chaebŏl*, were hit hard by the crisis and the number of NBFIs was substantially reduced. Among others, merchant banks were in the worst shape and two-thirds were closed. The remaining

TABLE 6.5
Share of Chaebŏl *in Bank/NBFIs Loans (Inflow, %)*

	Banks			NBFIs		
	December 1997	December 1998	June 1999	December 1997	December 1998	June 1999
Top 5 *Chaebŏl*	11.4	8.3	7.8	36.1	22.7	19.0
Top 30 *Chaebŏl*	20.0	16.5	15.1	62.1	40.3	34.9
Top 66 *Chaebŏl*	22.6	19.3	17.2	67.2	45.0	37.9
Total Bank Lending*	100.0	100.0	100.0	100.0	100.0	100.0
Total Lending (trillion won)	370	353	359	96.6	70.7	65.3

Source: IMF, "Republic of Korea: Economic and Policy Developments," IMF Country Report, no. 00/11 (February 2000), 105.

Note: *excluding guarantees.

NBFIs were burdened with a large amount of bad loans, whose share in the total outstanding loans surged up to 21.8 percent in June 1999. As NBFIs became nonviable and financial regulation over NBFIs strengthened, *chaebŏl* began to turn to their internal funds as well as to direct financing.

First, as the share of *chaebŏl* among bank lending as well as lending by NBFIs sharply decreased after the crisis (see Table 6.5), top *chaebŏl* began to increase their reliance on internal funds. Having realized the consequences of debt financing, they became more risk-averse and reluctant to continue high leverage. While internal funds had accounted for only about 30 percent of the annual inflow before 1997, half of all fund-raising came from the firms' own savings after the crisis.[59] Especially for the top five *chaebŏl,* the share of internal funds in total fund-raising was 37.2 percent on average during the period of 1987–1997 while the share increased by 31.6 percent to 68.8 percent during the period of 1997–2002.[60]

Second, direct financing had been a major source of funding for corporations since the mid-1990s and its share in corporate financing, although erratic, increased after the crisis. Especially with the stock market boom during 1998–1999, corporations had increased their reliance on the stock market. Nevertheless, when one examines the data of corporate financing in terms of balances, not flows, a significant share of corporate funds still depended on borrowing from banks. Table 6.6 and Table 6.7 show the mixed picture. While firms increasingly depended on direct financing, the amount

59 International Monetary Fund, "Republic of Korea: Selected Issues," IMF Staff Country Report, no. 02/20 (February 2002), 46–47.

60 Yi Yun-ho, *Chaebŏl ŭi chaemu kujo wa chagŭm chodal,* 201.

TABLE 6.6

Structure of Corporate Financing, 1998–2005 (Inflow, %)

	1997	1998	1999	2000	2001	2002	2003	2004	2005	2006
Indirect Finance (%)	**28**	**-7.3**	**4.1**	**17.9**	**-0.6**	**60.1**	**38.8**	**4.3**	**21.8**	**35.8**
Borrowing from Banks (%)	14	0.9	29.3	35.4	6.3	49.4	42.5	22.0	18.7	31.8
Borrowing from NBFIs (%)	13.9	-59.8	-25	-17.6	-7.3	10.3	-3.8	-17.5	3.1	3.9
Direct Finance (%)	**47.2**	**178.9**	**46.8**	**26.2**	**74.5**	**24**	**35.1**	**43.1**	**48.5**	**42.1**
Commercial Papers (%)	17.5	-42.2	-30.4	-7.2	8.7	-4.5	-5.7	-2.8	3.8	7.8
Corporate Bonds (%)	17.9	165.9	-5.3	-3.1	22.6	-9.4	-2.5	2.6	11.5	13.4
Stocks (%)*	10.9	48.9	77.6	31.6	32	34.5	35.9	43.6	32.6	20.5
Foreign Borrowing (%)	**10.4**	**-35.5**	**24.1**	**25.6**	**1.2**	**2.9**	**15.2**	**12.8**	**5.2**	**3.1**
Others** (%)	14.4	13.9	25	30.4	24.9	12.9	10.9	39.7	24.5	19.0

Source: Bank of Korea Quarterly Bulletin (various years).

Notes: *Includes stocks and equities other than stocks from 2004;

**Includes commercial trade credits, borrowing from government, bill payables, reserves for retirement allowances, etc.

TABLE 6.7

Structure of Corporate Financing, 1998–2005 (In Balance, %)

	1997	1998	1999	2000	2001	2002	2003	2004	2005
Indirect Finance	**67.1**	**59.2**	**61.5**	**62.6**	**56.7**	**57.2**	**59.1**	**63.9**	**66.9**
Borrowing from Banks	29.4	32.9	41.0	45.7	45.5	50.4	54.1	59.0	61.6
Borrowing from NBFIs	37.7	26.3	20.5	16.9	11.2	6.8	5.0	4.9	5.3
Corporate Bonds	18.6	27.8	28.6	30.3	35.2	36.4	35.7	31.3	28.5
Commercial Papers	14.3	13.0	9.9	7.1	8.1	6.4	5.2	4.8	4.6
Total	483.2	440.4	417.6	441.2	438.9	494.8	525.9	490.1	550.4
(trillion won, %)	100.0	100.0	100.0	100.0	100.0	100.0	100.0	100.0	100.0
Stocks (trillion won)	3.4	14.2	41.1	14.3	12.1	9.9	11.3	8.4	6.8

Source: Sin Hyŏn-yŏl and Kim Po-sŏng, "Kiŏp ŭi oebu chagŭm chodan kyŏngno rosŏ ŭnhaeng taech'ul kwa hoesa ch'aesijang ŭi taech'aesŏ punsŏk [Bank loans and corporate bonds as corporate fund-raising], *Bank of Korea Monthly Bulletin* (January 2007), 36.

of borrowing from banks in balance still accounted for a substantial portion of corporate financing. Given the significant share of borrowing from banks, we can expect that banks will continue to play a major role in corporate governance and restructuring. However, as *chaebŏl* become more independent from loans extended by financial institutions, it is very likely that the role financial institutions play in monitoring and changing *chaebŏl* will be limited. Rather, *chaebŏl* as key corporate clients will continue to exert a strong influence on financial institutions.

Moreover, a recent change in regulation on bank ownership can reinforce this lopsided relationship between *chaebŏl* and financial institutions. Until recently, non-financial companies had been prohibited from possessing more than 4 percent of voting shares of a bank. The amendment to this regulation in July 2009, however, eased this restriction and enabled non-financial companies to own up to 9 percent of voting shares of financial holding companies.[61] In the Korean context where top *chaebŏl* could become the largest shareholders to engage in bank management, this change could further strengthen the influence of *chaebŏl* on banks.

Last but not least, it is of great significance to see if the behavioral practices of banks have changed as a result of financial reform and restructuring. As Table 6.8 indicates, the share of collateralized loans in total loans continued to be large. This was so partly because banks had not developed a risk-assessment capacity in the context of the frequent changes in their relationship with debtor groups. This might also be a rational choice for them given the steady rise of real estate prices. A sudden collapse of the real estate sector, however, would result in a massive increase in NPLs in the banking sector and possibly another shock to the financial system.

Post-crisis corporate financing shows that *chaebŏl*—especially the largest ones—depended increasingly on direct financing and internal funds, which might suggest limited corporate monitoring by financial institutions in the future. However, a large amount of corporate financing still comes from banks. On the other hand, the influence of *chaebŏl* on banks as their major clients continued to be strong, not only because the shared risks between *chaebŏl* and financial institutions were significant but also because *chaebŏl* could change their MCBs and competition among banks provided additional leverage for *chaebŏl*. In addition, the role of NBFIs in corporate financing had irreversibly declined, both in flow and balance and *chaebŏl*

61 *Maeil kyŏngje sinmun* [MK Business News], "Taekiyŏp ŭnhaengŏp chinch'ul changbyŏk k'ŭke nachachŏ" [Entry barrier to the banking sector to be lowered significantly for big business], July 23, 2009.

TABLE 6.8

Collaterals in Bank Loans, 1993–2009 (%, Trillion Won)

	1993	1995	1997	1999	2001	2003	2005	2007	2009/09
Collateral	51.4	47.8	47.7	46.2	44.4	50.5	51.2	51.0	47.4
Real estate	—	38.1	37.6	38.3	39.9	45.5	46.6	46.9	43.8
Guarantor	9.1	7.9	10.0	12.6	12.4	10.2	7.9	5.8	7.5
Credit	39.5	44.3	42.3	41.2	43.2	39.3	40.8	43.3	45.1
Total	100	100	100	100	100	100	100	100	100
Amount (trillion won)	62.5	97.2	147.8	184.2	277.9	536.3	613.9	805.0	966.9

Sources: Financial Supervisory Service, Financial Statistics Information System (http://fisis.fss.or.kr/); adapted from Kim Hyŏn-jŏng, "Oehwan wigi ihu ŭnhaeng-kiŏp kwan'gye ŭi pyŏnhwa" [The change in bank-firm relations after the financial crisis], Kŭmyung kyŏngje yŏn'gu [Financial and economic studies] (2002), 16; Kang Chong-gu, "Ŭnhaeng ŭi kŭmyung chunggae kining yakhwa wŏnin kwa chŏngch'aek kwaje" [Banks' financial intermediary role in Korea] Economic Analysis (Institute for Monetary and Economic Research of the Bank of Korea) 11, no. 3 (2005): 7.

could not raise funds with the help of their affiliate financial institutions as much as they did before the crisis. Despite these changes, the lending practices of banks show little change in the post-crisis period, suggesting that this lack of proper risk assessment will be detrimental to improved corporate monitoring.

Foreign Participation and the Ownership Structure of Financial Institutions

Despite the expectation that increasing foreign participation would contribute positively to the financial and corporate restructuring process, foreign participation has produced mixed results. Advocates of foreign participation in the domestic financial market argue that foreign ownership of financial institutions involves not only the transfer of capital but also the transfer of technology, know-how, and human capital that will enhance efficiency.[62] Moreover, it was anticipated that changes in banks' lending practices with more emphasis on monitoring corporate investment behavior would affect corporate restructuring. Table 6.9 shows that the share of foreigners in the banking sector tripled during the period of 1998–2003. Accordingly, the number of foreigners on the boards of directors especially in NCBs increased.

Recent studies, however, cast doubt on the role of foreign participation in enhancing competition and efficiency in the domestic financial system. For instance, banks with higher levels of foreign participation did show better performance in some indicators such as share of NPLs than those with lower levels of foreign participation. However, as Table 6.10 shows, it might be an exaggeration to maintain that foreign participation generally increased productivity and efficiency. Also, the lending behavior shows little change in the post-crisis period regardless of the different levels of foreign participation.

Nevertheless, increasing foreign investment and foreign ownership in the Korean financial sector had a significant influence on the relationship between firms and financial institutions. At the initial stage of financial restructuring, foreign investment was instrumental to the recapitalization of the banking sector. Investment funds—Carlyle, Newbridge Holdings, and Lone Star—purchased Koram Bank, Korea First Bank, and Korea Exchange Bank respectively, although they were primarily interested in short-term returns. Because these new foreign owners had neither the intention nor the

---

62 Bank for International Settlements, "Foreign Direct Investment in the Financial Sector of Emerging Market Economies," report submitted by a working group established by the Committee on the Global Financial System (March 2004), www.bis.org/publ/cgfs22.pdf, 10.

TABLE 6.9

Share of Foreigners in the Banking Sector (%)

	1998	1999	2000	2001	2002	2003.9
All Commercial Banks	11.7	20	25.3	24.5	24.9	38.6
NCBs	12.3	21.7	27.7	27	26.7	43.4
Regional Banks	5.7	3.6	2.2	4.3	11.5	8.8

Source: Bank of Korea, "Oeguk chabon ŭi ŭnhaeng sanŏp chinip yŏnghyang mit chŏngch'aek sisa chŏm" [The effects of foreign participation in the banking industry and policy implications], Press Release (December 19, 2003), 9.

TABLE 6.10

Comparison Among Banks With Different Levels of Foreign Participation

Level of Foreign Participation		1998	1999	2000	2001	2002	2003.9
High*	NPLs		19.9	10	4.9	2.2	2.2
Medium**	NPLs		10.3	7.1	3.2	2.5	4.3
Low***			13.6	10.1	2.7	2.4	3
High	BIS Ratio		10.7	10.1	11.6	10.6	10.6
Medium	BIS Ratio		11.6	10.6	10.2	10.4	10.8
Low			10.3	10.7	11.2	10.6	10.6
High	ROA		−1.8	−0.5	0.6	0.4	0.1
Medium	ROA		−0.9	0.4	0.7	0.8	−0.1
Low			−0.14	−1.5	0.8	0.5	0.4
High	ROE		−34.6	−13.7	15	9.8	2.5
Medium	ROE		−18.9	8.4	13.9	13.4	−1.6
Low			−21.2	−27	17.9	10.6	8.9
High	Loans to Firms	82.9	73.4	63.5	54.8	50.1	49.6
Medium	Loans to Firms	47.6	47	42.8	38.1	37.4	37.2
Low		80.6	75	69.9	58.2	54.2	55.8
High	Loans to Households	10.4	17.9	26.1	38.6	44	45.6
Medium	Loans to Households	48.8	46.2	48.1	56.2	59.9	59.4
Low		14.3	19.3	23.6	35.7	42.1	40.7

Source: Adapted from Bank of Korea, "Oeguk chabon ŭi unhaeng sanŏp chinip yŏnghyang mit chŏngch'aek sisa chŏm."

Notes: *Korea First Bank, Korea Exchange Bank, and Citibank Korea Inc. (Koram Bank);

**Hana Bank and Kookmin Bank;

***Chohung Bank, Shinhan Bank, Woori Bank, and regional banks (Pusan Bank, Daegu Bank, Kwangju Bank, Jeonbuk Bank, Kyongnam Bank, and Jeju Bank).

capacity to transfer advanced skills and know-how, they sold their shares to strategic actors such as Citibank and Standard Chartered Bank as soon as they found it profitable. Unlike foreign investors at the initial stage, the latecomers in the Korean financial sector were more interested in long-term returns. To increase profitability, they introduced new financial products and skills. A data comparison among banks with different levels of foreign participation shows that banks with a high level of foreign investment increased their loans to households much more than others. Foreign owners, without capacity to properly assess risks in lending to firms, reduced the share of corporate financing sharply over time, from 82.9 percent in 1998 to 49.6 percent in 2003, while the share of retail financing increased from 10.4 percent to 45.6 during the same period. Domestically owned banks also increased loans to households, although the change during the same period was much less.

Foreign participation did not automatically result in increasing competition and efficiency, prudent loans, and better corporate monitoring. Increased foreign actors in domestic financial markets might not be a promoter of international best practices. Rather, they might be a good adapter to the domestic financial market. Decreasing corporate loans, combined with the firms' increasing reliance on direct financing and internal funds, indicates that the impact of more foreign participation on corporate restructuring will be limited.

Post-crisis Financial Regulation

The institutional legacies from the developmental period were instrumental in the successful reform during the initial stage of financial and corporate restructuring. Despite this initial success, old practices in financial regulation continued to undermine prudential regulation. The post-crisis regulatory system primarily comprised three agencies: the MOFE as financial policy-making authority; the FSC as supervisory decision-making body; and Financial Supervisory Service (FSS) as supervisory policy implementing agency. The new dual system of the FSC and FSS was purported to define responsibilities and mandates more clearly than before and to ensure independence from bureaucratic and political interference.

Post-crisis development in the financial regulatory system shows that financial reform failed to achieve what it had promised.[63] First, the bureaucratic influence on financial supervision has increased rapidly since 1999 when the MOFE was able to change the internal structure of the FSC by enlarging the executive office that was supposed to support only the basic functions of the FSC. Originally, the Act on the Establishment of Financial Supervisory Organizations (AEFSO) stipulated that the FSC "may have a *minimum level* of public officials" for administrative purposes in its executive office prescribed by presidential decree. However, the MOFE exploited

63 Heon Joo Jung, "Financial Regulatory Reform in South Korea Then and Now," *Korea Observer* 40, no. 4 (Winter 2009).

TABLE 6.11

Changes in the Number of Staff in the Executive Office of the FSC

	April 1, 1998	May 24, 1999	Dec. 31, 1999	Feb. 14, 2001	Feb. 2, 2002	Feb. 9, 2004	Mar. 22, 2004
Total Number	19	33	61	61	70	70	70
Number of Government Officials	11	25	50	50	58	58	58

Source: Adapted from Ministry of Legislation (http://www.moleg.go.kr/), accessed on May 30, 2010.

its authority to draft bills related to financial supervision and changed rules so that the organizational structure of the FSC could be altered by presidential decree.[64] As the number of bureaucrats in the FSC increased from 11 to 58 during the period from April 1998 to February 2002, the FSC's decision-making independence became compromised. More importantly, the executive office gradually became divided into several specialized bureaus and divisions to engage in the policy-making processes of the FSC, going well beyond the original intention of the institutional designers to administratively support the FSC commissioners.

The supervisory policy-making independence of the FSC would not necessarily be compromised by enlarging the executive office (Table 6.11). In practice, however, given the lack of sufficient resources of FSC commissioners, an increase in the MOFE's influence was predictable. As long as the MOFE retained the authority to establish financial policies and therefore remained as the center of policy coordination, the FSC had to rely on the MOFE in order to achieve its policy goals. To make matters worse, frequent changes of FSC chairmen increased the power of the executive office and undermined the credibility of supervisory independence.[65]

Moreover, the rotation system among the bureaus *within the* MOFE that had undermined the capacity-building of regulators and encouraged regulatory forbearance in the pre-crisis system was transformed into the new rotation system *between* the MOFE—especially, the Financial Policy Office—and the executive office of the FSC. As of September 2005, most key positions—director-generals and directors—in the FSC were taken over

64 Kim Tae-sik and Yun Sŏk-hŏn, "T'onghap kŭmyung kamdok kigu ŭi pyŏnch'ŏn kwa hyanghu ŭi kaep'yŏn panghyang" [Changes in the integrated financial supervisory agency and the future direction for reform], *Korea Money and Finance Association Review* 10, no. 1 (2005): 210.

65 World Bank, "Financial Sector Assessment: Korea," based on the Joint IMF-World Bank Financial Sector Assessment Program (June 2003), www1.worldbank.org/finance/assets/images/Korea_FSA.pdf, 6–7.

TABLE 6.12

Reemployment of Ex-regulators in Financial Institutions, 1998–2001

	Total Retirement	Reemployed among Retired Officials[2]	Reemployed in Financial Institutions	1998	1999	2000	2001
MOFE	81	55	40 (72.7%)	11	12	8	9
FSC[1]	6	6	5 (83.3%)	—	—	3	2
FSS	40	32	25 (78.1%)	—	2	7	16
Total	127	93	70 (75.3%)	11	14	18	27

Source: An Chong-bŏm, "Kim Tae-jung chŏngbu ŭi kyŏngje kaehyŏk ŭi p'yŏngga wa kwaje" [Evaluation and the problem of economic reform under the Kim Dae-jung administration], a paper presented at the Joint Conference organized by the Korean Association of Comparative Economics and the Korea Institute for Economic Research (November 2002); adapted by the author.

Notes: [1]Those who also held positions in the FSS are calculated as being included in the FSS;

[2]Includes those who retired due to age limits, those who did not seek reemployment, and those who could not be identified.

by the MOFE's career bureaucrats. The rotation system may have increased the potential of regulatory forbearance and undermined the operational independence of the FSC. As for the rotation system *within* the FSC, during the period of 1998-2005, the average term in one position (director level and above) was less than a year, suggesting that the rotation system made it hard for FSC officials to build up supervisory and inspection capacities.

Concerning the "parachute appointment" practice, the reemployment of retiring officials in regulatory agencies—MOFE, FSC, and FSS—to financial institutions has actually increased since 1998 (see Table 6.12). As of January 2002, "parachute appointments" at the end of the Kim Dae-jung administration seemed to be no less than those under previous administrations. Given the multi-dimensional functions of this practice, the roles ex-bureaucrats play in financial institutions are important. The fact that the majority of former regulators took positions of directors (*isa*) or auditors (*kamsa*) and did not take part in key business decisions confirms that their primary role was to maintain good relationships with incumbent regulators.[66] Especially those who were employed in NBFIs played a key role in establishing a close relationship between *chaebŏl* and financial regulators given that many NBFIs were the *chaebŏl*'s affiliate companies.

Post-crisis organizational changes for financial regulation show that the MOFE was successful in continuing its influence on financial regulation and supervision. One may argue that the influence of the MOFE on the supervisory policies of the FSC can contribute to effective financial supervision

66 *Chosun Ilbo*, "Kŭmkamwŏni kŭmyungsa imwŏn yangsŏngso inka" [Is the FSS a training school for executives of financial institutions?], October 1, 2004.

given that the newly established FSC may lack sufficient power and resources. Nevertheless, the real problem was that the supervisory policies of
the FSC were heavily influenced by the MOFE, whose policy preferences for
macroeconomic stability and growth might be different from those of the
FSC and FSS for rule-based prudential regulation and supervision. When
MOFE policies were incompatible with the supervisory policies of the FSC,
the final policy choice would favor those of the MOFE because the bureaucrats of the FSC expected that they would go *back* to the MOFE in the end.

The "Credit Card Crisis" of 2003 is a primary example of how prudential regulation had been compromised with the consideration of macroeconomic purposes. In 1999, when the immediate response to the crisis showed
positive signs for recovery and the sense of urgency melted away, the Kim
Dae-jung administration began to shift to policies to stimulate domestic demand in order to counter the credit crunch and unemployment.[67] Among
many other measures, the MOFE initiated deregulatory measures to encourage credit card usage such as removing the ceiling on cash advances in May
1999, removing corporate borrowing limits, implementing a lottery system
for credit card users in 2000 to increase tax revenue, and providing tax benefits for purchases with credit cards.[68] Consequently, credit card usage increased rapidly. Korean adults had an average of 1.8 credit cards in 1999
whereas they had 4.5 credit cards in 2002.[69] This rapid increase in credit
card usage and intense competition among credit card companies resulted
in high delinquency rates: 2.4 million became delinquent in 2003 (more than
6 percent of the population over the age of 14), an increase from 0.44 million in 2000; NPLs of credit card companies in total receivables were 34.2
percent in November 2003, increasing by 23 percent within less than a year.[70]
In December 2003, the largest credit card company, LG Card, encountered a
liquidity crisis, inviting government intervention.

This crisis showed that the new financial regulatory system of the FSC
and FSS failed to execute prudential regulation over credit card companies.
More important was that even when the FSC/FSS recognized the growing

67 Hong-Bum Kim and Chung H. Lee, "Financial Reform, Institutional Interdependency, and Supervisory Failure in Postcrisis Korea," *Journal of East Asian Studies* 6, no.
3 (September–December 2006).

68 IMF, "Republic of Korea: Selected Issues," IMF Country Report, no. 03/80,
(March 2003), 55.

69 Board of Audit and Inspection of Korea, *Kŭmyung kigwan kamdok silt'ae* [Inves-
tigation into supervision over financial institutions] (July 2004), 28.

70 IMF, "Republic of Korea: 2003 Article IV Consultation," IMF Country Report,
no. 04/44 (February 2004), 9; BAI, *Kŭmyung kigwan kamdok silt'ae*, 25.

risks in the rapid increase of credit card usage and tried to impose preemp-
tive measures, they could not implement these measures due to the opposition by the MOFE, which preferred demand-stimulus and macroeconomic
achievements over financial stability and prudential regulation.[71] Only after
it became clear that another crisis might occur, the MOFE changed its
stance and provided a legal foundation for the FSC/FSS to implement re-
regulatory measures. The relationship between the MOFE and the FSC/FSS,
in the context of the MOFE's lawmaking authority and personnel networks,
became just what financial reform was intended to prevent. The failure of
the FSC/FSS to initiate prudential measures in the face of opposition by the
MOFE was a clear indicator of continuing MOFE dominance in financial
regulation, undermining the credibility of the supervisory authorities.[72]

This event casts doubt on the policy autonomy and political independence of the FSC/FSS in initiating restructuring programs and prudential
regulation. When there existed clearly-defined reform programs in the
context of IMF conditionalities, a shared sense of national urgency, and
complementary institutional changes, the financial regulatory regime could
have effectively lead corporate restructuring. As the economic situation improved, however, the tradeoff between macroeconomic goals and prudential
regulation became a matter of choice and, under the MOFE's influence, the
choice tilted away from prudential regulation.

Conclusion

Korea's financial and corporate restructuring showed that initial reform
programs were facilitated by the presence of the IMF and a shared sense of
national urgency. Institutional legacies—the role of the presidency, financial
regulation as a policy tool, state interventionism, and the role of financial institutions in corporate financing—were instrumental in initiating various
institutional changes complementary to corporate restructuring, especially
when the government could exploit the weak positions of financial institutions and domestic financial markets were not yet open to strategic foreign
investors. Despite the initial expectation that successful financial restructuring
would promote corporate restructuring, the role of monitoring and corporate
control that financial institutions were expected to play in corporate restructuring turned out to be very limited, especially in their relationship with the
top *chaebŏl*. Instead, financial institutions were influenced by the top *chaebŏl*
because they had to keep their major clients alive for their own survival. The

71 Kim and Lee, "Financial Reform," 419.
72 Jung, "Financial Regulatory Reform," 722–23.

institutional arrangements designed to strengthen corporate control of financial institutions—the PTB and MCB systems—ironically became a stumbling block to *chaebŏl* restructuring.

The unprecedented economic crisis in 1997 opened a window of opportunity for corporate restructuring, especially *chaebŏl* reform. The crisis left little choice for President-elect Kim Dae-jung but to pursue financial and corporate reform at the same time. Institutional linkages between financial and corporate restructuring were taken seriously as the IMF presented comprehensive plans to change practices in corporate governance. While the five principles imposed by the IMF became the guidelines for corporate restructuring, Kim Dae-jung went beyond IMF conditionalities on *chaebŏl* reform by adding three more principles, not only because he needed to satisfy the IMF but also because he looked at those conditionalities as an opportunity to advance his own progressive agenda.

Successful corporate restructuring required concomitant reforms in other areas such as financial restructuring, labor market flexibility, and legal infrastructure for speedy bankruptcy procedures and new accounting standards. Among others, Kim Dae-jung decided to initiate financial restructuring prior to corporate restructuring because healthy financial institutions could be in a good position to lead corporate restructuring, and because the government could exploit its largest shareholder status of effectively nationalized financial institutions for corporate restructuring. New financial regulatory agencies—the FSC and the FSS—were established to lead financial and corporate restructuring and to implement prudential regulation. The credit control system was renewed and MCBs were expected to play a crucial role in corporate restructuring. Various measures were implemented simultaneously to facilitate corporate restructuring and improve corporate governance: a lower debt-to-equity ratio, limits on cross-shareholding and inter-subsidiary debt payment guarantees, more transparent consolidated financial statements, more accountability of *chaebŏl* owners, and so forth. Initial corporate restructuring seemed to be successful as the state allowed *chaebŏl*, even the second largest *chaebŏl*, to go bankrupt and then the remaining ones showed their willingness to change their corporate governance. However, despite Kim Dae-jung's perception of institutional linkages and opportunities provided by the IMF and the shared sense of national urgency, the reform processes began to create new challenges different from those immediately after the crisis. The collapse of the TBTF myth ironically increased the influence of the remaining top *chaebŏl* on the national economy as well as on financial institutions. This was because another *chaebŏl* bankruptcy would lead to a series of bank failures and negatively contribute to a rapid recovery, which was politically unacceptable. Moreover, while firms, especially top *chaebŏl*, relied increasingly on direct financing and internal funds, the influence that financial institutions could exert on them diminished. Foreign participation in the financial market has not produced tangible outcomes in corporate governance partly because international investors are more interested in retail banking.

The inability of financial institutions and regulatory decisions to change *chaebŏl* behavior in a significant way, however, does not exclude the possibility that financial institutions and regulation can play a significant role in changing corporate behavior in the future. Bank loans still account for a substantial portion of corporate financing and have become more significant in today's context of the global financial crisis and economic recession. In addition, the advent of mega-banks and financial holding companies will be able to change the current balance of power between *chaebŏl* and financial institutions, although a recent change in 2009 that eased the restrictions on bank ownership by *chaebŏl might* reinforce this lopsided relationship. A more serious problem for financial institutions is that they have not been able to change their own lending practices, such as reliance on collateral and failing to enhance risk-assessment capacities.

When changes and continuities are taken into consideration together, the financial restructuring that had been acclaimed as one of the most successful reform programs failed to fundamentally transform the ways of doing business in financial institutions and how they are regulated. A financial system where financial institutions can exert corporate control over *chaebŏl*, not the other way around, requires another round of financial restructuring at a deeper level.

7 The Role of Foreign (Direct) Investment in Corporate Governance Reform in South Korea

Eun Mee Kim, Nahee Kang, and Ji Hyun Kim[1]

The varieties of capitalism (VoC) approach provides conceptual tools, particularly the notions of institutional "coordination" and "complementarity" to examine diversity in systems, as well as providing interesting propositions about system change, namely that path-altering (and equilibrium-breaking) system change is difficult to come by.[2] Recently, informed by economic reality that suggests that system change is not so neat, but rather murky, writers of the VoC approach have underscored elements of incoherence, contradictions, and conflict.[3]

1 An earlier draft was presented at the international conference on "System Restructuring in East Asia," jointly sponsored by the Center for East Asian Studies, Stanford University, and the East Asia Institute, Seoul, South Korea, and held at the Walter H. Shorenstein Asia-Pacific Research Center, Stanford University, Stanford, California, USA, June 22–24, 2006. The authors would like to thank Byung-Kook Kim and Jean Oi for their helpful comments made since the planning stage of the paper. Eun Mee Kim acknowledges support by the WCU (World Class University) program through the Ministry of Education, Science and Technology (Grant number: R32-20077). Nahee Kang would also like to thank both the Economic and Social Research Council (ESRC) and the International Centre for Corporate Social Responsibility (ICCSR), Nottingham University Business School in the UK for sponsoring her research.
2 Peter A. Hall and David W. Soskice, "Introduction to Varieties of Capitalism," in *Varieties of Capitalism*, ed. Peter A. Hall and David W. Soskice (Oxford: Oxford University Press, 2001); Wolfgang Streeck and Kathleen Ann Thelen, eds., *Beyond Continuity: Institutional Change in Advanced Political Economies* (Oxford: Oxford University Press, 2005).
3 Bob Hancké, Martin Rhodes, and Mark Thatcher, eds., *Beyond Varieties of Capitalism: Conflict, Contradictions, and Complementarities in the European Economy* (Oxford: Oxford University Press, 2007).

South Korean capitalism from the 1980s to the present supports the latter view. The South Korean economy, since the beginning of its rapid development in the 1960s and through the 1970s, demonstrated strong state-led coordination, which involved exercising tight control and management of foreign investment, contributing to its economic success. However, growing incoherence and conflict began to materialize since the 1980s, ultimately leading to the Asian financial crisis of 1997.

In the post–Asian financial crisis period, using foreign investors as agents of change, the state—i.e., the dominant actor in the South Korean political economy—attempted to initiate corporate sector reform, which had been politically difficult to push through in the past. The Asian financial crisis in 1997 proved to be a historically contingent and politically opportune moment when path-altering change could be initiated. And foreign direct investment (FDI)-driven corporate governance reform can be seen as an attempt by the South Korean state to do just that.

The emergence of foreign investors as a new economic actor, along with the state, local capital (*chaebŏl*),[4] and, increasingly, nongovernmental organizations (NGOs) in what has traditionally been a nationalistic economy, has meant the re-shaping of interests and re-making of coalitions to both defend and challenge the existing system. While the outcomes of FDI-driven corporate governance reform are likely to be dependent on the playing out of such "politics" between reformers and defenders of the status quo, the active presence of FDI suggests that South Korea is experiencing path-altering and equilibrium-breaking system change.[5] Before we investigate the role of FDI in corporate governance reform in South Korea, we will examine FDI regimes since the 1960s, dividing the period into three different phases according to the government's stance toward FDI. In the next section, we begin by describing the FDI regime in the 1960s and 1970s. Then we examine the role of FDI in corporate governance reform during the pre– and post–Asian financial crisis. Since the Asian financial crisis presented an opportunity for possible path-altering and equilibrium-breaking system change, we compare the pre– and post–Asian financial crisis periods in terms of the effect of FDI

4 Business conglomerates in South Korea, which started out as family-owned and -managed businesses. They are noted for their collusive ties with the South Korean government during the 1960s–1970s, top-down management based on strong paternal chairmen, and diversified businesses. See Eun Mee Kim, *Big Business, Strong State: Collusion and Conflict in South Korean Development, 1960–1990* (Albany: State University of New York Press, 1997).

5 Andrew Walter, *Governing Finance: East Asia's Adoption of International Standards* (Ithaca, NY: Cornell University Press, 2008).

on corporate governance reform in the broader private sector as well as in a few cases where foreign capital was introduced.

During the post–Asian financial crisis period, our focus is on the claim that in the initial stage of drafting the post-crisis corporate reform agenda by the South Korean government, an important role was prescribed to FDI as an agent of change. We analyze the outcome of FDI-driven corporate governance reform, highlighting aspects of both change and resilience as well as key public policy debates surrounding the role of FDI in the corporate sector, which were voiced by a few NGOs and civil society. While a common focus with regard to FDI has been on the merits and demerits of FDI in terms of economic benefits and costs, we investigate a less tangible aspect of FDI; that is, the spill-over effect of FDI on management practices of corporate governance. Taking a political economy approach, we examine how the introduction of a new economic actor—i.e., foreign investors— in a traditionally "nationalistic" environment can possibly bring about a fundamental change in the economic system. We also note the growing role played by NGOs, which since the democratization in the late 1980s have assumed the role of watchdogs for many *chaebŏl* and their questionable business activities. They began to monitor foreign capital with a watchful eye, some with a nationalist sentiment and others with the hope that foreign capital may enforce transparent management practices in the South Korean *chaebŏl*. Finally, we conclude with a summary in the final section.

Foreign Direct Investment Regimes in South Korea

During South Korea's rapid economic development in the 1960s–1980s, foreign investment was not very significant and thus did not receive much attention. As Figure 7.1 shows, the amount of FDI was insignificant until the Asian financial crisis (1997–1998).

Figure 7.1 shows that FDI inflows to South Korea peaked in the immediate aftermath of the Asian financial crisis in 1999–2000 and again in 2004, but has dropped significantly since then. The most recent figure is for 2009, which stands at US$1,506 million.

Table 7.1, which shows FDI inflows to the Asia-Pacific countries, attests to the rather small FDI inflows to South Korea vis-à-vis its Asian and Pacific neighbors. The share of FDI in GDP shows a sharp contrast with the other nations in the region. Even in 1999 and 2000, during which FDI to South Korea reached its highest level in absolute amounts, the FDI/GDP ratio was only 2.1 percent and 1.7 percent respectively, far behind the average FDI/GDP ratio of the other nations in the region, where economic development was far more FDI-led.

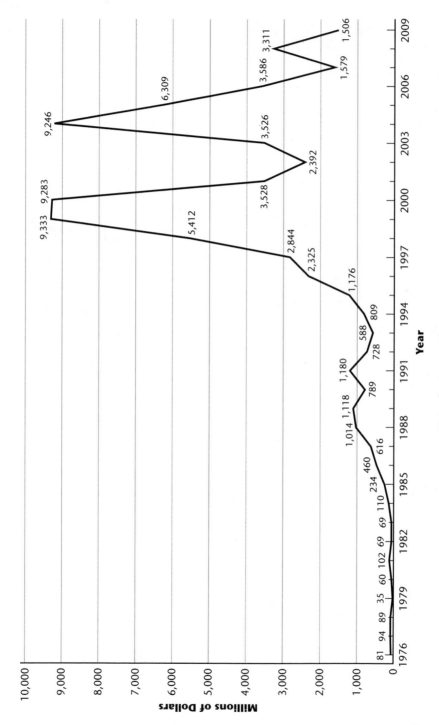

FIGURE 7.1 FDI inflows to South Korea, 1976–2009

Source: World Bank, www.worldbank.org.

TABLE 7.1

FDI Inflows and Shares of GDP in the Asian-Pacific Countries, 1990–2009
(Unit: Million $, Current USD)

	World		Korea		Australia		New Zealand		Malaysia		Singapore		Thailand	
	FDI	FDI/GDP	FDI	FDI/GDP	FDI	FDI/GDP	FDI	FDI/GDP	FDI	FDI/GDP	FDI	FDI/GDP	FDI	FDI/GDP
1990	204,494	0.9%	789	0.3%	8,111	2.7%	1,735	3.9%	2,332	5.3%	5,575	15.1%	2,444	2.9%
1991	157,355	0.7%	1,180	0.4%	4,312	1.3%	1,290	3.1%	3,998	8.1%	4,887	11.3%	2,014	2.1%
1992	167,853	0.7%	728	0.2%	5,699	1.8%	1,934	4.8%	5,183	8.8%	2,204	4.4%	2,113	1.9%
1993	220,234	0.9%	588	0.2%	4,318	1.4%	2,396	5.3%	5,006	7.5%	4,686	8.1%	1,804	1.4%
1994	248,393	0.9%	809	0.2%	5,001	1.6%	2,496	4.6%	4,342	5.8%	8,550	12.1%	1,366	0.9%
1995	328,380	1.1%	1,776	0.3%	12,026	3.3%	3,316	5.3%	4,178	4.7%	11,535	13.7%	2,068	1.2%
1996	373,934	1.2%	2,325	0.4%	6,181	1.6%	2,338	3.4%	5,078	5.0%	9,682	10.5%	2,336	1.3%
1997	468,216	1.6%	2,844	0.6%	7,631	1.8%	2,467	3.9%	5,137	5.1%	13,753	14.3%	3,895	2.6%
1998	696,466	2.3%	5,412	1.6%	5,957	1.5%	1,283	2.4%	2,163	3.0%	7,314	8.9%	7,315	6.5%
1999	1,094,494	3.5%	9,333	2.1%	3,311	0.9%	1,146	2.0%	3,895	4.9%	16,578	20.1%	6,103	5.0%
2000	1,518,702	4.7%	9,283	1.7%	13,618	3.4%	3,910	7.7%	3,788	4.0%	16,484	17.8%	3,366	2.7%
2001	794,780	2.5%	3,528	0.7%	8,261	2.2%	-68	-0.1%	554	0.6%	15,621	18.2%	5,061	4.4%
2002	737,539	2.2%	2,392	0.4%	16,992	4.4%	1,667	2.6%	3,203	3.2%	7,200	8.2%	3,335	2.6%
2003	641,571	1.7%	3,526	0.5%	8,024	1.8%	2,475	2.9%	2,473	2.2%	11,664	12.5%	5,235	3.7%
2004	751,652	1.8%	9,246	1.3%	36,827	6.2%	2,478	2.5%	4,624	3.7%	19,828	18.1%	5,860	3.6%
2005	1,116,371	2.5%	6,309	0.7%	-35,601	-5.3%	1,504	1.4%	3,966	2.9%	13,930	11.5%	8,055	4.8%
2006	1,457,091	3.0%	3,586	0.4%	26,415	3.6%	8,013	7.4%	6,064	3.9%	24,743	17.8%	9,004	4.5%
2007	2,139,338	3.9%	1,579	0.2%	39,596	4.8%	2,753	2.0%	8,456	4.5%	24,137	14.5%	9,498	4.0%
2008	1,826,910	3.0%	3,310	0.4%	47,281	4.5%	5,466	4.7%	7,376	3.3%	10,912	5.6%	8,570	3.1%
2009	1,116,270	1.9%	1,506	0.2%	—	—	4,701	0.4%	1,609	0.4%	16,809	9.2%	5,956	2.3%

Source: World Bank, www.worldbank.org.

TABLE 7.2

FDI Regimes and Key Elements of Change in South Korea

	Pre–Asian Financial Crisis		Post–Asian Financial Crisis
	1960–1983 Restrictive FDI Regime	1984–1997 Limited Liberalization of FDI Regime	1998–present Active Promotion of FDI Regime
State-Market Characteristics	Developmental state; market closed to FDI	Selective openness to foreign capital	Fully open to FDI
Major Types of Foreign Capital	Commercial loans / Aid	Commercial loans / FDI	FDI (esp., M&As in the post–Asian financial crisis)
Key Institutions	EPB, MoF, MOC/Ministry of Power and Resources	MoF, EPB, MOC	MOFE, PSPD, MOCIE, AS, IMF, FSS
Key Laws	Foreign Capital Inducement Law promulgated (1960)	Foreign Investment Promotion Act promulgated (1984)	Foreign Investment Promotion Act revised (1998)
Major Policy Direction	Foreign aid and loans rather than FDI	Foreign investment liberalization (5-Year Plan); friendly cross-border M&A allowed	Hostile cross-border M&As allowed; most restrictions on foreign land ownership ended
FDI and Corporate Governance	N/A	FDI reinforces the existing corporate governance system	FDI as agent of corporate governance reform

Source: Author.

Given the most recent global financial crisis since 2008, we do not expect to see any large jump in FDI to South Korea in that period either. While the reasons why South Korea lost its attractiveness as a FDI inducement site are debatable,[6] what is clear is that the influx of FDI to South Korea in the immediate aftermath of the Asian financial crisis was rather short-lived.

The VoC literature argues that institutional complementarity and coordination are important in understanding changes in the economy.[7] Key institutions for corporate governance reform in South Korea and their respective positions in three different FDI regimes are summarized in Table 7.2. The South Korean government has taken on different positions regarding FDI since the 1960s depending on the national development agenda, availability of different forms of foreign capital, and state and market dynamics. The South Korean economy in the pre–Asian financial crisis period can be classified as a Restrictive FDI Regime (1960–1983) and a Limited Liberalization of FDI Regime (1984–1997). In the post–Asian financial crisis period, it has been an Active Promotion of FDI Regime (1998-present). In terms of key actors, it is important to note that in the pre-crisis period, they were mainly government offices (ministries), while those in the post-crisis period included the IMF (international actor) and NGOs, along with government offices. This suggests a significant and systemic change in the FDI regime in South Korea that could potentially affect not only corporate governance reform, but also the economy as a whole.

Restrictive FDI Regime (1960–1983)

Those familiar with the South Korean political economy would be keen to point to the strong presence of the state as a key characteristic, particularly in the 1960s and 1970s.[8] In the developmental era that began with General Park Chung-hee's (Pak Chŏng-hŭi, 1961–79) rise to power, the authoritarian state subordinated all economic actors to its industrial policy.

6 Oh Yul Kwon, "Foreign Direct Investment in Korea: A Foreign Perspective," Korean Economic Research Institute, Major Research Paper, no. 2003–14 (2003).

7 Peter A. Hall and David W. Soskice, eds., *Varieties of Capitalism: The Institutional Foundations of Comparative Advantage* (New York: Oxford University Press, 2001); Bruno Amable, *The Diversity of Modern Capitalism* (Oxford: Oxford University Press, 2003).

8 Alice Amsden, *Asia's Next Giant: South Korea and Late Industrialization* (Oxford: Oxford University Press, 1989); Peter B. Evans, *The Embedded Autonomy: States and Industrial Transformation* (Princeton, NJ: Princeton University Press, 1995); Robert Wade, *Governing the Market: Economic Theory and the Role of Government in East Asian Industrialization* (Princeton, NJ: Princeton University Press, 1992).

This entailed gearing all scarce resources toward fostering the selected few local businesses—some of which later became *chaebŏl*—as "national champions." The economic reasoning behind the state's industrial policy is most simply encapsulated by the Gerschenkronian "infant industry" argument.[9]

In the 1960s–1970s, foreign investors were welcomed in the light-manufacturing export sector, especially in the two Free Export Zones at Masan and Iri (now Iksan) established in 1970 and 1974, respectively. However, the general position of the South Korean government was to keep FDI to a minimum.[10] FDI was heavily controlled and used only in cases where technology transfer was needed, and was allowed only in the form of a joint venture with local capital. This anti-FDI stance was based on the South Korean government's desire to take control of the available capital resources (both domestic and foreign) stemming from fear of foreign domination. Even in light industries where FDI was generally welcomed, performance requirements such as export or technology transfer requirements were imposed to raise foreign exchange earnings and induce absorptive capabilities to acquire advanced technology.[11] At the same time, foreign investors did not find South Korean firms to be particularly good investment sites due to political instability and lack of strong investment determinants such as a large market, low-cost raw materials, and accessibility.

In the absence of FDI, the South Korean government relied partly on domestic resource mobilization and foreign aid, which was available after the Korean War for postwar reconstruction. The South Korean government also actively utilized foreign capital loans, which were provided through the government.[12] Thus, foreign capital—i.e., aid and loans—"behaved" more like domestic capital rather than foreign investment.[13]

9 Ha-Joon Chang, *The Political Economy of Industrial Policy* (New York: St. Martin's, 1994); Hang-Sup Shin and Ha-Joon Chang, *Restructuring "Korea Inc.": Financial Crisis, Corporate Reform, and Institutional Transition* (New York: Routledge Curzon, 2003).

10 June-Dong Kim, "Impact of Foreign Direct Investment Liberalization: The Case of Korea," Korea Institute for International Economic Policy (KIEP) Working Paper, no. 97-01 (August 1997), 9.

11 Ibid., 9–10

12 Jung-en Woo, *Race to the Swift: State and Finance in Korean Industrialization* (New York: Columbia University Press, 1991).

13 Jeff Frieden, "Third World Indebted Industrialization: International Finance and State Capitalism in Mexico, Brazil, Argentina, and South Korea." *International Organization* 35, no. 3 (1981): 407–31; Kim, *Big Business, Strong State*; Barbara Stallings, "The Role of Foreign Capital in Economic Development," in *Manufacturing Miracles: Paths of Industrialization in Latin America and East Asia*, ed. Gary Gereffi and Donald L. Wyman (Princeton, NJ: Princeton University Press, 1990), 55–89.

Limited Liberalization of the FDI Regime (1984–1997)

Due to successful economic development during the 1960s and 1970s, which was unprecedented in world history except in a few other East Asian nations, South Korea became a target of challenges for economic liberalization by the early 1980s. The United States in particular led tough trade negotiations in Japan, South Korea, and Taiwan in the 1980s, requesting that each of these export-oriented nations, which had major trade surpluses with the United States, liberalize their economies. The political situation in South Korea had changed as well with the new Chun Doo-hwan (Chŏn Tu-hwan, 1979–88) regime coming to power in 1979 after the assassination of President Park Chung-hee (Pak Chŏng-hŭi, 1961–79) who had led South Korea during the developmental era of the 1960s–1970s. The new Chun administration sought economic policies different from its predecessor at the urging of its pro-market technocrats within the economic ministries, U.S. pressure, and also the *chaebŏl*-led business community. The latter expressed its collective opinion through the Federation of Korean Industries (FKI), which was composed of the CEOs of large enterprises. The FKI demanded that the government be less involved in industrial policy and planning.[14] Thus, the South Korean government decided to pursue economic liberalization measures in the 1980s due to a confluence of external as well as domestic pressures.

Policies on foreign capital and FDI were revised accordingly during this period to allow for liberalization of FDI. The new Foreign Investment Promotion Act was announced in 1983 and promulgated in 1984, followed by the Guideline for Foreign Direct Investment, which was also implemented in 1984. The Foreign Investment Law was again revised in 1987 to remove most of the restrictions regarding sectors previously closed to foreign direct investment, as well as the amount of investment allowed.[15] The two notable revisions were: 1) the lowering of the minimum amount allowed for FDI, and 2) the replacement of a positive list for sectors and industries eligible for FDI by a negative list.[16] As a result, the share of manufacturing industries that became open to FDI rose to 92.5 percent.[17] In addition, import were

---

14 Kim, *Big Business, Strong State.*

15 Ibid., 181.

16 A positive list is a much more restrictive system than a negative list. The former designates a small number of sectors that are open to FDI, while the latter designates only a small number of sectors that are closed to FDI, with all the others sectors open to FDI.

17 Economic Planning Board (EPB), "Analysis of Economic Policies of the 1980s" (Seoul, 1986).

further liberalized and tariff rates were reduced. The share of foreign banks in the lending market rose from 4 percent in 1975 to 12.9 percent in 1984 after the South Korean government announced a plan in 1981 to open its capital market to foreigners.[18] All of these changes since the early 1980s signaled an important change in the South Korean government's stance toward foreign capital, and in particular FDI.

The next stage of FDI liberalization came in the 1990s when President Kim Young-sam (Kim Yŏng-sam, 1993–98) introduced the New Economy Plan. Requirements including export quotas and technology transfer were abandoned, and a notification system replaced the approval system for FDI.[19] In accordance with the financial liberalization plan, limits on foreign ownership were removed in 1992 and in the mid-1990s, a one-stop service system for foreign investors was implemented. All of these measures helped the South Korean economy to become more receptive toward FDI.

With OECD membership in 1996, the South Korean government once again realigned its FDI regime with international norms and standards by amending the Foreign Capital Inducement Act to the Act on Foreign Direct Investment and Foreign Capital Inducement. The concept of FDI was expanded to encompass long-term loans of five years or more. Also in early 1997, foreign investors were allowed to pursue "friendly" mergers and acquisitions (M&As), which were defined as having the consent of the board of directors of the targeted company. Although the FDI liberalization ratio was constantly rising during the 1980s, and had risen to 97.7 percent in industrial sectors by December 1996,[20] the South Korean government's basic stance on FDI remained passive with little interest in removing various hidden impediments or aggressively promoting FDI.[21]

While liberalization policies were adopted by the South Korean government, they did not signal a profound change in the economy. For instance, there were no powerful foreign actors in what was still a very nationalistic political economy. From the viewpoint of foreign investors, implicit barriers to entry persisted in the form of a heavily regulated business environment and business practices that were often not very transparent. More importantly, despite liberalizing measures, the government did not actively solicit

18 Kim, *Big Business, Strong State*, 181.

19 Kyung Suh Park, "Bank-Led Corporate Restructuring," in *Economic Crisis and Corporate Restructuring in Korea: Reforming the Chaebol*, ed. Stephan Haggard, Wonhyuk Lim, and Euysung Kim (Cambridge: Cambridge University Press, 2003), 6.

20 Il Sagong, *Segye Sogui Hanguk Gyeongje* [The Korean economy in the world] (Seoul: Kimyoungsa, 1993), 116.

21 Kim, "Impact of Foreign Direct Investment Liberalization," 11.

FDI and still controlled foreign investment—in particular, greenfield investments where a foreign company enters another country to establish new operations—through a competition policy that was designed to complement
and even prolong the state-bank large-firms' "nationalistic" development.
The South Korean way of doing business—especially lack of transparency in
management—did not change in spite of the liberalization measures.

Nevertheless, as a result of the government's partial openness to FDI,
there was a rapid influx of FDI, as can be seen in Figure 7.1. FDI increased
from the late 1980s and quite dramatically since the mid-1990s. Yet the South
Korean government was not properly equipped to deal with this sudden and
rapid rise of FDI. Many argued that "under-regulated" FDI and short-term
foreign capital loans since the mid-1990s caused the Asian financial crisis to
run havoc in the South Korean economy.[22] In the arguments of the VoC perspective, there was a serious inconsistency and institutional incompatibility
that made South Korea vulnerable to the Asian financial crisis.[23]

Active Promotion of the FDI Regime (1998–present)

Although the massive exit of short-term foreign capital loans was seen as
a crucial symptom and cause of the Asian financial crisis, the South Korean
government decided that it was imperative to more fully and quickly liberalize the South Korean economy and induce FDI to help with its depleting
foreign exchange reserves. The Kim Dae-jung (Kim Tae-jung, 1998–2003)
government actively sought FDI, with President Kim himself leading the
crusade to solicit FDI. Although there was some public sentiment that the
South Korean government was selling out to foreign interests, the government appeared to have little choice but to attract FDI in order to salvage
the South Korean economy. Thus, gradual liberalization, which was pursued
in the earlier regimes, was replaced with fast and full liberalization after
the Asian financial crisis. The South Korean government revised the Foreign
Investment Promotion Act in September 1998, and switched its emphasis from "limited inducement" to "active inducement" of FDI.[24] The IMF,

22 Joon-Ho Hahm, "The Government, the *Chaebol* and the Financial Institutions
before the Economic Crisis," in *Economic Crisis and Corporate Restructuring in Korea*,
ed. Haggard, Lim, and Kim.

23 Nahee Kang, "Globalisation and Institutional Change in the State-Led Model:
The Case of Corporate Governance in South Korea," *New Political Economy* 15, no. 4
(2010).

24 Ministry of Strategy and Finance, "Oeguginjikjjeoptuja-ga Hwalbalhan Gukkaui Jiwonsarye-wa Uri-ui Jeongchaekbanghyang" [Policies of FDI-friendly countries and
Korea's policy direction], press release, November 30, 2001.

which was brought in to provide structural adjustment loans to rescue the South Korean economy from going bankrupt, also requested that the South Korean government undertake major reforms in the wide-ranging areas of financial system, corporate governance, labor relations, and the public sector.

Aggressive FDI Inducement (1998–2001)   In accordance with IMF requirements, the South Korean government took various measures to improve the climate for FDI inflows. The new Foreign Investment Promotion Act of 1998 guaranteed profit repatriations for foreign investors and provided various tax incentives. The government opened more industries and sectors to FDI, so that by 2001, nearly all sectors of the economy (99.8 percent to be exact) were open to FDI. The government reduced the processing time for FDI by streamlining the complicated and lengthy procedures with the introduction of the Comprehensive Processing System and the Automatic Approval System. Under the new system, the Korea Trade-Investment Promotion Agency (KOTRA) became a one-stop service institution for foreign investors.

Of the many regulatory changes in this period, the most important was that hostile M&As were allowed in 1998.[25] Foreign investors were allowed to purchase 100 percent of the targeted company's outstanding stock without the consent of its board of directors. In the past, any investor who intended to purchase 25 percent or more of a publicly-traded company's shares was obliged to make a tender offer bid to hold more than 50 percent of the firm's shares. The government abolished this to enable smoother M&A transactions between foreign and domestic companies, and introduced a corporate divestiture system to promote split-ups and to restructure business sectors within a corporation.

Reservations about FDI (2002–present)   However, as FDI flooded in immediately after the Asian financial crisis, there was a growing concern about some negative side effects of FDI on the South Korean economy. The public perceived that foreign capital does not behave like domestic capital in that the latter would put long-term national interests above short-term profits. This, of course, was not necessarily true given that many South Korean firms were investing abroad in China since the mid-1990s, not only to gain access to the large Chinese market, but most importantly to reduce their production costs with lower wages and other resources.[26] Nevertheless, this

25 KPMG Consulting, *Foreign Direct Investment in Korea*: A Summary Report (Seoul, 2001), 12–18.

26 Korea Export-Import Bank (EXIM), *Overseas Direct Investment Statistics Yearbook* (Seoul, various years).

perception, fueled by a sense of economic nationalism, made the public's mood more ambivalent, and sometimes outwardly hostile, toward FDI once the threat of national bankruptcy abated.

Reflecting such a sentiment, and wary of intensified competition as FDI entered the market, the FKI published a report warning about the detrimental effects of FDI.[27] In this report, the FKI highlighted a number of the following facts as a means of boosting support for protection of the ownership structure and managerial rights of domestic firms:

- Amid a rapid rise in inflow of foreign speculative funds into Asian markets, the imbalance between hostile M&A attacks and means of defense has threatened managerial rights of domestic enterprises. Of 604 listed companies, 58 blue-chip companies in which foreign shareholders hold a bigger stake than the largest shareholder are exposed to the possibility of hostile M&As.
- On the other hand, those facing lesser risks of hostile M&As with the largest shareholder's stake exceeding one-third of the total equity account for just 9.4 percent of the total listed companies.
- At present, the nation's M&A system is designed to favor attackers like the U.S.-style M&A system.

Accordingly, the FKI recommended that the government needed to introduce regulatory measures to protect the ownership structure and managerial rights, including the revival of a European-style mandatory offer system, which allows protection of minority shareholders and defense of managerial rights simultaneously, and the issuance of stocks with differential voting rights. Similarly, National Assembly members introduced new legislation, including that designed to restrict hostile M&As and to minimize transfer of core (local) technology to foreign companies.

With regard to hostile M&As, in 2006 Carl Icahn and hedge fund Steel Partners offered to the board of Korea Tobacco and Ginseng Corporation (KT&G) to buy the company, in what would have been the first unsolicited foreign takeover bid for a major South Korean firm. KT&G sought various measures to fend off the bid, including the involvement of Woori Financial Group and the Industrial Bank of Korea, to protect the ownership and control of the firm against such a hostile takeover through costly

27 The Federation of Korean Industries, *Haeoe Tugijabon Yuip Jeungga-e ttareun Jeokttaejeok M&A Wihyeop mit Daeeungbanghyang* [Threats of hostile M&As in the wake of an increase in inflows of foreign speculative funds and its countermeasures] (Seoul, 2006).

cross-shareholding arrangements.[28] The government sought to introduce a "poison pill" clause into commercial laws to help free up capital for corporations fending off hostile takeover bids.

FDI, NGOs, and Corporate Governance Reform since the Asian Financial Crisis

The Role of FDI in Corporate Governance Reform

In the last ten years, most industrialized economies have embarked on programs of corporate governance reform as an integral part of corporate restructuring, with developing countries following suit in more recent years.[29] Corporate governance—broadly defined as the problem of how firms are governed and managed—is a central issue for firms and for national competitiveness, and much attention has been given to the topic.[30] For this reason, and particularly in light of the fact that mismanagement by the top owners and managers of the *chaebŏl* was viewed to be a root cause of the crisis, in the post–Asian financial crisis period, South Korea's corporate restructuring has become synonymous with improving corporate governance, and thus has been an integral part of the economic adjustment.

In the comparative political economy tradition, the VoC literature has shown a keen interest in corporate governance, as corporate governance lies at the heart of how countries organize their political economies and why countries perform differently. An aspect of corporate governance that has received much attention is the relationship between two stakeholders, namely the external providers of finance and top management. According to the VoC perspective, pressures stemming from internationalization of finance, where developments have recently been dramatic, if not unprecedented, have shifted our attention to foreign investors as agents of change.

International flows of capital have grown exponentially over the past two decades, raising levels of both direct and portfolio investments.[31] Here, the

---

28 It is estimated that listed companies in South Korea held shares worth a combined 64 trillion won (US$54.8 billion) as of the end of January 2009 to defend their ownership and management (*Korea Times*, "Legalization of Poison Pill Planned in 2010," November 9, 2009).

29 Thankom Gopinash Arun and John Turner, eds., *Corporate Governance and Development: Reform, Financial Systems and Legal Frameworks* (Cheltenham, UK: Edward Elgar, 2009).

30 Peter Alexis Gourevitch and James J. Shinn, *Political Power and Corporate Control: The New Global Politics of Corporate Governance* (Princeton, NJ: Princeton University Press, 2005).

31 Hall and Soskice, *Varieties of Capitalism*, 60.

role of institutional investors, particularly those of Anglo-American origin, is considered to be vital in introducing shareholder value in corporate governance as they use both the "voice" arrangements and the threat of "exit" to impose their interests on the firm.[32] Even more important is the wave of international M&A activity that has taken place over the past decade as firms reposition themselves to take advantage of liberalized world markets. Firms are becoming increasingly attentive to the value of their shares and earnings in order to consolidate their positions in global markets through M&A contests and also to deter takeovers.[33]

An issue of much debate within VoC discussions is how "coordinated market economies" (CMEs) are managing such pressures for change. The VoC perspective views the economy as an arena in which multiple actors develop competencies by devising better ways of coordinating their endeavors with one another.[34] These developments threaten the traditional coordination practices of CMEs, where a high degree of non-market coordination exists between economic actors. In particular, the cooperative, long-term relationship between the main providers of finance (usually banks) and firms is at the heart of CMEs, e.g., Germany and Japan.[35] The growing reliance on the stock market and attentiveness to shareholders and rates of return or current profitability are likely to reduce the actors' capacity to make long-term commitments, which could engender shifts in firm management and strategy.[36] Drawing from Culpepper,[37] Hall and Soskice[38] posit that the problem facing the government or policymakers today is not so much the problem of inducing domestic economic actors to cooperate with the government, but rather one of inducing economic actors to cooperate more effectively with each other.

32 William Lazonick and Mary O'Sullivan, eds., *Corporate Governance and Sustainable Prosperity* (Basingstoke: Palgrave, 2002).

33 Hall and Soskice, *Varieties of Capitalism*, 61.

34 Ibid., 45.

35 Kozo Yamamura and Wolfgang Streeck, eds., *The End of Diversity? Prospects for German and Japanese Capitalism* (Ithaca, NY: Cornell University Press, 2003); Herbert Kitschelt and Wolfgang Streeck, eds., *Germany: Beyond the Stable State* (London: Frank Cass, 2004).

36 Christel Lane, "Institutional Transformation and System Change: Changes in the Corporate Governance of German Corporations," in *Changing Capitalisms? Internationalism, Institutional Change, and Systems of Economic Organization* ed. Glenn Morgan, Richard Whitley and Eli Moen (Oxford: Oxford University Press, 2005), 78–109.

37 Pepper Culpepper, "Rethinking Reform: The Politics of Decentralized Cooperation in France and Germany" (PhD diss., Harvard University, 1998).

38 Hall and Soskice, *Varieties of Capitalism*, 45.

The VoC literature is useful in analyzing South Korea in that it offers a framework for investigating the linkage between external investors and the firm within the broader national political economy. Somewhat different from the classic examples of CMEs, the traditional relationship between financial providers and firms in South Korea prior to mid-1980s consisted of the government actively and extensively coordinating with the two, i.e., banks and firms (or *chaebŏl*), in pursuit of "nationalistic" development.[39] Since the late 1980s, and especially after the Asian financial crisis, as a consequence of capital market liberalization, foreign investment—particularly in the form of portfolio investment—has emerged as a new actor. The insights derived from the VoC approach suggest that the growing presence of foreign investors may not be just another source of finance for firms, but may have a more profound impact on the dynamics of "state-led" coordination, and therefore the South Korean political economy. Below we examine the role of FDI in corporate governance reform within the purview of change and resilience in state-led coordination, focusing on the question of whether FDI has acted as an agent of change in the three FDI regimes in South Korea.

FDI and Corporate Governance Reform in South Korea

Corporate Governance Reform in the Restrictive FDI Regime (1960–1983)
Foreign capital, and particularly aid and foreign loans rather than FDI, played a significant role in shaping South Korean economic policies and its push toward industrialization. Approximately 22 percent of total investment during 1961–1991 was financed with foreign capital. More importantly, between 1961 and 1966, when the South Korean economy began to take off, over half of the total investment (53 percent) was financed with foreign capital. However, as discussed earlier, foreign capital in the form of aid and loans behaved more like domestic capital, with relatively little impact on corporate governance.

An example of the South Korean government's reluctance to open its economy to FDI can be best summarized in the following case. Until the late 1950s, the pharmaceutical industry in South Korea remained at a very early stage of development. Most of the production was based on herbal drugs, and the supply of modern drugs depended wholly on imports. After

---

39 In this sense, South Korea more closely resembles France than Germany and Japan (see Vivien A. Schmidt, *The Futures of European Capitalism* [Oxford: Oxford Oxford University Press, 2002]; Marco Orrù, "Dirigiste Capitalism in France and South Korea," in *The Economic Organization of East Asian Capitalism*, ed. Marco Orrù, Nicole Woolsey Biggart, and Gary Hamilton (London: Sage Publications, 1997).

the Foreign Capital Inducement Act was enacted in 1962, five joint ventures were established during the 1960s. However, due to the implicit desire of both the government and firms to maintain ownership and managerial control, technology licensing was much more preferred than joint ventures during this period.[40] The government also provided a series of policy measures to promote the local production of raw materials in the spirit of supporting an infant industry.

Thus, the total amount of FDI and its share in total investment was very small during this period, and other forms of foreign capital—i.e., aid and loans—behaved more like "domestic capital." Aid and loans were channeled through the South Korean developmental state, and the developmental state provided these funds to state-selected target industries.[41] The South Korean economy during this period was a tightly controlled and managed national economy, and foreign capital was no exception.

Corporate Governance Reform in the Limited Liberalization of FDI Regime (1984–1997)   From the mid-1980s, South Korea began to liberalize FDI due to rising pressure from trading partners, thereby opening more business categories to FDI and relaxing restrictive regulations. Also, as was discussed earlier, the FDI approval system was changed from a positive list to a negative list system, whereby FDI could readily enter any industries except for those that were specifically prohibited.

The pressure for change was both exogenous and endogenous. It came not only from foreign governments (especially the United States), but also from *chaebŏl* that wanted to take advantage of globalization and sought expansionist policies on a global scale aimed at capturing the markets of the newly emerging economies of the time. The *chaebŏl* exercised stronger influence over the banking sector in the more deregulated environment, but as the government placed a cap on bank lending to *chaebŏl*—in an attempt to deter its domination of bank lending by *chaebŏl* and to channel bank lending to more small- and medium-sized enterprises—other sources of financing needed to be explored for the kind of global expansion investments that they sought to pursue. The nonbanking financial institutions (NBFIs) accounted for a significant proportion of the credit made available to *chaebŏl*, as did high-interest short-term foreign capital loans.[42] The stock market, which was partially liberalized in the late 1980s, also gave

40 Kim, "Impact of Foreign Direct Investment Liberalization," 29.
41 Kim, *Big Business, Strong State*.
42 Hahm, "The Government."

the *chaebŏl* an alternative (direct) source of financing. Foreign institutional investors invested en masse, based on the commonly-held belief of "too big to fail," and aided by the fact that Asia was the hottest newly emerging market for investors.[43]

Nonetheless, foreign capital did not appear as a major actor given the short-term nature of the loans and stock markets, and it did not play any significant role in changing (but rather, reinforced) the existing corporate governance system. Meanwhile, the *chaebŏl* appeared to gain growing influence vis-à-vis the state, even to the point of a regulatory capture. There appeared to have been a serious inconsistency in that the state's liberalization measures toward FDI invited a rapid influx of FDI, which the *chaebŏl* used to their advantage, and yet there was an absence of corresponding and complementary regulatory measures. This was a period of incoherence as state-led coordination showed signs of weakening.

Corporate Governance Reform in the Active Promotion of FDI Regime (1998–present).

1) AGGRESSIVE FDI INDUCEMENT (1998–2001)

In the post–Asian financial crisis period, the state made a comeback, but not in the traditional sense; and this can be seen in the way the government dealt with foreign investors. The Kim government actively sought foreign investors, initially to inject more capital into firms, but also almost as a catalyst to reform the *chaebŏl*, particularly their corporate governance. In comparison, past attempts to reform the *chaebŏl* prior to 1997 had failed due to the intertwined interests between the state, banks, and *chaebŏl*.[44] And thus the foreign agent was seen as a force that could sever this link. The real question is whether foreign agents helped sever ties in order to promote corporate governance reform, or if they merely reinforced the opaque management practices of the *chaebŏl*. We suspect that it is the former, but the latter may also have occurred from time to time. While some may interpret this as an interventionist state at work again (or in the language of the VoC approach, state coordination on behalf of firms), the subtle difference is that by inviting foreign investors, the state had in fact to some extent tied its own hands because foreign investors were not like domestic actors that could be controlled, as they do not respond to the same incentives and penalties (e.g., in the case study of

43 Gourevitch and Shinn, *Political Power and Corporate Control*.
44 Byung-Kook Kim "The Politics of *Chaebol* Reform, 1980-1997," in *Economic Crisis and Corporate Restructuring in Korea*, ed. Haggard, Lim, and Kim.

KFB below where the new foreign management would not do as the state requested). As the SK Global incident demonstrates,[45] firms were faced with the task of coordinating with capital (in this case, foreign investors) through the market.

Then where is the state? Amid reforms, the state too was undergoing change, from an interventionist to a more market regulatory state.[46] Having introduced measures to attract foreign investment, it created and empowered regulatory bodies such as the Financial Supervisory Commission (FSC) with the intent of regulating foreign investment so as to deter monopolistic and speculative behavior on the part of foreign investors.

As was discussed, the Kim government carved out a greater role for FDI in post–Asian financial crisis South Korea. Policy to attract FDI became a central feature of the overall reform agenda, most immediately for balance of payment reasons, but gradually to assist with corporate governance reform. This naturally begs the question of why and how did the government go from being FDI-shy to using FDI for the purpose of corporate governance reform, particularly when foreign portfolio investment was seen to be one of the culprits of the crisis?

The very direness of the situation, not only in terms of the impending national default, but also corporate survival, coupled with the absence of domestic creditors able to take on the ailing firms, meant that FDI was an important and relatively untapped source of funds for corporate governance reform. Despite the expectation that corporate governance reform would be a "bank-led" process in a largely bank-based financial system, South Korean banks were not in a position to lead the reform since many of them were also suffering from governance problems of their own, and were faced with possible bankruptcy.[47] They themselves had to undergo restructuring according to the government-announced reform of the financial (including banking) sector in November 1997, prior to undertaking corporate restructuring.[48] For example, the financial supervisory authorities imposed BIS capital adequacy

45 See Dukjin Chang, Eun Mee Kim, and Chanwoong Park in Chapter 3 of this volume for a detailed discussion about how SK Global, a subsidiary of the SK *chaebŏl*, dealt with the M&A challenge from Sovereign Global, a multinational investment company.

46 Iain Pirie, "The New Korean State," *New Political Economy* 10 no. 1 (2005): 25–42; Il, *Segye Sogui Hanguk Gyeongje*; Kang, "Globalisation and Institutional Change in the State-Led Model."

47 Park, "Bank-Led Corporate Restructuring."

48 Ibid.

requirements and threatened to close any bank that could not meet the stringent 8 percent rule.[49] This means that banks and firms alike were pressured to rely on foreign capital to restructure.

Moreover, foreign actors were viewed to be the only viable (or relatively independent) agents for change that would sever the interwoven interests between the financial and corporate sectors. Attempted reforms of the corporate and financial sectors had proven to be politically impossible in 1995–1997.[50] Thus, after the initial shock, the government quickly began to regard the crisis as "a blessing in disguise,"[51] and the reforms were packaged as "turning crisis into opportunity."

Based on interviews with top bureaucrats and other insiders, Tiberghien[52] reveals that the government went beyond what was initially required by the IMF in the belief that in order to enact the IMF agreement, reform of the *chaebŏl* was crucial. The demands of the IMF and the U.S. Department of the Treasury (along with foreign lenders whose preferences were filtered through the U.S. Department of the Treasury and the IMF) pertained to monetary and fiscal policies, and the South Korean government accepted U.S. conditions regarding financial liberalization and market opening reforms. The clauses relating to *chaebŏl* reforms were included in the December 1997 Letters of Intent at the request of the South Korean side. As noted by Dore,[53] the use of foreign pressure by reform-minded policymakers to enforce politically difficult changes is not unusual.[54]

During the post–Asian financial crisis period, corporate restructuring involved lowering financial risks in the corporate sector, and thereby lowering the financial risks of the overall economy. This involved, in the short run, that FDI facilitate radical reduction in the corporate debt-equity ratio by providing capital to buy out business lines or assets of poorly performing

---

49 For more details, see Chapter 6 on financial liberalization by Heon Joo Jung in this volume.

50 Yves Tiberghien, "Political Mediation of Global Economic Forces: The Politics of Corporate Restructuring in Japan, France, and South Korea" (PhD diss., Stanford University, 2002); Kim, "The Politics of *Chaebol* Reform, 1980–1997."

51 Tiberghien, "Political Mediation of Global Economic Forces"; John A. Mathews, "Fashioning a New Korean Model Out of the Crisis," Japan Policy Research Institute (JPRI) Working Paper no. 46 (1998), cited in Ronald Dore, "Asian Crisis and the Future of the Japanese Model," *Cambridge Journal of Economics* 22, no. 6 (1998): 773.

52 Tiberghien, "Political Mediation of Global Economic Forces," 220.

53 Dore, "Asian Crisis and the Future of the Japanese Model," 773.

54 See Chapter 5 on state coordination in corporate restructuring by Joo-Yoon Jung in this volume.

companies, especially when capable local investors could not be found. In the long-run, expectations were that FDI would bring about corporate governance reform by introducing, and pressuring for, the adoption of international rules and practices (e.g., international accounting standards, arm's length monitoring mechanisms, etc.) aimed at enhancing transparency and accountability.

As a result, the following measures were introduced to attract FDI:

- The reform of the Securities Exchange Law eliminated ceilings on foreign equity ownership in the stock market as of May 1998;

- Restrictions on cross-border M&As were lifted in April 1997;

- The mandatory tender offer rule was abolished and merger procedures were streamlined in February 1998 to promote M&As;

- A number of pre-existing restrictions, such as the requirement that foreigners obtain board approval for ownership of more than one-third of the outstanding shares, were removed by May 1998, allowing hostile cross-border M&As;

- The Foreigner's Land Acquisition Act was amended in 1998, under which foreign land ownership was fully liberalized; and

- The Foreign Exchange Transaction Act was enacted in April 1999 to liberalize foreign exchange controls.

Responding to these regulatory changes, along with the depreciation of the South Korean won and asset values, FDI increased in 1998 and then almost doubled from 1998 to 1999, reaching more than US$10 billion on arrival basis. There was a substantial increase of FDI withdrawn in 1999, but the increase in FDI inflows compensated for the outflows. There has been a general increase in the volume of FDI inflows (albeit a decline in the share of FDI), reaching more than US$11 billion in 2006 on arrival basis. Of particular importance in the changing landscape of FDI was the emergence of new modes of FDI—namely, cross-border mergers and privatization—and that local governments became new channels for FDI.[55] The cross-border mergers and privatization became popular modes of entry, as in the general trend worldwide, and became increasingly significant in South Korea immediately after they were allowed in 1997.

55 Mikyung Yun, "Foreign Direct Investment and Corporate Restructuring After the Crisis," in *Economic Crisis and Corporate Restructuring in Korea*, ed. Haggard, Lim, and Kim, 243.

M&As by foreign firms increased after the Asian financial crisis in response to deregulation of laws restricting M&As, lower asset prices, and depreciation of the South Korean won. A plethora of acquisition opportunities emerged as distressed firms sold off parts of their business operations in the restructuring process. In many cases, rescue funds flowed in from existing foreign partners to ease liquidity constraints. Popular forms of M&As included buying out joint venture partners, existing investors expanding through acquisitions, and the creation of new establishments in collaboration with South Korean partners to acquire existing business units. In 1997, foreign acquisitions of outstanding shares amounted to approximately US$699 million, accounting for 10 percent of total FDI on notification basis. This figure increased to US$1.2 billion (or 14 percent of total FDI) in 1998 and roughly doubled to US$2.3 billion (or 15 percent of total FDI) in 1999.[56] Some of the well-known sales involving foreign investors that have changed the Korean corporate landscape include GM Daewoo (Taeu) and Renault Samsung (Samsŏng) Motors in the automobile industry, and Standard Chartered First Bank and Citibank (with its acquisition of Hanmi Bank) in the banking industry.

Another new channel for FDI has been privatization. Most foreign investment into the public sector has been in the form of portfolio investment, as the government preferred public offerings in capital markets to strategic sales. For example, Pohang (P'ohang) Iron and Steel Company (POSCO), Korea Electric Power Corporation (KEPCO), and Korea Telecom (KT)—all considered to be blue-chip companies—have issued depository receipts in international capital markets, and foreign ownership reached 51 percent, 25.8 percent, and 19.4 percent, respectively as of June 1999. These figures increased to 61.85 percent, 28.5 percent, and 48.98 percent as of 2006.[57] As of October 2010, the figures recorded 49.24 percent, 23.9 percent, and 49 percent each.

Finally, local governments have become a new channel for inducing greenfield investments, albeit less preferred than the other two modes discussed earlier. Local governments were given more freedom and financial support to attract foreign investors through local tax exemptions, land leases, or development and management of foreign investment zones. Regulatory changes that included streamlining procedures, strengthening

56 Ministry of Commerce, Industry, and Energy, "Trend Report of Foreign Direct Investment" (Seoul, 2000).

57 Mikyung Yun and Young-Ho Park, "The Role of Foreign Investment in Korean Privatization," *Journal of International Economic Policy Studies* 3, no. 2 (Summer 1999): 34.

incentives, and introducing a one-stop service for investors created a more investor-friendly environment in local areas.

The South Korean case demonstrates that foreign investors preferred M&As to any other form of entry mode, and actively participated in the FDI-welcoming environment of the post–Asian financial crisis period and sought M&As with highly indebted South Korean firms. Since 1999, however, there has been a shift in trend with greenfield investments increasing amid the general decline of FDI.

FDI was also utilized heavily in corporate sector debt reduction after the Asian financial crisis. The South Korean government mandated that the five largest *chaebŏl* reduce their debt ratios, which stood at 473 percent on average at the end of 1997, to below 200 percent by the end of 1999. And the results were overwhelmingly positive, at least on the surface, with all the targeted *chaebŏl* reducing their debt ratios to the government-recommended levels.

In the process, the government requested *chaebŏl* to detail the amount of foreign money that they were planning to bring in through asset sales by the end of 1999 in order to meet the deadline in 2000. The supporters of FDI-driven reforms—i.e., the government, the IMF, and the foreign business community—highlighted the fact that the firms "over-achieved" the target by reducing the debt ratio to 235 percent in 1998 and to 148.9 percent in 1999. The debt ratio of the thirty largest *chaebŏl* also went below 200 percent by 2000.[58] However, there were concerns that the fall in the debt-equity ratio was largely due to "financial engineering" and "distressed sales" through new stock issues, assets sales, and even asset revaluations, rather than through debt repayments and lowering of financial risks and enhancement of firm competitiveness.[59] As noted by Chang and Shin,[60] when the top four *chaebŏl* reported their "successful" restructuring at the end of 1999, it was reported that US$10.82 billion of their assets was transferred to foreigners.

However, the fact remains that FDI entered at a critical moment and helped to ease short-term liquidity constraints in the absence of willing or able domestic creditors, albeit at a high loss to domestic firms. The question of importance is whether foreign institutional investors had any positive impact in reforming corporate governance to enhance managerial transparency and accountability; that is, whether they were able either to engage in "voice" arrangements or to exercise their threat to "exit" when faced with opaque governance structures and questionable management practices.

58 Shin and Chang, *Restructuring "Korea Inc.,"* 85.
59 Ibid.
60 Ibid., 141.

The rights of minority shareholders were strengthened as follows, in part due to the work of influential NGOs including the People's Solidarity for Participatory Democracy (PSPD):

- The minimum proportion of shares required to bring a lawsuit against managers for misconduct was relaxed to 0.01 percent.
- The minimum requirements for inspecting accounting books were also relaxed from 3 to 1 percent of shareholdings (0.5 percent in the case of listed companies with more than 100 billion won worth of equity capital).
- A cumulative voting system was introduced in order to make it easier for minority shareholders to appoint board members representing their collective interests.

This raises the question, did foreign institutional investors help improve corporate governance? The answer is somewhat mixed. This is because foreign institutional investors generally invested in well-performing firms in high value-added sectors with relatively sound corporate governance structures, as demonstrated by the concentration of FDI in blue-chip firms (as discussed earlier), rather than taking on what were perceived to be "risky" investments.[61] And the influence of foreign investment on corporate governance reform is difficult to measure since blue-chip firms have already demonstrated themselves as having relatively good corporate governance and competitiveness in the open South Korean market, and thus the impact of foreign investors on raising their managerial transparency and accountability may have been limited. However, there have been cases where foreign investors have taken on the challenge of reforming the governance of firms that have been grossly mismanaged. Korea First Bank (KFB, now Standard Chartered First Bank) is widely regarded as a successful case of FDI-driven corporate governance reform, which we will examine below.

CASE 1. KOREA FIRST BANK (KFB): Before it became insolvent in 1998, KFB was regarded the largest and most competitive bank in the early 1990s.

---

61 In fact, the share of the top two companies in terms of net buying by foreign investors in 1998 was 47.33 percent. And it reached 63.65 percent in 1999 and 66.33 percent in 2000. This shows that foreign investors' preferences and concentration in a small number of blue-chip companies in the South Korean market were intensified during the period. The top two companies were Samsung Electronics and KEPCO in 1998; Kookmin Bank and Samsung Electro-mechanics in 1999; and Hyundai Electronics and Samsung Electronics in 2000. See Won Jong Han, "Jusiksijang-ui Chwiyaksseong-gwa Juga Hoebok Bangan" [Weakness of the stock market and bouncing strategies of share prices], *LG Weekly Economy* 10, no. 4 (2000): 9.

However, the story changed dramatically after the crisis. In fact, the misfortune of KFB started from the bankruptcy of Yoowon (Yuwŏn) E&C, which was one of the affiliates of the Hanbo Group, in March 1995. And due to a series of bankruptcies of relatively large companies, such as Hanbo Steel in January 1997, Sammi Special Steel in March 1997, and Kia Motors in July 1997, for which KFB was their correspondent (principal) bank, the bank's position quickly worsened. When KFB became insolvent in 1998, the bank was nationalized through recapitalization using public funds, with a plan to sell to a foreign investor in line with IMF recommendations. After a year of negotiations, Newbridge Capital (U.S.) acquired the controlling stake of 50.99 percent. The bank achieved a capital adequacy ratio of 13.7 percent, exceeding the standards of the BIS in the first half of 2000. During the same period, return-on-equity (ROE) and return-on-assets (ROA) ratios turned positive to 57 percent and 4.6 percent, respectively. The nonperforming loan ratio was reduced to 10 percent from 18.5 percent in 1999. KFB's financial position improved with the infusion of foreign capital.

However, it can also be argued that Newbridge Capital cannot take full credit for KFB's turnaround given that there has been a huge governmental subsidy (or "preferential treatment"). In fact, KFB received the greatest amount of government assistance of all Korean banks. From the time it was nationalized until September 2000, approximately 23 percent of initial public funds allocated to restructure the financial sector went into KFB.[62] As a part of the acquisition deal, the government contributed US$187.3 million (209.8 billion won) to increase the total net assets of the bank through the transfer of nonperforming assets, in effect giving the bank a clean balance sheet before the acquisition.[63]

What is significant, however, is the change in corporate governance, particularly in relation to transparency and accountability. The first innovative project that Newbridge Capital launched right after the M&A was to improve the "bad" corporate governance led by the president of the bank and to strengthen the internal monitoring system.[64] For this, Newbridge

62 Yun, "Foreign Direct Investment," 252.

63 Therefore, little risk was thought to have been assumed by Newbridge Capital. Newbridge Capital came under criticism when it sold its majority stake in KFB to Standard Chartered Bank in January 2005, and in the process earning more that 1 trillion won (or US$990 million) without paying tax.

64 Hyung-Chan Jung and Myung-Chul Lee, "Oegukjjabonui Gungnaeeunhaeng Insuwa Eunhaengsaneobui Gujo Byeonhwa: New Bridge Capital-ui Jeireunhaeng Insu Sarye" [Foreign acquisitions of Korean commercial banks and restructuring of the Korean banking industry: The case of Korea First Bank], *Journal of Money and Finance* 11, no. 1 (2006): 81–129.

Capital established an "acting" board of directors, independent from the management including the president of the bank. A new board of directors was subsequently appointed, which comprised 16 members including the president and 15 external directors, replacing the old board that comprised a balance of external and internal directors.

It has been claimed that the new president and independent board of directors of KFB turned down the government's request that KFB purchase a proportion of maturing corporate bonds to help stabilize the local bond market in 2000.[65] In a similar vein, KFB's new management introduced stronger financial discipline and a credit analysis system in line with international best practices, and refused to continue providing credit to Hyundai (Hyŏndae) Construction and Engineering Co., quoting its new and stricter lending policies. These are pace-setting examples of FDI-led corporate governance reform, and in light of the strong presence of foreign investors in the financial sector, their influence may also spill over to the rest of the economy.

At the same time, KFB received public criticism when it refused to aid a government-led initiative to restructure ailing firms of national importance, such as Daewoo Electronics and Ssangyong Motors, despite having been a recipient of a large government subsidy itself. Moreover, the sale of KFB to Standard Chartered Bank in 2005 raised concerns that foreign investors were selling cheaply acquired assets during the crisis period at staggering profits within a matter of a few years. The public was particularly outraged by the fact that many foreign funds such as Newbridge Capital did not pay taxes in South Korea because they were conducting deals through companies in tax havens.[66]

A more serious case that gripped public attention is that of Lone Star Equity Funds, which acquired controlling stakes in Korea Exchange Bank in 2003. Spec Watch Korea, an NGO established in 2004 with the support of national union federations and whose mission is to fight speculative funds operating in South Korea, filed a lawsuit to annul Lone Star, established in 2004 with the support of stock-price manipulation and financial data falsification, so as to acquire a 50.5 percent controlling stake in Korea Exchange for a bargain price of US$1.5 billion (1.4 trillion won).[67] In 2006, a South Korean court found the Lone Star original purchase illegal, undermining its plan to sell its shares in Korea Exchange Bank to Kookmin (Kungmin) Bank;

---

65 Yun, "Foreign Direct Investment," 254.

66 Newbridge Capital earned more than 1 trillion won (US$990 million) from the sale of KFB.

67 http://www.specwatch.or.kr.

a deal estimated to be a US$7.3 billion deal, which would have made it one of the largest corporate takeovers in South Korean history.

2) RESERVATIONS ABOUT FDI (2002–PRESENT)

After the initial honeymoon period with FDI immediately following the Asian financial crisis, the mood toward FDI began to change. A more cautious view on the role of FDI in corporate governance reform was supported by domestic businesses, including *chaebŏl*, *chaebŏl*-sponsored organizations (e.g., the FKI, the Korean Chamber of Commerce and Industry [KCCI]) and research institutes (e.g., Korea Economic Research Institute [KERI]). Their voice had been silenced in the initial stage of reforms given the prevailing public opinion that *chaebŏl* were the culprits of the economic crisis.

NGOs—another relatively new actor in the Korean political economy—grew very rapidly during the 1990s, and began to raise their voice on economic issues as well as social problems, reflecting the public's opinion on the *chaebŏl*, foreign capital, and corporate restructuring. The two most prominent NGOs that were concerned with economic matters were the Citizens' Coalition for Economic Justice (CCEJ) and the PSPD. Of the two, the PSPD took on a more progressive approach, and was more vocal in criticizing *chaebŏl* for their abuse of economic and political power. The PSPD was established in 1994, and became quite active during the aftermath of the Asian financial crisis in the midst of the economic reforms by leading the minority shareholder rights movement. In June of 1997, the PSPD succeeded in bringing a derivative suit against the past and current board of directors of the KFB, and eventually won a court decision upholding the rights of minority shareholders for the first time in South Korea.[68] This suit and others that followed were considered a catalyst in changing the corporate governance system by enhancing transparency in management practices and accountability on the part of top management.

A group of intellectuals known as Alternative Solidarity emerged in 2001 in an effort to provide a forum for discourse to counter-balance the dominant and prevailing influence of neo-liberal ideology in shaping the direction of South Korean capitalism. This group was critical of the unquestioning attitude toward liberalization and FDI, and highlighted the pitfalls of the shareholder-oriented corporate governance system found in the liberal

---

68 Sixty-one minority shareholders of KFB took part, with combined shares comprising 0.5 percent of total ownership. A suit requesting an estimated US$33 million in compensation was filed against top management for receiving bribes in return for providing credit to Hanbo Steel—the company that went bankrupt at the onset of the Asian financial crisis—thereby incurring substantial losses to the bank and its shareholders.

market economies (LMEs), such as the short-term and speculative nature of investors.[69] More specifically, Alternative Solidarity raised concerns that "minority" shareholders meant "foreign" shareholders, not South Koreans themselves. The average South Korean citizen stands to benefit little from these reforms, as Koreans do not have pension savings that could go into the reorganized firms.[70]

The public debates instigated by Alternative Solidarity—but actively promoted by the pro-*chaebŏl* community and forces of the left such as Spec Watch—played an important role in shifting public support for the stakeholder-oriented corporate governance system associated with the CMEs. What have emerged since the mid-2000s are divergent voices on the direction of corporate governance reform, and they were played out in the case of SK Corp. below. In this case, it is evident that the government was no longer the coordinator of FDI, but that a new system had yet to be established to take over the void left by the government.

CASE 2. SK CORP.: In early 2003, SK Corp.—a flagship of SK Group and the nation's largest oil refinery—was faced with great difficulty in management. SK Corp. Chairman Ch'oe T'ae-wŏn (Chey Tae-Won), the actual owner of SK Group, was jailed for alleged illegal stock transactions, and SK Global—the group's trading arm—admitted to bookkeeping irregularities worth US$1.2 billion. SK Shipping was also suspected of inflating its balance sheets. It is against this backdrop that Sovereign Asset Management (now known as Sovereign Global) emerged as a top shareholder of SK Corp., by purchasing a 14.99 percent stake in the company for US$143 million (170 billion won) when the company's share prices reached record-low levels.

Of all the foreign investors holding South Korean stocks, to this date, none has been as vociferous as Sovereign Asset Management Ltd. in pushing for corporate governance reforms.[71] Sovereign Asset Management and the management at SK Corp. came head to head in a legal battle over financially troubled SK Global, where SK Corp. is the largest shareholder with

---

69 Seong Il Jung, "Jeunggwonsijang Jabonjuui Bipangwa Chabol mit Eunhaenggae-hyeo-gui Daean" [Critics of stock-market capitalism and alternative reform measures for the *chaebŏl* and the banks], conference paper prepared for the Korea Socio & Economic Studies Association, 2003; Ha-Joon Chang, *Rethinking Developmental Economics* (London: Anthem Press, 2003).

70 The reasons have to do with prior decisions taken in the areas of pension funding and, to a lesser degree, the role of financial intermediaries in South Korea (see Gourevitch and Shinn, *Political Power and Corporate Control*, 130–131).

71 Sovereign Global Investment, "Sovereign Seeks Reform at SK Corporation," April 14, 2003, http://www.sovereignglobal.com/4_1_1en.asp?ItemID=6, accessed November 9, 2010.

a 36.88 percent stake. In stark contrast to Sovereign Asset Management's repeated recommendations that it was important for SK Corp. to disengage from the troubled affiliate, SK Group announced bail-out plans to revive SK Global by offering financial aid within legal limits, based on the decision that: 1) normalizing SK Global was the only way to minimize loss to the nation as well as to the nation's third-largest conglomerate, and 2) this was the best way to maximize shareholders' interests in the medium to long run.

On behalf of Hermes, a London-based fund manager with a 0.7 percent stake in SK Corp., Sovereign Asset Management filed a lawsuit against the three directors of SK Corp., including Ch'oe, pointing out a serious case of lack of confidence in the company's management, which should be both competent and ethical. Sovereign further argued that there was sufficient doubt as to whether shareholder value will be properly managed. Sovereign argued that taking out SK's top management could actually enhance the value of SK Corp.'s shares and dividends. Despite SK's reassurances of corporate governance reform, when the courts ruled against Sovereign, it terminated its involvement with SK Corp. Public sentiment was very critical when news came out that Sovereign earned approximately US$840 million (1 trillion won) in capital gains when it finally dissolved its relations with SK. The public was furious that "foreign capitalists" only had profits on their agenda rather than the national development of South Korea.

This is another example of FDI-led corporate governance reform, where Sovereign used both "voice" mechanisms and, eventually, the threat of "exit" to instigate corporate governance reform. However small and incremental, Sovereign's involvement provided incentives for the top management of SK Corp. to initiate change.

At the same time, critics of Sovereign would point to the fact that Sovereign was unsuccessful and chose to terminate its ties with SK Corp. It is not unreasonable to think that foreign investors are only interested in short-term capital gains and not interested in corporate governance reform, which can be a long, drawn-out process.

Although each assessment has some merits, and the extent of change can be debated, as was the case of Newbridge Capital (KFB), there is no denying that a foreign investor's active involvement had changed the corporate landscape and effected corporate governance reform. It appears that foreign capital in the form of FDI has become a critical agent of change.

Also important to note was the increasingly vocal role played by South Korean NGOs as watchdog, representing different voices from the South Korean public—i.e., both for and against foreign capital investment. An interesting development in recent years is that the joining of forces between

NGOs and foreign investors has driven corporate governance reform forward. In 2006 the leading figure behind the PSPD's minority shareholder movement, Chang Ha-sŏng (Jang Ha Sung), established the Center for Good Corporate Governance (CGCG), and, in collaboration with Lazard Asset Management (U.S.), launched the so-called "Korea Corporate Governance Fund." It is a socially responsible investment fund, capitalized at between US$120–200 million (which is almost 200 times the entire annual budget of the PSPD), focusing exclusively on improving corporate governance in South Korean firms. Lazard Asset Management oversees the technicalities of the daily management of the fund, and the CGCG provides the local knowledge, including identifying potential firms to be targeted as well as recommending specific sets of governance reform guidelines.[72] Both the CGCG and Lazard Asset Management have been keen to point out that the fund is a long-term player in the South Korean market, and the expected outcome of such a long-term commitment is that shareholder value would be routinized and embedded at the firm level.[73]

More than a decade after the Asian financial crisis, there are signs of corporate governance reforms slowing in South Korea.[74] And we have also witnessed a rather stark drop of FDI into South Korea since the mid-2000s. Given the relative scarcity of FDI in the current period, it is difficult to assess whether foreign capital can continue to act as a meaningful catalyst for change, as it seems to be the case in the CMEs.

Conclusion

Within the broader discussions on the VoC approach, this chapter examined the role of FDI in post–Asian financial crisis corporate restructuring in South Korea. The FDI regime in South Korea has undergone incremental yet substantial changes over the last five decades, from restrictive to limited, and to active promotion since the Asian financial crisis.

The sharp growth of FDI in the immediate aftermath of the Asian financial crisis appears to hint that the South Korean government's attempt to use FDI in order to alleviate the economy of low foreign exchange reserves and to improve corporate governance may have brought some positive effects. Although we were not able to examine a large number of cases involving

72 http://www.lazardnet.com/lam/us/index.shtml.
73 Nicholas Bratt and John Lee, "What Korea Needs: Good Corporate Governance," *The Korea Times,* January 1, 2009; Ihlwan Moon, "Cleaning Up in South Korea," *BusinessWeek*, August 17, 2006.
74 Walter, *Governing Finance,* 126–65.

FDI, it appears that the few celebrated cases we reviewed—i.e., the cases of Newbridge Capital (KFB) and Sovereign (SK Corp.)—suggest that FDI can drive corporate governance reform as agents of change.

However, we also note that the rather limited amount of FDI in the recent period questions the active role of FDI as a major agent of corporate governance reform. Because FDI has been fluctuating since the 2000s and has been quite low for some years, it will be important to examine the full effect of FDI on corporate governance reform once the influx of FDI is stabilized. Particularly important is an assessment of the long-term impact of corporate governance reform on competitiveness at both the firm and national levels. After all, although it is difficult to dispute the claim that more transparency and accountability would benefit South Korean firms, and in turn, national competitiveness as a whole, whether a corporate governance system that upholds shareholder value, as opposed to stakeholder value, enhances competitiveness has been an on-going debate within the VoC literature.

Furthermore, it was clear that the South Korean NGOs and civil society at large also played an increasingly vocal role in corporate governance reform in the cases examined in this chapter. What the FDI-led corporate governance reform shows is that South Korea has been experiencing what the VoC perspective calls path-altering (and equilibrium-breaking) system change. What the South Korean government probably did not foresee—or had no choice but to gamble on—is that the new foreign actors could resist governmental intervention, implying the beginning of a qualitatively different relationship between the government and the private sector, and therefore a different mode of coordination.

Section III

Consequences of Change

8 Enterprise Unions and the Segmentation of the Labor Market

LABOR, UNIONS, AND CORPORATE
RESTRUCTURING IN KOREA

Jiyeoun Song

One crucial economic policy issue faced by all countries is how to build institutional pillars of the labor market to encourage both capital and labor to agree on a sustainable economic growth formula, ensuring that labor productivity rises at least as fast as wage increases and welfare state expenditures. To achieve this policy goal, each country adopts political mechanisms that fit well with the institutional configurations of its national political economy. Despite its rapid economic growth during the past few decades, Korea failed to find a model for the labor market that would satisfy capital, labor, and government. All of the country's institutional experiments and its search for foreign labor models—ranging from Japanese decentralized enterprise unionism during the era of the developmental state, the neoliberal market ideology under the Kim Young-sam (Kim Yŏng-sam, 1993–98) administration, and social corporatism during the Kim Dae-jung (Kim Tae-jung, 1998–2003) administration, to the Dutch model of social partnership during the Roh Moo-hyun (No Mu-hyŏn, 2003–8) administration—did not come to fruition.

The two exogenous factors of democratization and globalization have complicated the state's political response to changes in the political and economic environments, depriving the state of its policy coordination capacity in the labor market. A top-down pattern of state-led labor coordination that had dominated labor politics during the period of development abruptly fell apart right after the 1987 political democratization. A series of state-led labor market reforms were not successful in moderating wage increases and institutionalizing cooperative industrial relations systems between management and labor unions. In particular, *chaebŏl* had to confront the dual challenges of sharp wage hikes driven by their enterprise unions, many of which were organized in conjunction with the 1987 democratic transition, and intensified international market competition.[1] Amidst the 1997 East Asian financial crisis, the Korean government undertook another conflict-ridden labor market reform to facilitate comprehensive corporate restructuring and alleviate firms' financial burdens to ultimately resuscitate its national economy, which was in serious trouble. In early 1998, then President-elect Kim Dae-jung initiated labor market reform to relax employment protection for regular workers in corporate restructuring and to deregulate rules and regulations for hiring nonregular workers.

Yet the political and economic consequences of the reform driven by Kim Dae-jung differed remarkably across the labor market. A majority of Korean workers, those hired in small- and medium-sized enterprises (SMEs) and smaller *chaebŏl*, experienced a high level of job insecurity during corporate restructuring.[2] Meanwhile, a very small fraction of well-organized workers in large *chaebŏl* were able to secure strong employment protection, high wage increases, and generous corporate welfare benefits, despite legislative changes in labor laws. The predominance of a few large *chaebŏl* over Korea's national political economy increasingly intensified after the financial crisis. A gap in economic performance and market profitability between the top five *chaebŏl* and the rest of the smaller ones became much wider. SMEs' heavy reliance on subcontracting systems did not change significantly. As of 2003, more than 60 percent of SMEs were locked in multiple layers of the subcontracting production system.[3] Ironically, the post-1997 labor market reform, whose aim was to increase labor market flexibility in the *chaebŏl* sector during corporate restructuring, contributed to the bifurcation of the Korean labor market: the reinforcement of the rigid internal labor market in large *chaebŏl* and the breakdown of the (weak) employment protection system for regular workers in SMEs and smaller *chaebŏl*.

Why were the policy outcomes of the post-1997 labor market reform different from those anticipated by state policymakers? Why have capital, labor, and government continued to search for an alternative model for the labor market? This chapter analyzes the benefits and limitations of emulating

1 *Chaebŏl* are family-owned large-sized Korean business conglomerates, most of which were created by the state-led developmental strategy during the Park Chung-hee regime (1961–79).

2 In Korea, small- and medium-sized enterprises are defined as firms with fewer than 300 full-time regular workers and/or with capital of less than 8 billion Korean won.

3 Pae Kyu-sik, Yi Sang-min, Paek P'il-gyu, Im Un-t'aek, and Yi Kyu-yong, *Chungso chejo ŏp ŭi koyong kwan'gye* [Employment relations in small- and medium-sized firms] (Seoul: Korea Labor Institute, 2006), 53–55.

foreign models for the labor market, and examines the ways in which labor market reform affected the political processes and outcomes of corporate restructuring, with a specific focus on post-1997 Korea. This study diverges from the existing literature on Korean labor politics, bringing in the concept of institutional complementarities and taking into account interactions among the key political actors in the labor market—firms, labor unions, government, and political parties. Building upon the theoretical insights of the varieties of capitalism literature, the chapter highlights a set of interdependent labor market institutions or the lack thereof to explain the effects of labor market reform on corporate restructuring.[4]

The next section begins with a brief history of Korean labor politics, dating back to the pre-1987 period, identifying the original institutional context of the Korean labor market, most of which was established under the authoritarian regime. The third section discusses a series of labor market reform attempts between 1988 and 1997 to examine the effects of the 1987 democratic transition on the sustainability of the old developmentalist labor model. Although significant formal institutional changes took place amidst the financial crisis, several precursors of the post-1997 labor market reform had already been undertaken. By delineating the pre-1997 labor market reform efforts, we can specify the factors that facilitated and/or hindered earlier reforms. The fourth section analyzes what has and has not changed after the post-1997 labor market reform, encompassing employment practices and wage systems as well as industrial relations during corporate restructuring. By closely analyzing the role of state policymakers, political parties, and societal interest groups (e.g., business associations and labor federations), I point out the political and institutional constraints on the post-1997 labor market reform. Finally, I conclude this chapter by addressing the policy implications of labor market reform for corporate restructuring in Korea.

The Origins and Development of Korea's State-led Labor Coordination during the Authoritarian Regime

The institutional foundations of Korean labor politics were established in the early 1960s when General Park Chung-hee (Pak Chŏng-hŭi, 1961–79), who had come to power through a military coup d'état, advanced the state-led developmental strategy. Park's industrial policies, targeting a few

---

4 Regarding the varieties of capitalism literature, see Peter A. Hall and David W. Soskice, eds., *Varieties of Capitalism: The Institutional Foundations of Comparative Advantage* (Oxford: Oxford University Press, 2001).

politically chosen large firms, gave rise to the formation of the dualistic labor market divided between *chaebŏl* and SMEs, but the state's labor coordination prevented labor market inequality (especially wage differentials according to firm size) from emerging under authoritarian rule. Selectively emulating the Japanese archetype of cooperative industrial relations centered on enterprise unions, the Park regime politically demobilized the working class and closely monitored the leadership of the national and industrial labor federations in order to preempt labor unrest and distributional conflicts.[5]

Only a couple of months after the coup, the military junta restored acquiescent national and industrial labor federations with the help of the clandestine political engineering of the Korean Central Intelligence Agency (KCIA).[6] Despite the state's reliance on a form of corporatist interest mediation in labor politics, the organizational weakness of the Federation of Korean Trade Unions (FKTU), the only national labor federation that had been founded by the Park regime, differentiated Park's labor model from state corporatism. The leadership of the FKTU did not possess any political authority to discipline its affiliated industrial federations and enterprise unions. As of 1970, only 47.58 percent of its affiliated unions paid their union dues to the FKTU and a few powerful industrial federations even delayed their payments if they had conflicts with the leadership of the FKTU.[7] A 1963 labor law prohibiting unions from participating in political activities further disempowered the FKTU in electoral politics, restricting the locus of Korea's labor movement to narrowly defined economic interests at the firm level.

The persistence of state-led labor coordination can also be attributed to the multifaceted institutional arrangements that preempted labor unrest, preventing the need to use coercive measures. First, the pro-state union leadership (*ŏyong nojo*) of the FKTU prevented workers from staging any political resistance to the state or firms. A few co-opted leaders at the FKTU and its affiliated industrial federations collaborated with the Park regime to demolish autonomous and democratic labor movements in return for political and economic incentives, such as political appointments and material compensation.[8] Secondly, national security agencies, like the KCIA and the National

5 Byung-Kook Kim, "The Park Era: Agent, Structures, and Legacies," paper presented at the annual meeting of the American Political Science Association, Boston, 2002.

6 Choi Jang-jip (Ch'oe Chang-jip), *Han'guk ŭi nodong undong kwa kukka* [Labor movements and the state in Korea] (Seoul: Nanam Publishing, 1997), 45–46.

7 Choi, *Han'guk ŭi nodong undong kwa kukka*, 185; Kim Su-gon, *Nosa kwan'gye chŏngch'aek kwa panghyang* [Policy agenda and direction of industrial relations in Korea] (Seoul: Korea Development Institute, 1983), 136.

8 Yu Pŏm-sang, *Han'guk ŭi nodong undong inyŏm* [An ideology of Korean labor movements] (Seoul: Korea Labor Institute, 2005), 124–40.

Police Agency (NPA), as well as the Ministry of Labor (MoL) were extensively engaged in monitoring labor unions to thwart any potential industrial disputes.[9] Despite the presence of co-opted union leadership, national security agencies kept watch on the FKTU, by dispatching KCIA agents to its headquarters.[10] The MoL, whose administrative role was to execute labor control policies to support Park's growth model, fell under the strong influence and control of other economic ministries—e.g., the Economic Planning Board and the Ministry of Trade and Industry—as well as national security agencies in monitoring labor unions.[11] The MoL's political role in pursuing the state-led developmental strategy can be inferred from the fact that between 1963 and 1982, five of the thirteen labor ministers were former security personnel in the military, the NPA, or the Ministry of Home Affairs (MHA) (see Figure 8.1).[12] This cooptation and intimidation enabled the state to manage industrial relations without resorting to harsh labor repression.

Last, organizationally weak and ideologically underdeveloped political parties, with few linkages to societal interest groups, could not assist workers in claiming political and economic rights. Park's institutional design on the party system strictly confined the role of the ruling Democratic Republican Party (DRP) to an auxiliary function in the policy-making processes, debilitating political incentives and preventing political parties from deepening their linkages to societal interest groups.[13] Opposition parties also did not have any organizational linkages with these groups. Although the New Democratic Party (*Sinmindang*), the major opposition party, supported the 1979 sit-in and hunger strike by YH Industry Company's female workers, there were few efforts on the part of opposition parties to forge a political coalition with societal interest groups in the realm of party politics.[14]

While the Park regime constrained the political rights of the FKTU and its affiliated labor unions, it imposed a system of political exchange for employment security and wage restraints on employers and workers in large

9 The Administration of Labor Affairs (*Nodong ch'ŏng*) was elevated to the Ministry of Labor (*Nodong pu*) in March 1981.

10 Yu, *Han'guk ŭi nodong undong inyŏm*, 124–25.

11 Choi, *Han'guk ŭi nodong undong kwa kukka*, 247–51.

12 During the Park regime, the Ministry of Home Affairs (MHA) was in charge of maintaining social order with the use of the National Police Agency. Hence, I classify it as a security ministry. Since the Administration of Labor Affairs was raised to the status of the Ministry of Labor in 1981, I place the commissioners of labor in the category of labor ministers.

13 Kim, "The Park Era: Agent, Structures, and Legacies."

14 Sunhyuk Kim, "From Resistance to Representation: Civil Society in South Korean Democratization" (PhD diss., Stanford University, 1996), 89–90.

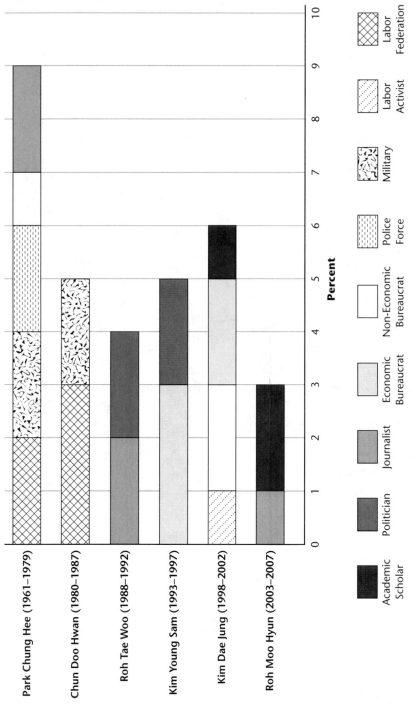

FIGURE 8.1 Composition of the Labor Ministers in Korea

Source: Byung-Kook Kim (Kim Pyŏng-guk), *Pundan kwa byŏngmyŏng ŭi tongbak* [The political dynamics of the divided nation and the revolution] (Seoul: Munhak kwa Chisŏngsa, 1994), 196; Korean Ministry of Labor (www.molab.go.kr).

firms to uphold its state-led developmental model. Given the Park regime's implicit pledge to guarantee employment security and rapid economic growth for future rewards, workers were forced to accept wage increases below labor productivity growth.[15] Indeed, high economic growth in the 1960s and 1970s delivered substantial wage increases to workers, although wages increased at a lower rate than the growth of labor productivity, except in the late 1970s. As illustrated by the fluctuations in the rate of real wage growth in Figure 8.2, however, the boom-and-bust cycle of the Korean economy exposed workers to the vagaries of the market and to high economic uncertainty. The only feasible policy option to maintain the state-led labor coordination system was to keep rapid economic growth and help firms survive in order to prevent massive unemployment and social and political dislocation—a critical challenge for the authoritarian regime. Therefore, when the first oil crisis hit the Korean economy in 1973, the Park regime continued to promote an immense heavy and chemical industrialization (HCI) drive to generate even more rapid economic growth, bail out ailing firms, and create more jobs, rather than subscribe to a conservative monetary policy.[16]

Park's state-led labor coordination also affected the formation and evolution of the dualistic labor market divided between *chaebŏl* and SMEs, facilitating the former to vigorously integrate and diversify businesses into heavy and chemical industries. The labor shortage that resulted from the HCI drive made *chaebŏl* develop a set of interdependent labor market institutions—permanent employment practices, seniority-based wage systems, and corporate welfare programs—to cope with the problems of high labor mobility.[17] As Figure 8.3 illustrates, the presence of these institutional pillars contributed to stabilizing labor market mobility in large firms, especially in

15 Wage restraints were partly sustained by a massive influx of unskilled workers from rural areas. Urbanization and industrialization fostered the rapid migration of the rural population into urban cities, and such a supply of labor contributed to curtailing wage increases during the 1960s. See Song Ho-gŭn, *Han'guk ŭi Nodong chŏngch'i wa sijang* [Labor politics and market in Korea] (Seoul: Nanam Publishing, 1991), 260–61; Kim Ji-hong (Kim Chi-hong), *Korean Industrial Policy in the 1970s: The Heavy and Chemical Industry Drive* (Seoul: Korea Development Institute, 1991), 260–71.

16 Stephan Haggard, "Macroeconomic Policy through the First Oil Shock, 1970–1975," in *Macroeconomic Policy and Adjustment in Korea 1970–1990*, ed. Stephan Haggard, et al. (Cambridge, MA: Harvard Institute for International Development and Korea Development Institute, 1994), 23–30; Kim, "The Park Era: Agent, Structures, and Legacies," 6–7; Jung-en Woo, *Race to the Swift: State and Finance in Korean Industrialization* (New York: Columbia University Press, 1991), 106–11.

17 According to a Korea Development Institute Mobility Survey from 1979, firms considered that the length of service was the most important criteria to determine wage levels.

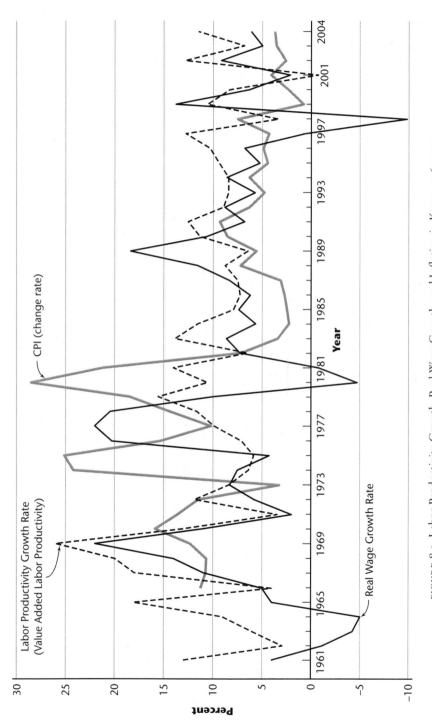

FIGURE 8.2 Labor Productivity Growth, Real Wage Growth, and Inflation in Korea, 1961–2004

Source: Bank of Korea (http://ecos.bok.or.kr); Korea Labor Institute, KLI *nodong t'onggye* [KLI labor statistics] (Seoul: Korea Labor Institute, 2002 and 2005); Korean Productivity Center Labor Productivity Statistics (www.kpc.or.kr); Song Ho-kŭn, "Kwŏnwi chuŭi Han'guk ŭi kukka wa imgŭm chŏngch'ak (II)" [Authoritarian government and wage policy in Korea (II)], *Han'guk chŏngch'i hakhoe po* [Korean political science review] 27, no.1 (1993): 81; T'ak Hŭi-jun, "Han'guk imgŭm chŏngch'a ŭi t'ŭksŏng" [The characteristics of Korean wage policies], *Han'guk kyŏngje* [Korean economics] 2 (1974): 111.

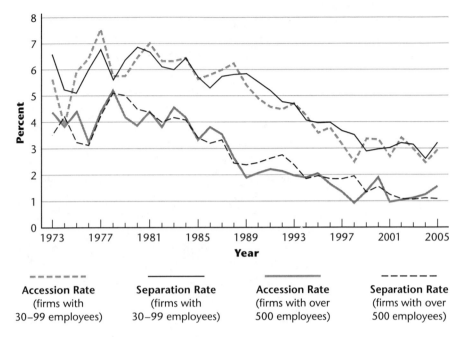

FIGURE 8.3 Labor Turnover Rates in the Korean Manufacturing Sectors, 1973–2005

Source: Korean Ministry of Labor, *Maewŏl nodong t'onggye chosa pogosŏ* [Report on monthly labor survey] (Seoul: Ministry of Labor, 1973–2005), various issues.

Note: Labor turnover rates are often measured by average monthly accession and separation rates in the labor market. Before 1973, firm size was classified into three categories: (1) firms with 10–99 employees, (2) firms with 100–499 employees, and (3) firms with over 500 employees. To make a consistent comparison over time, I compared firms with 30–99 employees and firms with over 500 employees since 1973.

comparison to that in SMEs, and to encouraging employers and workers to invest in long-term human capital.

Nonetheless, *chaebŏl* could not solve the dilemma of collective action in establishing firm-based skill formation systems in the labor market. The 1974 National Skill Training Legislation, which required firms with over 500 employees to establish education and training systems for workers at the firm level, did not stop *chaebŏl* from poaching skilled workers from other *chaebŏl*.[18] Two leading business associations—the Federation of Korean Industries (FKI) and the Korea Employers Federation (KEF)—could not coordinate their member firms over the issue of poaching skilled workers. Modeled after

18 Yang Chae-jin, "Han'guk ŭi sanŏp hwa sigi sungnyŏng kwa pokji chedo ŭi kiwŏn" [Skills formation systems and the origins of the Korean welfare system], *Han'guk chŏngch'i hakhoe po* [Korean political science review] 38 no. 5 (2004): 85–103; Kim, *Nosa kwan'gye chŏngch'aek kwa panghyang*; Kim Sŏng-jung and Sŏng Che-hwan, *Han'guk ŭi koyong chŏngch'aek* [Employment policies in South Korea] (Seoul: Korea Labor Institute, 2005), 73–200.

the Japan Federation of Economic Organizations (*Keidanren*), the FKI was founded in 1961 under the auspices of the military junta and represented the political, economic, and industrial policy interests of the big business community, namely the large *chaebŏl*. Meanwhile, the KEF, emulating the Japan Federation of Employers' Associations (*Nikkeiren*), was established in 1970 to specialize in industrial relations, but unlike the KFI, the KEF comprised large firms as well as SMEs. While both the FKI and KEF played the role of political representatives of the Korean business community, *chaebŏl* preferred to access individual state policymakers to receive selective policy benefits for their business projects. Similar to the problem confronted by the leadership of the FKTU, the lack of politically competent business associations to discipline their member firms complicated the high labor turnover and underdevelopment of skills formation systems, even in the *chaebŏl* sector.

The Park regime's political intervention in the labor market artificially suppressed high wage increases in the *chaebŏl* sector, mitigating the problems of wage inequality between *chaebŏl* and SMEs. When the Park regime embarked on the HCI drive in 1973, the wage differential between firms with 10-29 workers and firms with over 500 workers was at 66.4 percent, but the wage gap between these two groups dramatically narrowed to 91.74 percent by 1979.[19] Without the state's labor control policy to restrain wage increases in the *chaebŏl* sector, wage equality could not have been achieved. The Park regime let SME workers be paid market wages while preventing *chaebŏl* workers from exerting their organizational capacity to raise their wages even higher. In contrast to the trend of wage convergence across firm size, wage inequality across industrial sectors remained large. In comparing firms with over 500 workers in the garment industry and the industrial chemical industry, workers in the garment sector, where female workers comprised a disproportionate number, received only 42.8 percent of workers' wages in the industrial chemical industry.[20] This meant that in spite of the Park regime's political intervention, the law of supply and demand in the labor market pushed up wages in the heavy and chemical industries, in which *chaebŏl* pursued excessive expansion strategies during the late 1970s. Likewise, the state could not guarantee employment security against market forces, especially for workers in SMEs. During the recession of 1973–1974, firms with less than 50 workers experienced an aggregate decline of

19 Administration of Labor Affairs (currently Ministry of Labor), *Maewŏl nodong t'onggye chosa pogo sŏ* [Report on monthly labor survey] (Seoul, various issues, 1973–79).

20 Ibid.; Regarding the failure of the Park regime's wage guidelines see Song, *Han'guk ŭi Nodong chŏngch'i wa sijang*, 262–66.

74,726 employees, whereas firms with more than 200 workers increased by 164,872 employees during this period.[21] The HCI drive allowed large firms to create more jobs through aggressive investment projects, assisting them in retaining redundant workers even during economic downturns.

The Chun Doo-hwan regime (Chŏn Tu-hwan, 1980–87), which seized power by another military coup after the assassination of President Park, perfected the labor control policies bequeathed by the Park regime. Building upon Park's prohibition of political participation by labor unions, the 1980 labor laws revision reinforced political restrictions on labor unions: limiting the number of labor unions to one per work place; banning the intervention of third parties in labor disputes—not only by political parties but also by the FKTU, the only national labor federation; abolishing industrial federations to further decentralize labor unions at the firm level.[22] The Chun regime completed Park's labor model by legalizing *samgŭm* (three prohibitions on workers' basic rights). During the era of the developmental state, state-led labor coordination served to underpin the effective but fragile economic growth model, while exacerbating labor productivity, wage increases, and welfare expansion by the lack of autonomous coordination mechanisms between capital and labor. In the face of the 1987 political democratization and the 1997 East Asian financial crisis, sustaining the old developmentalist model of the Korean labor market was seriously challenged.

The Collapse of State-Led Labor Coordination and Partial Labor Market Reforms between 1988 and 1997

The 1987 political democratization broke down the institutional stability of the state-led labor coordination system in Korea. In the post-1987 period, the state proposed a series of labor market reforms to alleviate the financial burden on *chaebŏl*, which confronted wage hikes driven by their well-organized unions as well as cut-throat market competition from other developing countries, especially China. The state's diminishing political capacity for labor coordination, however, failed to bind capital and labor to abide by the state-imposed political exchange between employment security and wage restraints that had been established during the period of development. *Chaebŏl*, which had been shielded from the pressure of high wage increases and corporate welfare expansion, due to the state-led labor

---

21 Kim and Sŏng, *Han'guk ŭi koyong chŏngch'aek*, 91.
22 Byung-kook Kim and Hyun-chin Lim, "Labor Against Itself: Structural Dilemmas of State Monism," in *Consolidating Democracy in South Korea*, ed. Larry Diamond and Byung-kook Kim (Boulder, CO: Lynne Rienner Publishers, 2000), 115-16.

coordination, had to find their own ways to deal with political and economic challenges after 1987.

Immediately after Roh Tae-woo (No T'ae-u, 1988–93), President Chun's handpicked successor, pledged a direct presidential election on June 29, 1987, more than 3,000 industrial disputes broke out (see Table 8.1). The waves of industrial disputes led by *chaebŏl* workers in the heavy and chemical industries, whose political and organizational capacities had been suppressed by

TABLE 8.1

Unionization and Labor Disputes in Korea

	Labor Unions		Labor Disputes		
	Union Members (thousands)	Organization Rates (percentage)	Industrial Disputes	Participants (thousands)	Days Lost (thousand days)
1980	948	14.7	206	49	61
1981	966	14.6	186	35	31
1982	984	14.4	88	9	12
1983	1,009	14.1	98	11	9
1984	1,010	13.2	113	16	20
1985	1,004	12.4	265	29	64
1986	1,036	12.3	276	47	72
1987	1,267	13.8	3,749	1,262	6,947
1988	1,707	17.8	1,873	293	5,401
1989	1,932	18.6	1,616	409	6,351
1990	1,887	17.2	322	134	4,487
1991	1,803	15.4	235	175	3,271
1992	1,735	14.6	234	105	1,528
1993	1,667	14.0	144	109	1,308
1994	1,659	13.3	121	104	1,484
1995	1,615	12.5	88	50	393
1996	1,599	12.1	85	79	893
1997	1,484	11.1	78	44	445
1998	1,402	11.4	129	146	1,452
1999	1,481	11.7	198	92	1,366
2000	1,527	11.4	250	178	1,894
2001	1,569	11.5	234	89	1,083
2002	1,538	10.8	322	94	1,580
2003	1,550	10.8	320	137	1,299
2004	1,536	10.3	462	185	1,197

Source: Korea Labor Institute, Labor Statistics (www.kli.re.kr); Korean National Statistical Office (www.stat.go.kr).

Note: Union organization rates were calculated as the number of union members divided by the number of waged employees.

the authoritarian state, soon spread to other industrial sectors. Even without the political leadership of the FKTU, the only official labor federation,
chaebŏl workers wielded their organizational power, taking advantage of
the geographically concentrated industrial complex along the southern
shore, where the Park regime had strategically located the heavy and chemical industries.

In conjunction with the 1987 democratic transition, a large number
of *chaebŏl* workers became unionized with the help of dissident labor activists, whose union activities had been tightly controlled and monitored
by the state as well as by the *chaebŏl*. Also, pre-existing co-opted *chaebŏl*
unions were replaced by unions chosen through autonomous and democratic electoral procedures. While female workers in small- and medium-
sized textile and garment industries dominated Korea's labor movements
in the 1970s and early 1980s, *chaebŏl* unions, composed of male blue-collar
workers in the heavy and chemical industries, undertook a leading role in
the Korean labor movement after democratization. The institutional legacies of the state-led development strategy, centering on large firms, made
the Korean national political economy more vulnerable to industrial disputes in the *chaebŏl* sector since a series of strikes and work stoppages affected not only individual *chaebŏl* firms, but also a significant number of
their subcontracting SMEs, most of which were heavily dependent upon
business transactions with *chaebŏl*. Being aware of the political and organizational capacities that they could utilize, *chaebŏl* unions in heavy and
chemical industries took more aggressive and militant strategies in collective bargaining, demanding higher wage increases and more generous corporate welfare benefits.

Only a year after the 1987 Great Workers' Strike, the union organization
rate increased from 13.8 percent to 17.8 percent. Regional federations for
SMEs in manufacturing sectors, loose industry federations for white-collar
workers, and *chaebŏl* union councils were organized.[23] The 1987 political
democratization also triggered important changes in the political dynamics of the Korean labor movement. After several failed attempts to build
up another national labor federation, the Korean Confederation of Trade
Unions (KCTU) was finally founded in 1995 as the de facto second national

23 Kim and Hyun-chin Lim, "Labor Against Itself," 122–27; Choi Jang-jip (Ch'oe
Chang-jip), "Saeroun nodong undong ŭi panghyang mosaek ŭl wihayŏ" [In search of
a new direction for labor movements], *Sahoe p'yŏngnon* (June 1992): 233–46; Kim Se-
gyun, "1987-nyŏn ihu ŭi Han'guk nodong undong" [Korean labor movements after
1987], *Studies on Korean Politics* (Seoul: Institute of Korean Politics, Seoul National University, 2002), 197–244.

federation, in opposition to the official FKTU that had collaborated with the authoritarian regime to restrict the political and economic rights of workers and to impede development of the democratic labor movement. With the establishment of the KCTU, a large number of *chaebŏl* unions in the heavy and chemical industries defected from the FKTU to join the KCTU. The FKTU was able to maintain the political status of the largest national labor federation in terms of union membership even after *chaebŏl* unions left the organization. However, its organizational capacity was much weaker since a majority of its member unions were based in SMEs, which lacked financial and organizational resources in the labor movement. The state refused to recognize the legal status of the KCTU as a national labor federation. Yet the KCTU, consisting of well-organized *chaebŏl* unions in the heavy and chemical industries, consolidated its status in labor politics and pressured the state and *chaebŏl* to make political concessions for wage bargaining and labor policymaking.

Fractured business associations—e.g., the FKI and KEF—were also conducive to the persistence of the KCTU. Facing the new democratic labor movement driven by the KCTU, the Korean business community failed to coordinate individual *chaebŏl* firms in the labor market. Focusing only on the stabilization of contentious industrial relations in their own work places, individual *chaebŏl* firms often defected from the "implicit" wage guideline set by the business community by paying wages during strikes and securing industrial peace through even higher wage increases and more generous corporate welfare benefits.[24] Compliance with the demand of militant *chaebŏl* unions in wage bargaining at the firm level increased distrust among *chaebŏl* and made it far more difficult for them to formulate coherent political strategies toward new democratic labor movements.

This does not mean that the KCTU was able to coordinate the diverse political and economic interests of its affiliated enterprise labor unions. Since it encompassed a wide ideological and political spectrum of the Korean labor movement, the KCTU leadership was incessantly beset by factional conflicts, particularly between dovish and hawkish approaches to the state and *chaebŏl* in labor politics. Additionally, the very structure of the KCTU, with its membership composed of *chaebŏl unions,* undercut its internal cohesion and organizational capacity. Powerful *chaebŏl* unions swayed the (already) fragmented KCTU leadership and pressured it to disproportionately represent the political and economic interests of *chaebŏl* unions in the Korean labor movement. The organizationally weak

24 *Chosun Ilbo* (*Chosŏn Ilbo*), "Bulgŏjinŭn munodong muimgŭm" [Controversial debates on the principle of no work, no payment], July 4, 1996.

TABLE 8.2
Wage Gaps in the Korean Labor Market

Year	Female/Male (%)	Blue-Collar/ White-Collar (%)	30–99/over 500 Workers (%)
1980	44.1	47.0	99.4
1985	47.9	55.7	91.3
1990	53.5	70.7	77.2
1991	54.5	71.8	75.8
1992	55.9	73.8	77.9
1993	59.4	75.3	76.3
1994	58.4	77.7	74.4
1995	60.0	77.8	73.3
1996	60.9	80.5	72.8
1997	62.1	77.61	75.6
1998	63.7	n.a.	74.1
1999	62.8	n.a.	71.3
2000	62.5	n.a.	71.4
2001	63.6	n.a.	72.6
2002	63.5	n.a.	68.3
2003	62.9	n.a.	65.9
2004	62.3	n.a.	63.8

Source: Korea Labor Institute, *KLI nodong t'onggye* [KLI labor statistics] (Seoul: Korea Labor Institute, 2005), 48–89; Byung-Kook Kim and Hyun-chin Lim, "Labor Against Itself: Structural Dilemmas of State Monism," in *Consolidating Democracy in South Korea*, ed. Larry Diamond and Byung-Kook Kim (Boulder, CO: Lynne Rienner Publishers, 2000), 127.

Note: After 1998, a distinction between blue-collar and white-collar workers was no longer available.

leadership of the KCTU became a chronic problem in spite of its partial success in the democratic labor movement in the post-1987 period.

The combination of the declining capacity of state-led labor coordination and the surging power of well-organized *chaebŏl* unions gave rise to labor market inequality that had been previously curbed by the authoritarian regime (see Table 8.2). *Chaebŏl* unions in the heavy and chemical industries pushed for wage increases that often surpassed labor productivity growth. The economic boom during the period of 1986–1989, which had greatly benefited from the "three lows"—low interest rates, low oil prices, and a low won–U.S. dollar exchange rate—temporarily mitigated the distributional conflicts driven by *chaebŏl* unions. The end of hyper-economic growth in 1990, however, imposed a heavy burden on corporate finance due to rapidly increased labor costs since 1987. The state could not adopt its old labor adjustment strategy of imposing wage restraints on workers. Only a few large *chaebŏl* with monopoly market power were able to shift soaring labor costs to SME subcontractors and consumers and make a swift transition toward high-end product markets. Meanwhile, SMEs that were forced to bear the adjustment costs transferred from the *chaebŏl* resorted to hiring more nonregular workers and to subcontracting even smaller firms (see Figures 8.4 and 8.5).[25]

Beginning in the early 1990s, the Roh Tae-woo administration, which was democratically elected but staffed by the authoritarian ruling elite, stepped into industrial disputes to tame militant *chaebŏl* unions and quash democratic labor movements dominated by radical labor activists.[26] However, it is important to note that after the 1987 political democratization, the state could not forcefully employ labor control policies using the coercive measures of national security agencies as it had done under the authoritarian regime. The MoL, which had taken only a secondary part in administering labor control policies, also strove to transform itself into an "impartial" mediator between capital and labor. Interestingly, no labor ministers with political backgrounds in military or national security agencies were appointed after the Roh Tae-woo administration, as opposed to the predominance of labor ministers from both agencies during the authoritarian regime (see Figure 8.1 in the previous section).

The following Kim Young-sam administration attempted to further restrict the role of national security agencies in the realm of labor politics. As one of the important institutional changes, the Kim Young-sam administration reorganized the KCIA, which had played a pivotal role in implementing labor control policies in the earlier period.[27] Although Kim Young-sam was a political successor of President Roh Tae-woo as a presidential candidate of the ruling Democratic Liberal Party (DLP), he endeavored to distinguish the new government from that of his predecessor, which had continued policies inherited from the authoritarian regime, through proposing a wide array of

25 Yu Kyŏng-jun, ed., *Han'guk kyŏngje kujo pyŏnhwa wa koyong changch'ul* [Changes in the Korean economic structure and the creation of employment] (Seoul: Korea Development Institute, 2004).

26 Jongryn Mo, "Democratization, Labor Policy, and Economic Performance," in *Democracy and the Korean Economy*, ed. Jongryn Mo and Chung-in Moon (Stanford, CA: Hoover Institution Press, 1999).

27 *Hankyoreh (Han'gyŏre)*, "Minjudang Kim Young-sam chŏngbu 1gaewŏl pyŭngga juyo naeyong" [The Democratic Party's evaluation of the first month of the Kim Young-sam administration], March 31, 1993 and *Donga Ilbo (Tonga Ilbo)*, "Minju gaehyŭk ipbŏp sido" [The Democratic Party's reform-oriented policy proposal], April 29, 1993.

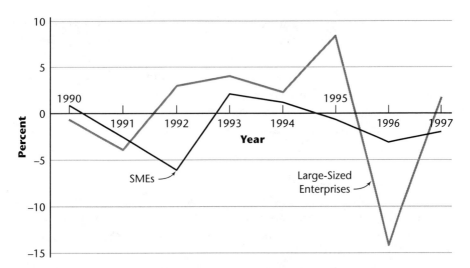

FIGURE 8.4 Gaps Between the Growth Rates of Gross Value-Added Per Capita and
Employment Costs Per Capita in Large-Sized Firms and SMEs in Korea
Source: Bank of Korea (http://ecos.bok.or.kr).

FIGURE 8.5 Percentage of Nonregular Workers Employed in SMEs in Korea
Source: Korean Ministry of Labor, *Nodong t'onggye yŏn'gam* [Yearbook
of labor statistics] (Seoul, 1991–1998).
Note: SMEs refer to firms with fewer than 300 employees.

pro-labor socioeconomic policies. Yi In-je, the first labor minister under the Kim Young-sam administration, provoked intense political conflicts with the economic bureaucracy, the ruling conservative DLP, and the business community, by formulating pro-labor policies that encompassed issues from the principle of "no work, but basic wage payments during strikes" to recognition of labor unions' rights to managerial discretion in collective bargaining.[28] His progressive policy proposals to enhance the political and economic rights of workers were withdrawn when the economic bureaucracy gained more political influence in the face of the massive industrial disputes in the Hyundai Group in June 1993.

While state policymakers acknowledged their diminished political capacity for state-led labor coordination after the 1987 democratic transition, they strenuously looked for alternative models for the labor market to replace the old developmentalist model. Distressed by wage hikes in the *chaebŏl* sector and consequent wage-push inflation after the end of its hyper-growth period, the Roh Tae-woo administration proposed labor market reforms to ensure firms' international market competitiveness: the institutionalization of wage coordination systems for wage restraints and the increase of labor market flexibility. In 1990, in an attempt to assume the role of coordinator in wage bargaining, the Roh administration ambitiously announced a single-digit wage increase policy, and designated major public corporations and large *chaebŏl* firms as pattern setters. Emulating Japan's inter- and intra-industry wage bargaining system, the "spring offensive" (or *shuntō*), in which a few large firms in export-oriented sectors take the primary role of informal wage coordinator, the state attempted to create an institutional mechanism of wage coordination to bind both capital and labor.[29] Yet the state's suggested wage guideline could not force presumed "followers"—i.e., SMEs and smaller *chaebŏl* firms—to comply with the single-digit wage increase policy, as indicated in the two-digit nominal wage growth rates in 1990 and 1991, which far exceeded the government's wage ceiling.[30] Even the pattern setters, many of which were concerned about the possibility of losing state-allocated financial

28 *Hankyoreh*, "Nodong chŏngch'aek buchŏgan daelip" [Inter-ministrial conflicts on labor policies], June 2, 1993 and "Saechŏngbu hu kŭpbyunhanŭn nodong chŏngch'aek" [Rapidly changing labor policies since the new administration], June 3, 1993.

29 Nobuhiro Hiwatari, "Employment Practices and Enterprise Unionism in Japan," in *Employees and Corporate Governance*, ed. Margaret Blair and Mark J. Roe (Washington DC: Brookings Institution Press, 1999).

30 Nominal wages increased 18.8 percent and 17.5 percent, respectively, in 1990 and 1991. See Korea Labor Institute, *KLI nodong t'onggye* [KLI labor statistics] (Seoul, 2005), 48.

resources,[31] offered militant labor unions generous corporate welfare benefits to compensate for state-imposed wage restraints.[32]

In July 1991, after the failure of the single-digit wage increase policy to moderate wage increases, the MoL proposed another wage restraint strategy, the "total wage system," which was designed to prevent major public corporations and large *chaebŏl* firms from subsidizing wages through the expansion of corporate welfare programs. However, the total wage system could not be implemented because of fierce opposition by labor unions and the ruling DLP that was worried about the upcoming National Assembly and presidential elections in 1992.[33] The wage bargaining that was further decentralized into the firm or, at best, group levels did not offer any political or economic incentives for *chaebŏl* to build disciplined wage coordination institutions at the industrial and/or national levels. There was no political leadership by business federations—e.g., the FKI and KEF—to coordinate political strategies of the business community in wage bargaining.

While the MoL executed wage restraint policies to solve the policy dilemmas of labor productivity growth and wage increases, the Ministry of Trade and Industry (MTI), which represented the interests of the business community, sought to resolve the same problem with different policy approaches. The nonliberal characteristics of the Korean economic structure, with its myriad of SMEs highly subordinated to *chaebŏl* in the production system, led MTI to undertake labor market reform to minimize the effects of *chaebŏl* unions' strikes on the national economy. The MTI's proposal aimed at increasing the opportunity costs for holding strikes, eliminating wage payments during strikes, and allowing *chaebŏl* to hire nonregular workers to replace striking union members. This business-friendly labor policy proposal angered labor unions, and the MTI was forced to withdraw the labor law revision in July 1990.[34]

31 *Hankyoreh*, "Hyundaicha paŏp ch'ŏdnal" [The first day of the Hyundai Motor strike], May 16, 1990.

32 Although large-sized firms extensively used corporate welfare programs to subsidize wages in order to bypass the government's wage guideline, SMEs also increased corporate welfare benefits after the 1987 democratization. Yet because of initial discrepancies in corporate welfare benefits across firm size, the gap in corporate welfare benefits did not narrow.

33 *Hankyoreh*, "Nodongbu, nodongbŏp gaejŏngan chŏlhoi" [The MoL's withdrawal of the Labor Law revision legislation], November 7, 1991.

34 *Hankyoreh*, "Giŏpju pyŏnhyang gaeak" [Employer-friendly labor reform], April 7, 1990 and "Nodongbŏp gaechŏng dangbungan angetta" [No labor reform for a while], July 22, 1990.

As another institutional experiment after the 1987 democratic transition, the MoL, which tried to take the initiative in labor policymaking by setting aside the economic bureaucracy, instituted the "Research Committee on the Revision of the Labor Law" (RCRLL) in April 1992, just a few months before the presidential election in December. Unlike the previous labor market reform attempts led by the state, the RCRLL represented business and labor equally, and delegated policy authority to public interest representatives— mostly academic scholars in industrial relations and other pertinent fields.[35] This signaled that the MoL was searching to redefine its role as the primary and neutral state agency to incorporate diverse societal interests into its labor policymaking. Although it was the first political attempt to implement the logic of the tripartite system in Korea's labor policymaking, the deadlock between business and labor, as well as the DLP's internal debates over labor law revision before the presidential election, impeded the submission of the draft bills to the National Assembly.[36] Another round of labor market reform came with the establishment of the Presidential Commission on Industrial Relations Reform (PCIRR) in May 1996.[37]

Led by Park Se-il, secretary to the president on social welfare, the PCIRR intended to establish new institutional foundations for the Korean labor market and industrial relations systems, embracing a neo-liberal ideology. As a reform initiator, Park, representing the intelligentsia (or policy intellectuals), envisioned "neutral" labor reform—based on political and social consensus between capital and labor. The PCIRR proposed a political exchange of granting workers' basic political rights and enhancing labor market flexibility for firms, and included both the official FKTU and the KCTU—the de facto second national federation, though still illegal—into policy discussions, two novel approaches to Korean labor politics.

The *samje* (three systems)—the rights of management to dismiss redundant workers in economic distress, to flexibly allocate workers' hours, and to hire nonregular workers during strikes on a temporary basis—stood for

35 Byung-kook Kim, "The Politics of *Chaebol* Reform," in *Economic Crisis and Corporate Restructuring in Korea: Reforming the* Chaebol, ed. Stephan Haggard, Won-hyuk Lim, and Euysung Kim (Cambridge: Cambridge University Press, 2003), 66.

36 *Hankyoreh,* "Sanŏp pyŏnghwa mokjŏk nodongbŏp jaechujin" [Push for another labor reform attempt with the goal of industrial peace], April 25, 1992; *Chosun Ilbo,* "Nodongbŏp gaechŏng" [Revision of the Labor Law], January 19, 1994.

37 Although the Kim Young-sam administration proposed labor market reforms in conjunction with Korea's accession to the Organisation for Economic Co-operation and Development (OECD), Kim's labor reforms were driven by domestic political actors (Author's interview with Park Se-il, August 2006, Seoul, Korea).

labor market flexibility, challenging two institutional pillars of the internal labor market in the *chaebŏl* sector: permanent employment practices and seniority-based wage systems.[38] Beginning in the early 1990s, several *chaebŏl*, pressed by wage hikes driven by their labor unions and the increasing financial costs of maintaining the internal labor market for regular workers, tried to introduce a wide range of new employment practices to increase intra-firm labor market flexibility, emulating Japan's multi-skill training systems. To accommodate the structural rigidity of the internal labor market in large Japanese firms, management possessed discretionary power over the allocation of a redundant internal workforce and the employment of nonregular workers (mostly female temporary and part-time workers), which helped to protect the jobs of male regular workers in economic downturns.[39] In so doing, large Japanese firms were able to adjust to temporary business fluctuations and technological changes. Yet *chaebŏl* unions, worrying that selective economic incentives and competition among workers would seriously undermine the solidarity of the union organization, fiercely opposed these changes and blocked new employment practices in the *chaebŏl* sector.[40] The only strategy left for *chaebŏl* to cope with the problems of the rigid internal labor market was to enhance labor market flexibility by hiring more nonregular workers and utilizing in-house subcontracting systems, as opposed to more efficiently using redundant regular workers.

In contrast, the *samgŭm* (three prohibitions) represented old repressive labor control policies that militated against workers' political rights: prohibiting labor unions' political participation; banning the intervention of third parties, including labor federations and political parties, in industrial disputes; and legally restricting the number of labor unions to one per work place. Although labor activists had called for the immediate removal of the *samgŭm*, controversy broke out between the two labor federations regarding the legal restriction of one labor union per work place. The FKTU and KCTU were sharply divided over the issue. The FKTU leadership was hesitant to support the legalization of the KCTU since it worried that the KCTU, composed of powerful *chaebŏl* unions in heavy and chemical industries, would take the initiative in labor politics if it could obtain legal recognition from the state.

38 Kim and Lim, "Labor Against Itself."

39 Mari Miura, *From Welfare through Work to Lean Work: The Politics of Labor Market Reform in Japan* (PhD diss., University of California, Berkeley, 2002).

40 *Labor Today*, "Sukryŏn, koyong ganŭngsŏng naega jikinda?" [Skills formation? can it protect job security?], December 7, 2005.

Meanwhile, it also thought that legalizing multiple labor unions at all levels might enhance the level of union political competition in *chaebŏl* firms, many of whose unions were affiliated with the KCTU, ultimately undermining the organizational capacity of the KCTU. Given its established status in *chaebŏl* unions, the KCTU would not gain any further political benefits by legalizing multiple labor unions at all levels. Therefore, the KCTU leadership preferred to introduce multiple labor unions at the national level only.[41]

The legalization of multiple labor unions triggered another set of intense conflicts between management and labor. As a precondition for allowing multiple labor unions, employers demanded a release from paying union officials' wages. They believed that allowing union officials' wages to remain on the firms' payroll encouraged labor strikes as a mode of expression. Therefore, the KEF, one of the two major business associations in charge of managing industrial relations, tried to prohibit the payment of union officials' wages from the firms' payroll in return for allowing workers to be represented by more than one union.[42] Yet the FKI, which represented the political and economic interests of the big business community (i.e., large *chaebŏl*) stubbornly refused the legalization of multiple labor unions at all levels.

The political deadlock over *samje* and *samgŭm* thwarted the PCIRR's attempt to draw up a draft bill based upon political compromise. As an advisory body to the president with no legal authority, the PCIRR could not enforce any political decisions on the state bureaucracy and societal interest groups. Besides, the critical power resource of the intelligentsia—the political backup provided by the presidential leadership—was too unstable to compete with the bureaucracy when it came to policymaking. After the failure of the PCIRR to initiate labor market reform, the inter-ministerial committee undertook the reform initiative in November 1996. The final version drafted by the MoL represented the policy position favored by businesses, incorporating all their demands: the rights of management to dismiss redundant workers in economic distress, to flexibly allocate workers' hours, and to hire nonregular workers on a temporary basis during strikes.[43]

---

41 A former official at the FKTU pointed out that the FKTU leadership was reluctant to embrace the idea of multiple unions, but indeed, numerous labor activists at the FKTU supported the legalization of the KCTU as the second national federation (Author's interview, June 2006, Seoul, Korea).

42 Kim and Lim, "Labor Against Itself"; Yu, *Han'guk ŭi nodong undong inyŏm*.

43 Yi Pyŏng-hun and Yu Pŏm-sang, "Nodong pŏp ŭi hyŏngsŏng kwa chiphaeng e kwanhan nodong chŏngch'i yŏn'gu" [Study of labor politics on the legislation and enforcement of labor laws], *Han'guk sahoe hak* [Korean sociology review] 35, no. 2 (2001): 177–204; Jongryn Mo, "Political Culture and Legislative Gridlock: Politics of

Two opposition leaders, Kim Dae-jung and Kim Jong-pil (Kim Chong-p'il) delayed the legislation on labor market reform bills in the National Assembly, arguing for the postponement of the reform until after the presidential election in December 1997. President Kim Young-sam and his party leadership, however, unilaterally passed the bills in the National Assembly without the consent of the opposition parties. Even worse, a few top party leaders of the ruling New Korea Party (NKP) inserted two additional conditions: a delay in introducing workers' representation by multiple unions at the national level for three years, and mergers and acquisitions (M&As) as a justified condition for management to dismiss workers.[44] Only after facing a general strike initiated by the two competing national labor federations, the FKTU and KCTU, the ruling and opposition parties, which had not actively participated in the political processes of labor market reform, agreed to revise the reform bills again.[45]

The political timing of additional labor market reform could not have been worse. Given the fact that Kim Young-sam was already in his fourth year of a nonrenewable five-year presidency, his government lost the political momentum necessary for driving conflict-ridden labor market reform. Furthermore, the bankruptcy of Hanbo Steel in January 1997 triggered the collapse of the Hanbo Group, the fourteenth largest *chaebŏl,* unveiling a huge scandal and entangling President Kim's son as well as a large number of politicians in the ruling and opposition parties. Neither political party was willing to invest in the intense bargaining and negotiations necessary to draft a labor reform bill that would transform the Korean labor market. The compromise bill recognized employers' rights to dismiss redundant workers, but only in the case of "urgent" business conditions, making the real-world implementation of this clause extremely difficult, especially in

---

Economic Reform in Precrisis Korea," *Comparative Political Studies* 34, no. 5 (2001): 467–92; Se-il Park, *Reforming Labor Management Relations: Lessons from the Korean Experience 1996–97* (Seoul: Korea Development Institute, 2000). The MoL proposed the abolition of the legal prohibitions on labor unions' political participation, third parties' intervention in industrial relations, and multiple unions at the national level. However, it delayed until 2002 the lifting of the limitation on the number of labor unions to one per working place at the firm level. See *Chosun Ilbo*, "Chŏngbu sae nodongbŏpan" [The government's new labor reform bill], December 4, 1996.

44 The New Korea Party (NKP) was renamed the Democratic Liberal Party (DLP) after the United Liberal Democrats (ULD) defected from the DLP in 1995. After the NKP merged with the Democratic Party in 1997, the Grand National Party (GNP) was renamed the NKP.

45 Yong Cheol Kim, "Industrial Reform and Labor Backlash in South Korea," *Asian Survey* 38, no. 12 (1998): 1142–60; Hagen Koo, "The Dilemmas of Empowered Labor in Korea: Korean Workers in the Face of Global Capitalism," *Asian Survey* 40, no. 2 (2000): 227–50.

large *chaebŏl* firms facing strong political opposition to corporate restructuring from well-organized *chaebŏl* unions. The bill also permitted multiple unions at the national level, but instituted a three-year grace period at the firm level. Directly reflected in the bill were the interests of the KCTU and its affiliated *chaebŏl* unions, whose firms would require a massive downsizing of unprofitable corporate structures. Already in early 1997, Korea's economy showed signs of serious recession. Even *chaebŏl*, often believed to be "too big to fail," fell under serious financial distress and were forced to streamline their business organizations. However, the new labor market reform enacted in February 1997 did not enable *chaebŏl* to carry out rapid and comprehensive corporate restructuring under the increasing pressure of economic distress. Another comprehensive labor market reform would have to wait until after the presidential election in December 1997, when a new political leadership would undertake the initiative in the midst of the 1997 East Asian financial crisis.

Labor Market Reform in the Post-1997 Period: New Institutional Changes, Old Legacies, and Segmentation of the Labor Market

The 1997 East Asian financial crisis bifurcated a very small fraction of workers in large *chaebŏl* from others in SMEs and smaller *chaebŏl*, reinforcing the institutional structure of the dualistic labor market divided between labor market insiders (i.e., regular workers in the *chaebŏl* sector) and labor market outsiders (i.e., nonregular workers and SME workers). In an attempt to save on increasing labor costs, firms' propensity to hire nonregular workers had accelerated since the mid-1990s (see Figure 8.6). Beginning in the 1990s, the size of the workforce in the *chaebŏl* sector also started to shrink. The share of employment of the thirty largest *chaebŏl* in the labor market rapidly declined from 6.5 percent to 3.9 percent between 1993 and 2002 because of labor restructuring, hiring more nonregular workers, and freezing new hirings in economic downturns.[46] By the end of 2000, seventeen of the thirty largest *chaebŏl* groups (according to 1997 rankings) were placed under court receivership or Workout programs, including the Daewoo (Taeu) Group, one of the four largest *chaebŏl*.[47] The dire financial

---

46 Song Wŏn-gŭn and Yi Sang-ho, *Chaebŏl ŭi saŏp kujo wa kyŏngjeryŏk chipjung* [The business structure and economic concentration of *chaebŏl*] (Seoul: Nanam Publishing, 2005), 107–10.

47 Jongryn Mo and Chung-in Moon, "Business-Government Relations under Kim Dae-jung," in *Economic Crisis and Corporate Restructuring in Korea*, ed. Haggard, Lim, and Kim, 131.

distress of these *chaebŏl* imposed a tremendous strain on workers' job security. The financial sector, at the center of the crisis, also could not avoid the pressure of extensive labor restructuring when the government injected massive public funds to nationalize two insolvent commercial banks—Korea First Bank and Seoul Bank—before selling them off to foreign capital investors. The government similarly bailed out other faltering commercial banks in return for comprehensive financial reforms, dictating a massive layoff of redundant workers in financial restructuring. In contrast to the high economic uncertainty that workers in SMEs, smaller *chaebŏl,* and the financial industry confronted, workers in large *chaebŏl* were shielded from the pressure of labor restructuring in the post-1997 period, fortifying the rigid, but shrinking internal labor market. The financial crisis and subsequent labor market reform promoted comprehensive corporate restructuring in SMEs, smaller *chaebŏl*, and the financial sector, altering the institutional arrangements of the labor market in these sectors in a more market-oriented direction. Meanwhile, the political and economic effects of the crisis and labor market reform on corporate restructuring were rather limited in large *chaebŏl*. This section discusses these two diverging processes and the consequences of corporate restructuring and labor adjustment in post-1997 Korea.

Amidst the financial crisis, in December 1997, then President-elect Kim Dae-jung advanced major labor market reform that would empower employers to hire workers on a temporary basis and dismiss redundant workers during corporate restructuring, including cases of M&As, in an attempt to salvage firms in intense financial distress. Despite his campaign promise to protect employment security for workers during corporate restructuring, the severity of the East Asian financial crisis and external pressure from the IMF and the U.S. government led him to abruptly shift his position, leaning toward neo-liberal labor reform but with the institutional configurations of societal corporatism (e.g., the Tripartite Commission). Although the IMF and the U.S. government strongly demanded that Kim Dae-jung enhance labor market flexibility to facilitate corporate restructuring, it was Kim himself who interpreted the increase in labor market flexibility as the legalization of collective dismissal during corporate restructuring.[48] Taking advantage of the logic of the two-level game between international and domestic bargaining, Kim adroitly utilized the external pressure of the IMF and the U.S. government to persuade the FKTU and KCTU to accept the

---

48 Ch'oe Yŏng-gi, Chŏn Kwang-sŏk, Yi Ch'ŏl-su, and Yu Pŏm-sang, *Han'guk ŭi nodong pŏp kaejŏng kwa nosa kwan'gye* [Labor law revisions and industrial relations in Korea] (Seoul: Korea Labor Institute, 2000).

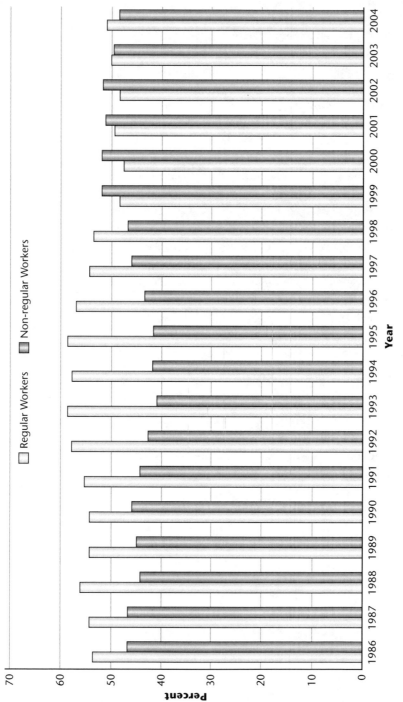

FIGURE 8.6 Trends in Regular and Nonregular Workers in the Korean Labor Market

Source: Korea Labor Institute, *KLI nodong t'onggye* [KLI labor statistics] (Seoul: Korea Labor Institute, 2005); Korean National Statistical Office (www.stat.go.kr).

Note: Korean government statistics do not clearly define categories of regular and nonregular workers. In this chapter, I use the Korean National Statistical Office distinction that divides waged workers into regular and nonregular workers based on the duration of the employment contract.

immediate legalization of employers' rights to dismiss redundant workers during corporate restructuring.[49]

Unlike the Kim Young-sam administration that embraced the neo-liberal ideology of labor market reform, Kim Dae-jung combined elements of societal corporatism into his market-oriented labor market reform, modeling it after that of Western European countries such as Sweden and Germany. With such a tripartite institutional mechanism in labor policymaking, he intended to forge a broader political coalition with the FKTU and KCTU so as to overcome the limitations of the minority ruling coalition of the National Congress for New Politics (NCNP) and the United Liberal Democrats (ULD) in the politics of labor market reform. To create social pacts for labor market reform, then President-elect Kim Dae-jung established the Tripartite Commission in January 1998 even before his inauguration.[50] Members of business associations and labor federations, as well as members of the ruling and opposition parties, were brought together to discuss labor market reform agendas. Less than a month after the Tripartite Commission convened, representatives of the FKTU and KCTU grudgingly accepted immediate implementation of the employers' rights to dismiss redundant workers in corporate restructuring for managerial reasons, including in cases of M&As, and the legalization of the hiring of nonregular workers on a temporary basis, issues that had been intensively debated among management, labor, and government since the early 1990s.[51] In return for the FKTU's and KCTU's political concessions to increasing labor market flexibility, the Tripartite Commission promised to improve workers' basic political rights, which organized labor had strongly demanded since the 1987 democratic transition. It agreed to lift the ban on labor unions' political participation, to legalize teachers' unions, and to expand public welfare programs, but it deferred the final decision on whether to allow workers to be represented by multiple unions at the firm level and whether to keep union officials on firm payrolls.[52]

49 Regarding two-level games, see Robert Putnam, "Diplomacy and Domestic Politics: The Logic of Two-Level Games," *International Organization* 42, no. 3 (Summer 1988): 427–60.

50 As briefly described in the previous section, the Roh Tae-woo and Kim Young-sam administrations implemented the components of a tripartite system when they attempted to initiate labor market reforms, but all of their efforts failed.

51 The hiring of nonregular workers on a temporary basis was permitted only in the 26 occupational categories stipulated by Presidential Decree No. 15828. See Korean Ministry of Labor (www.molab.go.kr).

52 Tripartite Commission, *Major Agreement of the Tripartite Commission between 1998–2005* (May 2005), http://www.lmg.go.kr/bbs/viewbody.asp?code=e_bbs52&page=2&id=17&number=17&keyfield=&keyword=&admin=, accessed December 18, 2011.

The Kim Dae-jung administration expanded previously neglected public welfare programs to complement corporate welfare programs in retrenchment and, more specifically, to persuade the two national labor federations, the FKTU and KCTU, to make political concessions to comprehensive and urgent labor market reform due to the financial crisis. It enlarged the coverage and duration of unemployment insurance programs to provide a social safety net for waged workers, and it also increased the budget for public works projects to create more temporary jobs in the aftermath of the crisis. The government's emphasis on public welfare programs could also be inferred from the increase in national public spending; while total public expenditure for public welfare programs as a percentage of GDP increased from 3.1 percent to 4.2 percent between 1990 and 1997, it increased to 5.9 percent in 1998.[53] Such state-financed welfare expansion signified an important policy transition in the Korean welfare system. While firms had, in the past, shouldered the bulk of the responsibility for welfare through corporate welfare programs, the state now actively intervened to provide social protection.[54]

The Tripartite Commission brought about the legislation of the *samje* and lifted the *samgŭm*, except for the legal limit of labor unions to one per work place at the firm level.[55] Nonetheless, these legal changes instituted by the Tripartite Commission could not change the militant political strategies of *chaebŏl* unions in corporate restructuring. The state's political efforts to expand public welfare programs in exchange for labor market reform could not speed up the processes of corporate restructuring, either. Well-organized *chaebŏl* unions blocked, or at least minimized, the implementation of the labor market reform at the firm level. The financial crisis opened a critical window of political opportunity for the state to drive comprehensive labor market reform, but the state was unable to force individual *chaebŏl* unions to abide by the political consent of the FKTU and KCTU to corporate restructuring in exchange for lifting the *samgŭm* and expanding public welfare programs.

Political compromise among a few political elites of the two labor federations, the FKTU and KCTU, could not bind the rank and file to abide

---

53 The OECD website, www.oecd.org/dataoecd/56/37/31613113.xls.

54 Since employment status is one of the most important criteria to determine the levels of welfare benefits that workers can obtain, the Korean welfare regime would be identified as a highly commodified system, according to Esping-Andersen. Regarding the concepts of commodification and decommodification, see Gøsta Esping-Andersen, *The Three Worlds of Welfare Capitalism* (Princeton, NJ: Princeton University Press, 1990).

55 The legalization of multiple labor unions at the firm level became effective as of July 2011.

by the social pact. The KCTU could not even make a credible commitment to the grand class compromise of the Tripartite Commission because of internal factional conflicts between the hard-liners and the soft-liners over the KCTU's political concessions to labor market reform. Just a few days after the announcement of the social pact for labor market reform at the Tripartite Commission, the rank and file union members of the KCTU voted no confidence and threw out the KCTU leadership that had consented to immediately recognize the rights of management to dismiss redundant workers in corporate restructuring. The KCTU, which had continuously threatened to withdraw from participation in the Tripartite Commission, finally backed out in 1999, leaving only the more externally docile and internally cohesive FKTU as representatives of the working class.[56] While the FKTU was always accused of taking more cooperative political stances toward the state and business, the FKTU leadership secured its political authority over affiliated SME labor unions, in comparison to its KCTU counterpart. In addition, the FKTU leadership publicly announced that it would support Kim Dae-jung during the 1997 presidential race, instead of Kwŏn Yŏng-gil who was another presidential candidate closely affiliated with the KCTU.[57] The different organizational features of the two labor federations and their political relationship with the Kim Dae-jung administration affected the divergent political strategies of the FKTU and KCTU in the politics of labor market reform and corporate restructuring.

Kim Dae-jung's superficial emulation of societal corporatism, which was not upheld by the correct institutional configurations for maintaining it, was troubled from the beginning. The organizational structure of the Tripartite Commission and the lack of support from political parties added to the limitations of its social pact for labor market reform. As a presidential advisory body, the Tripartite Commission was devoid of the legal authority and power to force societal interest groups and the state bureaucracy to adhere to the political compromise. For instance, the MoL, which Kim Dae-jung had disregarded in the labor market reform, did not respect policy recommendations suggested by the Tripartite Commission. The political status of the Tripartite Commission became further weakened by the miniscule role given to political parties and politicians in policy

56 Pak Tong, "Han'guk esŏ 'Sahoe hyŏbyak chŏngch'i ŭi ch'ulbal kwa kŭ pul anjŏng sŏng yoin punsŏk" [The emergence of the social pact and its instability in Korea], *Han'guk chŏngch'i hakhoe po* [Korean political science review] 34, no. 4 (2001): 161–77.

57 Because of the legal prohibition on political activities of labor unions (as of December 1997), FKTU president Pak In-sang issued a statement to support Kim Dae-jung as one of the union members of the FKTU, not as the political representative of the FKTU.

deliberations and labor market reform negotiations. Led by Kim Dae-jung, politicians from both the ruling coalition of the NCNP and the ULD and the majority-opposition GNP were engaged in discussing labor market reform at the First-Phase Tripartite Commission in early 1998. While a few political leaders of the NCNP, personally delegated by then President-elect Kim Dae-jung, actively participated in political negotiations with the representatives of business associations and labor federations, the ruling coalition was not enthusiastic about the drive for comprehensive labor market reform. The opposition GNP initially acquiesced to the labor market reform agenda proposed by the First-Phase Tripartite Commission, but eventually withdrew from it, criticizing the Tripartite Commission for making too many political concessions to organized labor.[58]

Given organizationally weak and ideologically underdeveloped political parties with few linkages to societal interest groups, myopic politicians and political parties calculated that it was too risky to adopt comprehensive labor market reform that would engender enormous adjustment costs on concentrated interest groups, despite the urgent necessity of advancing labor market reform under the pressure of financial distress (see Chapter 4 of this volume regarding the specific role of political parties in corporate restructuring). The adjustment costs generated by labor market reform would fall to the small but vocal interest groups, in particular *chaebŏl* unions and workers. For rational politicians and political parties, the optimal solution was to avoid undertaking any comprehensive labor market reform, whose political consequences would be extremely uncertain and which might cause a political backlash in electoral competition. Political parties with a well-developed ideological spectrum might provide incentives for politicians to initiate reform agendas vital to the national political economy, but saddled with immense short-term costs. Unfortunately, Korean political parties did not have such institutional capacity to expedite politically expensive labor market reform.

In 1998, more than one million workers in SMEs and smaller *chaebŏl* lost their jobs when their firms closed down, or entered into court receivership or Workout programs.[59] Even workers who survived corporate restructuring and

58 *Chosun Ilbo*, "Nosachŏng daetahyŏp" [Grand tripartite compromise on labor reform bills], February 6, 1998.

59 Wonduck Lee and Joohee Lee, "Will the Model of Uncoordinated Decentralization Persist? Changes in Korean Industrial Relations After the Financial Crisis," in *The New Structure of Labor Relations: Tripartism and Decentralization*, ed. Harry C. Katz, Wonduck Lee, and Joohee Lee (Ithaca, NY: Cornell University Press, 2004), 147.

labor adjustment confronted a high level of economic uncertainty, ranging from employment insecurity and a freeze in wages to the retrenchment of corporate welfare benefits. Contrary to policymakers' ex-ante predictions, the post-1997 labor market reform further consolidated the segmentation of the dualistic labor market, even across *chaebŏl*. A shrinking number of well-organized workers in large *chaebŏl*, who had benefited from the rigid internal labor market even before the financial crisis, still enjoyed the privileges of strong employment protection, high wage increases, and generous corporate welfare benefits. As presented in Table 8.3, labor unions affiliated with the KCTU dominated industrial disputes in the post-1997 period, indicating that large *chaebŏl* unions were more likely to raise strikes to pressure management in collective bargaining than those in SMEs affiliated with the FKTU. The militant political strategies of large *chaebŏl* unions in the industrial relations system did not change much after the financial crisis.

The rights of management to dismiss redundant workers under the pressure of financial distress were not fully recognized in large *chaebŏl* firms because of blockage by the labor unions in these firms. As a result, the expansion of unorganized nonregular workers became the firms' preferred option of labor adjustment to avoid intense political conflicts with unions and regular workers. The share of nonregular workers (e.g., temporary, part-time, or fixed-term contract workers) increased from 45.68 percent to 52.13 percent of the Korean labor market, although the percentage has declined slightly since 2001 (see Figure 8.6 presented earlier). Rarely covered by collective bargaining

TABLE 8.3

Composition of Industrial Disputes Across the Korean National Labor Federations

Year	National Labor Federations		Others (no union or no affiliation with national labor federations)
	FKTU	KCTU	
1997	38.5%	61.5%	0%
1998	27.9%	69.8%	2.3%
1999	21.7%	76.3%	2%
2000	12.8%	83.2%	4%
2001	17%	77.4%	5.6%
2002	10.6%	89.1%	0.3%
2003	22.2%	77.8%	0%
2004	13.6%	85.7%	0.7%

Source: Ministry of Labor, *Nodong paeksŏ* [White paper on labor] (Seoul, 2005).

and social welfare programs, a majority of nonregular workers in Korea had to bear the costs of the fluctuation in market conditions, unlike temporary and part-time workers in continental Western European countries, most of whom were equally protected by collective bargaining at the industrial and/ or national level as well as by social welfare programs. As of 2004, nonregular workers received 65 percent of the wages of regular workers and only 40 percent of nonregular workers benefited from four major national social welfare programs, namely unemployment insurance, health insurance, accidental injury insurance, and a national pension program, in comparison to 75 percent of regular workers.[60] To avoid political contestation with labor unions and to save labor costs in terms of wages and social welfare contributions, firms, including SMEs, smaller *chaebŏl*, and large *chaebŏl*, were more interested in expanding the use of these nonregular workers even after the Korean economy was resuscitated from the crisis. Rising inequality between regular workers and nonregular workers in the labor market was the unintended political and economic consequence of the post-1997 labor market reform in Korea.

SMEs, squeezed by transferring costs from *chaebŏl* firms in times of economic slowdown, had a much stronger tendency to hire nonregular workers. According to a survey conducted by the National Statistical Office in 2005, more than 60 percent of nonregular workers were concentrated in firms with less than 29 employees, while only 6.4 percent of them were hired in firms with over 300 employees. SMEs without adequate financial resources to retain their redundant workforce accelerated the hiring of nonregular workers to enhance labor market flexibility.

Firm size also influenced the quality of life for workers in the labor market. From 1997 until 2003, wage differentials and gaps in corporate welfare benefits across firm size consistently expanded, reflecting the exacerbation of labor market inequality (see Table 8.2 in the previous section and Figure 8.7). To cope with their unions' strong demand for higher wage increases, *chaebŏl* strove to sustain economic efficiency and market competitiveness by outsourcing a substantial portion of production lines to SME subcontractors within the firms. This system of subcontracting functioned as a primary mechanism for increasing labor market flexibility in response to changing market conditions and reducing labor costs without provoking *chaebŏl* unions' political resistance to corporate restructuring. As a result, the very bottom tier of SME subcontractors locked in the production system had to put up with the

---

60 Ministry of Labor, *Nodong paeksŏ* [White paper on labor] (Seoul, 2005).

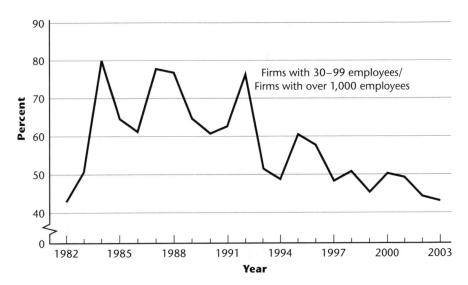

FIGURE 8.7 Corporate Welfare Benefit Differentials Across Firm Size in Korea

Source: Ministry of Labor, *Kiŏp nodong piyong chosa* [Survey report on enterprise labor costs] (Seoul, various issues, 1983–2004).

pressure of cost reductions from higher-tier SME subcontractors. The wage level of regular workers in the former group was even lower than that of non-regular workers in the latter, which indicates the extent of labor market inequality across firm size.[61]

The post-1997 labor market reform exacerbated labor market segmentation and wage inequality not only at the national level but also at the industrial and firm levels. The automobile industry, where a few large assemblers monopolized domestic market share, illustrated the characteristics of labor market segmentation within and across firms. After the financial crisis, a majority of automobile firms, regardless of size, increasingly hired nonregular workers[62] and started to assign them to positions that had previously been

61 Cho Sŏng-jae, Yi Pyŏng-hun, Hong Chang-p'yo, Im Sang-hun, and Kim Yong-hyŏn, *Chadongch'a sanŏp ŭi togŭp kujo wa koyong kwan'gye ŭi kyech'ŭng sŏng* [The subcontracting system and the stratification of the employment structure in the automobile industry] (Seoul: Korea Labor Institute, 2004), 180–89.

62 In the automobile sector, not only short-term temporary workers, but also SME subcontracted workers within the firm are considered nonregular workers because of the entrenched subcontracting system in production. Simply speaking, blue-collar union members are categorized as regular workers, whereas the rest of the blue-collar workers engaged in automobile production are regarded as nonregular workers.

TABLE 8.4

Annual Wage Differentials Across Firm Size in the
Korean Automobile and Manufacturing Industries

Firm Size	Automobile Industry		Manufacturing Industry		
	Wage (A) (10,000 won)	Ratio	Wage (B) (10,000 won)	Ratio	A/B (%)
5–49 Employees	1,377	40.4	1,390	47.7	99.1
50–99 Employees	1,623	47.6	1,699	57.6	95.5
100–299 Employees	2,005	58.8	1,955	66.3	100.3
300–499 Employees	2,558	75.0	2,334	79.2	109.6
Over 500 Employees	3,411	100	2,948	100	115.7

Source: Cho Sŏng-jae, Yi Pyŏng-hun, Hong Chang-p'yo, Im Sang-hun, and Kim Yong-hyŏn, *Chadongch'a sanŏp ŭi togŭp kujo wa koyong kwan'gye ŭi kyech'ŭng sŏng* [The subcontracting system and the stratification of the employment structure in the automobile industry] (Seoul: Korea Labor Institute, 2004), 155.

undertaken by regular workers.[63] Compared with other manufacturing industries, large firms in the automobile industry pressed subcontracting SMEs even more harshly into shouldering adjustment costs after the financial crisis. As demonstrated in Table 8.4, wage inequality in the automobile industry across firm size was even worse than in other manufacturing sectors.

The political strategies of firms and labor unions in corporate restructuring are better understood if labor adjustments within the automobile industry and firms are taken into account. The sector itself illustrated distinctly divergent patterns of corporate restructuring and labor union political responses to labor adjustments at the firm level. Except for Hyundai Motors, all major Korean auto assemblers—Asia/Kia, Daewoo, Samsung (Samsŏng), and Ssangyong—went bankrupt and were taken over by domestic and foreign capital investors. These insolvent firms, as well as Hyundai Motors, the sole survivor of the financial crisis, were forced to conduct comprehensive corporate restructuring to streamline their business organizations. Among a wide range of political and economic constraints, two factors influenced the political paths of corporate restructuring in the Korean automobile industry: 1) the degree to which the Korean government attempted to direct the processes of corporate restructuring and labor adjustment, and 2) how serious the firm's difficulty was—in other words, whether the firm was in financial distress, in court receivership, Workout programs, or even in bankruptcy.

Contrary to past contentious industrial relations, management and the labor union of Asia/Kia Motors forged a strong political coalition in

63 Cho Sŏng-jae, Yi Pyŏng-hun, Hong Chang-p'yo, Im Sang-hun, and Kim Yong-hyŏn, *Chadongch'a sanŏp ŭi togŭp kujo wa koyong kwan'gye ŭi kyech'ŭng sŏng*, 178 and 339.

opposition to the takeovers by other domestic firms, specifically the Samsung Group when it entered bankruptcy protection (*pudo yuye hyŏbyak*) in July 1997. While top managers stubbornly resisted giving up managerial rights in corporate restructuring, the labor union consented to moderate wage increases and a schedule of "gradual" employment restructuring suggested by management—e.g., natural attrition, freezing of new hiring, and so forth—in exchange for no collective dismissals. This political alliance between capital and labor, although very short-lived, halted comprehensive corporate restructuring for several months and blocked the intervention of the creditor banks and the government. In October 1997, the announcement of Asia/Kia's placement in court receivership (*pŏpjŏng kwalli*) swiftly turned around the corporate restructuring situation; top managers were displaced and the labor union raised industrial strikes against a third-party takeover, agitating for the nationalization of Asia/Kia and the guarantee of employment protection for workers in cvorporate restructuring. Almost a year later, the creditor banks and the government, which had vacillated between several corporate restructuring options, finally decided to sell off Asia/Kia to Hyundai Motors, which, in turn, pledged to protect workers' job security until the year 2000.

Unlike Asia/Kia Motors, the other ailing automobile assemblers were taken over by foreign capital investors. Samsung Motors, which had finally gotten into the business during the Kim Young-sam administration after several years of political lobbying, tried to rapidly expand its business by bidding for insolvent Asia/Kia Motors, but its strategy did not work. In the midst of the financial crisis, Kim Dae-jung proposed a "big deal" policy (or business swap among the top five *chaebŏl*) where the government would select a few competitive and uncompetitive industrial sectors for each *chaebŏl* to focus on and sell off in corporate restructuring. The Kim Dae-jung administration recommended (or even pressured) that the Daewoo Group take over Samsung Motors in exchange for handing Daewoo Electronics over to the Samsung Group.[64] The big deal policy symbolized another state-initiated industrial policy for rationalizing large *chaebŏl* that had always been blamed for inefficient investments in unrelated industrial diversification projects. This plan of corporate restructuring for Samsung Motors not only raised a series

64 The Roh Tae-woo administration had already implemented the industrial specialization of *chaebŏl* in the early 1990s, most of which had failed. The "big deal" policy was another extension of the past industrial specialization policy, but it was more directly informed by the government's specific guidelines. Regarding the industrial specialization policy during the Roh Tae-woo administration, see Kim, "The Politics of *Chaebol* Reform."

of labor strikes by its workers, but also inspired political rallies by SME sub-contractors and regional business associations, all of whom stood to suffer if Samsung Motors closed down its production lines. No political guarantee of the succession of employment and business contracts was seriously discussed at the bargaining table. A tedious seven-month-long "big deal" policy debate failed to result in an agreement between the two *chaebŏl* groups, and the Samsung Group decided to call for court receivership of Samsung Motors in July 1999. Although Samsung Motors' workers resisted the business swap and the foreign takeover, creditor bankers decided to sell off insolvent Samsung Motors to another foreign capital investor, Renault, in 2000.

Another small automobile assembler, Ssangyong Motors, which had triggered the critical financial distress of the Ssangyong Group, was merged with Daewoo Motors in December 1997. Instead of firing redundant workers in corporate restructuring, Daewoo Motors proposed that the labor union at Ssangyong Motors accept an unpaid vacation program.[65] The bankruptcy of the Daewoo Group in 1999, however, put Ssangyong Motors under a Workout program until Shanghai Motors purchased it in 2004. In contrast to the domestic takeover, the new foreign capital investor attempted to conduct comprehensive corporate restructuring, which brought management and the labor union into contention over issues of downsizing business structures and employment as well as moving production lines to China. Failing to recover its business competitiveness and profitability in the domestic market, Ssangyong Motors was placed under a Workout program again in January 2009. Shanghai Motors, the majority shareholder in Ssangyong Motors, finally gave up its managerial rights.

The collapse of Daewoo Motors, the second largest automobile assembler, posed a serious corporate restructuring challenge, not only for its creditor banks, but also for the government. The aggressive or even reckless investment strategies of the Daewoo Group drove Daewoo Motors into a Workout program in 1999 and then finally into bankruptcy in 2000. Haunted by the massive size of collective dismissals in corporate restructuring, the labor union opposed a foreign takeover and proposed the nationalization of the firm to protect employment. Given the fact that no domestic firms were

65 In contrast to Daewoo Motors' announcement of its intention to assure employment protection, 48.6 percent of Ssangyong employees had already left the firm in 1998, according to a report of the Korea Stock Exchange (*Hankyoreh*, "5 dae group jaknyŏn toesa 8man myŏng" [The number of the five top *chaebŏl*'s retired employees, 80,000], April 7, 1999). It would imply that other types of employment adjustment strategies, such as recruiting volunteers for early retirement programs or outsourcing business organizations, were comprehensively implemented although there was no massive collective dismissal in corporate restructuring.

interested in undertaking the restructuring of Daewoo Motors, burdened as it was with enormous liabilities and deficits, the only feasible solution was to look for foreign capital investors, notwithstanding the labor union's resistance. After the bankruptcy of Daewoo Motors, the impending necessity of corporate restructuring triggered more extensive employment restructuring, contrary to the firm's previous strategy of retaining redundant workers in financial distress. In addition to encouraging early retirement and expanding the number of nonregular workers, Daewoo Motors management announced in February 2001 that it would dismiss 1,750 workers, the largest collective dismissal ever reported since the financial crisis.[66] Although the labor union attempted to nullify the employment restructuring plan by raising a series of strikes and work stoppages, the political commitment of the Kim Dae-jung administration to corporate restructuring influenced management's decision.[67] After several rounds of failed biddings, in 2002 GM conditionally took over Daewoo Motors in exchange for industrial peace, demanding that the labor union keep industrial disputes at a lower than average level in GM factories around the world for the next five years.[68]

Unlike the previous four cases, Hyundai Motors was able to survive the financial crisis without resorting to court receivership or a Workout program, even though it was also under severe financial distress. In 1998, Hyundai Motors, which dominated the market with more than 40 percent of the domestic share, undertook extensive corporate restructuring programs.[69] To respond to the drastic decline in domestic sales, interest hikes, and loan recalls, Hyundai Motors, entangled in complicated cross-shareholding and cross-loan guarantees with other affiliate firms and suffering from a 490 percent debt-to-equity ratio as of 1997, announced its decision to lay off 8,189 workers in May 1998. The number comprised 18 percent of Hyundai Motors' total workforce.[70] The top management of Hyundai Motors tried

66 *Hankyoreh*, "Chŏngli haego, chongpaŏp jŏnmang" [Collective dismissal, prediction for a general labor strike], February 17, 2001.

67 Author's interview with a business executive at GM Daewoo Motors, August 2006 (Seoul, Korea).

68 *Hankyoreh*, "Daewoocha maegak hyŏpsang sasilsang tagyŏl" [A bargaining deal for Daewoo Motors is done], April 10, 2002; Author's interview with a business executive at GM Daewoo Motors, August 2006 (Seoul, Korea).

69 Cho Sŏng-jae, Yi Pyŏng-hun, Hong Chang-p'yo, Im Sang-hun, and Kim Yong-hyŏn, *Chadongch'a sanŏp ŭi togŭp kujo wa koyong kwan'gye ŭi kyech'ŭng sŏng*, 25–26.

70 Chu Mu-hyŏn, "Kyŏngje wigi ihu ŭi kiŏp pyŏl naebu nodong sijang ŭi kujo pyŏnhwa: Hyŏndae chadongch'a ŭi sarye" [Structural changes in the internal labor market after the financial crisis: A case study of Hyundai Motors], *Sanŏp nodong yŏn'gu* [Industry and labor studies] 8, no. 1 (2002): 75–110; *Chosun Ilbo*, "Hyundaicha 8,189 chŏngli haego bangchim" [Hyundai Motors' plan to lay off 8,189 workers], May 20, 1998.

to push forward labor restructuring since it expected to benefit from the legalization of management's rights to dismiss redundant workers in corporate restructuring. Since it was the first attempt by large *chaebŏl* firms to implement these rights since their legislation, the outcome of labor adjustment at Hyundai Motors was expected to affect not only the firm, but also the automobile industry and the Korean national political economy.

After a three-month tug of war between management and the labor union over labor restructuring, the industrial dispute was finally resolved, with the political intervention of a few NCNP political leaders dispatched by President Kim Dae-jung. Despite hawkish sentiment arguing for the dispersal of union members of Hyundai Motors by police forces, the NCNP politicians, including Roh Moo-hyun—then vice-chairman of the NCNP and the next president of Korea—strove to arbitrate between management and the labor union at the bargaining table.[71] Management and the labor union at Hyundai Motors agreed to lay off 277 workers, including 144 female cafeteria service workers, and implement an unpaid vacation program for 1,961 workers in August 1998.[72] Neither business associations nor labor federations played a pivotal role in facilitating the political mediation of conflicting interests between management and the labor union at Hyundai Motors. The KCTU, the national federation affiliated with Hyundai Motors' labor union, further complicated political negotiations by threatening to raise a general strike to block the scheduled layoffs at Hyundai Motors. Business associations also did not make any political efforts to bargain with labor on behalf of the business community.

As a result of the state-led political intervention in corporate restructuring and labor adjustment, management at Hyundai Motors could lay off redundant workers in corporate restructuring, but due to the stubborn opposition of the labor union, it could not conduct the extensive labor adjustment programs that it had proposed in the first place. The political turmoil over corporate restructuring further exacerbated distrust between management and the labor union. In June 2000, the labor union at Hyundai Motors, haunted by fears of massive layoffs in corporate restructuring, urged management to sign a contract on an "Agreement to Employment Security" to assure employment protection for its union members. Furthermore, it asked that management notify and consult with the union in advance regarding any corporate strategies pertinent to labor adjustments brought

---

71 *Hankyoreh*, "Hyundaicha gyŏngchal tuip sinjungron" [A cautious approach to the use of the police force in the Hyundai Motors' strike], August 18, 1998.

72 As of 2000, most of the laid-off workers had returned to Hyundai Motors because of the firm's rapid economic turnaround.

to the collective bargaining table in 2003, such as moving production sites abroad, introducing new car models, divesting its business organization, and subcontracting production lines. Management consented to all of these conditions.[73] For management at Hyundai Motors, using nonregular workers could be the only solution to replace its rigid internal labor market. Not surprisingly, nonregular workers hired on a temporary basis and employed by SME subcontractors within the firm became a buffer zone for union members in subsequent corporate restructuring. In exchange for employment security for its rank and file, the labor union at Hyundai Motors agreed to a 16.9 percent increase in the hiring rate of nonregular workers. As a result, the number of nonregular temporary workers rose from 1,808 to 3,517 between 1999 and 2000.[74]

The institutional structures of the rigid internal labor market in a few large *chaebŏl* remained intact or became even more consolidated, regardless of the legislative changes in labor laws and regulations. The consequences of the limited implementation of the post-1997 labor market reform in corporate restructuring affected the freezing of new hirings for regular workers in the labor market, which resulted in an increase in the unemployment rate for youth after the financial crisis.[75] As of 2003, the percentage of large firms (with more than 300 workers) in the Korean manufacturing industry was 0.2 percent, but the share of the workforce hired in these firms was 20.8 percent, implying that labor restructuring in these firms would have far-reaching effects on the conditions of the Korean labor market.[76] After the 1997 financial crisis, a significant number of large *chaebŏl* firms implemented labor adjustment strategies in corporate restructuring, by expanding the hiring of nonregular workers, limiting/freezing new hirings of regular workers, and transferring the increasing financial burdens of *chaebŏl* firms' production costs to SMEs. In addition, numerous large *chaebŏl* resorted to early retirement programs if they desperately needed to shed regular workers, in order to minimize the resistance of labor unions and workers in cases of corporate restructuring.[77]

73 Cho Sŏng-jae, Yi Pyŏng-hun, Hong Chang-p'yo, Im Sang-hun, and Kim Yong-hyŏn, *Chadongch'a sanŏp ŭi togŭp kujo wa koyong kwan'gye ŭi kyech'ŭng sŏng*, 82.

74 Chu Mu-hyŏn, "Kyŏngje wigi ihu ŭi kiŏp pyŏl naebu nodong sijang ŭi kujo pyŏnhwa," 84 and 87.

75 The youth unemployment rate, referring to people between the ages of 20–29, was recorded at 7.7 percent, which was almost twice as high as the total unemployment rate of 3.7 percent. See Korean National Statistics Office, www.stat.go.kr.

76 Pae Kyu-sik, Yi Sang-min, Paek P'il-gyu, Im Un-t'aek, and Yi Kyu-yong, *Chungso chejo ŏp ŭi koyong kwan'gye*, 57.

77 Ch'oe Kang-sik and Yi Kyu-yong, *Uri nara kiŏp ŭi koyong chojŏng silt'ae* (III) [Employment adjustment in Korean firms (III)] (Seoul: Korea Labor Institute, 1995), 28.

Like management's rights to dismiss redundant workers in corporate re-structuring, a performance-based wage system was very discriminately implemented. One of the core institutional pillars that sustained the old model of the labor market in Korea—a seniority-based wage system—had eroded since the financial crisis, especially in the majority of *chaebŏl* firms. While only 1.3 percent of firms—mostly large *chaebŏl* firms—adopted a performance-based wage system in 1996, the percentage increased remarkably to 19.4 percent as of 2002, although the wage system was still a combination of performance-based and seniority-based elements.[78] Interestingly, the performance-based wage system applied primarily to white-collar workers who became the main target of corporate restructuring after the financial crisis, lacking the protection of labor unions. Blue-collar workers (in the *chaebŏl* sector) were left in the old seniority-based wage system due to the union's skepticism of "fair" evaluation criteria of performance-based remuneration systems.

After the financial crisis, several industrial sectors attempted to build industry unions in order to overcome the political and organizational limitations of enterprise unions in preventing massive layoffs in corporate re-structuring, many of which were only interested in very narrowly defined economic interests within individual firms. The Korean Metal Workers' Federation (KMWF), affiliated with the KCTU, and the Korean Financial Industry Union (KFIU), affiliated with the FKTU, were two prime examples of both the strengths and limitations of industry unions in Korea. The KMWF tried to establish an industry union, encompassing the automobile, shipbuilding, steel, and machinery industries. However, powerful *chaebŏl* union members, namely Hyundai Motors and Daewoo Shipbuilding, voted against joining the industry union since their workers already enjoyed guaranteed employment protection and high wage increases, and did not believe that they would reap any extra political and economic benefits by participating in the industry union.[79] A majority of *chaebŏl* unions in heavy industries finally decided to join the KMWF to prepare for the legalization of multiple labor unions at the firm level, which was originally scheduled for 2007 but once again postponed. Nonetheless, it remains to be seen whether or not *chaebŏl* unions are willing to cooperate with SMEs and the KMWF leadership at the collective bargaining table on the industrial level. Despite a few successful trials of collective bargaining among the SMEs at the industry level, the *chaebŏl* unions' halfhearted response to an industry union has been the KMWF's most serious organizational obstacle.

78 Wonduck Lee and Byung-yoo Chun, "Flexibility in the Korean Labor Market," paper presented at the KCESRI-OECD Seminar on Korea issues, Paris, 2004, 19.

79 *Hankyoreh*, "Daewoo Chosun dŭng 3 g'od sanbyŏl bugyŏl" [Three large chaebŏl firms' rejection to join the industrial union], June 28, 2003.

Similarly, the KFIU for the commercial banking industry confronted a collective action dilemma.[80] In exchange for the IMF's financial rescue package, the Korean government pledged to restructure its backward financial sector and open the financial market to foreign investment. In the first phase of financial restructuring, five commercial banks were closed down and seven others were to maintain their businesses under the condition that they reduce the number of nonperforming loans and eliminate their redundant workforce. Consequently, by 1998, 34 percent of workers in the commercial banking sector had to leave their jobs.[81] In opposition to the government-led financial restructuring, the KFIU, which encompassed the commercial banking sector, was established in March 2000.[82] Yet the KFIU could not effectively control its enterprise unions since most financial and human resources for union activities still remained at the firm level.[83] More seriously, member unions diverged in their economic interests in financial restructuring, further complicating collective action at the industry level. When the KFIU organized the first strike against the Kim Dae-jung administration's financial restructuring, its rank and file of enterprise unions in competitive banks—the Hana, Hanmi, and Shinhan banks—refused to join the strike since employees in these profitable commercial banks regarded financial restructuring as a great opportunity to rapidly expand their businesses.[84] By contrast, employees of banks that received massive public funds from the state in return for extensive financial restructuring tried to block mergers and acquisitions

80 Mansur Olson, *The Logic of Collective Action* (New York: Schochen Books, 1965).

81 Yi Chong-sun, "Han'guk ŏi sin chayu chuŭi chŏk kujo kaehyŏk kwa nodong sijang pyŏnhwa" [Neo-liberal economic restructuring and the change in the Korean labor market], *Han'guk sahoe hak* [Korean sociology review] 36 no. 3 (2002): 30.

82 Chŏng Ihwan and Yi Pyŏng-hun, "Kyŏngje wigi wa koyong kwan'gye ŭi pyŏnhwa: Tae kiŏp sarye rŭl chungsim ŭro" [Changes in employment relations after the 1997 economic crisis: A case study with a focus on large-sized firms], *Sanŏp nodong yŏn'gu* [Industry and labor studies] 6, no. 1 (2000), 27–58; Kim Myŏn-hŭi, "Han'guk kŭmyung sanŏp kujo chojŏng kwa nodong chohap undong" [Financial restructuring and labor movements in Korea], *Han'guk chŏngch'i hakhoe po* [Korean political science review] 38, no. 2 (2004): 167–88; Yu Ki-rak, "Nodong chohap ŭi kwŏllyŏk chawŏn kwa chiphap haengwi e taehan yŏn'gu: Kŭmyung kujo chojŏng kwa chŏn'guk kŭmyung nodong chohap yŏnmaeng ŭi taeŭng 1997–2000" [Power resources and labor unions' collective actions: Political responses of the Korean financial industry union to financial restructuring, 1997–2000], *Sanŏp nodong yŏn'gu* [Industry and labor studies] 7, no. 2 (2001): 129–64.

83 *Labor Today*, "Yŏchŏnhi giŏpbyŏl nojogwanhaeng" [Still enterprise union-centered labor movements], December 19, 2005.

84 *Chosun Ilbo*, "Kŭmyung nojo paŏp tupyŏ" [The KFIU's vote for a labor strike], July 3, 2000; *Hankook Economic Daily*, "Kŭmyung nojo paŏp choeso 5 ilgan jisok" [The KFIU's strike will last for the five days at least], July 11, 2000; *Seoul Economic Daily*, "11 il kŭmyung nojo chongpaŏp yŏgo" [The KFIU's July 11 labor strike announcement], July 3, 2000.

that might bring about large-scale labor restructuring. Several general strikes or strike threats against financial restructuring did not bear fruit since the affiliated enterprise unions refused to follow the KFIU leadership, prioritizing their own banks' profits. Still, enterprise unions dominated industrial relations, in spite of the labor sector's initiative to organize industry unions. The fundamental organizational weakness of enterprise unionism—narrowly defined economic interests at the firm level—could not overcome the collective action dilemma in the post-1997 period.

Under the Roh Moo-hyun administration, the Dutch labor model of social partnership was chosen as another foreign labor model for adoption by Korea. A few top policymakers, like Yi Chŏng-u, policy chief of the Presidential Office, envisioned that a system of social consensus embedded in the Dutch model of social partnership, which included both capital and labor in socioeconomic policy deliberations with a focus on economic efficiency, would stabilize Korea's conflict-ridden contentious industrial relations.[85] However, the Roh Moo-hyun administration persuaded neither the big business community, which was reluctant to embrace the idea of union participation in management, nor organized labor, which was very skeptical of the intention behind this new institutional design of labor policymaking.

After the failed reform attempt to institutionalize the Dutch model of social partnership, in December 2006 the Roh Moo-hyun administration passed labor reform bills by building a political consensus with the majority-opposition GNP and the cooperative FKTU. By stipulating a mandatory change of nonregular employment status to regular status after the first two years of the employment contract, the government endeavored to improve employment protection and working conditions for nonregular workers, most of whom were exposed to high job insecurity, low wages, and the lack of social welfare programs. Once again, the new legislation, which had intended to achieve greater protection for disadvantaged nonregular workers in the labor market, yielded divergent processes and consequences through its implementation. In July 2009 when the government started to enforce implementation of changing employment contract terms from nonregular status to regular status, a few large *chaebŏl* firms with financial resources guaranteed job security for nonregular workers who had already served the first two years of temporary employment, but with limitations of promotion opportunities and wage increases. Meanwhile, SMEs and smaller *chaebŏl* firms either laid off nonregular workers after the two-year employment contract or continued to hire them as nonregular workers in violation of labor laws.

85 *Hankyoreh*, "Yi Chŏng-woo chŏngchaek siljang shin nosagwangye naedal yung-wak" [New outline for industrial relations], July 4, 2003.

Conclusion

Labor market reforms are driving forces behind corporate restructuring that aim to bring about firms' quick economic turnaround during financial distress. Expecting positive returns of institutional complementarities between labor market reform and corporate restructuring in the Korean national economy, the Kim Dae-jung administration proposed comprehensive labor market reform, ranging from relaxing employment protection for regular workers to deregulating the hiring of nonregular workers in order to accelerate corporate restructuring in the midst of the financial crisis. However, the Kim Dae-jung administration's labor market reform proceeded in a very different direction from what policymakers had predicted. Despite important legal changes in labor laws and regulations, the weakening of the employment protection system for regular workers had been implemented in a very discriminating way, leaving a shrinking fraction of well-unionized regular workers in the large *chaebŏl* shielded from the pressure of labor adjustments in corporate restructuring. A small group of these privileged workers who belonged to large *chaebŏl* impeded corporate restructuring that would undermine their employment security and working conditions, wielding monopoly market power and a strong organizational capacity at the collective bargaining table. In contrast, a majority of workers hired in SMEs and smaller *chaebŏl* encountered much more volatile employment conditions after legalization of management's rights to lay off redundant workers in times of distress.

Korea experienced two critical turning points in the labor market and the national political economy: the 1987 political democratization and the 1997 financial crisis. Political democratization resulted in the collapse of the state-led labor coordination system in the labor market, and the economic shock triggered the shift of the Korean business community toward the adoption of more neo-liberal labor market institutions. The primary purpose of Korea's labor market reforms in the period before and after the financial crisis was to facilitate corporate restructuring, particularly in large *chaebŏl,* many of which had already been suffering from surplus production capacities, redundant workers, and low market profitability. The post-1997 labor market reform was not successful in transforming the rigid internal labor market of large *chaebŏl* into a labor market with more flexibility in corporate restructuring, and it further consolidated the segmentation of the dualistic labor market. For SMEs and smaller *chaebŏl*, the labor market reform accelerated corporate restructuring during financial distress, allowing them to shed even redundant *regular* workers. The political and economic effects of the post-1997 labor market reform on corporate restructuring have been mixed. Despite the intent of the state and policymakers, Korea's labor market reform strengthened the privileges of core regular workers in large *chaebŏl* firms, as opposed to weakening the rigid internal labor market.

Korea is still looking for an alternative labor model that will fit well with the institutional configurations of its national political economy. Confronting the global financial crisis since 2008, the government responded to the increasing pressure of economic distress on the Korean labor market by increasing budget allocations for public works projects to absorb the unemployed and the underemployed as well as providing employment subsidies for SMEs. Additionally, a large number of firms opted for retaining redundant workers in return for wage restraints or wage reductions, as opposed to layoffs. As a result, Korea's unemployment rates remained relatively low (3.4 percent as of October 2009) during economic distress, compared with those of the United States (10 percent as of November 2009) and Japan (5.1 percent as of October 2009).[86]

While the state and policymakers focused on the increase in labor market flexibility by undermining the privileges of regular workers in large *chaebŏl*, most labor market reforms led to the consolidation of the strong, but shrinking internal labor market for these workers. Korea's dualistic labor market may sustain economic growth centered on large *chaebŏl*, but it will ultimately undermine the social and political stability of the country by exacerbating labor market inequality across employment status and firm size. As alternative strategies to resolve intricate problems of labor market flexibility and labor market inequality, state policymakers have recently proposed the expansion of performance-based wage systems to alleviate firms' financial burdens from increasing labor costs and the improvement of wages and social welfare benefits for nonregular workers to reduce firms' incentives to hire "cheap" nonregular workers. Considering intensified global market competition and the fragmented structure of enterprise unionism, neither firms nor labor unions are willing to make concessions to political exchanges for employment security and wage restraints. Without any government subsidies and labor union compromise, firms are less likely to pay equal wages and social welfare benefits for nonregular workers. To complement the underdevelopment of institutional mechanisms to foster either market-based or strategic coordination, the state will need to undertake the role of coordinator in forging a consensus between business and labor for economic, social, and political sustainability.

86 Bank of Korea (www.bok.or.kr); Japanese Ministry of Internal Affairs and Communication (www.stat.go.jp); U.S. Bureau of Labor Statistics (www.bls.gov).

9 Welfare Institutional Change in South Korea

Ito Peng

This chapter examines relationships between corporate restructuring and the reform of the welfare institution in South Korea (hereafter Korea).[1] Specifically, it will address the following two questions: 1) how have Korea's changing political economic institutions affected welfare restructuring and vice versa, and 2) if, how, and why changes required for welfare institutions to facilitate corporate restructuring also triggered complementary measures in other areas that resulted in not only corporate but also system restructuring. To answer these questions, I will first discuss how the welfare institution in Korea is integrated with other key institutions, such as corporate and labor market institutions in the context of the Korean political economy. Here, I emphasize that the welfare institution in Korea is closely interlocked with other key institutions to provide institutional complementarity. I use the varieties of capitalism (VoC) perspective to show how this institutional complementarity has afforded Korea a competitive advantage in pursuing its economic development objectives.

1 In this chapter, I use the term "welfare" to include a wide range of public, corporate, and private provisions and services provided to individuals and families to ensure their social and economic well-being. These include social security and social insurance programs such as pensions, health care, employment or unemployment insurance, family allowances, and income maintenance and public assistance, as well as services such as personal and social services and a variety of child and elderly care services and provisions. I also use Peter Hall and Kathleen Thelen's conceptualization of institution here: "a set of regularized practices with a rule-like quality in the sense that the actors expect the practices to be observed, whether they are backed by sanctions or not." See Peter Hall and Kathleen Thelen, "Institutional Changes in Varieties of Capitalism," paper presented at ISA RC-19 Conference, Chicago, Illinois, September 8, 2005, 3. These practices may range from legislations to formal and informal organizational procedures/norms.

Second, I illustrate how changes in the Korean welfare regime affect, and are in turn affected by, systems restructuring in that country. Korea's developmental welfare regime was originally instituted as a part of the Park Chung-hee (Pak Chŏng-hŭi, 1961–79) government's economic and industrial development strategy in the 1960s.[2] Over the years, however, this welfare regime gradually evolved in response to changes in the country's social, economic, and political contexts. The evolutionary changes in welfare institutions did not happen by themselves; rather, they occurred in conjunction with changes in other sectors such as the state, labor market, and business. Thus welfare regime changes were closely articulated with other institutional changes taking place at the time. The political democratization of 1987 and the Asian economic crisis of 1997 mark two critical junctures in postwar Korean history. During these two critical moments, significant changes were made to the welfare state institution, leading to an expansion of the welfare state. It is therefore useful to divide the evolutionary trajectory of the postwar Korean welfare institution into three periods marked by the two junctures: 1) the authoritarian developmentalist period (1961–1987); 2) the political democratization period (1987–1997); and 3) the post-economic crisis period (1997-now). Even though the political democratization and the economic crisis were two high points in Korea's welfare institutional changes, we need to be mindful that less visible and incremental changes were taking place during the period of relative stability. It is therefore important that we examine the dynamics of the welfare institution in Korea during the periods before, in between, and after the two critical junctures.

In the next section I will first elaborate on how the Korean welfare institution interlocks with other key institutions, particularly corporate and labor market institutions. Using the VoC perspective on institutional complementarity, I describe the institutional interlock among welfare, the state, the corporate sector, and the labor market in Korea. I use Kathleen Thelen and Wolfgang Streeck's concept of slow evolutionary changes to show changes and continuities in relation to the Korean welfare regime.[3] In the

2 Ian Holliday, "Productivist Welfare Capitalism: Social Policy in East Asia," *Political Studies* 48, no. 4 (2000): 706–23; Huck-Ju Kwon, "Reforming of the Developmental Welfare State in Korea: Advocacy Coalition and Health Politics," in *Transforming the Developmental Welfare State in East Asia*, ed. Huck-Ju Kwon (New York: Palgrave, 2006), 27–49.

3 Wolfgang Streeck and Kathleen Thelen, eds., *Beyond Continuity: Institutional Changes in Advanced Political Economies* (Oxford: Oxford University Press, 2005); Kathleen Thelen, *How Institutions Evolve: The Political Economy of Skills in Germany, Britain, the United States and Japan* (New York: Cambridge University Press, 2004).

third section, I elaborate on the evolutionary trajectory of the Korean welfare institution since the 1960s. Here, I show not only the significant welfare state expansion that followed the political democratization of 1987 and the economic crisis of 1997, but also how changes associated with these events have, in fact, masked the less visible but incremental changes that were taking place during the period of relative stability. Finally, in the last section, I summarize key lessons from the Korean case.

Theoretical Framework

Institutional Complementarity

It is now widely accepted that the Korean welfare regime, like other East Asian welfare regimes, is highly productivist in nature. It has been argued that by limiting social rights to the productive sectors of society, the Korean welfare state subordinates social policy to serve the state's economic development objectives.[4] But how exactly does the Korean welfare regime configure and function with other key institutions to achieve the country's economic objectives? The VoC literature suggests that core institutions making up a country's political economy—financial, corporate, vocational, and welfare state institutions—are organized in such a way that they are integrated as a whole, and, moreover, they serve to mutually reinforce each other. Peter Hall and David Soskice contend that national economic institutions often integrate themselves to produce institutional complementarity.[5] According to these authors, institutions located in different spheres of the political economy eventually arrive at a complementary arrangement as they organize themselves to generate increased returns.[6] Once established, it would be difficult to break such an institutional equilibrium because changes in one institutional sphere will necessitate complementary changes in other spheres, raising the overall transactional costs. Wolfgang Streeck, however, points out that institutional complementarity, or systems integration, is not as self-evident or rational as Peter Hall and David Soskice portray. Rather, systems integration is a deeply political process that involves constant inputs and negotiations among political and societal actors. For Wolfgang Streeck, such systems integration is "continuously established, restored, redefined,

4 Soonman Kwon and Ian Holliday, "The Korean Welfare State: A Paradox of Expansion in an Era of Globalisation and Economic Crisis," *International Journal of Social Welfare* 16, no. 3 (2007): 242–48; Holliday, "Productivist Welfare Capitalism."

5 Peter A. Hall and David W. Soskice, eds., *Varieties of Capitalism: The Institutional Foundations of Comparative Advantage* (Oxford: Oxford University Press, 2003), 17–21.

6 Ibid., 17–21.

and defended against all sorts of disorganizing forces, from special sectoral interests to the accidents of local decision making in limited time and with restricted information."[7]

From the VoC perspective, we can see how the Korean welfare regime is interlocked with corporate and labor market institutions to create institutional complementarity. The limited and occupationally segregated social insurance programs that were initially introduced in the 1960s and the 1970s complemented very well the Korean corporate and labor market institutions that were developed to achieve rapid economic development. By limiting social protection to core workers in large industries, civil servants, military personnel, and public and private teachers, the original social insurance programs not only served to reward and to co-opt workers who were most important to the country's economic development objectives, but also to keep the level of public welfare spending low. In turn, the limited and occupationally segregated social insurance programs served to reinforce Korea's dual labor market system whereby wages, working conditions, and company welfare benefits differ significantly between the core and the periphery (see Chapter 8 by Jiyeoun Song).

Having a dual labor market system is beneficial for employers not only because they can keep overall labor costs low by limiting high wages and welfare provisions to core workers, but it also reinforces corporate objectives of attracting and retaining skilled workers. The structure of the original social insurance programs, specifically the decentralized and firm-managed fund-holding system (for example, the national health insurance scheme before the consolidation of health insurance funds under a single pipe system in 2000), coordinates well with the corporate strategy to discourage inter-firm mobility among core and skilled workers. The generous company welfare, employment security, and seniority-based wage system for core workers also serve as an important exchange for worker loyalty and wage control. Finally, the system of enterprise unions and industrial relations mediated through firm-specific labor management councils has also served to reinforce the support for particularistic social insurance, and helped undermine labor support for universal welfare. In sum, the Korean welfare regime centered on limited and occupationally segregated social insurance schemes and a company welfare system well integrated with the authoritarian state's economic and industrial development agenda.

---

7 Wolfgang Streeck, "Introduction," in *The Origins of Nonliberal Capitalism: Germany and Japan in Comparison*, ed. Wolfgang Streeck and Kozo Yamamura (Ithaca, NY: Cornell University Press, 2001), 31.

However, the fact that the welfare institution in Korea is well integrated with corporate and labor market institutions does not mean that this configuration was a natural outcome of the Korean political economy, or that this institution has remained fixed since the 1960s. Rather, the Korean welfare institution also changed over the years in response to the changes in the country's social, economic, and political contexts. Indeed, by the 1970s, the very success of the economic and industrial development strategies had fostered labor and societal demands for better welfare. At the same time, the limits of foreign capital had also begun to create pressures on the Park Chung-hee government to readjust its economic planning. It was during this period that the authoritarian government made a decisive shift to the development of heavy and chemical industries, and at the same time proposed to develop a National Pension Scheme in order to fund the new industrial strategy.[8] The outcome of welfare policymaking in the 1970s in fact resulted in expansion of the limited occupation-based health insurance schemes to workers in other sectors of the labor market. In other words, while political democratization in the late 1980s and the Asian economic crisis of 1997 may be key junctures for the development of the Korean welfare state, the welfare institution was by no means in stasis before or in between those moments. Rather, changes had been taking place, albeit less dramatically, since the 1960s.

Institutional Change and Continuity

Kathleen Thelen and Wolfgang Streeck's notion of gradual institutional change can be usefully applied to the case of the Korean welfare institution.[9] Looking at the institution of training and skills formation in Germany, Britain, Japan, and the United States, Thelen argues that even during periods of exogenous shocks, the institutions in these countries did not undergo dramatic transformation; rather, changes happened throughout the period of equilibrium through incremental layering and grafting of policies and programs.[10] Over time, these institutions changed as a result of cumulative alterations. Institutional changes are thus path-dependent in the sense that radical transformation is rare; instead, institutions change through steady

8 Its implementation was, however, postponed until 1988. See Shinyoung Kim, "Towards a Better Understanding of Welfare Policy Development in Developing Nations: A Case Study of South Korea's Pension System." *International Journal of Social Welfare* 15, no. 1 (2006): 75–83.

9 Thelen, *How Institutions Evolve*; Streeck and Thelen, *Beyond Continuity*.

10 Thelen, *How Institutions Evolve*.

incremental adjustments. To stress this point, Streeck and Thelen point to the idea of changes amidst apparent institutional continuity. Separating the *processes* of change from the *consequences*, they highlight "incremental changes with transformative results."[11] Looking at welfare state changes in Japan and Korea, Ito Peng and Joseph Wong also note that the institutional purposes and formats of the welfare state in these countries have changed over time without necessarily altering their structure.[12] The point here is that institutional changes can occur in many different ways, and that radical rupture of the system leading to paradigmatic shift is not the only path.

We can use ideas of institutional complementarity and incremental institutional changes to understand the mechanism of changes and continuities in the Korean welfare institution, and how it in turn articulates with institutional changes in other spheres of the national economy. I argue that in the case of Korea, two kinds of institutional changes are evident: in the foreground are radical changes marked by the political democratization of 1987 and the economic crisis of 1997; but in the background there are more incremental changes as the system tried to adjust to new social, political, and economic conditions. Table 9.1 summarizes the dynamics of changes related to the welfare institution in Korea since 1961. Here, changes in the welfare institution are conceptualized in terms of changes in institutional purposes, policy format, articulation with other policy sectors, and policymaking coalitions. As shown in the table, significant changes have occurred in all these sectors since 1961. Briefly, during the authoritarian developmental period, the welfare institution was seen primarily as a means to facilitate the nation's economic and industrial development objectives. Social insurance programs were designed to be limited, selective, and employment-based to protect workers in productive sectors of the economy. Welfare programs were thus formatted precisely to be productive. Furthermore, this welfare policy format closely interlocked with policies of *chaebŏl*-led industrial development, enterprise unionism and firm-specific labor management councils, and illegalization of mass labor unions and their political activities.

During the 1980s and early 1990s, however, the process of political democratization helped to redefine the purpose of the welfare institution. As welfare purposes were re-interpreted to ensure more social and economic redistribution, the earlier selective and occupation-specific social insurance was reformed into a more universalistic social insurance. The implementation of the National Pension Scheme and the universalization of health insurance are

11 Streeck and Thelen, *Beyond Continuity*.

12 Ito Peng and Joseph Wong, "Institutions and Institutional Purpose: Continuity and Change in East Asian Social Policy," *Politics and Society* 36, no. 1 (2008): 61–88.

TABLE 9.1

Welfare Institution Patterns, Articulations, and Modes of Policymaking

	Authoritarian Developmental Period (1961–1987)	Political Democratization Period (1987–1997)	Post-crisis Period (1997–present)
Primary Welfare Purpose	• Facilitate economic and industrial development • Legitimate political regime	• Social and economic redistribution	• Labor market activation • Social safety net • Creation of economic growth engines
Policy Format	• Selectivity • Occupational specificity • Employment-based social insurance • Company welfare • State intervention in economic and welfare policies	• Universalism and population coverage through national social insurance • Shift from company welfare to public welfare • Relaxation of the state role in the economy • Increased state policy emphasis on welfare	• Targeting • Social investment and social care • Productive welfare • Labor market flexibilization
Articulation with Policies in Other Institutions	• *Chaebŏl*-led industrial development strategy • Illegalization of labor unions; labor suppression • Labor-management councils; enterprise unionism	• *Chaebŏl*-led industrial development strategy • Labor market deregulation; employment flexibilization • Legalization of labor unions' political activities	• *Chaebŏl* reforms • Financial sector reforms • Labor market deregulation; employment flexibilization • Investing in a knowledge-based economy through industry and educational reforms.
Dominant Policy-making Coalitions	• The president, economic bureaucrats (EPB, KDI, MoF, MCI) and sometimes business	• The president, economic bureaucrats, big business (*chaebŏl*)	• Trilateral policy council made up of the labor, business, and the state • Social bureaucrats (MHSA/MOHW MOGE/MOGEF) and economic bureaucrats • Civil society groups supporting DJ administration.

Source: Ito Peng and Joseph Wong, "Institutions and Institutional Purpose: Continuity and Change in East Asian Social Policy," *Politics and Society* 36, no. 1 (2008): 61–88.

Note: Social expenditure as a percentage of GDP; company welfare as a percentage of total labor costs.

cases in point. The expansion of the welfare state and the increased social-ization of welfare during this period were results of political pressures from business, labor, and civil society. Having gained political space through de-mocratization, labor and civil society groups actively lobbied for welfare ex-pansion. The corporate sector also pressured the government for more labor market flexibility to help Korean industries maintain international economic competitiveness and to reduce the burden of company welfare by externalizing costs. The increased socialization of welfare during this period thus was co-ordinated with with the introduction of labor market flexibilization policies.

After 1997, the institutional purposes of welfare in Korea were once again altered to articulate with corporate and labor market reforms. Institutional purposes shifted, this time from focusing primarily on socio-economic re-distribution to labor market activation and strengthening of the social safety net and social investment. During this period, the universalization of social insurance programs was further overlaid with targeted social investment programs specifically aimed at poverty reduction, human capital develop-ment, and job creation. To maintain national competitiveness while manag-ing negative social impacts of competitiveness-enhancing policy measures and risks of political backlash, policymakers in Korea further expanded welfare while at the same time pushing forward on neo-liberal economic reforms. This was accomplished by: 1) socializing more of the welfare costs that were hitherto assumed by employers (see Table 9.1), 2) extending uni-versal social security programs while trying to get rid of inefficiencies within the existing system (for example, reform of the health insurance financing system under a single pipe), and 3) institutionalizing safety net measures to prevent social crisis.

Underlying the institutional processes were political actors and coali-tions that mobilized around specific policy issues and negotiated with other stakeholders to reach a settlement. As shown on the bottom row of Table 9.1, changes in institutional purposes and policy format during the three his-torical periods occurred in conjunction with changes in key political coali-tions. During the authoritarian developmental period, social policymaking was highly insulated and centralized, with many of the social policies being made by economic bureaucrats in key governmental bureaucracies such as the Economic Planning Board (EPB), Ministry of Finance (MoF), and Ministry of Commerce and Industry (MOCI), with the consent of the president. Societal actors were excluded altogether from the policy process during this period, as political activities by labor unions or civil society groups were banned. During the democratization period, both labor and civil society organiza-tions emerged as important policy actors. Even military-backed presidents, such as Chun Doo-hwan (Chŏn Tu-hwan, 1981–88), were forced to invite the Federation of Korean Trade Unions (FKTU) to participate in policymaking processes such as the Preparation Committee for the National Pension Scheme, along with the Korean Employers Association (KEA).[13] Despite its continuing reliance on economic bureaucrats, particularly the EPB, Kim Young-sam (Kim Yŏng-sam, 1993–98) did try to form a trilateral state-business-labor policy council to negotiate labor and social policies. Unfortunately, the attempt failed to achieve any consensus. After the economic crisis, however, the Tripartite Commission composed of state, business, and labor did finally set a new format for social and economic policymaking. Under the Kim Dae-jung (Kim Tae-jung, 1998–2003) administration, civil society groups also emerged as an important political actor in the social policymaking process.[14] As illustrated in Table 9.1, since 1961, the Korean welfare regime has rearticulated itself in relation to other political economic institutions in response to changes in the country's social, economic, and political contexts. The following section describes the evolution of the Korean welfare institution, with emphasis on the post-economic crisis period.

The Evolutionary Trajectory of Korean Welfare Institution

Authoritarian-Developmentalist Period (1961–1987)

During the authoritarian period, the governments of Park Chung-hee and Chun Doo-hwan sought to legitimate their political regimes through economic growth. The Park Chung-hee government began its economic development strategies with export-oriented light manufacturing industries in the early 1960s, and then switched to heavy and chemical industries in the 1970s. During this period, and particularly during the Park Chung-hee administration, the EPB played a key role in policymaking. Created in 1961, the EPB became a "super-ministry" that took over the main policymaking and policy coordination roles within the Korean state, with the EPB minister (who was also concurrently the deputy prime minister) assuming the authority to "control, coordinate, and adjudicate among the other ministries on economic matters [and to] preside over the fortnightly Economic Minister's Meeting attended by eleven economic ministries and the minister of Foreign Affairs."[15]

13 Kim, "Towards a Better Understanding," 75–83.

14 Huck-Ju Kwon, "Advocacy Coalitions and the Politics of Welfare in Korea after the Economic Crisis," *Policy and Politics* 31, no. 1 (2003): 69–83; Hye-Kyung Lee and Ito Peng, "Civil Society and Social Policy Reforms in Japan and Korea," presented at the annual meeting of the Association for Asian Studies, Chicago, March 31–April 3, 2005.

15 Byung-Nak Song, *The Rise of the Korean Economy*, 2nd ed. (Oxford: Oxford University Press, 1997), quoted in Kelley K. Hwang, "South Korea's Bureaucracy and the Informal Politics of Economic Development," *Asian Survey* 36, no. 3 (1996): 308.

The EPB's impacts on social policy were significant. The 1963 health insurance bill proposed by the Ministry of Health and Social Affairs (MHSA) Special Committee on Social Security—a fairly modest bill to cover employees in large firms—was unilaterally amended by the EPB and the Supreme Council for National Reconstruction (the official name of the military junta in control of the Korean government, 1961–1963), and made into a voluntary insurance scheme. In its place, the compulsory Industrial Accident Insurance was introduced to cover work place injuries sustained by workers in firms with 500 or more employees. In reality, the coverage was limited as very few firms had 500 or more workers at that time. Joseph Wong contends that the diminution of employee health insurance in 1963 to a voluntary scheme was motivated by economic bureaucrats who feared the political backlash from big businesses by mandating employer contributions for health insurance.[16] Sungnam Cho, on the other hand, argues that the failure of the 1963 Health Insurance Act had more to do with the Korean government's primary concern for economic development at the time.[17] Accordingly, economic bureaucrats were not interested in any social welfare programs because they expected that economic growth would eventually address social welfare issues. In the end, very few firms participated in the voluntary health insurance scheme and the program was eventually scrapped.[18] In the meantime, the Park regime's reliance on the economic expertise of EPB technocrats and other bureaucrats to manage economic growth, and on the military to maintain social order, was reflected in the introduction of the Civil Servants' Pension Scheme in 1961, and the extension of the pension scheme to military personnel in 1963. Thus until the 1970s, very little happened with regard to social welfare beyond these two pension schemes.

In the 1970s, however, a number of socio-economic changes prompted the government to expand social welfare. First, rapid economic growth, industrialization, and urbanization had resulted in noticeable changes in class and social composition. The proportion of the population economically active in the agricultural, forestry, and fisheries sectors had shrunk from 79.5 percent in 1960 to 8.7 percent in 1980, while those in mining and

16 Joseph Wong, *Healthy Democracies: Welfare Politics in Taiwan and South Korea* (Ithaca, NY: Cornell University Press, 2004).

17 Sungnam Cho, "The Emergence of a Health Insurance System in a Developing Country: The Case of South Korea," *Journal of Health and Social Behavior* 30, no. 4 (1989): 467–71.

18 Hye-Hoon Lee and Kye-Sik Lee, "A Korean Model of Social Welfare Policy: Issues and Strategies," in *An Agenda for Economic Reform in Korea: International Perspectives*, ed. Kenneth Judd and Yoong-Ki Lee (Stanford, CA: Hoover Institution Press, 2000).

manufacturing, and social overhead capital and other sectors grew from 5.4 percent to 22.5 percent, and 15.1 percent to 43.5 percent, respectively. By 1980, most Koreans were living in cities, and they considered themselves working or middle class. Indeed, those classified as "middle class" rose from 19.6 percent to 38.5 percent, while the "working class" grew from 8.9 percent to 22.6 percent between 1960 and 1980, respectively.[19] The increase in the middle-class population also corresponded with the rise in the general educational level of the population. For example, post-secondary educational attainment as a percentage of the population over 15 years of age more than tripled from 2.6 percent in 1960 to 9.2 percent in 1980.[20] These socio-economic changes in turn raised public awareness of social and income inequality, and facilitated the growth of civil activism.

Second, the very success of Korea's economic development strategies also highlighted the problem of growing social and income inequality under authoritarian regimes, creating a condition for social and political instability. The Korean economy grew at a rate of more than 8 percent per year throughout the 1960s and the 1970s. The positive economic growth initially helped equalize incomes, but this trend had begun to reverse in the 1970s, leading to a widening income gap. The Gini index declined from 0.448 in 1960 to 0.332 in 1970, but increased again to 0.391 by 1975. To be sure, by the mid-1970s, the question of equity and class inequality had become a serious source of social and political instability."[21]

Third, the widening income gap also coincided with substantial changes in workers' attitudes toward distributive justice and collective action in the 1970s. This was particularly evident among women in the manufacturing industries, the lowest-paid sector of Korea's industrial workers. As women's employment rate in the manufacturing industries increased, the unionization rate among women workers in the manufacturing industries also rose, from 20.1 percent in 1970 to 37.1 percent in 1976, surpassing the union membership rate of male workers.[22] During the 1970s, the government faced growing labor unrest as women workers in the manufacturing industries spearheaded labor actions against low wages, poor working conditions,

19 Doo-Seung Hong, "Social Change and Stratification," *Social Indicators Research* 61/63 (2003): 39–50.

20 Jong-Wha Lee, "Economic Growth and Human Development in the Republic of Korea," UNDP Occasional Paper no. 24, at http://hdr.undp.org/en/reports/global/hdr1997/papers/jong-wha_lee.pdf, accessed December 18, 2011.

21 Hagen Koo, "The Political Economy of Income Distribution in South Korea: The Impact of the State's Industrialization Policies," *World Development* 12, no. 10 (1984): 1029–37.

22 Jeong-Lim Nam, "Labor Control of the State and Women's Resistance in the Export Sector of South Korea," *Social Problems* 43, no. 3 (1996): 327–38.

and state control of labor.[23] Jeong-Lim Nam argues that women workers in Korea were more compelled to organize themselves and to take collective action because they were concentrated in a few industries, paid low wages, and constantly exposed to discrimination.[24] The barrier to women's political action therefore was relatively low compared to that for men. Women workers were also compelled to form their own independent unions because the officially sanctioned peak union, the FKTU, was uninterested in their concerns. Having no support from the mainstream unions, women workers turned to civil society groups such as church groups, students, and other grassroots organizations for collective action. Eighty-six percent of labor dispute cases in the 1970s were led exclusively by female union members or female workers; similarly, the majority of the labor clashes during the early 1980s were also led by young female workers.[25]

Fourth, from the employer side, the shift in the industrial structure from light manufacturing to heavy and chemical industries also increased the demand for skilled workers, making the issue of worker recruitment and retention increasingly imperative.[26] Employers therefore became more concerned about workers' health and safety issues, while at the same time pushing for higher productivity through retention of skilled workers and keeping general labor costs low. The tighter labor market had, however, increased the influence of labor, and along with this, the pressure for wage increases. The FKTU did attempt to raise the issue of wage increases, but its capacity to make demands was limited due to state intervention and a ban on the union's political activities. The shift to heavy and chemical industries also created a nascent protest movement of pollution victims seeking economic and welfare compensation from polluting companies. Unable to gain support from the labor for their causes, the anti-pollution movement began to create its own grassroots organization, often centered in certain regions and local areas, such as Ulsan and Onsan, and by lobbying the members of the parliament in those districts.[27]

Finally, the government also came under increasing financial and political problems in the early 1970s. The problem of declining capital accumulation

23 Ibid.; Chang Dae-oup, "Korean Labor Relations in Transition: Authoritarian Flexibility?" *Labour, Capital and Society* 35, no. 1 (2002): 10–40; Hagen Koo, *Korean Workers: The Culture and Politics of Class Formation* (Ithaca, NY: Cornell University Press, 2002).

24 Nam, "Labor Control."

25 Ibid.

26 Cho, "The Emergence of a Health Insurance System."

27 Jaehyun Joo, "Dynamics of Social Policy Change: A Korean Case Study from a Comparative Perspective," *Governance* 12, no. 1 (1999): 57–80.

forced the government to rethink its industrial development strategy and ways to accumulate capital to achieve industrial transfer. Despite the expansion of manufacturing exports in the 1960s, the import of machineries and other materials had outstripped the value of total exports, leading to a net trade deficit by the end of the decade. Korean export growth in light and textile industries also began to decline after 1967 as a result of increased trade protectionism in the West, particularly the United States.[28] The Park Chung-hee regime's attempt to shift to heavy and chemical industries in 1972 was therefore motivated by the understanding that the country needed to move beyond light manufacturing industries; however, this move was hampered by limitations in raising foreign capital due to huge foreign debts.[29] In fact, under pressure from the IMF, the Park government had to severely cut down on external borrowing by the end of the 1960s.[30] On the political side, the 1971 election also revealed significant public resistance to Park Chung-hee's authoritarian state, despite the economic growth.

In response to these socio-economic changes, the Park Chung-hee regime therefore began to apply different policy tools to manage economic growth and to control potential social and political crises. The government's initial responses to labor unrest and the threat of political opposition were to crack down on labor unions and protest groups and to tighten media control. The Yushin (Yusin) Constitution passed in 1972 banned all unions and associational activities and strengthened the president's power: it gave the president unlimited terms in office and power to appoint a large portion of the National Assembly. However, as social protests continued, the repressive policy levers became less effective. While maintaining policies of labor suppression, the Park government turned to economic and social policy measures to stave off social unrest.

In 1973 the EPB proposed a limited National Pension Scheme to cover workers in companies with 30 or more employees as well as high-income self-employed individuals.[31] The response of the employers' association to the proposed National Pension Scheme was lukewarm. It considered the proposed pension scheme expensive. Rather, it was more interested in health insurance because it would be less costly compared to pensions, and the maintenance of healthy workers was more directly useful to its

28 Chang, "Korean Labor Relations."

29 Korea's capacity to raise foreign capital was severely limited by the fact that its total foreign debt had soared from US$200 million in 1964 to US$2.922 billion in 1971. See Martin Hart-Landsberg, *The Rush to Development: Economic Change and Political Struggle in South Korea* (New York: Monthly Review Press, 1993).

30 Hwang, "South Korea's Bureaucracy."

31 Kim, "Towards a Better Understanding."

needs.[32] As the demand for, and maintenance of, skilled labor increased, the provision of medical services began to be more economically important for employers.[33] The employers thus advocated employee health insurance as an alternative to the National Pension Scheme. Workers were also more concerned about health insurance than pensions. The increase in medical technology was beginning to drive up the cost of medical care, and by the mid-1970s, even the middle class was finding the cost of medical services too expensive and wanting some kind of health insurance. Workers were therefore interested in a health insurance scheme as well. The employers thus advocated employee health insurance as an alternative to the National Pension Scheme. The Park Chung-hee government consulted with both the KEA and FKTU on a pension proposal, but these groups had little power to influence policymaking at the time. The National Pension Act was passed in 1973, but implementation of the scheme was postponed indefinitely. In the meantime, the Second Health Insurance Amendment Act was passed in 1976, making health insurance enrolment compulsory for all workers in firms with 500 or more employees. In the following year, the Environmental Protection Law was passed to dampen the rising claims for compensation for pollution victims.[34] Once the new Health Insurance Act was passed, a steady expansion of the health insurance program ensued as workers in other key occupational sectors were brought into the insurance coverage.

During the Chun Doo-hwan regime the authoritarian state came under increasing opposition and political setbacks arising from changes in social and economic contexts. U.S. pressure to open the East Asian markets— Japan and Korea in particular—intensified.[35] Following the Washington Consensus, international financial institutions such as the IMF and the World Bank also called for the elimination of the statist development paradigm in developing countries. These global policy changes influenced some pro-reform policymakers within the Korean government—particularly those in the EPB—to advocate liberal market reform.[36]

The tightening of government control over labor activism under the Yushin Constitution had, instead of acquiescing social protest, fueled more

32 Ibid.
33 Hwang, "South Korea's Bureaucracy."
34 Joo, "Dynamics of Social Policy Change."
35 Bruce Cumings, "The Korean Crisis and the End of the 'Late' Development," *New Left Review I,* no. 231 (1998).
36 David Hundt, "A Legitimate Paradox: Neo-Liberal Reform and the Return of the State in Korea," *Journal of Development Studies* 41, no. 2 (2005): 242–60.

widespread public demand for democracy and social justice.[37] In 1980, the government tried to suppress a student- and labor-led uprising in Kwangju with military force, killing several hundred civilians. Rather than quashing labor activism, this further strengthened the labor-radical alliance and fueled labor militancy and further student uprisings.[38] In response to the public unrest, General Chun Doo-hwan who replaced Park Chung-hee following Park's assassination in 1979 quickly revised the constitution in 1981, restricting the presidential term to seven years. This, however, did little to assuage public discontent. Public attitude surveys in the mid-1980s show that not only the working class, but also the Korean middle class, was extremely dissatisfied with the authoritarian regime.[39] The ruling Democratic Justice Party's (DPJ) poor performance in the 1985 National Assembly election, the first election since Chung Doo-hwan took power in 1980, and the huge electoral support for the opposition New Democratic Party in urban areas, also reflected public discontent toward the government. The ruling DJP had just managed to secure a parliamentary majority with only 35 percent of the popular vote, thus prompting a change in political strategy.[40] In 1986, Chun announced "Three Measures for the Promotion of Social Welfare," pledging to establish universal health insurance by 1989, to implement the National Pension Scheme, and to introduce the Minimum Wage Law. The measures were aimed specifically to co-opt the middle class and less radical segments of the growing anti-government democracy movement. The measures were also carefully timed to coincide with the next National Assembly election scheduled in 1988, thus to ensure a DJP victory.

The Chun regime did not survive to see through the completion of the three measures. In the meantime, pressed by increasing mass democracy protests and changes in the U.S. position vis-à-vis support for the Chun regime, then-DJP president, Roh Tae-woo (No T'ae-u, 1988–93), made a surprise announcement in June 1987, accepting all of the opposition's demands, including fully democratic political elections, starting with the presidential election at the end of the year. After more than a decade of labor demands and government repression, the Minimum Wage Law was passed in 1986, a year before the first fully democratic presidential election. The

37 Nam, "Labor Control"; Chang, "Korean Labor Relations"; Sunhyuk Kim, *The Politics of Democratization in Korea: The Role of Civil Society* (Pittsburgh, PA: University of Pittsburgh Press, 2000).

38 Kim, *The Politics of Democratization.*

39 Hagen Koo, "Middle Classes, Democratization, and Class Formation: The Case of South Korea." *Theory and Society* 20, no. 40 (1991): 485–509.

40 Kim, "Towards a Better Understanding"; Wong, *Healthy Democracies.*

National Pension Scheme was finally implemented in 1988, shortly after the presidential election to cover workers in firms with ten or more employees, while in the same year, health insurance was extended to workers in firms with five or more employees and self-employed individuals in rural areas. In 1989, health insurance was further expanded to bring in the last group of workers who had been hitherto uncovered—urban self-employed individuals—thus making health insurance universal. Although the EPB continued to play the leading role in social policymaking under the Chun administration, the KEA and FKTU were also given larger roles in policymaking. In sum, the process of democratization had set in motion rapid expansion and reforms of social welfare policies in Korea, starting with the two most important social security programs, the National Health Insurance and the National Pension Scheme. As shown in Table 9.2 below, while welfare reforms had been taking place throughout the 1960s and 1970s, they were limited in scope; only after 1987 do we see a serious push toward universalization of social insurance schemes.

Democratization Period (1987–1997)

The political democratization brought about more changes in social welfare. First, President Roh Tae-woo's narrow electoral victory and the loss of the ruling DJP's parliamentary majority in the 1987 election made it imperative for the government to make political compromises. Second, the democratization process also led to new political competition and shifts in the political cleavages away from traditional regional/personal lines to demographic and social policy issues.[41]

Social and economic contexts also continued to change throughout the 1980s and the 1990s, making policy adjustments highly contentious. Throughout the 1980s the external pressures for economic liberalization continued. Both the Reagan and Bush administrations continued to push the U.S. demand for trade liberalization. Within the government bureaucracy there was also an increasing divide between pro-liberalization and conservatively oriented policymakers. In the early 1980s, the EPB was successful in pushing for the Industrial Assistance Law against the MOCI and MoF that limited the amount of subsidies and other forms of state protection given

41 See Byung-Kook Kim, "The U.S.-South Korean Alliance: Anti-American Challenges," *Journal of East Asian Studies* 3, no. 2 (2003): 225–58 on cleavages along demographic lines; Wong, *Healthy Democracies* on cleavages along social policy lines; also Ito Peng, "Postindustrial Pressures, Political Regimes Shifts, and Social Policy Reform in Japan and South Korea," *Journal of East Asian Studies* 4, no. 3 (2004): 389–425 on political realignments along social and demographic lines.

TABLE 9.2

Summary of Social Policy Developments in South Korea, 1960–2006

Major Social Welfare Programs	Authoritarian Period (1961–1987)	Democratization Period (1987–1997)	Post-Economic Crisis Period (1997–present)
Health Care	**1963: Health Insurance Act** required voluntary insurance to workers in work places with 300+ employees **1964: Industrial Accident Insurance** required compulsory insurance against industrial accidents to workers in work places with 500+ employees **1976: Second Health Insurance Amendment Act** mandated compulsory insurance to workers in work places with 500+ employees **1977: Amendment of the Health Insurance Act** made health insurance compulsory for government employees and private school teachers **1977: Third Health Insurance Amendment Act** opened health care institutions to non-members of health societies **1981: Fourth Health Insurance Amendment Act** set up occupational and self-employed health insurance societies	**1988:** Expansion of health insurance and health assistance programs to workers in work places with 5+ employees, and self-employed in rural areas **1988:** Expansion of Industrial Accident Insurance **1989:** Extension of health insurance and health assistance programs to urban self-employed	**1999: Unification of national health insurance** unified separate health insurance carriers under a single body, the Health Insurance Review Agency **2000: Separation of medical services and drug dispensing** **2008: Introduction of long-term care insurance** mandated universal social care insurance for people over age 65

TABLE 9.2 (*continued*)

Major Social Welfare Programs	Authoritarian Period (1961–1987)	Democratization Period (1987–1997)	Post-Economic Crisis Period (1997–present)
Pensions	**1961: Civil Servants' Pension Scheme** established for government employees **1963:** Military personnel added to civil servants pension scheme **1974:** Private school teachers added to civil servants pension scheme **1973: National Pension Act** introduced but implementation delayed until 1988, all through company-based retirement pay	**1988: National Pension Scheme** first legislated in 1973, but not implemented until 1988, for workers in work places of 10+ people **1989:** Introduction of a legal retirement payment system **1992:** National Pension Scheme extended to workers in work places with 5+ people **1995:** Inclusion of people in rural areas in the National Pension Scheme **1997:** Retirement insurance introduced	**1998**—Integration of regional and company pensions **1999:** Compulsory participation in the National Pension Scheme for all people between the ages of 18 and 60 in work places with 10+ employees. (70 percent of the economically active population covered) **1999:** Urban self-employed pensions included in the National Scheme **2003:** National Pension Scheme made compulsory for all workers in work places with 1+ people **2003:** Revision of the National Pension Scheme reorganized national pension and retirement pay **2007:** National Pension Reform Scheme reduced benefit level from 60 percent to 50 percent by 2008, and thereafter to 40 percent by 2028, while maintaining the same contribution rate of 9 percent
Social Welfare	**1961: Livelihood Protection Act** provided public assistance to deserving poor (based on Japan's Daily Livelihood Protection Law of 1929) **1979:** Educational support for children of recipients of livelihood protection assistance who attend middle school	**1987:** Expansion of educational support for children of people receiving public assistance and those living in subdivisions and designated areas to attend secondary and vocational high schools **1991: National Child Care Plan** established child care institutions	**1997:** Extension of educational support to children of all public assistance recipients up to secondary and vocational high school **1998:** Introduction of active labor market policies, or "productive welfarism" **1998: Promotion of Disabled, the Elderly, and Pregnant Women Law**, put into effect

1982: Welfare of the Disabled Act, put into effect

1993: Employment Support Allowance (one time cash benefit) to people completing job training programs

1999: National Basic Livelihood Security Act established and implemented in 2000

2005: National Child Care Act— expansion of child care institutions, public subsidies for child care for families with preschool-age children, new regulatory mechanisms for child care services and work place child care

2006: Saessak Plan introduced to strengthen the role of the government in child care, including doubling the number of child care space, by 2010, and increasing in number of child care subsidy recipients

2006: Saromazi Plan introduced to address low fertility issues, including expansion of public child care, subsidies for infant care, and other forms of child care and possible child allowances

2006: Framework Plan introduced to expand social services, increase public investment in social welfare, and create a social welfare market and jobs in the social welfare sector

2008: Child Development Account introduced providing matching grants for families saving for children's education

2008: Act on Management of Marriage Brokerage Business enacted to legislate and regulate the international marriage brokerage business

2008: Transnational Marriages & Family Support Services introduced to provide education and counseling to Koreans marrying foreigners

2006: Elderly Care Insurance Act introduced; to be implemented in 2008

TABLE 9.2 (*continued*)

Major Social Welfare Programs	Authoritarian Period (1961–1987)	Democratization Period (1987–1997)	Post-Economic Crisis Period (1997–present)
Economic/Labor Market	**1977: Environment Protection Law** **1986: Minimum Wage Law**	**1988: Equal Employment Act** **1990:** Encouragement to employ the elderly and the disabled **1990: Environment Pollution Dispute Settlement Law** **1990: Employment Promotion and Vocational Rehabilitation for Disabled Persons Act** **1995: Employment Insurance Program** **2000:** Employment legislation reform to allow increased labor market flexilization **2004: Job Creation and Advancement of Industrial Relations Policy** introduced to deal with labor market flexibilization **2006: Non-regular Workers' Act** **2007:** Industrial trainee system unified under the Employment Permit System **2008:** Youth training programs expanded	**1998:** Expansion of Employment Insurance **1999: Maternity Leave Law** **2001: Maternity Protection Law** **2008: Paternity Leave Law**

Source: Ministry of Labor; Ministry of Health, Welfare, and Family Affairs.

to industries and the corporate sector.[42] The pro-liberalization–oriented EPB saw this as a moment to advocate the state to withdraw its intervention in the market economy. The result was a loosening of the state policy instrument to intervene in the economy and labor market.[43] With the liberalization of labor union activity, labor unions also quickly strengthened their political power. Organized labor union membership and labor activism soared. The number of trade unions rose from 2,742 in 1987 to 7,883 in 1989, while union density increased from 11.7 percent to 18.6 percent, respectively. Workers took this political opening to demand wage increases. The total number of labor disputes escalated from 276 in 1986 to 3,749 in 1987, and then stabilized at 1,616 in 1989.[44] The first two years of democratization thus saw a sharp increase in nominal industrial wages, on an average of 12 percent a year,[45] along with increased company welfare.[46] Overall, the combination of labor laws that made it difficult for employers to dismiss workers, growing labor power, and positive economic growth had led to an increase in workers' employment stability, particularly for blue-collar workers, after 1987.[47]

In the meantime, welfare expansion continued. Following the implementation of the National Pension Scheme in 1988, the government legalized the retirement payment system. In 1992, the National Pension Scheme was extended to workplaces with five or more employees, bringing an additional 2.3 million workers into the existing scheme that already had about 4.2 million participants. Then, in 1995, rural workers were also brought into the National Pension Scheme, adding another 2.1 million workers.[48] External pressures to liberalize trade and market also intensified once Korea achieved its political democratization. By the beginning of the 1990s, the opening of the Korean market to the global economy, combined with a rise in wages, had made Korean industries, especially textiles, much less competitive. In addition, Korea was also aiming for entry into the OECD, an objective that required a number of labor reforms in line with the other OECD countries. Pressured by employer

42 Hwang, "South Korea's Bureaucracy."

43 Hundt, "A Legitimate Paradox."

44 Wonduck Lee and Joohee Lee., *Industrial Relations: Recent Changes and New Challenges* (Seoul: Korea Labor Institute, 2004).

45 Ibid.

46 Ho Keung Song, "The Birth of a Welfare State in Korea: The Unfinished Symphony of Democratization and Globalization," *Journal of East Asian Studies* 3, no. 3 (2003): 405–32.

47 Ee-Hwon Jung and Byung-You Cheon, *Employment Changes in Japan and Korea* (Seoul: Korea Labor Institute, 2004).

48 Jae-jin Yang, "Democratic Governance and Bureaucratic Politics: A Case of Pension Reform in Korea," *Policy and Politics* 32, no. 2 (2004): 193–206.

demands for a more flexible labor market, particularly more flexibility in hiring and firing, on the one hand, and labor's demand for further wage increases and social welfare, on the other hand, the government once again turned back to its more interventionist wage control policies in 1991 and 1992.

The Kim Young-sam (1993–97) government, which inherited this highly volatile social and economic situation in 1993, attempted to direct the national economy in a more neo-liberal direction, while at the same time, expanding social welfare to help people adjust to the changes in the labor market. Kim Young-sam's "Korean welfare model" advocated the role of the family and a new partnership between the private and public sectors in providing social welfare. The National Child Care Plan was introduced in 1991 to facilitate married women's employment. The government expanded job and skills training programs to help people adjust to labor market changes. The Employment Support Allowance Program was established in 1993 to provide people with a one-time cash benefit to complete job and skills training programs. Employment insurance was introduced in 1995, providing coverage to workers in firms with more than thirty employees. These programs were introduced in conjunction with a relaxation of the employment policy that gave employers more flexibility to use contract workers. To be sure, Employment insurance was not meant to be an extension of social rights: the coverage was meager and conditions were strict. In 1996, it covered only 35.5 percent of waged and salaried workers. Rather, along with other employment-related social programs, it was more aimed to mollify labor and the public's anxiety over the relaxation of employment legislation, and to socialize the costs of the skills training and labor adjustments under the increasingly flexible labor market conditions. This was followed by the beginning of the reform plan to universalize the National Pension Scheme in the following year.

Again, changes in political processes and welfare policy need to be considered in the context of other structural and ideational institutional changes that were taking place in the 1980s and 1990s. Korea began to experience the process of de-industrialization in the 1990s. For example, the proportion of the population that was economically active in the mining and manufacturing industries declined from 27.6 percent in 1990 to 20.6 percent in 2000, while those in social overhead capital and other occupations rose from 54.5 percent to 70.7 percent in 1990, respectively. By 2000, people claiming to be middle class had grown to 48.7 percent, up from 38.5 percent in 1980; while those in the working class gained a slight increase, from 22.6 percent to 29.7 percent during the same time.[49] In the meantime, the percentage of men

49 Hong, "Social Change and Stratification."

and women over the age of 25 with a post-secondary education rose from 12.0 percent and 3.6 percent, respectively, in 1980 to 31.0 percent and 18.0 percent, respectively, in 2000.[50] Using data from the World Values Surveys between 1982 and 1996, Aie-Rie Lee found a significant value shift in a libertarian direction among Koreans, with age and education being the two strongest predictors of the change. Younger and better-educated Koreans were significantly more likely to embrace liberal and progressive ideas about politics and social policies.[51]

Simply put, by the early 1990s the previous patterns of economic and labor market systems were already showing signs of strain, and the political economic system from the authoritarian developmental state era had begun to disarticulate. The internal and external pressures toward economic liberalization and labor, as well as civil society pressures for more economic redistribution and social welfare, meant that the state had to carefully chart a policy path that would support and facilitate market reform, while at the same time instituting social policies to prevent crisis. The result was a rapid universalization of social insurance programs and the institution of market-oriented social policies on the one hand, and neo-liberal labor market reform policies on the other.

Post-economic Crisis Period: 1997–Present

The political economic situation in Korea changed even more after the economic crisis of 1997. Stunned by the magnitude of the crisis, Koreans directed their shock and anger to the government, bureaucrats, and big business. A survey in 1998 found that nearly 60 percent of the respondents blamed the financial crisis on *chaebŏl* and government bureaucrats.[52] The EPB in particular came under severe criticism, resulting in a significant loss of its political support within the bureaucracy. Public discontent over Kim Young-sam government's handling of the economy gave his long-time political opponent and opposition leader, Kim Dae-jung, a decisive victory in the presidential election of December 1997. Kim Dae-jung pledged to undertake radical corporate and economic reform, including *chaebŏl* reform, and to help improve the lives of the middle and working classes.

The Kim Dae-jung government signified not just a political regime change, but also marked a shift in the government's powerbase from an economic

50 Korean Women's Development Institute (KWDI), *Gender Statistics in Korea, 2009* (Seoul, 2010).

51 Aie-Rie Lee, "Stability and Change in Korean Values," *Social Indicators Research* 62/63 (2003): 93–117.

52 Yang, "Democratic Governance."

development–oriented and EPB-dominated political coalition to a social welfare–oriented political coalition made up of the MHSA and civil society groups that supported the democratization movement and Kim Dae-jung's National Congress for New Politics Party. Changes in the political terrain were immediately evident. The outlawed KCTU was legalized and brought into the policy-making process along with the FKTU. Civil society groups, social movement leaders, and academics were also brought into the policy-making process as members of government commissions and policy committees, or more directly through the migration of civil society group leaders and activists into the government bureaucracy, particularly the MHSA (later renamed the Ministry of Health and Welfare [MOHW]) and the newly created Ministry of Gender Equality (MOGE—renamed the Ministry of Gender Equality and Family in 2005, and then changed back to the MOGE in 2009 under Lee Myung-bak [Yi Myŏng-bak, 2008-present]). The MHSA's and MOGE's status within the government also increased. The EPB was dismantled, while the "super-ministry" for finance and the economy created by Kim Young-sam was partitioned into the Ministry of Finance and Economy, Ministry of Planning and Budget, the Financial Supervisory Commission (FSC) and the Financial Supervisory Service (FSS).[53] Lee Myung-bak, however, established the Ministry of Strategy and Finance in 2009, thus bringing back the budgeting function back to the Ministry of Finance and Economy.

Policy-making processes did not always go smoothly, however. As one of its first tasks, the Kim Dae-jung government formed a Tripartite Commission in early 1998, consisting of the government, labor, and business to negotiate labor demands for job security and wage increases, employer demands for easier layoffs and more labor market flexibility, and IMF economic bailout conditions, mandating corporate and labor market restructuring. Having agreed to work together to resolve the economic crisis and having signed the Social Compact of 1998, which included a wide range of labor market and social policy reforms, the Tripartite Commission fell back into a state of dysfunction as disagreements and mistrust beset the social partners. Almost as soon as the initial social pact was signed, the KCTU membership protested against its leadership for conceding too much, thus prompting them to withdraw from the commission. They returned to the second round, which resulted in legalization of a teachers' union and integration of a health insurance system, but again withdrew and resorted to boycotting the process in 1999. *Chaebŏl* also resisted acting once the social

---

53 Joo-Youn Jung, "The End of the Old System? Coordination within the Korean Bureaucracy in Transformation," paper presented at the conference on "System Restructuring in East Asia," Stanford University, Stanford, CA, June 22–24, 2006.

pact was signed. Instead of complying with the new financial regulations on corporate restructuring, some *chaebŏl* groups—such as Daewoo—simply ignored them and continued to borrow from the banks and to extend their debt-to-equity ratio.[54] Between 1998 and 2002, the commission broke off and re-launched no less than five times as labor and business took turns walking out on the process. Finally, in 2003, the KTU walked out of the commission permanently, leaving the FKTU as only labor representative in the group.

The social compact reached by the Tripartite Commission in 1998 consisted of a number of economic and market reform measures, including market liberalization, expansion of the social safety net, and *chaebŏl* reforms. The employers' demands were addressed by lifting restrictions on company layoffs, expanding of temporary employment, and privatizing of temporary employment agencies. Labor conceded to a wage freeze and reductions in benefits and bonuses in exchange for a broadening of the social safety net, including expansion of unemployment insurance, pensions and health care reforms, and improvements in labor rights (e.g., legalization of labor union right to engage in political activities, legalization of the Teachers' Union, and establishment of work councils for government officials).[55] The subsequent social agreements among social partners added the rail sector, postal services, and financial deregulation, an agreement on shorter working hours, restructuring of the power industry, an agreement on job creation, improvements in occupational accident insurance, and improved wages. Through the tripartite policy-making process, the Kim Dae-jung government also satisfied the IMF conditions, including implementation of financial and corporate reforms and active labor market policies.

On the one hand, systems restructuring involving reforms of employment, corporate, and welfare sector institutions proceeded in loose coordination with one another; on the other, different institutional actors continued to fight to protect their interests and to grasp opportunities throughout the process. For employers, the economic crisis had forced many to restructure and downsize. Corporate restructuring did not only result in multiple bankruptcies among many small- and medium-sized enterprises. Many big businesses also went under, with the closure of fifteen financial institutions and more than fifty *chaebŏl* subsidiaries within the first year of the crisis.[56] However, for some it was also an opportune moment to renegotiate

54 Hundt, "A Legitimate Paradox."

55 Wonduck Lee and Joohee Lee, "Will the Model of Uncoordinated Decentralization Persist? Changes in Korean Industrial Relations after the Financial Crisis," in *The New Structure of Labor Relations*, ed. Harry C. Katz, Wonduck Lee, and Joohee Lee (Ithaca, NY: Cornell University Press, 2004).

56 Song, "The Birth of a Welfare State."

long-term employment and seniority-based wage systems as well as company welfare. There was a significant increase in the dismissal rate following the crisis for companies of all sizes, with white-collar (i.e., non-unionized) workers more affected than blue-collar workers.[57] In some cases, companies tried to use the new employment legislation to introduce mass layoffs. Hyundai, for example, attempted to lay off over 4,800 workers in 1998, after having already laid off about 4,000 through honorary retirement.[58] The economic crisis was therefore an excellent opportunity for employers to rethink their industrial relations strategies.

For labor, the economic crisis also implied not only a struggle to maintain their hard-won rights since 1987, but also a moment to broaden their base beyond traditional enterprise unions. Even though labor unions in Korea are largely enterprise-based, they increasingly took collective action to protect common interests. Through the economic crisis both national labor union federations, the KCTU and FKTU, saw reasons to extend beyond enterprise unionism to form industry-wide unions. They sought to build membership in sectors that were particularly vulnerable in the economic crisis: the financial and service sectors. The formation of the banking sector union, the Korean Financial Industry Union, under the FKTU in 2000, is a good example. Between 1998 and 2003, Korean labor unions also used the "block the restructuring" strategy to emphasize cross-sector interests in the labor movement. After 2003, the FKTU continued to work with the government while the KCTU focused its efforts on deepening engagement with the international labor movements.

The economic crisis and the change in political regime was also an important opportunity for the pro-welfare policy group to advocate and influence social policy within and outside of the government.[59] The Kim Dae-jung administration replaced the old welfare ideology represented by the "developmental coalition" consisting of the authoritarian regime, economic bureaucrats (e.g., the former EPB and MoF bureaucrats), and big business, with a "pro-welfare coalition" made up of the new government, social bureaucrats (e.g., particularly in the MOHW and the MOGEF), business, and civil society groups, that supported the idea of productive welfare. For example, many civil society groups, such as the People's Solidarity for Participatory Democracy (PSPD) and the Korean Women's Association

---

57 Jung and Cheon, *Employment Changes.*

58 In this case, fierce labor union resistance involving sit-in strikes managed to stop the company from taking full action. In the end only 227 people were laid off. See Jung and Cheon, *Employment Changes.*

59 Lee, "Stability and Change"; Lee and Peng, "Civil Society."

United (KWAU) that supported Kim Dae-jung, took on active and prominent roles in negotiating for social policy after 1998. The conspicuous role
of the PSPD in pushing for National Basic Livelihood Security (NBLS) legislation is a case in point.[60]

Adding to this, there were also some economic bureaucrats within the
government who saw the economic crisis and IMF conditions as an opportunity to reform Korea's developmental state and *chaebŏl* system that
formed the legacy of the past authoritarian regimes. These were not pro-
welfare actors; to be sure, they were pro-liberal market reform policymakers
(many of them coming from the previous EPB) who saw market liberalization and *chaebŏl* reform as a way to refashion Korea's political economy in
line with neo-liberal reforms.[61] But their interests intersected with those of
key actors within the Kim Dae-jung government, who were also keen to cut
"the chains of power and protection of power" afforded between the previous authoritarian developmental state and the *chaebŏl*.[62] The FSC's ability
to push forward on *chaebŏl* reform in the face of fierce *chaebŏl* resistance
can be attributed to this confluence of interests among pro-liberal market
reform bureaucrats—who were not natural allies of the Kim Dae-jung government—and the Kim Dae-jung government, backed by Kim Dae-jung's
anti-authoritarian supporters.

The picture of the post-crisis period thus reveals significant instabilities,
disruptions, and contestations as changes in social, political, and economic
contexts shifted after 1997. This in turn created both constraints and open-
ings for institutional actors, old and new, to navigate, contest, and secure, if
not to expand, their positions and interests. This is not to say, however, that
this was an entirely new phenomenon. Social, political, and economic contexts changed dramatically after political democratization. Indeed, throughout the 1980s institutional and social actors were actively negotiating with
each other in response to the changing environment. What makes the economic crisis remarkable, however, is the combination of cumulative changes
that transpired from the economic crisis and made the transformative process more clearly evident and urgent. This in turn pushed public and policy
debates forward, expediting the process of social and economic policy reforms. In the following section I will highlight some major policy changes
in social welfare after 1997, and how they in turn interlock with changes in
other policy sectors, particularly the corporate and labor markets.

60 Lee and Peng, "Civil Society."
61 Hundt, "A Legitimate Paradox."
62 Kim Dae-jung, quoted in Hundt, "A Legitimate Paradox," 248.

Welfare Policy Changes Post-1997

First, although there was a gradual erosion of long-term employment and wage security systems throughout the 1990s, it became much more visible after 1997, as employers applied various measures to lay off workers and reduce labor costs. A result of a more flexible employment policy is increased nonstandard and nonregular employment, especially temporary work (see Table 9.3A and 9.3B). These changes, however, have been to some extent offset by social welfare expansion and strategic social investment in human capital development and social care. Korea's de facto system of lifetime employment and the seniority wage system have eroded since 1997. The unemployment rate in Korea rose from 2.5 percent in 1997 to 6.8 percent in 1998 and gradually leveled off to 3.6 percent in 2004, where it remains relatively unchanged until now.[63] The trajectory toward greater labor market flexibility continued even after the economic recovery in 1999. The dismissal rate for both small and large companies increased. For example, the rate for companies with 30 or more employees rose from 1.2 percent in 1996 to 9.4 percent in 1998, and eventually settled at 5.5 percent in 2001. Similarly, the rate for companies with more than 1,000 employees rose from 0.2 percent in 1996 to 3 percent in 1999.[64] The 2001 Establishment Survey found in that year, the rates of layoffs, "honorary retirements,"[65] contract suspensions, and transfers to affiliated companies came to 8.6 percent, 10.2 percent, 1.2 percent, and 3.8 percent, respectively, much higher than the pre-crisis levels.[66] The Ministry of Labor's survey of companies with 100 or more employees also found a noticeable increase in companies adopting an annual salary system: 1.6 percent in 1996 to 12.7 percent in 1999. Ee-Hwon Jung and Byung-You Cheon's analysis based on the Survey on the Wage Structure shows rapid adoption of an annual salary system among Korean companies after 1997.[67]

As illustrated in Table 9.3B, the proportion of nonregular workers (temporary and daily workers) to the total employees increased from 35.4 percent in 1990 to 40.1 percent in 2007 for women, and from 22.4 percent to 25.1 percent, respectively, for men.[68] Between 1997 and 2000, the banking sector

63 OECD, *OECD Employment Outlook: Statistical Annex* (Paris: OECD, 2005).

64 Jung and Cheon, *Employment Changes.*

65 Ibid.,

66 Ibid.,

67 Ibid.,

68 Korean Women's Development Institute (KWDI), *Statistical Handbook, 2008: Women in Korea* (Seoul, 2008).

TABLE 9.3A

Proportion of Nonstandard Workers in Relation to the Distribution of Workers by Gender and Status of Employment of All Employees in Korea, 1990–2007

Gender	Year	Total	Employer	Own Account Holders	Unpaid Family Workers	Regular Employees	Temporary Workers	Daily Workers
Female	1980	100.0	1.8	21.5	37.4	30.9*	—	8.3
	1990	100.0	2.7	16.0	24.5	21.4	22.5	12.9
	2000	100.0	3.0	16.2	19.2	19.1	28.5	13.9
	2007	100.0	3.5	15.0	12.7	28.7	29.9	10.2
Male	1980	100.0	6.5	34.1	7.3	41.9*	—	10.2
	1990	100.0	9.0	25.4	2.5	40.7	14.1	8.3
	2000	100.0	9.6	24.1	2.0	38.1	17.1	9.2
	2007	100.0	8.9	22.2	1.2	42.7	16.4	8.7

Source: KWDI, *Statistical Handbook, 2008: Women in Korea* (2008).

Note: *Both regular and temporary workers were included in the Employees category in the 1980 Survey of Economically Active Persons

TABLE 9.3B

Proportion of Nonstandard Workers in Relation to Distribution of All Employees in Korea, 1990–2007

Country	Year	Part-time workers (%)	Contract/Temporary and Other Workers (%)
Korea	1995	Total 4.4 Male: 2.9 Female: 6.7	Total: 41.9
	2000	Total (2001): 7.5 Male: 5.3 Female: 10.5	Total: 52.9

Source: Wonduck Lee and Joohee Lee, *Industrial Relations: Recent Changes and New Challenges* (Seoul: Korea Labor Institute, 2004).

Note: Social welfare programs, however, have expanded to some extent to compensate for the increased labor market dualism.

saw a 35 percent reduction in regular employment, and a doubling in the proportion of temporary and part-time employees from 11.8 percent to 21.8 percent. Time series data of the two-year job retention rate before, during, and after the 1997 economic crisis also show that while all groups of workers were adversely affected by the crisis, long-tenured workers (i.e., those in core employment and older workers) were able to regain their job stability once the crisis was over, whereas the situation for short-tenured workers remained insecure or became worse. This can be seen from the increase in the two-year job retention rate for the former group and the decline for the latter, indicating a dualistic pattern of economic recovery.[69] In sum, these changes add up to increased flexibility of the labor market, erosion of the core, and a deepening of labor market dualization.[70]

Social welfare programs have expanded to some extent to compensate for the increased labor market dualization, however. Table 9.4 shows the expansion of social insurance coverage since 1997. As shown in the table, the Employment Insurance Program was expanded to workers in firms with less than five employees in 1998, and subsequently, to daily and temporary workers in the public sector. In addition, the duration of unemployment benefit coverage was also increased to ensure adequate coverage. In fact, the government's total expenditure on the Employment Insurance Program increased from 52.5 billion won in 1996 to 988.8 billion won in 2000.[71] The Workers Compensation Insurance Program also expanded after 1998, while the pension reform of 1999 universalized pension coverage. [72] In addition, a variety of social policy measures were introduced after 1998; for example, the active labor market policies were initiated in 1998 as a part of the government's efforts to help unemployed workers and married women enter the labor market. These included skills training, employment support, public works, and a variety of macro- and micro-economic measures to support small- and medium-sized firms and to develop venture capital and small businesses. The NBLS was also introduced in 1999 (implemented in 2000) to provide cash benefits to low-income individuals and families. Unlike other social security programs, the NBLS guarantees income support to low-income families and individuals regardless of labor market attachment or ability to work. It is the first welfare program in Korean history that is premised on the principle of citizenship rights.[73] Admittedly the program is small, but the conceptual shift in the basic principles behind this program should not

69 Joonmo Cho, "Assessing Dualism and Institutional Insecurity in the Korean Labor Market," in *Beyond Flexibility: Roadmaps for Korean Labor Policy*, ed. Richard B. Freeman, Sunwoo Kim, and Jaeho Keum (Seoul: Korea Labor Institute, 2008), 99–130.

70 Ito Peng, "Economic Dualization in Japan and South Korea," paper presented at the Labor Market Dualization Workshop, Green Templeton College, Oxford University, January 14–16, 2010.

71 Jacob Keum, et al. *Employment Insurance in Korea: The First Ten Years* (Seoul: Korea Labor Institute, 2006). The total figure for Employment Insurance Program includes: the Employment Stabilization Program, Job Skill Development Program, and Unemployment Benefit Program.

72 The 2006 National Pension Reform Scheme, however, reduced pension payouts.

73 For a discussion of the political processes culminating in the introduction of this program, see Lee and Peng, "Civil Society."

TABLE 9.4

Changes in the Population Coverage of the Four Major Social Insurances in Korea

	1997				2000			
	EI	WCI	PI	HI	EI	WCI	PI	HI
Firm Size (number of regular employees)	X	X	X	O	O	O	O	O
–5	X	X	X	O	O	O	O	O
5–9	X	X	O	O	O	O	O	O
10–29	O	O	O	O	O	O	O	O
30+	X	O	O	O	O	O	O	O
Daily Workers	X	X	X	O	△	△	O	O
Temporary Workers	X	X	X	O	△	△	O	O
Self-employed	X	X	X	O	X	O	O	O
Unpaid Family Workers	X	X	X	O	X	O	O	O

Source: Hye-Kyung Lee, "Welfare Reforms in Post-Crisis Korea: Dilemmas and Choices," *Social Policy and Society* 3, no. 3 (2004): 291–99.

Notes: O=covered, △=partially covered; X=uncovered; EI=employment insurance; WCI=workers compensation insurance; PI=pension insurance; HI=health insurance.

be underestimated. Finally, Long-Term Care Insurance, a compulsory social care insurance aimed to provide long-term care for the elderly was implemented in 2008.

The new social policy emphasis on labor market activation is most evident in the targeted support to women. To incentivize women to enter and remain in the labor market, the Kim Dae-jung government significantly expanded the 1991 National Child Care Plan and the budget for child care rose by over tenfold, from 42 billion won to 437 billion won between 1991 and 2002, while the number of day care centers increased from just over 9,000 to over to 22,000 over the same period. The total number of children enrolled in child care facilities also increased from 294,000 in 1995 to 801,000 in 2001.[74] Following Kim Dae-jung's active labor market policies, the Roh Moo-hyun (No Mu-hyŏn, 2003–8) government redoubled its commitment to social welfare expansion, further extending government support for child care. The National Child Care Act of 2005 promised to increase financial

74 Hye-Kyung Lee and Yeong-Ran Park, "Families in Transition and the Family Welfare Policies in Korea," paper presented at the Canada-Korea Social Policy Research Symposium, Seoul, November 22–23, 2003.

support for child care for 70 percent of all children (up to the age of 4) and to raise the total government contribution for child care expenses to 50 percent by 2008 from the 2004 levels of 23 percent and 37 percent, respectively.[75] The Saessak Plan in 2006 aimed to strengthen government support for families with small children by proposing to double the number of child care spaces from 2005 to 2010, and enlarging child care subsidies to middle-class families. The Maternity Leave Law was also passed in 1999, granting women 60 days of unpaid leave. In 2001, the Maternity Protection Law was added, increasing maternity leave from 60 to 90 days, with a benefit of 300,000 won per month. The benefit was increased to 500,000 won per month in 2006. In anticipation of rapid population aging, a Ten-Year Master Plan was introduced in 2001 to expand health and welfare facilities for the elderly.

The Korean government's new social policy focus on women after 1997 was not an accident. By the end of the 1990s, both economic and social policy bureaucrats within the government had come to understand the value of women's human capital in the context of the country's new economy. The growth of knowledge-intensive and service-sector industries has meant economic opportunities for people with new kinds of skill sets. In addition, given the increasing flexibilization of the labor market, there also has been a huge demand for nonregular (part-time and contract) workers. On all accounts, women fill the needs of the new economy. Second, recent demographic changes have also prompted government and business to take more proactive measures. Korea's extremely low fertility rate has raised concerns about the rapidly aging population and its implications for future labor shortages and downturns in economic growth.[76] As a pronatalist strategy, Korea has been following Japan and other OECD countries by developing family-work harmonization policies to encourage young couples to have

---

75 Ministry of Gender Equality and Family (MOGEF), "50 Percent of Child-Care Cost to be Shouldered by the Government by 2008 / The Committee of the Aging and Future Society," Ministry of Gender Equality and Family Announcement (November 30, 2004); MOGEF, "Information on Changes Made in Child-care Policies in 2005," Ministry of Gender Equality and Family Announcement (January 17, 2005); MOGEF, "Information on Changes Made in Child-care Policies in 2005: Increase in Financial Support for Needy Families," Ministry of Gender Equality and Family Announcement (January 17, 2005).

76 Korea's total fertility rate declined from 2.0 in 1980 to 1.3 in 2002. In 2000, the proportion of people aged 65 or over was 7.2 percent. Demographic projections show that the aged population will reach 20 percent by 2026. See Korea National Statistics Office, *Highlights of Population Projections* (Seoul, 2006); Ministry of Health and Welfare, *Health and Welfare Services, 2003* (Seoul, 2003).

children.[77] Finally, the increased feminist voice within and outside the government bureaucracy has also contributed to the increased policy attention to women. Indeed, feminists and women's organizations, and feminist bureaucrats within the government have been lobbying for more social policy support to address women's employment and welfare issues.

To sum up, significant changes have been made to the welfare institution in consort with the market and corporate sector restructuring since 1997. Total social security expenditures as a proportion of GDP rose from 3.9 percent in 1990 to 10.8 percent in 1998 and stabilized at around 8 percent thereafter.[78] A breakdown of social security expenditures by category in the 1990s shows in particular a large increase in expenditures on unemployment insurance benefits, retirement pay, active labor market policies, and old-age cash benefits. It is, however, important to be mindful of the fact that despite the changes, the social safety net and active labor market policies remain inadequate to solve problems of economic insecurity and income inequality. Evidence shows that Korea's Gini index has increased since the end of the 1990s. Studies also suggest that expansion of the social insurance scheme may have reinforced rather than minimized labor market dualism.[79] The welfare state expansion in Korea since 1997 therefore needs to be understood, neither as a result of government largess nor as a labor victory. Rather, it was a product of the political economic coordination process in which labor market flexibilization and corporate sector restructuring necessitated a parallel and compensatory expansion of the welfare institution.

Conclusion

This chapter examined the relationship between systems restructuring and reform of the welfare institution in South Korea. Through a historical

77 OECD, *Babies and Bosses—Reconciling Work and Family Life* (Volume 2): *Austria, Ireland, and Japan* (Paris: OECD, 2003); Ito Peng, "Political and Social Economy of Care in the Republic of Korea," United Nations Research Institute for Social Development, Gender and Development Paper, no. 6 (2009), at http://www.unrisd.org/unrisd/website/document.nsf/(httpPublications)/2B5879FBCD1DBD3FC12576A200479FA3?OpenDocument; Ito Peng, "Social Policy Reforms and Gender in Japan and South Korea," in *Gender and Social Policy in a Global Context*, ed. Shahra Razavi and Shireen Hassim (New York: Palgrave Macmillan, 2006), 130–50.

78 OECD, *Social Expenditure Database*, at http://www.oecd.org/document/9/0,3343,en_2649_34637_38141385_1_1_1_1,00.html

79 Cho, "Assessing Dualism and Institutional Insecurity"; Byung You Cheon, "Labor Market Flexicurity in Korea and Labor Market Policy Tasks," proceedings from the International Symposium on the National Employment Strategy and Its Vision for Job Creation, Seoul, 2006.

analysis of social welfare development, it specifically addressed the questions of how Korea's changing political economic institutions affected welfare restructuring and vice versa, and if, how, and why changes required in welfare institutions to facilitate corporate restructuring triggered complementary measures in other issue areas that added up to not only corporate but also system restructuring. The analysis of social welfare development in Korea since 1961 shows that through social policies, the welfare institution has, and continues to, coordinate with other institutions, particularly the corporate and labor market institutions, to achieve institutional complementarity.

The analysis of social welfare development presented in this chapter highlights three points. First, the way in which welfare policies developed in Korea was not accidental. Rather, welfare policy developments often have been coordinated with policy changes in other institutions. During the authoritarian period, social welfare policies were organized to complement the state's economic development priorities. Limited and occupationally divided social insurance schemes were introduced as a way to selectively protect and co-opt core workers in key sectors of the economy. Because of limited state support for social welfare, the corporate sector played an important social welfare role by providing job security and company welfare benefits. The state during this period played a key role in directing and coordinating national economic and industrial development. After democratization, however, the state's political economic logic changed. During the first decade after democratization, economic development objectives were eclipsed by a social and economic redistribution agenda from below. While managing liberal economic restructuring, the government also pushed to universalize the existing social insurance schemes. The increased socialization of social welfare responsibilities was matched by a gradual decline in company welfare benefits. After the economic crisis, the Korean political economy underwent yet another shift. This time, hit by both global and domestic pressures to liberalize markets on the one hand, and domestic political pressures to expand social welfare on the other, both labor market deregulation and welfare state expansion policies were implemented. Once the crisis was averted, the government embarked on strategic human capital investment policies, in particular those targeted to promote women's labor market participation. Throughout these changes, social welfare policies were developed in close articulation with employment, labor market, and corporate reform policies. The close policy articulation between these institutions, as shown in this chapter, illustrates a high level of coordination between the welfare institution and other institutions.

Second, the historical examination of social welfare development also reveals both continuities and changes in the Korean welfare institution. First, the purposes of the Korean welfare institution have changed dramatically since the 1960s. During the authoritarian regimes, the welfare institution was seen primarily as a tool to facilitate economic growth; however, after political democratization, the welfare institution's economic growth objective was eclipsed by social and economic redistributional objectives. After the economic crisis, the purposes of the welfare institution changed again, this time to achieve both redistributional and economic growth objectives. Yet, despite these changes, certain features of the welfare institution in Korea have also remained stable. For example, the reliance on the social insurance model, despite changes in institutional purposes, suggests that changes have been path-dependent. Indeed, the welfare institution in Korea has not been totally abolished and replaced by a new institutional form. Rather, it has reoriented its purposes while maintaining its original structure. Second, while significant changes have taken place during political democratization and the economic crisis period, it is also clear that the welfare institution did not remain fixed the rest of the time. As illustrated in this chapter, small incremental changes were made throughout the periods before, after, and in between these two critical junctures as social, economic, and political contexts shifted. Put simply, institutional changes occurred steadily and incrementally as well as abruptly. The case of the Korean welfare institution thus helps us gain insights into ways in which institutions change and continue over time.

Finally, an analysis of institutional changes in Korea also highlights the mechanisms of change. By focusing on changes in political coalitions and the behavior of political actors, I have shown that mechanisms of institutional changes are, in fact, highly political. Like the process of institutional complementarity, institutional changes are neither rational nor self-evident; rather, they are shaped by political agents through constant processes of contestation and negotiation. As illustrated in this chapter, welfare institutional changes in Korea have been about changes in key political actors and political coalitions in response to changes in social, economic, and political contexts.

Bibliography

Administration of Labor Affairs. *See* Ministry of Labor.

Amable, Bruno. *The Diversity of Modern Capitalism*. Oxford: Oxford University Press, 2003.

Amsden, Alice H. *Asia's Next Giant: South Korea and Late Industrialization*. Oxford: Oxford University Press, 1989.

An Chong-bŏm. "Kim Tae-jung chŏngbu ŭi kyŏngje kaehyŏk ŭi p'yŏngga wa kwaje" [Evaluation and the problem of economic reform under the Kim Dae-jung administration]. Paper presented at the Joint Conference organized by the Korean Association of Comparative Economics and the Korea Institute for Economic Research, November 2002.

Aoki, Masahiko. *Toward a Comparative Institutional Analysis*. Cambridge, MA: MIT Press, 2001.

Arun, Thankom Gopinash and John Turner, eds. *Corporate Governance and Development: Reform, Financial Systems and Legal Frameworks*. Cheltenham: Edward Elgar, 2009.

Balassa, Bela and John Williamson. *Adjusting to Success: Balance of Payments Policy in the East Asian NICs*. Washington, DC: Institute for International Economics, 1987.

Baliño, Tomás J.T. and Angel J. Ubide. "The Korean Financial Crisis of 1997: Strategy of Financial Sector Reform," IMF Working Paper, no. 99/28 (March 1999).

Bank for International Settlements. "Foreign Direct Investment in the Financial Sector of Emerging Market Economies," report submitted by a working group established by the Committee on the Global Financial System, March 2004, at www.bis.org/publ/cgfs22.pdf.

Bank of Korea, "Oeguk chabon ŭi ŭnhaeng sanŏp chinip yŏnghyang mit chŏngch'aek sisa chŏm" [The effects of foreign participation in the banking industry and policy implications], Press Release (December 19, 2003).

Bedeski, Robert E. *The Transformation of South Korea: Reform and Reconstruction in the Sixth Republic under Roh Tae Woo, 1987–1992*. New York: Routledge, 1994.

Board of Audit and Inspection of Korea (BAI). *Kongjŏk chagŭm kamsa paeksŏ* [White paper for public fund inspection], 2003.

Board of Audit and Inspection (BAI). *Kŭmyung kigwan kamdok silt'ae* [Investigation into supervision over financial institutions] (July 2004).

Bonacich, Phillip. "Power and Centrality: A Family of Measures," *American Journal of Sociology* 92, no. 5 (March 1987): 1170–82.

Bonacich, Phillip and Paulette Lloyd. "Eigenvector-like Measures of Centrality for Asymmetric Relations," *Social Networks* 23, no. 3 (2001): 191–201.

Boorman, Jack, Timothy Lane, Marianne Schulze-Ghattas, Aleš Bulíř, Atish R. Ghosh, Javier Hamann, Alexandros Mourmouras, and Steven Phillips, "Managing Financial Crisis: The Experience in East Asia," IMF Working Paper WP/oo/107 (June 2000).

Bratt, Nicholas and John Lee. "What Korea Needs: Good Corporate Governance," *The Korea Times*, January 1, 2009.

Camdessus, Michel. "Crisis, Restructuring, and Recovery in Korea," remarks at the Conference on Economic Crisis and Restructuring, Seoul, December 2, 1999. IMF 99/27.

Carey, John and Andrew Reynolds. "Parties and Accountable Government in New Democracies," *Party Politics* 13, no. 2 (March 2007): 255–74.

Chang, Dae-oup. "Korean Labor Relations in Transition: Authoritarian Flexibility?" *Labour, Capital and Society* 35, no. 1 (April 2002): 10–40.

Chang, Dukjin. "Financial Crisis and Network Response: Changes in the Ownership Structure of Chaebol Business Groups Since the Asian Crisis." Paper presented at the Georgetown Conference on Korean Society, 1999.

Chang, Dukjin. "Privately Owned Social Structures: Institutionalization-Network Contingency in the Korean Chaebol." PhD diss., Department of Sociology, University of Chicago, March 1999.

Chang, Ha-Joon. *The Political Economy of Industrial Policy*. New York: St. Martin's, 1994.

Chang, Ha-Joon. *Rethinking Developmental Economics*. London: Anthem Press, 2003.

Cheng, Tun-jen. "Political Institutions and the Malaise of East Asian New Democracies," *Journal of East Asian Studies* 3, no.1 (2003): 1–41.

Cheng, Tun-Jen, Stephan Haggard, and David Kang. "Institutions and Growth in Korea and Taiwan: The Bureaucracy," *Journal of Development Studies* 34, no. 6 (August 1998): 87–111.

Cheon, Byung You. "Labor Market Flexicurity in Korea and Labor Market Policy Tasks." Proceedings from the the International Symposium on the National Employment Strategy and its Vision for Job Creation, Seoul, 2006.

Cho Dong-sŏng. *Han'guk chaebŏl yŏn'gu* [A study on Korean chaebŏl]. Seoul: Maeil Kyŏngje Sinmunsa, 1990.

Cho, Joonmo. "Assessing Dualism and Institutional Insecurity in the Korean Labor Market," in *Beyond Flexibility: Roadmaps for Korean Labor Policy*, ed. Richard B. Freeman, Sunwoong Kim, and Jaeho Keum. Seoul: Korea Labor Institute, 2008, 99–130.

Cho, Myeong-Hyeon. "Reform of Corporate Governance," in *Economic Crisis and Corporate Restructuring in Korea: Reforming the* Chaebol, ed. Stephan Haggard, Wonhyuk Lim, and Euysong Kim, New York: Cambridge University Press, 2003, 286–305.

Cho Sŏng-jae, Yi Pyŏng-hun, Hong Chang-p'yo, Im Sang-hun, and Kim Yong-hyŏn. *Chadongch'a sanŏp ŭi togŭp kujo wa koyong kwan'gye ŭi kyech'ŭng sŏng* [The subcontracting system and the stratification of the employment structure in the automobile industry], Seoul: Korea Labor Institute, 2004.

Cho, Sungnam. "The Emergence of a Health Insurance System in a Developing Country: The Case of South Korea," *Journal of Health and Social Behavior* 30, no. 4 (December 1989): 467–71.

Cho, Yoon Je and Kim Joon Kyung. "Credit Policies and the Industrialization of Korea," Korea Development Institute Research Monograph 9701 (December 1997).

Ch'oe Kang-sik and Yi Kyu-yong. *Uri nara kiŏp ŭi koyong chojŏng silt'ae* (III) [Employment adjustment in Korean firms (III)]. Seoul: Korea Labor Institute, 1995.

Ch'oe Kyŏng-su. "Nodong sijang yuyŏnhwa ŭi koyong hyogwa punsŏk: Kohyŏng poho kyuje wanhwa rŭl chungsim ŭro" [An analysis of the employment impact of flexible labor market measures: A focus on the relaxing of employment security regulations], Korea Development Institute Research Paper 01–09 (2001).

Ch'oe Yŏng-gi, Chŏn Kwang-sŏk, Yi Ch'ŏl-su, and Yu Pŏm-sang. *Han'guk ŭi nodong pŏp kaejŏng kwa nosa kwan'gye* [Labor law revisions and industrial relations in Korea]. Seoul: Korea Labor Institute, 2000.

Choi, Byung-Sun. "Financial Policy and Big Business in Korea: The Perils of Financial Regulation," in *The Politics of Finance in Developing Countries*, ed. Stephan Haggard, Chung H. Lee, and Sylvia Maxfield. Ithaca, NY: Cornell University Press, 1993, 23–54.

Choi Doo-Yull. P*idaech'ingjŏk kiŏp kŭmyung kyuje wa oehwan wigi* [Asymmetric corporate financial regulation and Korea's 1997 currency crisis]. Seoul: Korea Economic Research Institute, 2002.

Choi Jang-jip (Ch'oe Chang-jip). *Han'guk ŭi nodong undong kwa kukka* [Labor movements and the state in Korea]. Seoul: Nanam Publishing, 1997.

Choi Jang-jip (Ch'oe Chang-jip). "Saeroun nodong undong ŭi panghyang mosaek ŭl wihayŏ" [In search of a new direction for labor movements], *Sahoe p'yŏngnon* (June 1992): 233–46.

Choi, Jin-Wook. "Regulatory Forbearance and Financial Crisis in South Korea," *Asian Survey* 42, no. 2 (March/April 2002): 251–75.

Chŏn Hong-t'aek. "Kŭmnyung kaehyŏk: Chungang ŭnhaeng mit kŭmnyung kamdok chedo kaep'yŏn sarye" [Financial reform: The case of the central bank and the reorganization of financial supervisory institutions], in *Han'guk kyŏngje kaehyŏk sarye yŏn'gu* [Case studies on economic reform in Korea], ed. Mo Chong-nin, Chŏn Hong-t'aek, and Yi Su-hŭi. Seoul: Orŭm, 2002, 485–500.

Chŏng Ihwan and Yi Pyŏng-hun, "Kyŏngje wigi wa koyong kwan'gye ŭi pyŏnhwa: Tae kiŏp sarye rŭl chungsim ŭro" [Changes in employment relations after the 1997 economic crisis: A case study with a focus on large-sized firms], *Sanŏp nodong yŏn'gu* [Industry and labor studies] 6, no. 1 (2000): 27–58.

Ch'ong Yong-dŏk. "Han'guk ŭi chŏngbu chojik ŭi kaep'yŏn" [Korean government reorganization], *Han'guk chŏngch'aek hak'oebo* [Korean policy studies review] 4, no. 1 (1995): 58–84.

Chu Mu-hyŏn. "Kyŏngje wigi ihu ŭi kiŏp pyŏl naebu nodong sijang ŭi kujo pyŏnhwa: Hyŏndae chadongch'a ŭi sarye"[Structural changes of the internal labor market after the financial crisis: A case study of Hyundai Motors], *Sanŏp nodong yŏn'gu* [Industry and labor studies] 8, no. 1 (2002): 75–110.

Claessens, Stijn. "Policy Approaches to Corporate Restructuring around the World: What Worked, What Failed?" in *Corporate Restructuring: Lessons from Experience*, ed. Michael Pomerleano and William Shaw. Washington DC: World Bank, 2005, 11–58.

Corrales, Javier. "Presidents, Ruling Parties, and Party Rules: A Theory on the Politics of Economic Reform in Latin America," *Comparative Politics* 32, no. 2 (January 2000): 127–49.

Cox, Gary W. "The Organization of Democratic Legislatures," in *The Oxford Handbook of Political Economy*, ed. Barry R. Weingast and Donald A. Wittman. New York: Oxford University Press, 2006, 141–61.

Croissant, Aurel. "Electoral Politics in South Korea," in *Electoral Politics in Southeast and East Asia*, ed. Croissant, Gabriele Bruns, and Marei John. Singapore: Friedrich Ebert Stiftung, 2002, 233–275.

Croissant, Aurel. "Legislative Powers, Veto Players, and the Emergence of Delegative Democracy: A Comparison of Presidentialism in the Philippines and South Korea," *Democratization* 10, no. 3 (August 2003): 68–98.

Crouch, Colin. "Complementarity and Fit in the Study of Comparative Capitalisms," in *Changing Capitalisms?: Internationalization, Institutional Change, and Systems of Economic Organization*, ed. Glenn Morgan, Richard Whitley, and Eli Moen. New York: Oxford University Press, 2005, 167–89.

Culpepper, Pepper. "Rethinking Reform: The Politics of Decentralized Cooperation in France and Germany." PhD diss., Harvard University, 1998.

Cumings, Bruce. "The Asian Crisis, Democracy, and the End of Late Development," in T.J. Pempel, *The Politics of the Asian Economic Crisis*. Ithaca, NY: Cornell University Press, 1999, 17–44.

Cumings, Bruce. "The Korean Crisis and the End of the 'Late' Development," *New Left Review* I, no. 231 (September-October 1998): 43–72.

Deeg, Richard. "Path Dependency, Institutional Complementarity, and Change in National Business Systems," in *Changing Capitalisms? Internationalization, Institutional Change, and Systems of Economic Organization*, ed. Glenn

Morgan, Richard Whitley, and Eli Moen. Oxford: Oxford University Press, 2005, 21–49.

Diamond, Larry and Doh Chull Shin. "Introduction: Institutional Reform and Democratic Consolidation in Korea," in *Institutional Reform and Democratic Consolidation in Korea*, ed. Larry Diamond and Doh Chull Shin. Stanford, CA: Hoover Institution Press, 2000) 1–41.

Dore, Ronald. "Asian Crisis and the Future of the Japanese Model," *Cambridge Journal of Economics* 22, no. 6 (1998): 773–87.

Economic Planning Board. "Analysis of Economic Policies of the 1980s." Seoul (1986).

Esping-Andersen, Gøsta. *The Three Worlds of Welfare Capitalism*. Princeton, NJ: Princeton University Press, 1990.

Evans, Peter B. *The Embedded Autonomy: States and Industrial Transformation*. Princeton, NJ: Princeton University Press, 1995.

Export-Import Bank of Korea (EXIM). *Overseas Direct Investment Statistics Yearbook*. Seoul, various years.

Federation of Korean Industries. *Haeoe Tugijabon Yuip Jeungga-e ttareun Jeokttaejeok M&A Wihyeop mit Daeeungbanghyang* [Threats of hostile M&As in the wake of an increase in inflow of foreign speculative funds and its countermeasures]. Seoul, 2006.

Financial Team, Korea Development Institute. *1998-nyŏn kŭmyung pumun Chŏngch'aek yŏn'gu charyo moŭm chip* [A 1990 collection of policy study materials on the financial sector]. Seoul: Korea Development Institute, 1998.

Frieden, Jeff. "Third World Indebted Industrialization: International Finance and State Capitalism in Mexico, Brazil, Argentina, and South Korea," *International Organization* 35, no. 3 (1981): 407–31.

Geddes, Barbara. *Politician's Dilemma: Building State Capacity in Latin America*. Berkeley: University of California Press, 1994.

Gourevitch, Peter Alexis and James J. Shinn. *Political Power and Corporate Control: The New Global Politics of Corporate Governance*. Princeton, NJ: Princeton University Press, 2005.

Graham, Edward M. *Reforming Korea's Industrial Conglomerates*. Washington DC: Institute for International Economics, 2003.

Granovetter, Mark. "Business Groups and Social Organization" in *The Handbook of Economic Sociology*, ed. Neil J. Smelser and Richard Swedberg. Princeton, NJ: Princeton University Press, 2005, 429–50.

Grzymała-Busse, Anna. *Rebuilding Leviathan: Party Competition and State Exploitation in Post-Communist Democracies*. New York: Cambridge University Press, 2007.

Haggard, Stephan. "Macroeconomic Policy through the First Oil Shock 1970–1975," in *Macroeconomic Policy and Adjustment in Korea 1970–1990*, ed. Stephan Haggard et al. Cambridge, MA: Harvard Institute for International Development and Korea Development Institute, 1994, 23–48.

Haggard, Stephan. *Pathways from the Periphery: The Politics of Growth in the Newly Industrializing Countries*. Ithaca, NY: Cornell University Press, 1990.

Haggard, Stephan. *The Political Economy of the Asian Financial Crisis*. Washington, DC: Institute for International Economics, 2000.

Haggard, Stephan and Robert R. Kaufman. *The Political Economy of Democratic Transitions*. Princeton, NJ: Princeton University Press, 1995.

Haggard Stephan, Wonhyuk Lim, and Euysong Lim, eds., *Economic Crisis and Corporate Restructuring in Korea: Reforming the* Chaebol. New York: Cambridge University Press, 2003.

Haggard, Stephan and Jongryn Mo. "The Political Economy of the Korean Financial Crisis," *Review of International Political Economy* 7, no. 2 (April 2000): 197–218.

Hahm, Joon-Ho. "Financial System Restructuring in Korea: The Crisis and its Resolution," in *East Asia's Financial Systems: Evolution and Crisis*, ed. Seiichi Masuyama, Donna Vandenbrink, and Chia Siow Yue. Tokyo and Singapore: Nomura Research Institute and Institute of Southeast Asian Studies, 1999, 109–43.

Hahm, Joon-Ho. "The Government, the Chaebol and the Financial Institutions Before the Economic Crisis," in *Economic Crisis and Corporate Restructuring in Korea: Reforming the* Chaebol, ed. Stephan Haggard, Wonhyuk Lim, and Euysung Kim. New York: Cambridge University Press, 2003, 79–101.

Hall, Peter A. and Daniel W. Gingerich. "Varieties of Capitalism and Institutional Complementarities in the Macroeconomy: An Empirical Analysis," Max-Planck Institute for the Study of Societies, Discussion Paper 4, no. 5 (2004).

Hall, Peter A. and David W. Soskice, "An Introduction to Varieties of Capitalism" in *Varieties of Capitalis: The Institutional Foundations of Comparative Advantage*, ed. Peter A. Hall and David Soskice. Oxford: Oxford University Press, 2001, 1–68.

Hall, Peter A. and David Soskice, eds. *Varieties of Capitalism: The Institutional Foundations of Comparative Advantage*. Oxford: Oxford University Press, 2001.

Hall, Peter A. and Kathleen Thelen. "Institutional Change in Varieties of Capitalism." Paper presented to the Conference of Europeanists, Chicago, March 2006.

Hall, Peter and Kathleen Thelen. "Institutional Changes in Varieties of Capitalism." Paper presented at the ISA RC-19 Conference, Chicago, September 8, 2005.

Hamilton, Gary G. *Cosmopolitan Capitalists: Hong Kong and the Chinese Diaspora at the End of the 20th Century*. Seattle: University of Washington Press, 1999.

Han, Joon and Dukjin Chang. "Changing Corporate Governance in Korea: Rise of a Market for Corporate Control or the Strategic Adaptation of *Chaebol?*" *Development and Society* 32, no. 2 (December 2003): 253–70.

Hancké, Bob, Martin Rhodes, and Mark Thatcher, eds. *Beyond Varieties of Capitalism: Conflict, Contradictions, and Complementarities in the European Economy*. Oxford: Oxford University Press, 2007.

Hart-Landsberg, Martin. *The Rush to Development: Economic Change and Political Struggle in South Korea*. New York: Monthly Review Press, 1993.

Hayo, Bernd. "Mass Attitudes toward Financial Crisis and Economic Reform in Korea," *Socio-Economic Review* 3, no. 3 (2005): 419–515.

Heo, Uk and Hans Stockton. "The Impact of Democratic Transition on Elections and Parties in South Korea," *Party Politics* 11, no. 6 (November 2005): 674–88.

Hiwatari, Nobuhiro. "Employment Practices and Enterprise Unionism in Japan," in *Employees and Corporate Governance*, ed. Margaret M. Blair and Mark J. Roe. Washington DC: Brookings Institution Press, 1999, 275–46.

Holliday, Ian. "Productivist Welfare Capitalism: Social Policy in East Asia," *Political Studies* 48, no. 4 (September 2000): 706–23.

Hollingsworth, J. Rogers and Robert Boyer. "Coordination of Economic Actors and Social Systems of Production," in *Contemporary Capitalism: The Embeddedness of Institutions*, ed. J. Rogers Hollingsworth and Robert Boyer. New York: Cambridge University Press, 1997, 1–48.

Hong Chae-bŏm and Hwang Kyu-sŭng. "Han'guk kiŏp ŭi tagakhwa wa kyŏngje chŏk sŏnggwa e kwanhan yŏn'gu" [A study on the diversification and economic performance of Korean firms], *Kyŏngyŏnghak yŏn'gu* [Research in business administration] 26 (1997): 493–511.

Hong, Doo-Seung. "Social Change and Stratification," *Social Indicators Research* 62/63 (April 2003): 39–50.

Hundt, David. "A Legitimate Paradox: Neo-Liberal Reform and the Return of the State in Korea," *Journal of Development Studies* 41, no. 2 (2005): 242–60.

Hwang, Kelley K. "South Korea's Bureaucracy and the Informal Politics of Economic Development," *Asian Survey* 36, no. 3 (March 1996): 306–19.

Il Sagong. *Segye Sogui Hanguk Gyeongje* [The Korean economy within the world]. Seoul: Kimyoungsa, 1993.

Im, Hyug Baeg. "Politics of Democratic Transition from Authoritarian Rule in South Korea," *Korean Social Science Journal* 21, no. 1 (1995): 134–51.

International Monetary Fund. "Republic of Korea: Economic and Policy Development," IMF Staff Country Report, no. 00/11 (February 2000).

International Monetary Fund. "Republic of Korea: Selected Issues," IMF Country Report, no. 02/20 (February 2002).

International Monetary Fund. "Republic of Korea: Selected Issues," IMF Country Report, no. 03/80 (March 2003).

International Monetary Fund. "Republic of Korea: 2003 Article IV Consultation," IMF Country Report, no. 04/44 (February 2004).

Iverson, Torben. *Capitalism, Democracy, and Welfare*. New York: Cambridge University Press, 2005.

Jayasuriya, Kanishka. "Authoritarian Liberalism, Governance and the Emergence of the Regulatory State in Post-crisis East Asia," in *Politics and Markets in the Wake of the Asian Crisis*, ed. Mark Beeson, Kanishka Jayasuriya, Hyuk-Rae Kim, and Richard Robison. New York: Routledge, 2000, 315–30.

Ji, Donghyun and Jaeha Park. "The Korean Banking Sector: Current Issues and Future Direction," in *Rising to the Challenge in Asia: A Study of Financial Markets*, Vol. 7, Republic of Korea. Manila: Asian Development Bank, 1999, 29–54.

Johnson, Chalmers. "The Developmental State: Odyssey of a Concept," in *The Developmental State*, ed. Meredith Woo-Cumings. Ithaca, NY: Cornell University Press, 1999, 32–92.

Johnson, Chalmers. *MITI and the Japanese Miracle: The Growth of Industrial Policy*, 1925–1975. Stanford, CA: Stanford University Press, 1982.

Johnson, Chalmers. "Political Institutions and Economic Performance: The Government-Business Relationship in Japan, South Korea, and Taiwan," in *The Political Economy of the New Asian Industrialism*, ed. Frederic C. Deyo. Ithaca, NY: Cornell University Press, 1987, 136–64.

Joo, Hagen. "Middle Classes, Democratization, and Class Formation: The Case of South Korea," *Theory and Society* 20, no. 40 (August 1991): 485–509.

Joo, Jaehyun. "Dynamics of Social Policy Change: A Korean Case Study from a Comparative Perspective," *Governance* 12, no. 1 (January 1999): 57–80.

Jung, Ee-Hwon and Byung-You Cheon. *Employment Changes in Japan and Korea*. Seoul: Korea Labor Institute, 2004.

Jung, Heon Joo. "Financial Regulatory Reform in South Korea Then and Now," *Korea Observer* 40, no. 4 (Winter 2009): 701–34.

Jung Hyung-Chan and Myung-Chul Lee. "Oegukjjabonui Gungnaeeunhaeng Insuwa Eunhaengsaneobui Gujo Byeonhwa: New Bridge Capital-ui Jeireunhaeng Insu Sarye" [Foreign acquisitions of Korean commercial banks and restructuring of the Korean banking industry: The case of Korea First Bank], *Journal of Money and Finance* 11, no. 1 (2006).

Jung, Joo-Youn. "The End of the Old System? Coordination within the Korean Bureaucracy in Transformation." Paper presented at the conference on System Restructuring in East Asia, Stanford University, June 2006.

Jung, Joo-Youn. "Reinventing the Interventionist State: tThe Korean Economic Bureaucracy Reform under the Economic Crisis," *Pacific Focus* 23, no. 1 (April 2008): 121–38.

Kang, C. S. Eliot. "*Segyehwa* Reform of the South Korean Developmental State," in *Korea's Globalization*, ed. Samuel S. Kim. New York: Cambridge University Press, 2000, 76–101.

Kang Chong-gu. "Ŭnhaeng ŭi kŭmyung chunggae kinŭng yakhwa wŏnin kwa chŏngch'aek kwaje" [Banks' financial intermediary role in Korea], *Economic Analysis* (Institute for Monetary and Economic Research of the Bank of Korea) 11, no. 3 (2005).

Kang, David C. "The Institutional Foundations of Korean Politics," in *Understanding Korean Politics: An Introduction*, ed. Soong Hoom Kil and Chung-in Moon. Albany: State University of New York Press, 2001, 71–105.

Kang Kyŏng-sik. *Hwallan ilgi* [A diary of the financial crisis]. Seoul: Munyedang, 1999.

Kang Man-su. *Hyŏnjang esŏ pon Han'guk kyŏngje 30-nyŏn* [Thirty years of Korean economy from a first-hand view]. Seoul: Samsŏng kyŏngje yŏn'guso, 2005.

Kang, Nahee. "Globalisation and Institutional Change in the State-Led Model: The Case of Corporate Governance in South Korea," *New Political Economy* 15, no. 4 (December 2010): 519–42.

Katz, Leo. "A New Status Index Derived from Sociometric Analysis," *Psychometrica* 18, no. 1 (March 1953): 39–43.

Kawai, Masahiro, Ira Lieberman, and William P. Mako. "Financial Stabilization and Initial Restructuring of East Asian Corporations: Approaches, Results, and Lessons," in *Managing Financial and Corporate Distress: Lessons from Asia*, ed. Charles Adams, Robert E. Litan, and Michael Pomerleano. Washington, DC: Brookings Institution Press, 2003, 77–136.

Keum, Jacob et al. *Employment Insurance in Korea: The First Ten Years*. Seoul, 2006.

Khatkhate, Deena and Ismail Dalla. "Regulated Deregulation of the Financial System in Korea," World Bank Discussion Paper, no. 292 (1995).

Kihoek yesan wiwŏnhoe (PBC). *Chŏngbu chojik kaep'yŏn paeksŏ* [White paper on government reorganization]. Seoul: Kihoek yesan wiwŏnhoe, 1998.

Kihoek yesanch'ŏ (MPB). Chŏngbu kaehyŏk paeksŏ [White paper on government reform]. Seoul: Kihoek yesanch'ŏ, 2000.

Kim, Byung-Kook. "Bringing and Managing Socioeconomic Change: The State in Korea and Mexico." PhD diss., Harvard University, 1987.

Kim, Byung-Kook. "Electoral Politics and Economic Crisis, 1997–1998," in *Consolidating Democracy in South Korea*, ed. Larry Diamond and Byung-Kook Kim. Boulder, CO: Lynne Rienner, 2000, 173–201.

Kim, Byung-Kook. "Ideology, Organization and Democratic Consolidation in Korea," in *Democracy and Communism: Its Ideals and Realities*, ed. Sangyang Chul. Seoul: Korean Political Science Association, 1997, 135–77.

Kim, Byung-Kook. "The Leviathan: Economic Bureaucracy under Park Chung Hee." Paper presented at the annual meeting of the American Political Science Association, Boston, 2002.

Kim, Byung-Kook. "The Park Era: Agent, Structure, and Legacies." Paper presented at the annual meeting of the American Political Science Association, 2002.

Kim, Byung-Kook. "Party Politics in South Korea's Democracy: The Crisis of Success," in *Consolidating Democracy in South Korea*, ed. Larry Diamond and Byung-Kook Kim. Boulder, CO: Lynne Rienner, 2000, 53–85.

Kim, Byung-Kook. "The Politics of *Chaebŏl* Reform, 1980–1997," in *Economic Crisis and Corporate Restructuring in Korea: Reforming the* Chaebol, ed. Stephan Haggard, Wonhyuk Lim, and Euysung Kim. New York: Cambridge University Press, 2003, 53–78.

Kim, Byung-Kook. "The Politics of Crisis and a Crisis of Politics: The Presidency of Kim Dae-Jung," in *Korea Briefing, 1997–1999: Challenges and Change at the Turn of the Century*, ed. Kongdan Oh. Armonk, NY: ME Sharpe, Inc., 2000, 35–74.

Kim, Byung-Kook. "The Politics of Financial Reform in Korea, Malaysia, and Thailand: When, Why, and How Democracy Matters?" *Journal of East Asian Studies* 2, no. 1 (February 2002): 185–240.

Kim Byung-Kook (Kim Pyŏng-guk). *Pundan kwa hyŏngmyŏng ŭi tonghak: Han' guk kwa Meksiko ŭi chŏngch'i kyŏngje* [The dynamics of national division and revolution: The political economy of Korea and Mexico]. Seoul: Munhak kwa chisŏngsa, 1994.

Kim, Byung-Kook. "The U.S.-South Korean Alliance: Anti-American Challenges," *Journal of East Asian Studies* 3, no. 2 (May-August 2003): 225–58.

Kim, Byung-Kook and Hyug Baeg Im. "'Crony Capitalism' in South Korea, Thailand, and Taiwan: Myth and Reality," *Journal of East Asian Studies* 1, no. 1 (February 2001): 5–52.

Kim, Byung-Kook and Hyun-Chin Lim. "Labor against Itself: Structural Dilemmas of State Monism," in *Consolidating Democracy in South Korea*, ed. Larry Diamond and Byung-Kook Kim. Boulder, CO: Lynne Rienner, 2000, 111–37.

Kim, Dae Jung. *Mass-Participatory Economy: A Democratic Alternative for Korea.* Lanham, MD: University Press of America, 1985.

Kim, Eun Mee, *Big Business, Strong State: Collusion and Conflict in South Korean Development, 1960-1990.* Albany: State University of New York, 1997.

Kim, Eun Mee. "From Dominance to Symbiosis: State and *Chaebol* in Korea," *Pacific Focus* 3, no. 2 (September 1988): 105–21.

Kim Eun Mee (Kim Ŭn-mi), Dukjin Chang (Chang Tŏkjin) and Mark Granovetter. *Kyŏngje wigi ŭi sahoehak: kaebalkukka ŭi chŏnhwan-kwakiŏpchiptan yŏn'gyŏlmang* [The sociology of economic crisis: The transformation of the developmental state and business group networks]. Seoul: Seoul National University Press, 2005.

Kim Hong-bŏm. *Han'guk kŭmyung kaep'yŏn ron* [Reforming the institutional structure of financial supervision in Korea]. Seoul: Seoul National University Press, 2006.

Kim, Hong-Bum and Chung H. Lee. "Financial Reform, Institutional Interdependency, and Supervisory Failure in Postcrisis Korea," *Journal of East Asian Studies* 6, no. 3 (September-December 2006): 409–31.

Kim Hyŏn-jŏng. "Oehwan wigi ihu ŭnhaeng-kiŏp kwan'gye ŭi pyŏnhwa" [The change in bank-firm relations after the financial crisis], *Kumyung kyŏngje yŏn'gu* [Financial and economic studies] (2002).

Kim Hyŏn-uk. "Oeguk chabon ŭi ŭnhaeng sansŏp chinip hwakdae e taehan ihae wa kyuje" [An understanding of and regulation of the expansion of entry into the banking industry by foreign capital], in *Kiŏp kyŏngyŏngkwŏn e taehan yŏn'gu: Siljŭng punsŏk kwa chedo chŏngbi pangan ŭl chungsim ŭro* [Studies on corporate management control in Korea: An empirical analysis and a measure of institutional modification], ed. Yŏn T'ae-hun. Korea Development Institute Research Paper, no.05–07 (2005), 185–258.

Kim, June-Dong. "Impact of Foreign Direct Investment Liberalization: The Case of Korea," Korea Institute for International Economic Policy Working Paper, no. 97–01 (August 1997).

Kim Ki-t'ae and Hong Hyŏn-p'yo. "Chaebŏl ŭi t'ŭksŏng kwa ŭiŭi"[The characteristics and meaning of chaebŏl], in *Han'guk kyŏngje ŭi kujo* [The structure of Korea's economy], ed. Kim Ki-tae et al. Seoul: Hanul Academy, 1993.

Kim Myŏn-hŭi. "Han'guk kŭmyung sanŏp kujo chojŏng kwa nodong chohap undong" [Financial restructuring and labor movements in Korea], *Han'guk chŏngch'i hakhoe po* [Korean political science review] 38, no. 2 (2004): 167–88.

Kim, Pyung Joo. "Financial Institutions," in *Korea's Political Economy: An Institutional Perspective*, ed. Lee-Jay Cho and Yoon Hyung Kim. Boulder, CO: Westview Press, 1994.

Kim Se-gyun. "1987-nyŏn ihu ŭi Han'guk nodong undong" [Korean labor movements after 1987], *Studies on Korean Politics*. Seoul: Institute of Korean Politics, Seoul National University, 2002, 197–244.

Kim, Shinyoung. "Towards a Better Understanding of Welfare Policy Development in Developing Nations: A Case Study of South Korea's Pension System," *International Journal of Social Welfare* 15, no. 1 (2006): 75–83.

Kim Sŏng-jung and Sŏng Che-hwan. *Han'guk ŭi koyong chŏngch'aek* [Employment policies in South Korea]. Seoul: Korea Labor Institute, 2005.

Kim Su-gon. *Nosa kwan'gye chŏngch'aek kwa panghyang* [Policy agenda and direction of industrial relations in Korea]. Seoul: Korea Development Institute, 1983.

Kim, Sunhyuk. *The Politics of Democratization in Korea: The Role of Civil Society*. Pittsburgh: University of Pittsburgh Press, 2000.

Kim, Sunhyuk. "From Resistance to Representation: Civil Society in South Korean Democratization." PhD diss., Stanford University, 1996.

Kim Tae-sik and Yun Sŏk-hŏn. "T'onghap kŭmyung kamdok kigu ŭi pyŏnch'ŏn kwa hyanghu ŭi kaep'yŏn panghyang" [Changes in the integrated financial supervisory agency and the future direction for reform], *Korea Money and Finance Association Review* 10, no. 1 (2005).

Kim Tong-hun. "Han'guk chaebŏl ŭi chibae kujo" [The corporate governance structure of Korean *chaebŏl*], in *Han'guk chaebŏl kaehyŏkron* [The theory of chaebŏl reform], ed. Kim T'ae-hwan and Kim Kyun. Seoul: Nanam Publishing, 1999, 65–104.

Kim, Yong-Ho. "Korea," in *Political Party Systems and Democratic Development in East and Southeast Asia*, vol. 2: East Asia, ed. Wolfgang Sachsenröder and Ulrike E. Frings. Aldershot: Ashgate, 1998, 132–78.

Kim Yonghwan. *Imja, Chane ka saryŏnggwan anin'ga* [You are the commander]. Seoul: Maeil kyŏngje sinmunsa, 2002.

Kim, Yŏngmin. "Munmin chŏngbu chŏngbu chojik kaep'yŏn ŭi naeyong kwa munje chŏm" [Issues regarding government reorganization during the Kim Young-sam administration], *Inha taehakkyo sahoe kwahak yŏn'guso nonmun chip* [Social science treatise, Inha University] 17 (1999): 329–48.

Kim, Young Cheol. "Industrial Reform and Labor Backlash in South Korea: Genesis, Escalation, and Termination of the 1997 General Strike," *Asian Survey* 38, no. 12 (December 1998): 1142–60.

Kim Young-sam. *Kim Yŏng-sam taet'ongnyŏng hoegorok, ha-gwŏn* [Memoirs of President Kim Young-sam, vol. 2]. Seoul: Chosŏn ilbosa, 2001.

Kitschelt, Herbert and Wolfgang Streeck, eds. *Germany: Beyond the Stable State*. London: Frank Cass, 2004.

Kitschelt, Herbert and Steven I. Wilkinson."Citizen-Politician Linkages: An Introduction," in *Patrons, Clients, and Policies: Patterns of Democratic Accountability and Political Competition*, ed. Kitschelt and Wilkinson. New York:
Cambridge University Press, 2007, 1–49.

Kong, Tat Yan. *The Politics of Economic Reform in South Korea: A Fragile Miracle*. London: Routledge, 2000.

Kongboch'ŏ [Government Information Agency]. *Munmin chŏngbu 5-nyŏn kyehoek paeksŏ* [A comprehensive report on the five years of reform during the
Kim Young-sam administration]. Seoul: Kongboch'ŏ 1997.

Koo, Hagen. "The Dilemmas of Empowered Labor in Korea: Korean Workers in
the Face of Global Capitalism," *Asian Survey* 40, no. 2 (March/April 2000):
227–50.

Koo, Hagen. *Korean Workers: The Culture and Politics of Class Formation*. Ithaca,
NY: Cornell University Press, 2001.

Koo, Hagen. "The Political Economy of Income Distribution in South Korea: The
Impact of the State's Industrialization Policies," *World Development* 12, no. 10
(October 1984): 1029–37.

Korea Chamber of Commerce. "Kiŏp yuboyul hyŏnhwang kwa sisajŏm" [The current situation of corporate retained earnings and its implications], July 4, 2007.

Korea Development Institute (KDI). *DJnomics*. Seoul: Korea Development Institute, 1999.

Korea Labor Institute. *KLI nodong t'onggye* [KLI labor statistics]. Seoul: Korea
Labor Institute, various years.

Korea National Statistics Office, *Highlights of Population Projections*. Seoul, 2006.

Korean Women's Development Institute (KWDI). *Gender Statistics in Korea, 2009*.
Seoul, 2010.

Korean Women's Development Institute (KWDI). *Statistical Handbook 2008:
Women in Korea*. Seoul, 2008.

KPMG Consulting. *Foreign Direct Investment in Korea* Summary Report. Seoul,
2001.

Kwon, Huck-Ju. "Advocacy Coalitions and the Politics of Welfare in Korea after the
Economic Crisis," *Policy and Politics* 31, no. 1 (2003): 69–83.

Kwon, Huck-Ju. "Reforming of the Developmental Welfare State in Korea: Advocacy Coalition and Health Politics," in *Transforming the Developmental Welfare State in East Asia*, ed. Huck-Ju Kwon. New York: Palgrave, 2006, 27–49.

Kwon, Soonman and Ian Holliday."The Korean Welfare State: A Paradox of
Expansion in an Era of Globalisation and Economic Crisis," *International
Journal of Social Welfare* 16, no. 3 (July 2007): 242–48

Lane, Christel. "Institutional Transformation and System Change: Changes in the
Corporate Governance of German Corporations," in *Changing Capitalisms?
Internationaliism, Institutional Change, and Systems of Economic Organization*, ed. Glenn Morgan, Richard Whitley, and Eli Moen. Oxford: Oxford University Press, 2005, 78–109.

Lane, Timothy, et al. *IMF-Supported Programs in Indonesia, Korea, and Thailand: A Preliminary Assessment*. Washington, DC: International Monetary Fund, 1999.

Lazonick, William and Mary O'Sullivan, eds. *Corporate Governance and Sustainable Prosperity*. Basingstoke: Palgrave Macmillan, 2002.

Lee, Aie-Rie. "Stability and Change in Korean Values," *Social Indicators Research* 62/63 (April 2003): 93–117.

Lee, Chung H. "The Political Economy of Institutional Reform in Korea," *Journal of the Asia Pacific Economy* 10, no. 3 (August 2005): 257–77.

Lee, Dong Gull. "The Restructuring of Daewoo," in *Economic Crisis and Restructuring in Korea: Reforming the* Chaebol, ed. Stephan Haggard, Wonhyuk Lim, and Euysong Kim. New York: Cambridge University Press, 2003, 150–77.

Lee, Doowon. "South Korea's Financial Crisis and Economic Restructuring," in *Korea Briefing 1997–1999: Challenges and Change at the Turn of the Century*, ed. Kongdan Oh. Armonk, NY: ME Sharpe, 2000, 9–34.

Lee, Hye-Hoon and Kye-Sik Lee. "A Korean Model of Social Welfare Policy: Issues and Strategies" in *An Agenda for Economic Reform in Korea: International Perspectives*, ed. Kenneth Judd and Yoong-Ki Lee. Stanford, CA: Hoover Institution Press, 2000, 203–45.

Lee, Hye-Kyung. "Welfare Reforms in Post-Crisis Korea: Dilemmas and Choices," *Social Policy and Society* 3, no. 3 (July 2004): 291–99.

Lee, Hye-Kyung and Yeong-Ran Park. "Families in Transition and the Family Welfare Policies in Korea." Paper presented at the Canada-Korea Social Policy Research Symposium, Seoul, November 2003.

Lee, Hye-Kyung and Ito Peng. "Civil Society and Social Policy Reforms in Japan and Korea." Paper presented at the annual meeting of the Association for Asian Studies, Chicago, 2005.

Lee, Jong-Wha. "Economic Growth and Human Development in the Republic of Korea, 1945–1992" UNDP Occasional Paper, no. 24, at http://hdr.undp.org/en/reports/global/hdr1997/papers/jong-wha_lee.pdf, accessed December 18, 2011.

Lee, Suk-jun. "Accounting Reform Gathers Momentum in Korea," in *Korea's Economy 2004*. Seoul: Korea Economic Institute and Korea Institute of International Economic Policy, vol. 20, 2004.

Lee, Wonduck and Byung-yoo Chun. "Flexibility in the Korean Labor Market." Paper presented at the KCESRI-OECD seminar on Korea issues, Paris, 2004.

Lee, Wonduck and Joohee Lee. *Industrial Relations: Recent Changes and New Challenges*. Seoul: Korea Labor Institute, 2004.

Lee, Wonduck and Joohee Lee, "Will the Model of Uncoordinated Decentralization Persist? Changes in Korean Industrial Relations after the Financial Crisis," in *The New Structure of Labor Relations: Tripartism and Decentralization*, ed. Harry C. Katz, Wonduck Lee, and Joohee Lee. Ithaca, NY: Cornell University Press, 2004, 143–65.

Lee, Yeon-ho. *The State, Society, and Big Business in South Korea*. London: Routledge, 1997.

Lee, Yeonho. "Participatory Democracy and Chaebol Regulation in Korea: State-Market Relations under the MDP Governments, 1997–2003," *Asian Survey* 45, no. 2 (March/April 2005): 279–301.

Leipziger, Danny M. "Industrial Restructuring in Korea," *World Development* 16, no.1 (1988): 121–35.

Levitsky, Steven and María Victoria Murillo. "Conclusion: Theorizing About Weak Institutions: Lessons from the Argentine Case," in *Argentine Democracy: The Politics of Institutional Weakness*, ed. Steven Levitsky and María Victoria Murillo. University Park: Pennsylvania State University Press, 2005, 269–89.

Lim, Wonhyuk. "The Emergence of the *Chaebol* and the Origins of the *Chaebol* Problem," in *Economic Crisis and Corporate Restructuring in Korea: Reforming the* Chaebol, ed. Stephan Haggard, Wonhyuk Lim, and Euysung Kim. New York: Cambridge University Press, 2003, 35–52.

Lim,Wonhyuk and Joon-Ho Hah. "Turning a Crisis into an Opportunity: The Political Economy of Korea's Financial Sector Reform,' in *From Crisis to Opportunity: Financial Globalization and East Asian Capitalism*, ed. Jongryn Mo and Daniel I. Okimoto. Stanford, CA: Walter H. Shorenstein Asia-Pacific Research Center, Stanford University, 2006, 85–122.

Lim, Youngjae. "The Corporate Bankruptcy System and the Economic Crisis," in *Economic Crisis and Corporate Restructuring in Korea: Reforming the* Chaebol, ed. Stephan Haggard, Wonhyuk Lim, and Euysong Kim. New York: Cambridge University Press, 2003, 207–30.

Lindgren, Carl-Johan, Tomas J. T. Baliño, Charles Enoch, Anne-Marie Gulde, Marc Quintyn, and Leslie Teo. "Financial Sector Crisis and Restructuring: Lessons from Asia," IMF Occasional Paper 188 (2000).

Lukauskas, Arvid and Susan Minushkin. "Explaining Styles of Financial Market Opening in Chile, Mexico, South Korea, and Turkey," *International Studies Quarterly* 44, no. 4 (2000): 695–723.

Maeil kyŏngje sinmun [MK Business News]. "Taekiyŏp ŭnhaengŏp chinch'ul changbyŏk k'ŭke nachachŏ" [Entry barrier to the banking sector to be lowered significantly for big business], July 23, 2009.

Mathews, John A. "Fashioning a New Korean Model Out of the Crisis," Japan Policy Research Institute (JPRI) Working Paper, no. 46 (1998).

McKinnon, Ronald I. and Huw Pill. "Credible Liberalizations and International Capital Flows: The 'Overborrowing Syndrome,'" in *Financial Deregulation and Integration in East Asia*, ed. Takatoshi Ito and Anne O. Krueger. Chicago: University of Chicago Press, 1996, 7–50.

Ministry of Commerce, Industry, and Energy. "Trend Report of Foreign Direct Investment." Seoul, 2000.

Ministry of Finance and Korea Development Bank. *Han'guk oeja toip samsip-nyŏnsa* [Thirty years of foreign capital imports] (1993).

Ministry of Government Administration. *Kongmuwŏn t'ongkye* [Statistics on public officials], various years.

Ministry of Health and Welfare, *Health and Welfare Services, 2003*. Seoul, 2003.

Ministry of Labor, *Kiŏp nodong piyong chosa* [Survey report on enterprise labor costs]. Seoul, various issues.

Ministry of Labor (formerly Administration of Labor Affairs). *Maewŏl nodong t'onggye chosa pogosŏ* [Report on monthly labor survey]. Seoul, 1973–2005.

Ministry of Labor, *Nodong paekŏ* [White paper on labor]. Seoul, 2005.

Ministry of Labor. *Nodong t'onggye yŏn'gam* [Yearbook of labor statistics]. Seoul, various years.

Ministry of Labor. *Yearbook of Labor Statistics* (2005).

Ministry of Strategy and Finance. "Oeguginjikjjeoptuja-ga Hwalbalhan Gukkaui Jiwonsarye-wa Uri-ui Jeongchaekbanghyang" [Policies of FDI-friendly countries and Korea's policy direction], November 30, 2001.

Ministry of Trade, Industry, and Resources. "Tae kyumo kiŏp chipdan ŭi ŏpjong chŏnmunhwa yudo pangan" [A measure to induce sectoral specialization of large-scale business groups], May 1993.

Miura, Mari. "From Welfare through Work to Lean Work: The Politics of Labor Market Reform in Japan." PhD diss., University of California, Berkeley, 2002.

Mo, Jongryn. "Democratization, Labor Policy, and Economic Performance," in *Democracy and the Korean Economy*, ed. Jongryn Mo and Chung-in Moon. Stanford, CA: Hoover Institution Press, 1999, 97–134.

Mo, Jongryn. "Political Culture and Legislative Gridlock: Politics of Economic Reform in Precrisis Korea," *Comparative Political Studies* 34, no. 5 (June 2001): 467–92.

Mo, Jongryn and Chung-in Moon. "Business-Government Relations under Kim Dae-jung," in *Economic Crisis and Corporate Restructuring in Korea: Reforming the Chaebol*, ed. Stephan Haggard, Wonhyuk Lim, and Euysung Kim. New York: Cambridge University Press, 2003, 127–49.

Mo, Jongryn and Chung-in Moon. "Korea after the Crash," *Journal of Democracy* 10, no. 3 (1999): 150–64.

Moon, Chung-in. "Changing Patterns of Business-Government Relations in South Korea," in *Business and Government in Industrialising Asia*, ed. Andrew MacIntyre. Ithaca, NY: Cornell University Press, 1994, 222–46.

Moon, Chung-in and Song-min Kim. "Democracy and Economic Performance in South Korea," in *Consolidating Democracy in South Korea*, ed. Larry Diamond and Byunk-Kook Kim. Boulder, CO: Lynne Rienner, 2000, 139–72.

Moon, Chung In and Sang-young Rhyu. "The State, Structural Rigidity, and the End of Asian Capitalism: A Comparative Study of Japan and South Korea," in *Politics and Markets in the Wake of the Asian Crisis*, ed. Mark Beeson, Kanishka Jayasuriya, Hyuk-Rae Kim, and Richard Robison. New York: Routledge, 2000, 77–98.

Moon, Ihlwan. "Cleaning Up in South Korea," *BusinessWeek*, August 17, 2006.

Na Chung-sik. "Han'guk chungang chaejŏng kigu pyŏnch'ŏn ŭi yŏksa chŏk punsŏk—Pak Ch'ŏng-hŭi, Kim Yŏng-sam, Kim Tae-jung chŏngbu ŭi chaemu haengjŏng chojik kaep'yŏn e kwanhan sarye punsŏk ŭl chungsim ŭro" [A historical analysis of Korean national financial institutions' transformation under

the Park Chung-hee, Kim Young-sam, and Kim Dae-jung administrations],
Han'guk haengjŏngron chip [Korean public administration quarterly] 11, no. 3
(1999): 541–61.

Nam, Jeong-Lim. "Labor Control of the State and Women's Resistance in the Export
Sector of South Korea," *Social Problems* 43, no. 3 (August 1996):327–38.

Nam, Sang-Woo and Dong-Won Kim. "The Principal Transactions Bank System
in Korea," in *The Japanese Main Bank System: Its Relevance for Developing
and Transforming Economies*, ed. Masahiko Aoki and Hugh Patrick. Oxford:
Oxford University Press, 1994, 450–93.

Nam, Sang-Woo and Dong-Won Kim. "The Principal Transactions Bank System in
Korea and Its Comparison with the Japanese Main Bank System." World Bank
Economic Development Institute (1994).

Nemoto, Kuniaki. "Mixed Incentives for Legislative Behaviors: Party Label, Office
Benefits, and Party Discipline in Korea." Paper prepared for the Annual Meeting of the Midwest Political Science Association, April 2009.

O Sŭngyong, *Punjŭm chŏngbu wa Han'guk chŏngch'i* [Divided government and
Korean politics]. Seoul: Han'guk haksul chŏngbo, 2005.

O'Donnell, Guillermo. "Delegative Democracy," in *The Global Resurgence of
Democracy*, 2nd ed., ed. Larry Diamond and Marc F. Plattner. Baltimore, MD:
Johns Hopkins University Press, 1996, 94–108.

Oh Yul Kwon, "Foreign Direct Investment in Korea: A Foreign Perspective," Korean
Economic Research Institute, Major Research Paper, no. 2003–14 (2003).

Olson, Mansur, Jr. *The Logic of Collective Action" Public Goods and the Theory
of Groups*. New York: Schochen Books, 1965.

Organisation for Economic Co-operation and Development. *Babies and Bosses:
Reconciling Work and Family Life*. Vol. 2: Austria, Ireland, and Japan. Paris:
2003.

Orrù, Marco. "Dirigiste Capitalism in France and South Korea," in *The Economic
Organization of East Asian Capitalism*, ed. Marco Orrù, Nicole Woolsey Biggart, and Gary Hamilton. London: Sage Publications, 1997, 368–82.

Pae Kyu-sik, Yi Sang-min, Paek P'il-gyu, Im Un-t'aek, and Yi Kyu-yong. *Chungso
chejo ŏp ŭi koyong kwan'gye* [Employment relations in small- and medium-
sized firms]. Seoul: Korea Labor Institute, 2006.

Pak Tae-sik. "Chŏngbu chojik kaep'yŏn e taehan chedo sŏnt'aek chŏk punsŏk:
Kungmin ŭi chŏngbu chojik kaep'yŏn ŭl chungsim ŭro" [An institutional choice
analysis of government reorganization: Government reform under the Kim
Dae-jung administration], *Han'guk haengjŏng hakpo* [Korean review of public
administration] 35, no. 3 (2001): 1–19.

Pak T'ae-gyun. *Kwallyo mangguk ron kwa chaebŏl sinhwa ui Bungkwoi* [National
ruin by the bureaucracy and the collapse of the *chaebŏl* myth]. Seoul: Sallim
Publishing, 1997.

Pak Tong, "Han'guk esŏ 'Sahoe hyŏbyak chŏngch'i' ŭi ch'ulbal kwa kŭ pul anjŏng
sŏng yoin punsŏk" [The emergence of the social pact and its instability in

Korea], *Han'guk chŏngch'i hakhoe po* [Korean political science review] 34, no. 4 (2001): 161–77.

Park, Kyung Suh. "Bank-led Corporate Restructuring," in *Economic Crisis and Corporate Restructuring in Korea: Reforming the* Chaebol, ed. Stephan Haggard, Wonhyuk Lim, and Euysung Kim. New York: Cambridge University Press, 2003, 181–206.

Park, Se-il. "Reforming Labor Management Relations: Lessons from the Korean Experience, 1996–1997" Korea Development Institute (June 2000).

Park, Yoon-Shik. "Financial and Corporate Restructuring Lessons from Korea to Latin America and the Caribbean." Paper prepared for the Inter-American Development Bank, April 2003.

Park, Yung Chul and Dong Won Kim. "Korea: Development and Structural Change of the Banking System," in *The Financial Development of Japan, Korea, and Taiwan: Growth, Repression, and Liberalization*, ed. Hugh T. Patrick and Yung Chul Park. New York: Oxford University Press, 1994, 188–221.

Patrick, Hugh T. "Comparisons, Contrasts, and Implications," in *The Financial Development of Japan, Korea, and Taiwan: Growth, Repression, and Liberalization*, ed. Hugh T. Patrick and Yung Chul Park. New York: Oxford University Press, 1994, 325–72.

Peng, Ito. "Economic Dualization in Japan and South Korea." Paper presented at the Labor Market Dualization Workshop, Green Templeton College, Oxford University, January 2010.

Peng, Ito. "Political and Social Economy of Care in the Republic of Korea," United Nations Research Institute for Social Development, Gender and Development Paper, no. 6 (2009), at http://www.unrisd.org/unrisd/website/document.nsf/ (httpPublication s)/2B5879FBCD1DBD3FC12576A200479FA3?OpenDocument.

Peng, Ito. "Postindustrial Pressures, Political Regimes Shifts, and Social Policy Reform in Japan and South Korea," *Journal of East Asian Studies* 4, no. 3 (September-December 2004): 389–425.

Peng, Ito. "Social Policy Reforms and Gender in Japan and South Korea" in *Gender and Social Policy in a Global Context: Uncovering the Gendered Structure of "the Social"*, ed. Sharha Razavi and Shireen Hassim. New York: Palgave Macmillan, 130–50.

Peng, Ito and Joseph Wong. "Institutions and Institutional Purpose: Continuity and Change in East Asian Social Policy," Politics and Society 36, no. 1 (March 2008): 61–88.

Pierson, Paul. "Increasing Returns, Path Dependence, and the Study of Politics," *American Political Science Review* 94, no. 2 (2000): 251–67.

Pierson, Paul. "The Limits of Design: Explaining Institutional Origins and Change," *Governance* 13, no. 4 (2000): 475–99.

Pirie, Iain. "The New Korean State," *New Political Economy* 10, no. 1 (2005): 25–42.

Putnam, Robert D. "Diplomacy and Domestic Politics: The Logic of Two-Level Games," *International Organization* 42, no. 3 (Summer 1988): 427–60.

Radelet, Stephen and Jeffrey Sachs. "The East Asian Financial Crisis: Diagnosis, Remedies, Prospects," *Brookings Papers on Economic Activity* 1, no. 1 (1998): 1–90.

Radelet, Steven and Jeffrey Sachs. "What Have We Learned, So Far, from the Asian Financial Crisis?" Harvard Institute for International Development, CAER Discussion Paper, no. 37, presented at the annual meeting of the American Economic Association, January 1999.

Rius, Andres and Nicolas van de Walle. "Political Institutions and Economic Policy Reform," in *Understanding Market Reforms*, vol. 1: *Philosophy, Politics and Stakeholders*, ed. José Maria Fanelli and Gary McMahon. New York: Palgrave Macmillan, 2005, 176–202.

Roger, Scott. "The Asian Crisis Four Years On," *Finance and Development* 38, no. 1 (March 2001): 1–2.

Root, Gregory, Paul Grela, Mark Jones, and Anand Adiga. "Financial Sector Restructuring in East Asia" in *Managing Financial and Corporate Distress: Lessons from Asia*, ed. Charles Adams, Robert E. Litan, and Michael Pomerleano. Washington, DC: Brookings Institution Press, 2003, 149–222.

Samuels, David J. and Matthew Søberg Shugart. "Presidentialism, Elections and Representation," *Journal of Theoretical Politics* 15, no. 1 (January 2003): 33–60.

Schmidt, Vivien A. *The Futures of European Capitalism*. Oxford: Oxford University Press, 2002.

Securities Exchange Supervisory Commission. *Chabon sijang nyŏnbo* [Capital markets annual] (various issues).

Securities Exchange Supervisory Commission. "Kukhoe kukchŏng kamsa yogu charyo" [The materials demanded for a National Assembly audit] (September 1989).

Segyehwa ch'ujin wiwŏnhoe [The Globalization Promotion Committee], *Segyehwa paeksŏ* [White paper on globalization]. Seoul: Segyehwa ch'ujin wiwŏnhoe, 1998.

Segyehwa ch'ujin wiwŏnhoe [The Globalization Promotion Committee]. *Segyehwa ŭi bijyŏn-kwa chŏllyak* [Globalization: Visions and strategies]. Seoul: Segyehwa ch'ujin wiwŏnhoe, 1995.

Seong Il Jung. "Jeunggwonsijang Jabonjuui Bipangwa Chabol mit Eunhaenggaehyeo-gui Daean" [Critics of stock-market capitalism and alternative reform measures for the *chaebŏl* and the banks]. Conference paper prepared for the Korea Socio & Economic Studies Association, 2003.

Shin, Hang-Sup and Ha-Joon Chang. *Restructuring "Korea Inc.": Financial Crisis, Corporate Reform, and Institutional Transition*. New York: RoutledgeCurzon, 2003).

Sin Hyŏn-yŏl and Kim Po-sŏng. "Kiŏp ŭi oebu chagŭm chodan kyŏngno rosŏ ŭnhaeng taech'ul kwa hoesa ch'aesijang ŭi taech'aesŏ punsŏk" [Bank loans and corporate bonds as corporate fund raising], *Bank of Korea Monthly Bulletin* (January 2007).

Sŏ Chae-jin. *Han'guk ŭi chabon kwa kyegŭp* [The capitalist class of Korea]. Seoul: Nanam Publishing, 1991.

Son Uk and Yi Sang-jae. "Kŭmyung sŏbisŭ sŏnjinhwa rŭl wihan kwaje" [Agendas for the advancement of financial service], in *Sŏbisŭ pumun ŭi sŏnjinhwa rŭl wihan chŏngch'aek kwaje* [The policy agendas for advancing the service sector], ed. Kim Ju-hun and Ch'a Mun-jung. Korea Development Institute Policy Paper, no 07-04 (2007).

Song, Byung-Nak. *The Rise of the Korean Economy*, 2nd ed. Oxford: Oxford University Press, 1997.

Song Ho-gŭn. *Han'guk ŭi nodong chŏngch'i wa sijang* [Labor politics and the labor market of Korea]. Seoul: Nanam Publishing, 1991.

Song, Ho Keung. "The Birth of a Welfare State in Korea: The Unfinished Symphony of Democratization and Globalization," *Journal of East Asian Studies* 3, no. 3 (2003): 405–32.

Song Ho-kŏn. "Kwŏnwi chuŭi Han'guk ŭi kukka wa imgŭm chŏngch'ak (II)" [Authoritarian government and wage policy in Korea (II)], *Han'guk chŏngch'i hakhoe po* [Korean political science review] 27, no.1 (1993).

Song Wŏn-gŭn and Yi Sang-ho. *Chaebŏl ŭi saŏp kujo wa kyŏngjeryŏk chipjung* [The business structure and economic concentration of *chaebŏl*]. Seoul: Nanam Publishing, 2005.

Stallings, Barbara. "The Role of Foreign Capital in Economic Development," in *Manufacturing Miracles: Paths of Industrialization in Latin America and East Asia*, ed. Gary Gereffi and Donald L. Wyman. Princeton, NJ: Princeton University Press, 1990, 55–89.

Stokes, Susan C. "What Do Policy Switches Tell Us About Democracy?" in *Democracy, Accountability, and Representation*, ed. Adam Przeworski, Stokes, and Bernard Manin (New York: Cambridge University Press, 1999), 98–130.

Streeck, Wolfgang. "Introduction: Explorations in the Origins of Nonliberal Capitalism in Germany and Japan," in *The Origins of Nonliberal Capitalism: Germany and Japan in Comparison*, ed. Wolfgang Streeck and Kozo Yamamura. Ithaca, NY: Cornell University Press, 2001, 1–38.

Streeck, Wolfgang and Kathleen Ann Thelen, eds., *Beyond Continuity: Institutional Change in Advanced Political Economies*. Oxford: Oxford University Press, 2005.

Suh, Jin-Young and Byung-Kook Kim. "The Politics of Reform in Korea: Dilemma, Choice, and Crisis," in *The World after the Cold War: Issues and Dilemmas*, ed. Jin-Young Suh and Changrok Soh. Seoul: Graduate School of International Studies, Korea University, 1999, 17–53.

T'ak Hŭi-jun. "Han'guk imgŭm chŏngch'a ŭi t'ŭksŏng" [The characteristics of Korean wage policies], *Han'guk kyŏngje* [Korean economics], 2 (1974).

Tiberghein, Yves. "Political Mediation of Global Economic Forces: The Politics of Corporate Restructuring in Japan, France, and South Korea." PhD diss., Stanford University, 2002.

Thelen, Kathleen. *How Institutions Evolve*. New York: Cambridge University Press, 2004.

Tripartite Commission. *Major Agreements of the Tripartite Commission between 1998–2005* (May 2005), at http://www.lmg.go.kr/bbs/viewbody.asp?code=e_bbs 52&page=2&id=17&number=17&keyfield=&keyword=&admin=, accessed December 18, 2011.

Velasco, Andrés, ed. *Trade, Development and the World Economy: Selected Essays of Carlos F. Díaz-Alejandro*. Oxford: Basil Blackwell, 1988.

Wade, Robert. *Governing the Market: Economic Theory and the Role of Government in East Asian Industrialization*. Princeton, NJ: Princeton University Press, 1990).

Wade, Robert and Frank Veneroso. "The Asian Crisis: The High Debt Model versus the Wall Street Treasury-IMF Complex," *New Left Review* I, no. 228 (March-April 1998): 3–23.

Walter, Andrew. *Governing Finance: East Asia's Adoption of International Standards*. Ithaca, NY: Cornell University Press, 2008.

Wang, Yunjong. "Capital Account Liberalization: The Case of Korea." Unpublished manuscript, 2002.

Wasserman, Stanley and Katherine Faust. *Social Network Analysis: Methods and Applications*. Cambridge: Cambridge University Press, 1994.

Won Jong Han. "Jusiksijang-ui Chwiyaksseong-gwa Juga Hoebok Bangan" [Weakness of the stock market and bouncing strategies of share prices], *LG Weekly Economy* 10, no. 4 (2000).

Wong, Joseph. *Healthy Democracies: Welfare Politics in Taiwan and South Korea*. Ithaca, NY: Cornell University Press, 2004.

Woo, Jung-en. *Race to the Swift: State and Finance in Korean Industrialization*. New York: Columbia University Press, 1991.

Woo-Cumings, Meredith. "Miracle as Prologue: The State and the Reform of the Corporate Sector in Korea," in *Rethinking the East Asia Miracle*, ed. Joseph E. Stiglitz and Shahid Yusuf. New York: Oxford University Press, 2001, 343–77.

World Bank. *The East Asian Miracle: Economic Growth and Public Policy*. New York: Published for the World Bank by Oxford University Press, 1993.

World Bank. "Financial Sector Assessment: Korea," based on the Joint IMF-World Bank Financial Sector Assessment Program (June 2003), at www1.worldbank. org/ finance/assets/images/Korea_FSA.pdf.

Yamamura, Kozo and Wolfgang Streeck, eds. *The End of Diversity? Prospects for German and Japanese Capitalism*. Ithaca, NY: Cornell University Press, 2003.

Yang Chae-jin. "Han'guk ŭi sanŏp hwa sigi sungnyŏng kwa pokji chedo ŭi kiwŏn" [Skills formation systems and the origins of the Korean welfare system], *Han'guk chŏngch'i hakhoe po* [Korean political science review], 38, no. 5 (2004): 85–103.

Yang, Jae-jin. "Democratic Governance and Bureaucratic Politics: A Case of Pension Reform in Korea," *Policy and Politics* 32, no. 2 (2004): 193–206.

Yi Chong-sun, "Han'guk ŭi sin chayu chuŭi chŏk kujo kaehyŏk kwa nodong sijang pyŏnhwa" [Neo-liberal economic restructuring and the change in the Korean labor market], Han'guk sahoe hak [Korean sociology review], 36, no. 3 (2002).

Yi Pyŏng-hun and Yu Pŏm-sang. "Nodong pŏp ŭi hyŏngsŏng kwa chiphaeng e kwanhan nodong chŏngch'i yŏn'ngu" [Study of labor politics on the legislation and enforcement of labor laws], Han'guk sahoe hak [Korean sociology review] 35, no. 2 (2001): 177–204.

Yi Yun-ho. Chaebŏl ŭi chaemu kujo wa chagŭm chodal [The capital structure and financing of Korean chaebŏl]. Seoul: Nanam Publishing, 2005.

Yoo, Seong Min. "Evolution of Government-Business Interface in Korea: Progress to Date and Reform Agenda Ahead," Korea Development Institute Working Paper (November 1997).

Yu Ki-rak. "Nodong chohap ŭi kwŏllyŏk chawŏn kwa chiphap haengwi e taehan yŏn'gu: Kŭmyung kujo chojŏng kwa chŏn'guk kŭmyung nodong chohap yŏnmaeng ŭi taeŭng 1997–2000" [Power resources and labor unions' collective actions: Political responses of the Korean financial industry union to financial restructuring, 1997–2000], Sanŏp nodong yŏn'gu [Industry and labor studies] 7, no. 2 (2001): 129–64.

Yu Kyŏng-jun. "Pijŏng'gyujik munje wa koyong ch'angch'ul" [The problem of temporary workers and job creation], in Han'guk kyŏngje kujo pyŏnhwa wa koyong ch'angch'ul [Economic structural changes and job creation in Korea], ed. Yu Kyŏng-jun. Seoul: Korea Development Institute, 2004, 464–518.

Yu Kyŏng-jun, ed. Han'guk kyŏngje kujo pyŏnhwa wa koyong changch'ul [Changes in the Korean economic structure and the creation of employment]. Seoul: Korea Development Institute, 2004.

Yu Kyŏng-jun and Yi Hŭi-suk. "IMF ihu nodong sijang ŭi pyŏnhwa mit chŏnmang" [The change and forecast of the Korean labor market after the crisis], Korea Development Institute Research Paper 99–02 (1999).

Yu Pŏm-sang. Han'guk ŭi nodong undong inyŏm [An ideology of Korean labor movements], Seoul: Korea Labor Institute, 2005.

Yu Sŏng-min. Chaebŏl wigi ŭi chubŏm in'ga [Are chaebŏl the culprit of the crisis]. Seoul: Pibong ch'ulp'ansa, 2000.

Yu Sŭng-min. Chaebŏl, kwayŏn wigi ŭi chubŏm in'ga: Wigi ihu chaebŏl chŏngch'aek ŭi p'yŏngga wa kwaje [Is the chaebŏl the villain behind the crisis? An evaluation of the post-crisis chaebŏl policy and its agendas]. Seoul: Korea Development Institute, 2000.

Yu Sŭng-min. "Chaebŏl ŭi kong'kwa: chaebŏl nonjaeng e taehan pip'an" [The merits and demerits of the chaebŏl: A critique of the polemic over the chaebŏl], in Han'guk kyŏngje ŭi chillo wa tae kiŏp chipdan [The path of the Korean economy and its large business group], ed. Korean Academic Society of Industrial Organization. Seoul: Kia Economic Institute, 1996, 239–96.

Yun, Mikyung. "Foreign Direct Investment and Corporate Restructuring After the Crisis," in Economic Crisis and Corporate Restructuring in Korea: Reforming *the* Chaebol, ed. Stephan Haggard, Wonhyuk Lim, and Euysung Kim. New York: Cambridge University Press, 2003, 233–64.

Yun, Mikyung and Young-Ho Park. "The Role of Foreign Investment in Korean Privatization," *Journal of International Economic Policy Studies* 3, no. 2 (Summer 1999).

Zysman, John. *Governments, Markets, and Growth: Financial Systems and the Politics of Industrial Change.* Ithaca, NY: Cornell University Press, 1983.

Index

RECENT PUBLICATIONS OF THE WALTER H. SHORENSTEIN ASIA-PACIFIC RESEARCH CENTER

BOOKS (distributed by the Brookings Institution Press)

Lim, Dong-won. *Peacemaker: Twenty Years of Inter-Korean Relations and the North Korean Nuclear Issue.* 2012.

Byung Kwan Kim, Gi-Wook Shin, and David Straub, eds. *Beyond North Korea: Future Challenges to South Korea's Security.* 2011.

Jean C. Oi, ed. *Going Private in China: The Politics of Corporate Restructuring and System Reform.* 2011.

Karen Eggleston and Shripad Tuljapurkar, eds. *Aging Asia: The Economic and Social Implications of Rapid Demographic Change in China, Japan and South Korea.* 2010.

Rafiq Dossani, Daniel C. Sneider, and Vikram Sood, eds. *Does South Asia Exist? Prospects for Regional Integration.* 2010.

Jean C. Oi, Scott Rozelle, and Xueguang Zhou. *Growing Pains: Tensions and Opportunity in China's Transition.* 2010.

Karen Eggleston, ed. *Prescribing Cultures and Pharmaceutical Policy in the Asia-Pacific.* 2009.

Donald A. L. Macintyre, Daniel C. Sneider, and Gi-Wook Shin, eds. *First Drafts of Korea: The U.S. Media and Perceptions of the Last Cold War Frontier.* 2009.

Steven Reed, Kenneth Mori McElwain, and Kay Shimizu, eds. *Political Change in Japan: Electoral Behavior, Party Realignment, and the Koizumi Reforms.* 2009.

Donald K. Emmerson. *Hard Choices: Security, Democracy, and Regionalism in Southeast Asia.* 2008.

Henry S. Rowen, Marguerite Gong Hancock, and William F. Miller, eds. *Greater China's Quest for Innovation.* 2008.

Gi-Wook Shin and Daniel C. Sneider, eds. *Cross Currents: Regionalism and Nationalism in Northeast Asia.* 2007.

Stella R. Quah, ed. *Crisis Preparedness: Asia and the Global Governance of Epidemics.* 2007.

Philip W Yun and Gi-Wook Shin, eds. *North Korea: 2005 and Beyond.* 2006.

STUDIES OF THE WALTER H. SHORENSTEIN ASIA-PACIFIC RESEARCH CENTER
(published with Stanford University Press)

Erik Kuhonta. *The Institutional Imperative: The Politics of Equitable Development in Southeast Asia*. Stanford, CA: Stanford University Press, 2011.

Gene Park. *Spending Without Taxation: FILP and the Politics of Public Finance in Japan*. Stanford, CA: Stanford University Press, 2011.

Erik Martinez Kuhonta. *The Institutional Imperative: The Politics of Equitable Development in Southeast Asia*. Stanford, CA: Stanford University Press, 2011.

Yongshun Cai. *Collective Resistance in China: Why Popular Protests Succeed or Fail*. Stanford, CA: Stanford University Press, 2010.

Gi-Wook Shin. *One Alliance, Two Lenses: U.S.-Korea Relations in a New Era*. Stanford, CA: Stanford University Press, 2010.

Jean Oi and Nara Dillon, eds. *At the Crossroads of Empires: Middlemen, Social Networks, and State-building in Republican Shanghai*. Stanford, CA: Stanford University Press, 2007.

Henry S. Rowen, Marguerite Gong Hancock, and William F. Miller, eds. *Making IT: The Rise of Asia in High Tech*. Stanford, CA: Stanford University Press, 2006.

Gi-Wook Shin. *Ethnic Nationalism in Korea: Genealogy, Politics, and Legacy*. Stanford, CA: Stanford University Press, 2006.

Andrew Walder, Joseph Esherick, and Paul Pickowicz, eds. *The Chinese Cultural Revolution as History*. Stanford, CA: Stanford University Press, 2006.

Rafiq Dossani and Henry S. Rowen, eds. *Prospects for Peace in South Asia*. Stanford, CA: Stanford University Press, 2005.